Random Order

OCTOBER BOOKS

Rosalind E. Krauss, Annette Michelson, George Baker, Yve-Alain Bois, Benjamin H. D. Buchloh, Leah Dickerman, Hal Foster, Denis Hollier, Mignon Nixon, and Malcolm Turvey, editors

Broodthaers, edited by Benjamin H. D. Buchloh

AIDS: Cultural Analysis/Cultural Activism, edited by Douglas Crimp

Against Architecture: The Writings of Georges Bataille, by Denis Hollier

Painting as Model, by Yve-Alain Bois

The Destruction of Tilted Arc: Documents, edited by Clara Weyergraf-Serra and Martha Buskirk

Techniques of the Observer: On Vision and Modernity in the Nineteenth Century, by Jonathan Crary

Looking Awry: An Introduction to Jacques Lacan through Popular Culture, by Slavoj Žižek

Cinema, Censorship, and the State: The Writings of Nagisa Oshima, by Nagisa Oshima

The Optical Unconscious, by Rosalind E. Krauss

Gesture and Speech, by André Leroi-Gourhan

Compulsive Beauty, by Hal Foster

Continuous Project Altered Daily: The Writings of Robert Morris, by Robert Morris

Read My Desire: Lacan against the Historicists, by Joan Copjec

Fast Cars, Clean Bodies: Decolonization and the Reordering of French Culture, by Kristin Ross

Kant after Duchamp, by Thierry de Duve

The Duchamp Effect, edited by Martha Buskirk and Mignon Nixon

The Return of the Real: The Avant-Garde at the End of the Century, by Hal Foster

October: The Second Decade, 1986–1996, edited by Rosalind Krauss, Annette Michelson, Yve-Alain Bois, Benjamin H. D. Buchloh, Hal Foster, Denis Hollier, and Silvia Kolbowski

Infinite Regress: Marcel Duchamp 1910–1941, by David Joselit

Caravaggio's Secrets, by Leo Bersani and Ulysse Dutoit

Scenes in a Library: Reading the Photograph in the Book, 1843–1875, by Carol Armstrong

Neo-Avantgarde and Culture Industry: Essays on European and American Art from 1955 to 1975, by Benjamin H. D. Buchloh

Bachelors, by Rosalind Krauss

Suspensions of Perception: Attention, Spectacle, and Modern Culture, by Jonathan Crary

Leave Any Information at the Signal: Writings, Interviews, Bits, Pages, by Ed Ruscha

Guy Debord and the Situationist International: Texts and Documents, edited by Tom McDonough

Random Order: Robert Rauschenberg and the Neo-Avant-Garde, by Branden W. Joseph

Random Order

Robert Rauschenberg and the Neo-Avant-Garde

Branden W. Joseph

An OCTOBER Book

The MIT Press
Cambridge, Massachusetts
London, England

Publication of this book has been aided by a grant from the Publications Committee, Department of Art and Archaeology, Princeton University.

This book was set in Bembo by Achorn Graphic Services, Inc., and was printed and bound in the United States of America.

Library of Congress Cataloging-in-Publication Data

Joseph, Branden Wayne.

Random order : Robert Rauschenberg and the neo-avant-garde / Branden W. Joseph.

p. cm.

"An October book."

Includes bibliographical references and index.

ISBN 0-262-10099-1 (hc. : alk. paper)

1. Rauschenberg, Robert, 1925–—Criticism and interpretation. I. Rauschenberg, Robert, 1925– II. Title.

N6537.R27J67 2003

709′.2—dc21

2003043620

for Fel

Contents

Acknowledgments

During the course of writing this book, I have benefited from the support of a great number of individuals and institutions. Certain chapters originally formed part of my Ph.D. thesis at Harvard University, and I owe the first debt to my advisors Yve-Alain Bois, Norman Bryson, and Benjamin H. D. Buchloh. I would also like to thank those individuals who read and offered valuable comments on this book's contents at various stages of its evolution: Callie Angell, George Baker, Thierry de Duve, Hal Foster, Ellsworth Kelly, Rosalind Krauss, and, in different ways, Tony Conrad and David Grubbs. Leah Dickerman, Helen Molesworth, and Douglas Nickel provided me with opportunities to present segments of this work in public forums. An anonymous reader provided helpful critiques of this manuscript in its final stages. Special thanks are also due to Larry Cohen, Lisa Reeve, and especially Roger Conover at MIT Press for their support of this project at crucial moments. I would also like to thank Alice Falk and Matthew Abbate for the care and expertise with which they treated this manuscript.

Research and reproductions for this book have been enabled by many people, all of whom have gone out of their way to accommodate my needs and requests: Thomas Buehler and Matt Magee at Robert Rauschenberg's New York studio; Deborah Campana, while she was at the Northwestern University

Music Library; Harry Cooper, Laura Muir, and Peter Nisbet at the Harvard University Art Museums; Don Gillespie at C. F. Peters; Beth Guynn and Nancy Perloff at the Getty Research Center Library; Robert Haller and Jonas Mekas at Anthology Film Archives; Jon Ippolito at the Solomon R. Guggenheim Museum; Tommy Jackson at Black Mountain Press; Bruce Kirby at the Smithsonian Institution Archives; Harry Miller and the other staff of the Wisconsin Center for Film and Theater Research; Sid Sachs of the gallery of the University of the Arts, Philadelphia; and Neal Turtell, Ted Dalziel, and the library staff of the National Gallery of Art. Special thanks are due to Susan Davidson, formerly of the Menil Collection and currently at the Solomon R. Guggenheim Museum; Laura Kuhn of the John Cage Trust; and David White of Robert Rauschenberg's New York studio, all of whom provided invaluable assistance. I would also like to acknowledge the generosity Robert Rauschenberg has shown toward this project.

My graduate studies would not have been possible without the support of an Agnes Mongan Fellowship in Art History, Mellon Fellowships for Summer Research and Dissertation Research, a Jacob K. Javits Graduate Fellowship, and a Wyeth Pre-doctoral Fellowship at the Center for Advanced Study in the Visual Arts at the National Gallery of Art. A summer research support grant from the Getty Research Institute allowed me important access to their archives.

Portions of this book were written when I was a visiting lecturer at Rice University and a Cotsen Fellow in the Society of Fellows in the Liberal Arts at Princeton University. I would like to thank my colleagues at Rice, especially Bill Camfield, Hamid Naficy, and Heghnar Watenpaugh, for helping to make it a rewarding year. At Princeton, I am grateful to all those who made my time particularly successful, especially Alexander Nehamas and Mary Harper. I would also like to thank the Princeton University Committee on Research in the Humanities and Social Sciences for a generous grant toward the procurement of images and reproduction rights, and the Publications Committee, Department of Art and Archaeology, Princeton University, for an equally generous subvention toward publication and production costs.

Earlier versions of chapter 1 appeared in *Critical Inquiry* (autumn 2000) and in French in *Les Cahiers du Musée National d'art moderne* (spring 2000). An earlier version of chapter 4 was published in *October* (winter 2001), and a brief section of chapter 3 appeared in different form in *Celebrating Modern Art: The Anderson Collection* (San Francisco: San Francisco Museum of Modern Art, 2000).

For their support, I would like to thank my family: Carol and Clarence Haught, Steven and Linda Joseph, Gail Joseph, and Jennifer Joseph. I would also like to express my gratitude to the many students and intellectual acquaintances with whom I've worked and whose discussions have benefited me in innumerable ways. Of all of the individuals with whom the ideas in this book have been shared, however, one must be singled out as having truly played the role of a colleague: Felicity D. Scott. With her has come the insight, support, and discussion necessary not only to make such an enterprise interesting but indeed to make it bearable. The personal support I have also received from her over many years simply cannot be adequately acknowledged.

Note on the text: The titles of Rauschenberg's artworks (for example, *White Paintings* but black paintings) follow the conventions established with the artist in Walter Hopps, *Robert Rauschenberg: The Early 1950s* (Houston: Houston Fine Arts Press, 1991), and Walter Hopps and Susan Davidson, eds., *Robert Rauschenberg: A Retrospective* (New York: Solomon R. Guggenheim Museum, 1997). In quoting John Cage, I have chosen not to reproduce the chance-derived typographical layouts of the composer's published writings.

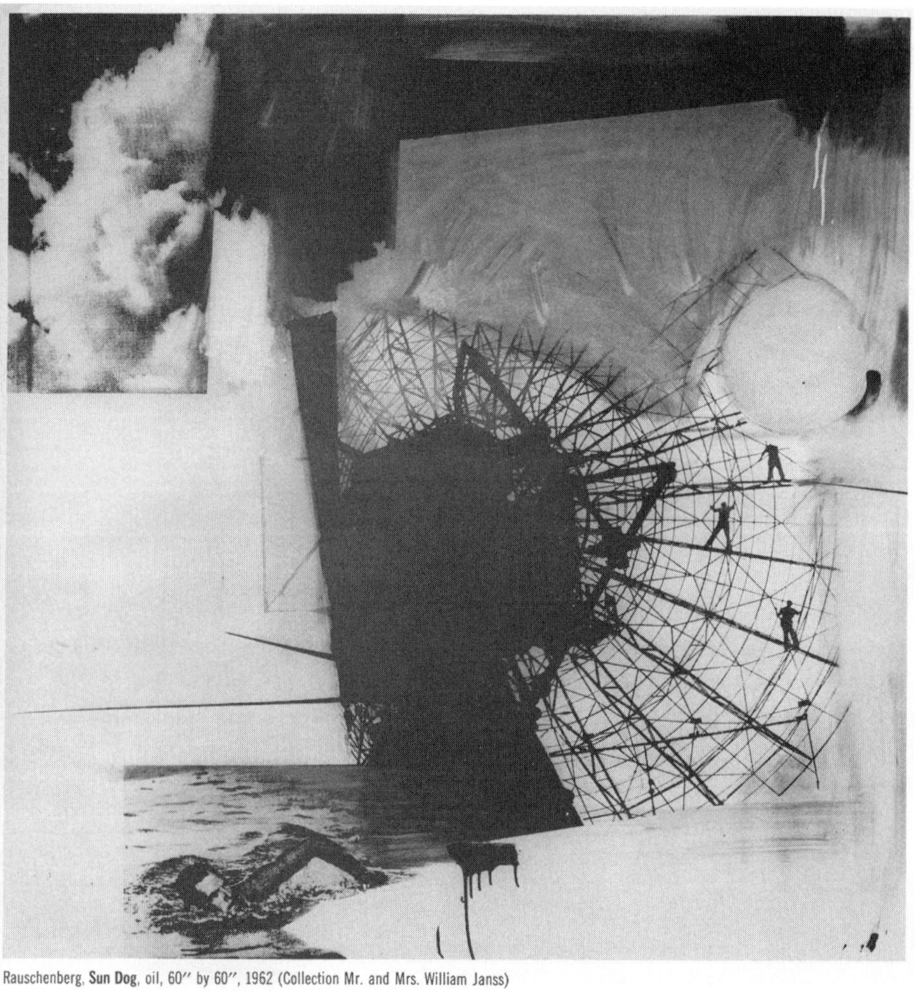

Rauschenberg, **Sun Dog**, oil, 60″ by 60″, 1962 (Collection Mr. and Mrs. William Janss)

Random Order

by ROBERT RAUSCHENBERG

"Random Order." *Location* 1, no. 1 (spring 1963): 27.

Introduction: The Art of Assemblage

Opening the symposium organized for the exhibition *The Art of Assemblage* at the Museum of Modern Art in New York in 1961, William C. Seitz, the exhibition curator and moderator for the night, promised his audience that their experience would be "as full as a Rauschenberg combine painting."[1] The reference was natural enough, as Rauschenberg was seated at the table with Seitz, one of an invited panel that also included Lawrence Alloway, Roger Shattuck, Richard Huelsenbeck, and Marcel Duchamp. In a sense Rauschenberg was the pivotal member of this group. For although the exhibition had initially been intended to feature works of collage, montage, and assemblage created during the first half of the century, it quickly, as Seitz put it, "evolved by its own logic and the pressure of events into a survey of an international wave at its moment of breaking."[2] As the creator of the Combine paintings and Combines, Rauschenberg occupied a position at the crest of that wave.

When it came his turn to present, Rauschenberg, proclaiming himself "an old collage man," started reading from a brief prepared statement. As with "Random Order"—his "manifesto," published two years later in the art periodical *Location*[3]—Rauschenberg attempted to provide a written equivalent to the material heterogeneity in his Combines. Poetically, if somewhat cryptically, he strung together apparently disparate observations and images in a

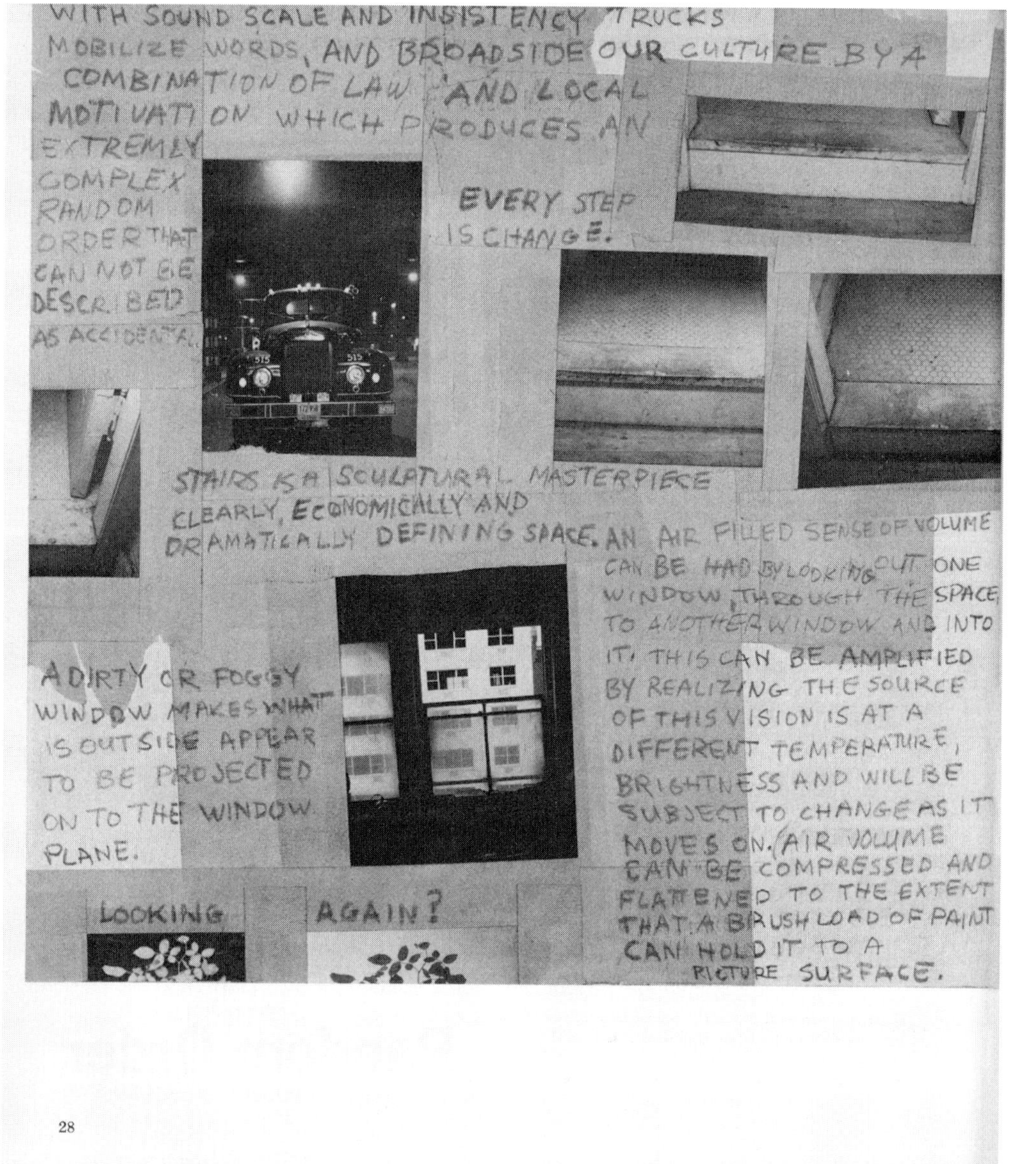

"Random Order," p. 28.

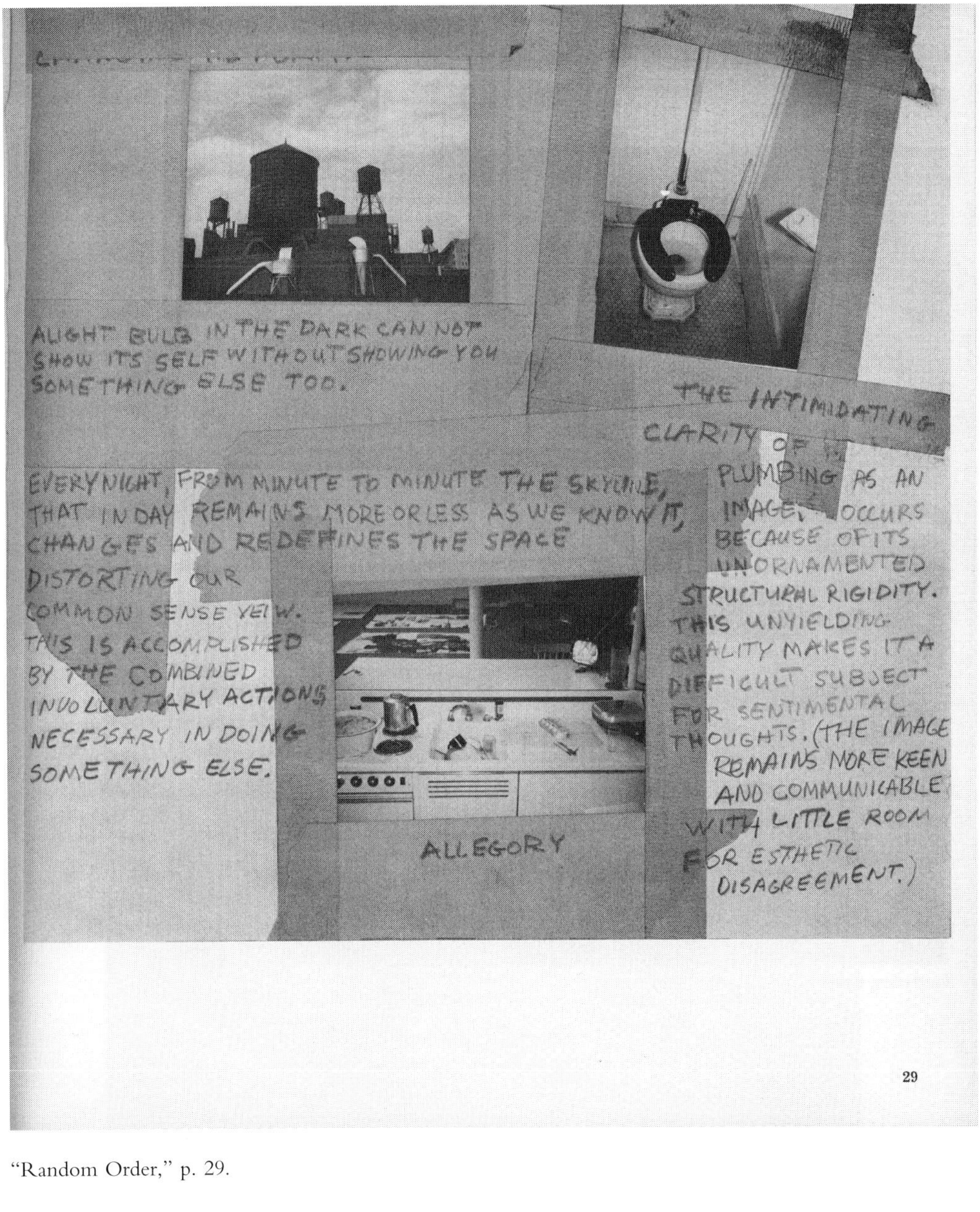

"Random Order," p. 29.

loosely aleatory fashion. As Seitz indicated, it was a strategy similar to that employed in John Cage's article "On Robert Rauschenberg, Artist, and His Work" (the connection between the two men is discussed further below). Rauschenberg began, "Validity cannot exist without standards. How long are standards fresh?" To which he then added, "Two images: a starched stiff shirt unworn responding to the wind is a board; frozen meat that would rot in the sun."[4]

From today's perspective, Rauschenberg's statement opens in a manner that is relatively easy to decipher. While defending a certain notion of artistic "validity," he prefigures its inevitable transformation by juxtaposing an image of fresh, unused laundry—stiff as a board, or a modernist picture plane—with one of frozen meat, changing via the processes of thawing and, eventually, rotting when moved from the freezer into the sunshine and other elements. Purity versus decay, stasis versus change, protection from versus exposure to "natural" forces, the inside versus the outside of the museum, modernism versus what standards of validity are to follow: these are some of the primary tropes by which Rauschenberg's Combines would be characterized and that will form much of the subject matter of this book. At the *Art of Assemblage* symposium, however, Rauschenberg would not even be allowed to finish. After reading just a few more lines, he was interrupted by a series of questions posed first by Seitz and then by Huelsenbeck. As agreed on beforehand, members of the panel were free to interject their thoughts into each others' statements as they pleased. Unlike in the evening's other exchanges, however, Rauschenberg's interlocutors consistently expressed more a genuine perplexity than a considered difference of opinion. When nearly two dozen replies failed to clarify the points being made, Seitz used Rauschenberg's momentarily losing his place on the page as an opportunity to turn the microphone over to Alloway. "All right," Rauschenberg responded with good-natured but nonetheless palpable frustration, "but next time don't ask for collage from your friends."[5]

Rauschenberg's experience at the Museum of Modern Art appears retrospectively as a telling moment in his reception. In the midst of the most apparently fitting context, flanked by curators, historians, and members of the older dadaist avant-garde, his viewpoint proved most difficult to understand. Such difficulties undoubtedly derived in part from his peculiar manner of expression. Yet there was, as we will see, a larger and more profound difference in the underlying presuppositions about art and the avant-garde separating Rauschenberg from his fellow participants (with the important exception of Duchamp). The goal of this book is to investigate and theorize the specificity of Rauschenberg's position, ultimately arguing that it forms part of a distinct strain of avant-garde production heretofore unrecognized in its consistency, seriousness, and oppositional intent. Since the dominant complex of conceptions about the postwar neo-avant-garde forms the backdrop against which this thesis will be argued, it is worthwhile to begin by mapping the larger discursive fields that constitute that backdrop, starting at the *Art of Assemblage* symposium.

◆

As an exercise in curatorial legitimation, *The Art of Assemblage* gave Rauschenberg and those "neo-dada" artists seen as traveling in his wake both a historical pedigree and an interpretive context. According to Seitz's exhibition catalogue, the contemporary artistic developments documented by the show derived from the same feelings of anxious uprootedness and pessimistic rebellion found in futurism and dada a half century before. Indeed, so closely did Seitz identify the pre- and postwar moments of the avant-garde that he questioned whether there was any justification at all for appending the prefix "neo" to dada's contemporary manifestation. Referring to the artists of Rauschenberg's generation, Seitz wrote:

> Certain of their attitudes are comparable to those of the dada period; but why (especially considering the overtone of tired academicism which it can imply) is the prefix "neo" more applicable in 1961 than it was in 1921? Social and emotional life is scarcely more secure

> at present than it was during the youth of Jarry, Vaché, Schwitters, or Duchamp.[6]

In order to understand both dada and neo-dada, Seitz drew on the discussion of the aesthetics of juxtaposition found at the end of Roger Shattuck's study of the early Parisian avant-garde, *The Banquet Years*.[7] No doubt, it was for this reason that Seitz chose Shattuck to open the symposium with a statement titled "The Mode of Juxtaposition."[8] But rather than endorsing Seitz's position, as might have been expected, Shattuck declared it insufficient. Although certain forms of juxtaposition characterized all the works on display, Shattuck maintained that it was necessary to distinguish them according to the result that juxtaposition had within each work. He proposed to divide the works into two categories: the first, those that achieved a certain shock or scandal that was powerful but, according to Shattuck, only temporary; the second, those in which the juxtaposition of disparate elements led to lasting aesthetic tensions:

> In the first category, the event can happen once per customer. As in a short circuit, the desired effect blows the fuse: scandal is unique. The second form of juxtaposition, on the other hand, brings as close together as possible, without ignition, elements that create a large difference in potential. We react not to a brief, bright spark that jumps the gap and thus destroys the whole rig, but to a field of forces sustained by the association.[9]

With this distinction Shattuck only partially succeeded in differentiating the avant-garde strategy of shock or negation from traditional aesthetic effect. Although not unaware of the avant-garde's more socially and politically extreme attempts to undermine the division between "art" and "life," he clearly valued what he saw as legitimate, lasting works of art over the period's more radical manifestations. From this perspective, Shattuck characterized most products of dada as artifacts of an ultimately failed artistic movement. When pressed to publicly declare his sympathies by Huelsenbeck (who largely shared Seitz's view that the contemporary era was socially and artistically analogous to the period of the original dadas), Shattuck avowed only that he was "*for* the *spirit* of Dada" but that "Dada was principally an historical movement."[10]

For Shattuck, dada was now relegated to the status of historical document—"cultural fireworks that cannot be recaptured today"—and he even went so far as to state that the indiscriminate exhibition of such pieces alongside lasting works of art (as in *The Art of Assemblage* itself) "damages both the historical interest of the former *and* the aesthetic values of the latter." Toward the end of the evening Shattuck expressed this view directly to Duchamp, explaining that to his mind the assisted readymade *Bicycle Wheel* (1913) was "no longer a work of art."[11] Duchamp, seeing the situation from the perspective of the avant-garde, took Shattuck's observation as a compliment. "Maybe it is no longer a work of art," he replied, "and if this is so I am delighted to have tried to do something to destroy art, if you want to say, and succeeded."[12]

When turning to the subject of neo-dada assemblage, Shattuck voiced the opinion that it fell short on both of the levels outlined above. Unlike dada, which had been able to mount a challenge, if only temporarily, to the established artistic and social order—to "get beyond the aesthetic block," as Shattuck phrased it on this occasion—neo-dada was deemed unable *either* to escape *or* to achieve an aesthetic outcome. Although admitting to being not thoroughly familiar with recent artistic developments, Shattuck nonetheless declared, "I don't believe there is a neo-Dada which fulfills the same function of applying what has been discovered in the arts and allowing it to come out in our lives, and if anyone would like to comment about that, I'd like to hear."[13]

As these exchanges indicate, even Rauschenberg's earliest reception took place within the now familiar terms of a neo-avant-garde revival of the aesthetic and political strategies of the prewar avant-garde.[14] With Duchamp and, to some extent, Huelsenbeck on one side advocating the more radical "destruction" of art, and Seitz and Shattuck—despite their different valuations of neo-dada—on the other, arguing from a more traditional point of view, the major terms by which Rauschenberg's production would henceforth be judged were already set.

Rauschenberg, however, was not to be found only on the receiving end of the night's interruptions. As opposed to Duchamp, whose disagreements were voiced with reserve and a characteristically understated wit, Rauschenberg, who was in a spirited mood, sparred openly with the symposium's other participants, particularly Shattuck. What Rauschenberg found objectionable in Shattuck's position was not so much on which side of the distinction art/non-art the historian thought to place his work ("I mean the idea of art," he declared, "being for it or against it, I find ridiculous"), but rather the entire notion of shock. Before Shattuck had even fully explained his understanding of the distinction between shock and aesthetic effect, Rauschenberg interrupted him to take issue with the metaphor he had chosen. Against Shattuck's characterization of shock in terms of "the association of two elements that cancel each other out and return us spiritually and aesthetically to zero," Rauschenberg immediately contended, "No, no! There's *no* zero . . . which returning implies."[15]

Throughout the symposium, Rauschenberg consistently denied that the categories of shock or negation were in any way valid when applied to an understanding of contemporary, neo-dada art. Seeking to claim the older artist for his side, Rauschenberg even questioned the idea that "there was any element of threat or shock" to Duchamp's strategy of choosing a readymade.[16] Furthermore, he rejected as invalid the very terms through which Seitz and Shattuck approached an understanding of assemblage, flatly telling both of his interlocutors, "The kind of isolation you're talking about is the most classical form of juxtaposition—which I don't find a very interesting idea."[17]

Despite the bluntness and vigor with which Rauschenberg expressed his disagreements, both Seitz and Shattuck continued to greet him with almost total incomprehension. ("I don't *quite* know what you're referring to," Shattuck was forced at one point to admit.)[18] Nevertheless, Rauschenberg would continue to reject an aesthetics of shock or negation throughout his career. Asked for instance by Emile de Antonio about the attitude behind his black paintings and *White Paintings* of the early 1950s, Rauschenberg reiterated, "None of those early things was about negativism or nihilism."[19]

In 1963, when organizing Rauschenberg's first retrospective for the Jewish Museum in New York, Alan Solomon would take such protestations to heart. In the catalogue, Solomon clearly dissociated Rauschenberg from Seitz's previous conflation of his work with the spirit of dada. Presenting Rauschenberg as the leader of a new generation of artists, he explained:

> The apparently negative attitude of the Dada group toward art and society actually grew out of a deep sense of esthetic and political frustration. The new artists operate, by contrast, in complete esthetic freedom, and politically they have disengaged themselves totally. By way of explanation one might say that both the art battles and the historical battles have been fought for them by their predecessors, but whatever the explanation, the result seems to be that this new generation is wholly engaged in life and the process of art, in a direct, intense and optimistic way, without commitment to any of the familiar existing institutions.[20]

As anyone acquainted with Rauschenberg's language will recognize, much of Solomon's description—such as the opposition to negation (a "negative attitude") and politics and the commitment to engage with "process" and "life"—undoubtedly derived from conversations with the artist. Yet Solomon's assimilation of Rauschenberg's position merely reinscribed it within the same notion of a lasting art that Rauschenberg had so strenuously rejected when voiced by Shattuck or Seitz. In Solomon's text, ideas of Rauschenberg's, such as that of his works' "causing changes of focus and providing multiplicity," lost their specificity and were transformed into such anodyne statements as "Resolved images would destroy the tense and precarious balance of elements maintaining the whole dynamic fabric of the work" (before being related to safe artistic precedents such as Cézanne).[21]

No doubt, Solomon's recasting of Rauschenberg's opposition to the tenets of the historical avant-garde as a form of quietism (by which it is still often understood) was a necessary complement to comfortably inserting his work into the museum.[22] Yet, while Rauschenberg's assimilation into the realm of traditional high art has garnered him worldwide acclaim, it has long been recognized as sacrificing much, if not all, of his works' critical interest. Reflecting on the Jewish Museum retrospective a decade later, the artist and critic Brian O'Doherty perceptively diagnosed the art historian's task in words still applicable today. "Works such as Rauschenberg's," he observed,

> thus have a lost mode of perception buried in them, as the esthetic of "museum perception" instructs academic modes of looking quite alien to the original. . . .
>
> The task for anyone writing about Rauschenberg now is to construct, from the museum-broken residues of his work and intentions, a rationale that does not ignore this perceptual history but which does ignore the myth of careless superficiality that disqualifies his work from the strenuous examinations of high seriousness.[23]

Although going beyond questions of perception, *Random Order* should be viewed as a response to O'Doherty's challenge. It seeks to construct, or reconstruct, an understanding of the importance that Rauschenberg's early production had in its time and might (beyond its status as mere luxury objects) continue to have in ours.

In this endeavor, I am far from alone. In fact, examinations of Rauschenberg's seriousness have never been as strenuous as they are now. Over the past two decades, in particular, the reception of Rauschenberg's work has developed into a highly contested arena of differing historical, methodological, epistemological, and political approaches. With the purportedly apolitical discourse of the museum standing, to some degree, in the center, one pole of this reception is represented by those who view Rauschenberg's importance through the very academic modes of looking that O'Doherty warned against. The status of Rauschenberg's work as high art has brought forth increasingly intense attempts to read it through the most traditional paradigms of signification, including that of iconography.[24] Such readings have recently gained in prominence as the artist's work has come to be seen as expressing coded messages about his sexual orientation.[25] Although, as Rosalind Krauss has observed, "the convinced iconographer is almost impossible to dissuade,"[26] nearly three decades of such analyses (which at their most reductive condense a work's evident heterogeneity into a single sentence or illustration of a mythic event) have yielded only partial and unsatisfactory results. Indeed, those relatively few of Rauschenberg's pieces that seem to invite such readings are far outweighed by the majority that do not.[27] The arguments put forth here issue from an entirely different perspective, as I propose that Rauschenberg pursued forms of aesthetic signification and spectatorial reception that challenge traditional signifying means. Such a claim is not to deny Rauschenberg a politics of identity. Rather, it is, as others have also argued, to see in his position a wider challenge to reification, conformity, and, ultimately, the very subjective forms through which modern relations of power operate (see, in particular, chapter 1).

◆

Despite the persistence of Rauschenberg's "museum-broken" and iconographic receptions, the issues broached four decades ago at the *Art of Assemblage* symposium—the "failure" of the first moment of the avant-garde, the nature of the distinction between art and life, and the definition and role played by shock and negation—have not disappeared but instead have continued to structure more theoretical discussions of Rauschenberg's role within postwar art. By the 1980s, however, Shattuck's *The Banquet Years* had been displaced as the central reference point by Peter Bürger's much discussed *Theory of the Avant-Garde,* first published in 1974.[28]

Like Shattuck, Bürger saw the history of the avant-garde as discontinuous and the earlier, historical moment of the avant-garde as ending in failure. Unlike

Shattuck, however, Bürger viewed the situation from the perspective of the avant-garde rather than the traditional arts, and he therefore judged success not according to lasting aesthetic potential but according to radical political effect.[29] Like Duchamp, Bürger would not define the failure of the avant-garde in terms of the non-art status of its production. Instead, as he argued, the avant-garde's failure lay precisely in its being accepted as nothing more than the producer of legitimate works of art. Unlike the historical avant-garde—which achieved a level of self-criticism about the conditions of its production from which it strove to criticize the means-ends rationality of the social realm and attempted to refashion the latter according to a different set of criteria (derived from "art"; see pp. 18–22)—the neo-avant-garde, according to Bürger, merely rehearsed earlier avant-garde strategies within an institutional context, thereby nullifying their radical potential (p. 34). As put forward in the *Theory of the Avant-Garde*'s most famous contention, it was in the very repetition by the postwar neo-avant-garde of the strategies pioneered by the historical avant-garde that the demise of the radical avant-garde project was conclusively proven:

> To the extent that the means by which the avant-gardistes hoped to bring about the sublation of art have attained the status of works of art, the claim that the praxis of life is to be renewed can no longer be legitimately connected with their employment. To formulate more pointedly: the neo-avant-garde institutionalizes the *avant-garde as art* and thus negates genuinely avant-gardiste intentions. (p. 58)

While Bürger's theoretical formulation of the relationship between the pre- and the postwar avant-garde attained a much higher level than is found in Shattuck's remarks, it similarly revolved around the interrelated notions of shock and negation. Like Shattuck, Bürger regarded shock as the central strategy in the avant-garde assault on the division of art and life. Starting from an investigation into the aesthetics of montage, Bürger theorized that the avant-garde work of art, in its disarticulation of the organic artwork's integrated form, invalidated the traditional cognitive approaches that formerly characterized artistic reception. If sympathetic, the viewer, in attempting to understand the work of the avant-garde, is led to a level of interpretation no longer predicated solely on the work's appearance but focused on the underlying principles of its construction—including those deriving from the conventions and, eventually, the institutions governing its production and reception (pp. 52–82).[30] The ascetic refusal of the avant-garde artwork to provide readily recognizable and assimilable meaning further leads the viewer to a measure of critical distance by which the world's governing conventions and institutions can also be understood, judged, and eventually opposed. "This refusal to provide meaning," Bürger explains,

> is experienced as a shock by the recipient. And this is the intention of the avant-gardiste artist, who hopes that such a withdrawal of meaning will direct the reader's attention to the fact that the conduct of one's life is questionable and that it is necessary to change it. Shock is aimed for as a stimulus to change one's conduct of life; it is the means to break through aesthetic immanence and to usher in (initiate) a change in the recipient's life praxis. (p. 80)

According to Bürger, the effects of such provocative dadaist manifestations "are certainly collective in nature" (p. 53), and this collective reception is a fundamental aspect of the dissolution of art into the praxis of everyday life. With these considerations, the scope of Bürger's position goes beyond the specifics of dada or montage toward a more general theorization of historical avant-garde practices.

The notion of shock or, rather, of the effective lack of shock effects also plays an important role in Bürger's judgment of the neo-avant-garde. As Bürger recognized, avant-garde provocation cannot last indefinitely (in this he is once again in agreement with Shattuck). The welcoming of a work such as a readymade or an aleatory collage into the museum heralds its reinscription within the paradigms of symbolic meaning and individual creativity that reinforce the "failure" of the historical avant-garde (p. 53). What is more, the failure to escape or oppose the institutionalization of art destroys not only the avant-garde's political effectiveness but art's historical progression as well. Once sealed off from the realm of life praxis, the fractured, inorganic structure pioneered by the avant-garde becomes, in the still-autonomous neo-avant-garde artwork, a historicist pastiche that merely reflects, rather than questions, the irrationality of society under late capitalism (p. 94).

Despite Rauschenberg's unparalleled importance in the postwar revival of montage, his work goes unmentioned by Bürger. Nevertheless, as the *Art of Assemblage* symposium made particularly clear, issues of the revival, repetition, and institutionalization of avant-garde practices have always been central to the understanding of Rauschenberg's work.[31] And whether or not they draw explicitly on Bürger (whose position must be understood within the larger context of Frankfurt School aesthetics), contemporary discussions of Rauschenberg's production have not failed to regard it in Bürgeresque terms of an etiolation of effective shock effects, a reassertion of individual authorship, and a comfortable inscription within artistic institutions.[32]

This is not to say that Rauschenberg has lacked powerful proponents who have investigated his challenge to traditional forms of artistic production and reception. Beginning with Leo Steinberg's celebrated "Other Criteria," important discussions by O'Doherty, Krauss, Craig Owens, Douglas Crimp, and others have argued variously for its critical importance.[33] Their writings form the second major pole of Rauschenberg's reception: a line of analysis that regards the meaning of his work as residing not in its iconography but in its more structural reflections of the social, subjective, and commercial transformations that Steinberg already in 1972 termed "post-Modernist."[34]

This is the side of Rauschenberg's reception that I consider the most insightful and to which the arguments put forward in the following pages are indebted. Yet it is in the very success of such investigations into the complex, postmodern heterogeneity (or "random order") of Rauschenberg's work that the specter of Bürger's argument continues to haunt Rauschenberg's project most persistently. For within a Frankfurt School analysis, both Rauschenberg's promiscuous imagistic interactions and the postmodern critiques of autonomy, totality, and subjectivity to which they have been related would be understood as reflecting, rather than challenging, the development of late capitalism. From this perspective—which shifts the terrain from Bürger's analysis to Fredric Jameson's more extensive and powerful discussions of postmodernity[35]—Rauschenberg would seem, at best, to be a forerunner and, at worst, a merely complicitous presence in the development of a late-capitalist, postindustrial society: a society into which he is subsumed without the critical remainder that such a discourse can understand only in terms of the autonomy, shock, negation, and critical distance that Rauschenberg opposed. Where the supposed "free play of the signifier" appears as an ideological obfuscation of increased social administration or an entropic dissolution of avant-garde critique or modernist autonomy, Rauschenberg's optimistic advocacy of involvement, participation, and creation appear, almost by definition, as illegitimate.

Ultimately, perhaps, such apparent illegitimacy is less a result of art-historical investigation than the development of postwar art. Artists who came to prominence in the 1960s such as Carl Andre, Robert Morris, and Yvonne Rainer combined a renewed understanding of the historical avant-garde with contemporary discussions of phenomenology, structuralism, and Marcusean dialectics to produce a powerful neo-avant-garde practice distinctly at odds with its neo-dada predecessor. Recent years have seen Bürger's study thoroughly critiqued, criticized, extended, and transformed. Nevertheless, when speaking from a standpoint aligned with the minimalist and postminimalist practices of the 1960s, even Bürger's most sophisticated and thoroughgoing critics have conceded the applicability of his thesis to Rauschenberg and other members of the 1950s neo-avant-garde. It is the one place, symptomatically, that Bürger continues to hold sway.[36]

Yet is it not possible to displace this perspective with regard to Rauschenberg as well? to view the postmodernization heralded by his production as still critical in intent and effect? Since the ideas of shock, protest, and negation play such pivotal roles in Bürger's analysis, cannot Rauschenberg's objections to them be seen as directed not merely at Shattuck but also at Bürger? Admittedly, such an attempt to invert the priority of Rauschenberg and Bürger significantly raises the stakes beyond those involved in the *Art of Assemblage* symposium. It requires that one understand Rauschenberg's position in a manner that those at the MoMA symposium did not and move as far beyond the apparent level of Rauschenberg's comments on that occasion as Bürger's discussion of the avant-garde surpassed Shattuck's. Yet, as unlikely as the characterization of Rauschenberg as Bürger's theoretical equal may at first appear, that is exactly what I propose. Indeed, it is my position that a satisfactory comprehension of Rauschenberg's work requires nothing less than an understanding of the particularly "neo" aspects of his avant-garde project and the ways in which they differ from the dominant practices and understandings of both his predecessors in the 1910s and 1920s and his minimalist contemporaries in the 1960s and beyond.[37]

In part, this argument demands a theorization of Rauschenberg's work that pushes toward its furthest and most radical implications, placing a weight on his images and statements that some readers may initially find untenable. As I see it, however, the impetus behind such an approach is not merely academic but historical and art critical as well. For I believe that to theorize an artist's work at its most radical, constructing a comprehension of what it might entail and imply, is one means of understanding the impact that it had in its time. In this case, it is one, though by no means the only, way to rediscover something of the excitement, strangeness, and possibility that are evident in the contemporary responses to Rauschenberg's work but that have been all but forgotten in the course of its comfortable inscription within the museum.

Moreover, such a resituation of Rauschenberg's position makes it necessary to displace the overarching historical framework inherited from the Frankfurt School, which sees the socioeconomic transformations following World War II as the ultimate phase in capitalist development—either to be overthrown or, more probably, succumbed to as the demonically realized end of history.

Despite inevitable moments of economic crisis, it no longer seems tenable that the latest of what Ernest Mandel termed "long waves of capitalist development" will be the last.[38] Indeed, today it is not so much the avant-garde that must be understood as "neo" but capitalism itself. For as Gilles Deleuze, Félix Guattari, and others have proposed, postwar capitalism, far from being "late," is always and already a "neocapitalism" that unfolds through a perpetually altering dynamic of de- and reterritorialization.[39] Although this dynamic entails a certain repetition, as the processes of capitalist deterritorialization recur again and again, it is accomplished under social, cultural, and economic conditions that are qualitatively and not simply quantitatively altered.

To understand capitalism as operating in this manner is not so much to discount the analyses and warnings of the Frankfurt School and its followers as it is to take them very seriously. According to theorists such as Deleuze and Guattari and, more recently, Michael Hardt and Antonio Negri, any analysis of the postwar period must begin from a point that resembles the Frankfurt School's worst nightmare: that of a world everywhere totalized such that capitalism has effectively liquidated any stable or autonomous realm of the outside.[40] Importantly, this perspective views the socioeconomic transformations in the postwar era as primarily characterized not by the passage from an earlier phase of capitalism to a later one but by the transformation from a disciplinary society to a society of control.[41]

My thesis here follows a similar line of analysis to propose that rather than being seen as the end of a long and increasingly impoverished line of avant-garde history, Rauschenberg should be viewed as among the first avant-gardists of an era of control or what Hardt and Negri have more recently termed "Empire." As Hardt and Negri describe them, the discourses of postmodernism in which Rauschenberg has been so pivotal (though they do not mention Rauschenberg) are most productively understood as critiquing the transcendent and dialectical structure of modern sovereign or disciplinary power.[42] Seen through this lens, what they call "the deconstructive phase of critical thought" (which includes the positions advanced by the Frankfurt School as well as the philosophy of Jacques Derrida) is understood as a particular historical stance that indicates, but does not succeed in passing beyond, the last remnants of modernist transcendence and autonomy.[43] Only a thought of immanence, multiplicity, and posthuman subjective becoming such as that developed by Deleuze and Guattari, they argue, adequately addresses a fully saturated or foreclosed postmodern condition. Although not identical to the position put forth in *Empire,* my argument regards Rauschenberg's production as demonstrating a related movement beyond a modernism allied with subjective and artistic autonomy and opening onto a condition that traffics in immanent and differential forces. Hence the particular tension that runs throughout this book between analyses derived from deconstruction, on the one hand, and the insights of Deleuze and Guattari, on the other. Together, these serve to characterize the particular moment of historical and theoretical passage reflected by Rauschenberg's work during this time.

From within this framework, terms, concepts, and practices familiarly applied to Rauschenberg's art will have to be grasped with a new specificity—even, indeed especially, when they most seem to be mere repetitions of the earlier avant-garde. Such will also be the case with regard to Rauschenberg's position within postmodernism; for we will begin to see the criticality of his work as residing not in the much-discussed strategies of appropriation but rather in the opening of the appropriated, commercial realm to subrepresentational forces of multiplicity and temporal difference. The end result will be to problematize current understandings of postwar art by posing the "neo-dada" aesthetic spearheaded by Rauschenberg as a distinct strain of neo-avant-garde production, incompatible with but equally as productive and provocative as that developed by minimalism.

◆

Whether or not he was in the auditorium during the *Art of Assemblage* symposium, there was one person who would undoubtedly have understood Rauschenberg's comments better than any other: his longtime friend and collaborator

John Cage.[44] At the time, the two shared what may be described as an almost telepathic relationship. "There was," Cage said, "from the beginning a sense of absolute identification, or utter agreement, between us. So much so that there have been times, for example on a lecture platform when Bob was answering questions from the audience, that I've had the feeling I would have given the same answer in almost the same words."[45] Indeed, Rauschenberg's metaphorical description of art as frozen meat and the museum as an icebox at the *Art of Assemblage* symposium recalls Cage's similar discussion from "Composition as Process." Making an analogy between "contemporary music" and "contemporary milk," Cage explained:

> At room temperature it is changing, goes sour etc., and then a new bottle etc., unless by separating it from its changing by powdering or refrigeration (which is a way of slowing down its liveliness) (that is to say museums and academies are ways of preserving) we temporarily separate things from life (from changing).[46]

It is in the frequently remarked but surprisingly little investigated relationship with Cage that Rauschenberg would find the means to reformulate his avant-garde project in the direction discussed above. We should not find this entirely unexpected, since theorists such as Deleuze and Guattari long regarded Cage as an important source for their own thinking.[47] The relationship between Cage's outlook and that of the more recent theorists of control society surely also arises from the composer's early recognition of the capitalist totalization of the globe. It was in the context of his years at Black Mountain College (where he came to know Rauschenberg) and his own transformation from an avant-garde to a neo-avant-garde aesthetic that Cage came to the realization—sparked initially in 1948 by Buckminster Fuller—that "the world is one world now."[48] Fuller's perspective, as I have argued elsewhere, was deeply imbricated with the dynamics of capitalist deterritorialization, and it revealed to Cage that the outside—which he had previously located in the East and precapitalist West, and from which he sought to relativize and critique "Western commercialism"—had become foreclosed.[49] Lacking any stable, localizable, autonomous, or subjective outside, Cage would set himself the task of articulating an understanding of difference, or what he still termed the "outside," as an immanent force within the totalized sphere itself.[50]

Though he has frequently been characterized as something of a holy fool, Cage adopted neither the historical nor the theoretical implications of this neo-avant-garde transformation naively. While he did not explicitly address Rauschenberg's relationship to the historical avant-garde in his article "On Robert Rauschenberg, Artist, and His Work," he did broach the issue in the foreword to his book *Silence.* "It is possible," Cage wrote, "to make a connection between the two, but neither Dada nor Zen is a fixed tangible. They change; and in quite different ways in different places and times, they invigorate action. What was Dada in the 1920's is now, with the exception of the work of Marcel Duchamp, just art."[51] In this brief but nonetheless significant comment, Cage conveyed an awareness both of the historical foundation of avant-garde practices and of the "failure" of the first avant-garde's radical program as represented by its acceptance within the category of art. Although Cage keyed into two aspects that would become important to subsequent conceptualizations of the avant-garde, his judgment of its two periods, not surprisingly, reversed that of theorists such as Bürger. Although dada's earlier period is plainly deemed historical, the current one—of which Cage and Rauschenberg as much as Duchamp were the exemplars—was understood as having maintained its viability.

As will become clear in chapter 1 of this book, "White on White," Cage's estimation of the postwar situation differs from Bürger's in large part because he did not similarly value the notion of negation or shock. Like Rauschenberg, Cage explicitly rejected shock aesthetics. As he explained in 1956 in a letter to Paul Henry Lang, the music critic for the *New York Herald Tribune,*

> I gather that you find me concerned with shocking the man on the street. . . . But I have never gratuitously done anything for shock,

> though what I have found necessary to do I have carried out, occasionally and only after struggles of conscience, even if it involved actions apparently outside the "boundaries of art."[52]

For Cage, the difference between the two eras of the avant-garde was understood not through the continued viability of shock but via the interrelated concepts of "space" and "emptiness." This he proclaimed in *Silence*'s foreword, a few lines below the above-quoted discussion of dada and Zen: "I often point out that Dada nowadays has in it a space, an emptiness, that it formerly lacked."[53]

Cage's ideas of space and emptiness relate integrally to his famous concept of silence, defined in 1951 as not the complete absence of sound but the presence of unintentional noises. "Silence, like music, is non-existent," he contended; "There are always sounds."[54] In 1959 (the year Cage's comments on dada and Zen originally appeared in the liner notes to his recording *Indeterminacy*)[55] Rauschenberg also addressed a similarly paradoxical notion of "emptiness." In the last line of his artist's statement for the Museum of Modern Art's exhibition *Sixteen Americans,* Rauschenberg declared simply, "A canvas is never empty."[56]

Cage would quote this idea of an empty canvas that is not empty twice in his article on Rauschenberg. And it is this notion of the *White Paintings'* emptiness—before which, Cage observed, "you just wait to see what you will see"[57]—that characterized and catalyzed the composer's reception of those works. Likewise, as chapter 1 will make clear, it was to such a transvalued concept of emptiness that Rauschenberg was referring at the *Art of Assemblage* symposium in his comments about there existing "no zero . . . which returning implies." This being the case, an understanding of Rauschenberg and Cage's idea of "neo-dada" will have to begin not with the issues of montage and juxtaposition brought up by Rauschenberg's Combines, but by first investigating how their concepts of space and emptiness redefined the avant-garde strategy of the monochrome.

◆

Starting with a discussion of the *White Paintings,* this book investigates several succeeding phases of Rauschenberg's development to the early 1970s. Chapter 2, "Pedestrian Colors," examines the manner in which the black paintings, *Red Paintings,* and *Elemental Sculptures* both deepened Rauschenberg's understanding of historical avant-garde strategies and led him to recognize the complete capitalist foreclosure of the aesthetic realm. Chapter 3, "Mole Archaeology," then follows the evolution of the Combines and Combine paintings as they developed a mode of multiplicitous signification that opened perception to forces of differentiation and opposed the perceptual regimes of traditional iconography and commercial culture. Chapter 4, "Split Screens," on Rauschenberg's silkscreen paintings, presents these works in relation to his engagement with the realm of electronic mass media, speculating on their place within an emergent understanding of, and opposition to, a society of control. Finally, chapter 5, "Moving Images," investigates Rauschenberg's endeavors in dance, performance, and "experiments in art and technology" in light of his attempt to forge a sacrificial economy of signifying excess that he hoped to position against the oppressive social assemblage he termed "industry."

Though spanning two decades of artistic production, this study does not purport to encompass the entirety of Rauschenberg's work, nor to exhaust its various implications. (Omitted from consideration are, for instance, the majority of Rauschenberg's pre-1951 production and his photography, printmaking, and much of his sculpture.) On one level, the thesis I propose is straightforward: that beginning at Black Mountain College in the summer of 1952, the meeting between Rauschenberg and Cage initiated a new paradigm of avant-garde production, in which the idea of difference was conceived not in terms of negation but rather as a positive force. This analysis will lead to a better understanding of the art and importance of these two influential figures, rendering more complex and thereby deepening our current understanding of the neo-avant-garde, its history and formulation, the questions it raised, and the stakes for which it worked. If successful, such an investigation will also indicate some of the reasons why, from the moment of the *Art of Assemblage* symposium, Rauschenberg's position has been so difficult to assimilate within the dominant theorizations of the neo-avant-garde.

More than that, however, the focus on Rauschenberg and his relationship to Cage will lead to an understanding of how their work forged an avant-garde project that did not depend on recovering the already-liquidated spaces of subjective autonomy or stable, critical distance but nevertheless opposed the instrumental signification and stultifying pseudo-differentiation of commodity production. That such an analysis might aid in understanding aesthetico-political programs of relevance within the current era of untrammeled capitalism is not the least of my motivations for having undertaken this study.

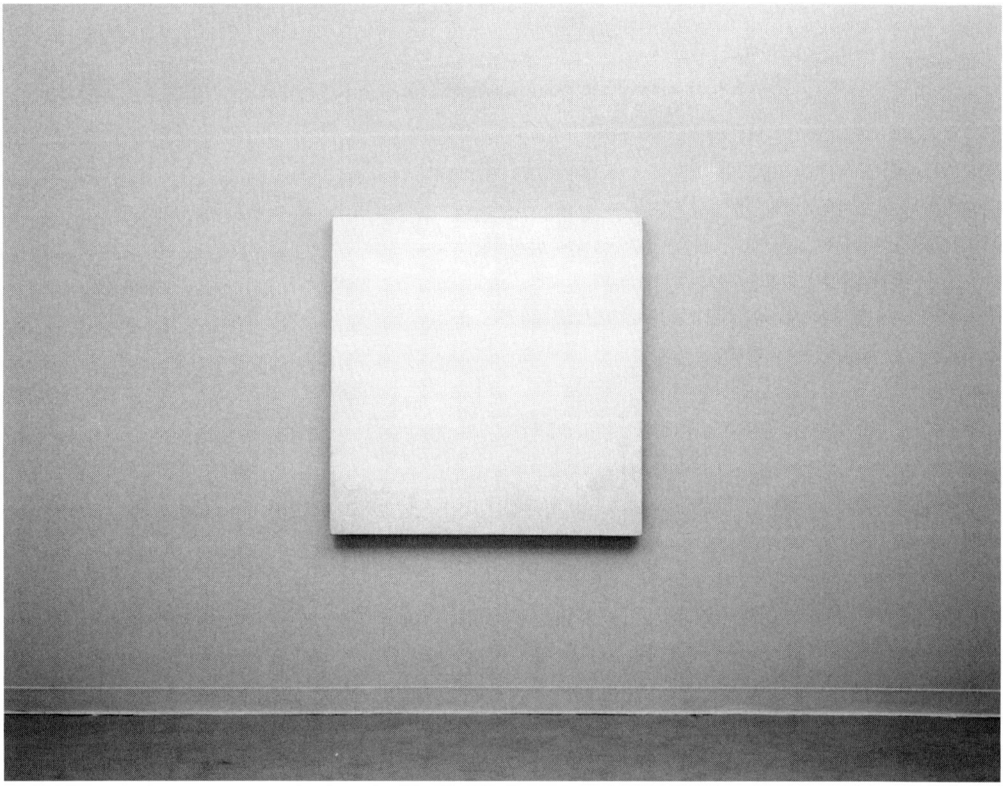

White Painting, 1951. Oil on canvas. One panel, 48 × 48 in. Collection of the artist, New York.

1

White on White

On 18 October 1951, just four days before his twenty-sixth birthday, Robert Rauschenberg sent a letter to Betty Parsons from Black Mountain College to announce the completion of his *White Paintings.* Although Parsons had given Rauschenberg his first one-person show the previous May, presenting earlier work in the gallery's second room, he was already entreating her for another opportunity to exhibit. "I will be in N.Y. Nov. 1st," he informed her, "and will forfeit all right to ever show again for their being given a chance to be considered for this year's calender."[1] Rauschenberg could hardly have been unaware of how unusual was his request for another show. At the time, after all, he was a virtually unknown artist whose previous exhibition had failed to inspire a single purchase.[2] Clearly, however, he felt that this situation was exceptional. As he explained to Parsons, he considered his group of *White Paintings* "almost an emergency."

This letter—the only contemporary statement about the *White Paintings* that we have—reveals Rauschenberg in transition. In its very first lines, he claims for himself a newfound maturity, implying that he had left his earlier work behind and embarked on a new stage in his artistic career. "I have," he writes, "since putting on shoes sobered up from summer puberty and moonlit smells. Have felt that my head and heart move through something quite different than the hot dust the earth threw at me." But despite such claims, Rauschenberg had not entirely broken with either his past work or his past thinking. Many of the pieces shown at the Parsons Gallery in May were products of what he later characterized as "a short lived religious period";[3] these ranged from the more representational *Eden* (ca. 1950) and *Trinity* (ca. 1949)—the first a sparse, somewhat Klee-like depiction of the prelapsarian paradise, the second depicting three lights shining out from their dark surrounds—to the more formal and abstract *Crucifixion and Reflection* and *Mother of God* (both ca. 1950).

With its emphasis on the rectilinearity of the support and the way in which the two areas of paint appear to form separate, conjoined panels, *Crucifixion and Reflection* anticipates the modular aspect of the *White Paintings*. Yet it is *Mother of God* that more clearly indicates the artistic paradigm from which the *White Paintings* seem to have been born. There, Rauschenberg used a field of city maps to depict the earthly realm, employing collage as a means of directly incorporating elements of the outside world into the work and emphasizing their (and its) materiality. Despite initial appearances, this collage ground does not continue beneath the white circle further than a small edge running around its circumference. By keeping collage from the center of the painting, Rauschenberg not only produced a brighter white than that in *Crucifixion and Reflection,* he also signified that the white was at once in the world and to be understood as somehow separate from it. The white would thereby seem to be symbolic of the divine, with Rauschenberg presenting painting as the result of a sort of incarnation.[4] Like the body of the Virgin Mary, Rauschenberg's *Mother of God* serves as a material or bodily vessel for the manifestation of the divine. Rauschenberg's collaging of a newspaper clipping from the *Catholic Review* to the bottom right corner only reinforced the connection.

To some extent, this line of thinking seems to have continued in Rauschenberg's initia! conception of the *White Paintings*. Rauschenberg described them in his letter to Parsons:

> they are large white (1 white as 1 GOD) canvases organized and selected with the experience of time and presented with the innocence of a virgin. Dealing with the suspense, excitement and body

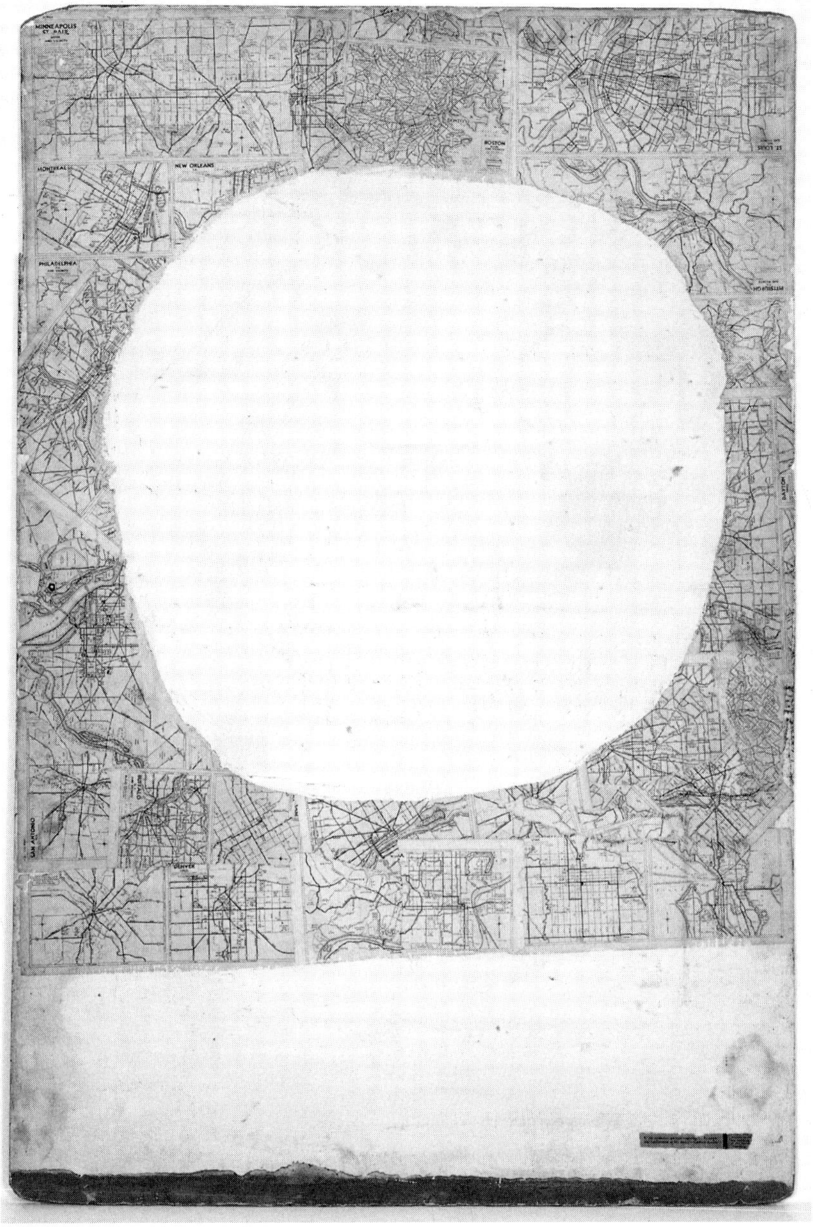

Mother of God, ca. 1950. Oil, enamel, printed paper, newspaper, and copper and metallic paints on masonite. 48 × 32⅛ in.Collection of the artist, New York.

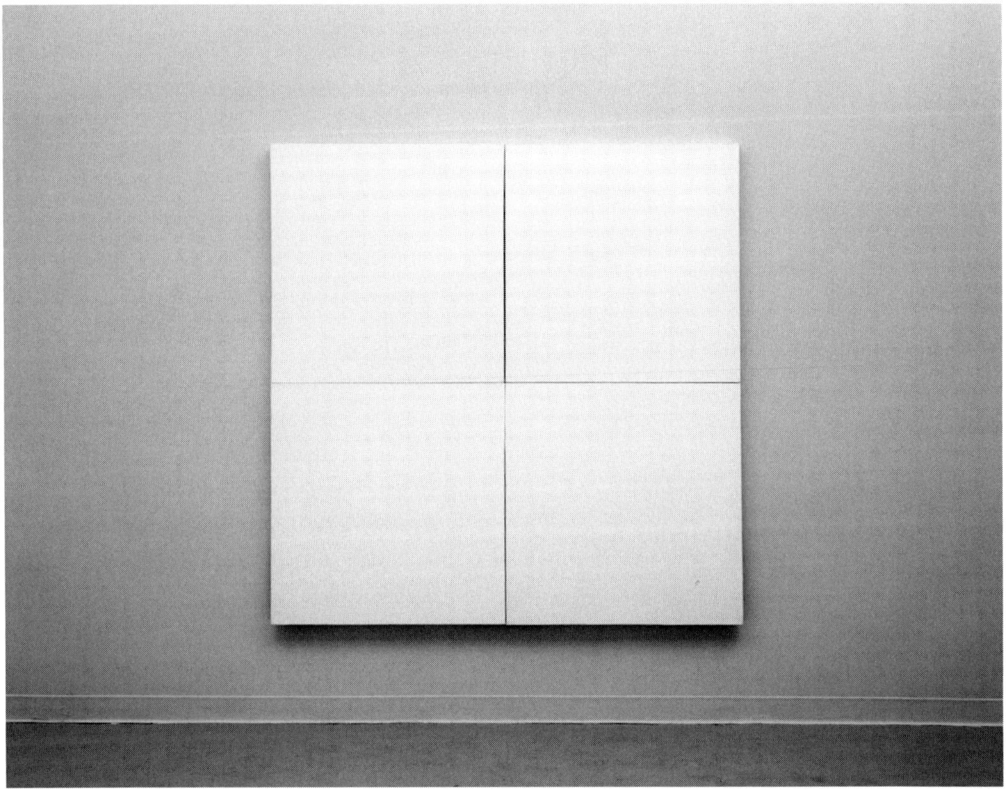

White Painting, 1951. Oil on canvas. Four panels, 36 × 36 in. each; 72 × 72 in. overall. Collection of the artist, New York.

> of an organic silence, the restriction and freedom of absence, the plastic fullness of nothing, the point a circle begins and ends. they are a natural response to the current pressures of the faithless and a promoter of intuitional optimism. It is completely irrelevant that I am making them—*Today* is their creater.[5]

What is different here is that it is no longer the *painting* that serves as the "Mother of God," but the *artist* who presents the work with "the innocence of a virgin." Correspondingly, white paint now covers the entirety of the canvas—the whole work seemingly figuring as an incarnation of the divine, to be placed directly within its worldly surroundings instead of evoking or representing them.

A more profound change in Rauschenberg's thinking, however, seems to have been signaled in the final line of the passage quoted above. Despite the residual traces of religious implications in the description, Rauschenberg's urgency seems also to have resulted from a newfound engagement with the developmental logic of modernist painting. What Rauschenberg meant by the enigmatic declaration that "*Today* is their creater" would be more fully explained by another of the letter's comments on the *White Paintings*: "they bear the contriditions that deserves them a place with other outstanding paintings and yet they are not Art because they take you to a place in painting [where] art has not been. (therefore it is)." Here, Rauschenberg is invoking the modernist trope by which artistic progress proceeds via the transgression and subsequent reformation of the historically specific, conventional definitions of artistic genre.[6] Though the *White Paintings* transgressed the heretofore accepted, canonic standards of art (signaled by Rauschenberg with the capital A), this canon would eventually, or so Rauschenberg believed, be reformed to accommodate his most recent additions. In the end—as indicated by his parenthetical, elliptical reminder, "therefore it is"—their status as "Art" would be ensured by this very transgression. So that Parsons would not miss this point, Rauschenberg explained to her: "that is the pulse and movement[,] the truth of the lies in our pecul[i]ar preoccupation."

Rauschenberg had been absent from Black Mountain College in the summer of 1950 when Clement Greenberg taught courses on Kantian aesthetics and the history of modernism.[7] Nevertheless, Greenberg's specter hovers over Rauschenberg's observations, as it was in the critic's writings that the underlying tenets of modernist painting were most clearly developed. For Greenberg, painting's medium specificity was defined in terms of its flatness.[8] Thus one way to take painting to a place where art had not yet been would be to pursue it further toward its "essential" two-dimensionality. In 1951 Rauschenberg seems not only to have discovered such a logic underlying modernist painting but to have jumped immediately to its conclusion: the *White Paintings* were purged of all remnants of image, mark, or color that could represent or imply illusionistic depth. Rauschenberg's pure white, monochrome canvases therefore occupy a terminal point in this modernist development, reprising the historical role played by the monochrome as the degree zero of painting.[9] Indeed, the language Rauschenberg used to describe his achievement—terms such as "silence," "restriction," "absence," "nothing," and "the point a circle begins and ends"—clearly conveys an aura of finality.

Despite Rauschenberg's passionate advocacy, Parsons failed to give him a show. When Rauschenberg finally exhibited the *White Paintings* in New York at the Stable Gallery in 1953, Hubert Crehan, the reviewer for *Art Digest,* duly noted their culminating role within the history of modernist painting. Of the two *White Paintings* on view Crehan wrote:

> They do make an extraneous impression: they are a climax to an esthetic that began to enchant a cult of painters some time ago—I mean the esthetic of the purge, with its apparatus of elimination, its system of denials, rejections and mortifications. In the drama of this cult the bare canvas has always been the spectral hero.
>
> Rauschenberg's pair of albinos (one is made up of seven tall panels, the other of two wider panels), of course, are the image of these ascetic ideas reduced to their ultimate plastic reality. Their exhibition is a *chef-d'oeuvre* of [canvas] duck pressed to the point of no return.[10]

Although sharing Rauschenberg's view of the paintings' radicality, Crehan did not join in the artist's enthusiasm, judging that these works had gone too far.

"White canvas," Crehan concluded unequivocally, "conceived as a work of art, is beyond the artistic pale. If anything, it is a *tour de force* in the domain of personality gesture." This last term, "personality gesture," was code for arbitrary or anarchic negation—in other words, shock, or what Crehan called "dada shenanigans."[11]

Crehan's opinion would later be echoed by Greenberg. Although he encountered the *White Paintings* in 1953, Greenberg withheld commentary until 1967; then, in the article "Recentness of Sculpture," he denigrated them as being "familiar looking and even slick."[12] Unlike Crehan, Greenberg did judge the *White Paintings* to be valid as art, albeit certainly not good art. But like Crehan, Greenberg also saw Rauschenberg as succeeding only in crossing into the dadaist realm of gratuitous, "far-out" gestures. For both Crehan and Greenberg, Rauschenberg's *White Paintings* signified that art had crossed the razor-thin dividing line between a determinate negation (upon which the dialectic of formalist modernism's perpetual self-critique was founded) and an indeterminate or abstract form of negation that marked a revival of earlier avant-garde shock.[13] Indeed, in "Recentness of Sculpture," Greenberg more than implied that Rauschenberg's monochromes were responsible not only for the advent of minimalism (against which he was principally arguing) but also for the rise of pop, op, assemblage, and all those other manifestations of "Novelty art" that disavowed the role of taste and "aesthetic surprise" in legitimate artistic production.[14]

Of these dissident movements, as Hal Foster and Thierry de Duve have shown, it was minimalism that depended most directly on formalism's discursive framework and on the continuation of its determinate negation and dialectical critique.[15] Following the evolution of modernist painting from perspectival illusion to the picture plane's evident and self-reflexive flatness, the minimalists transgressed the canvas's two-dimensionality by moving outward into real space. As Annette Michelson and Rosalind Krauss have established with regard to Robert Morris's play with gestalt forms, the result was a type of "specific object" or "blank form" sculpture that led to an active engagement with the phenomenological processes of perception.[16] This shift in the locus of self-reflexivity from the internal dynamics of the work to the viewer's interaction with it formed a crucial stage in the development of a series of critical art practices, leading

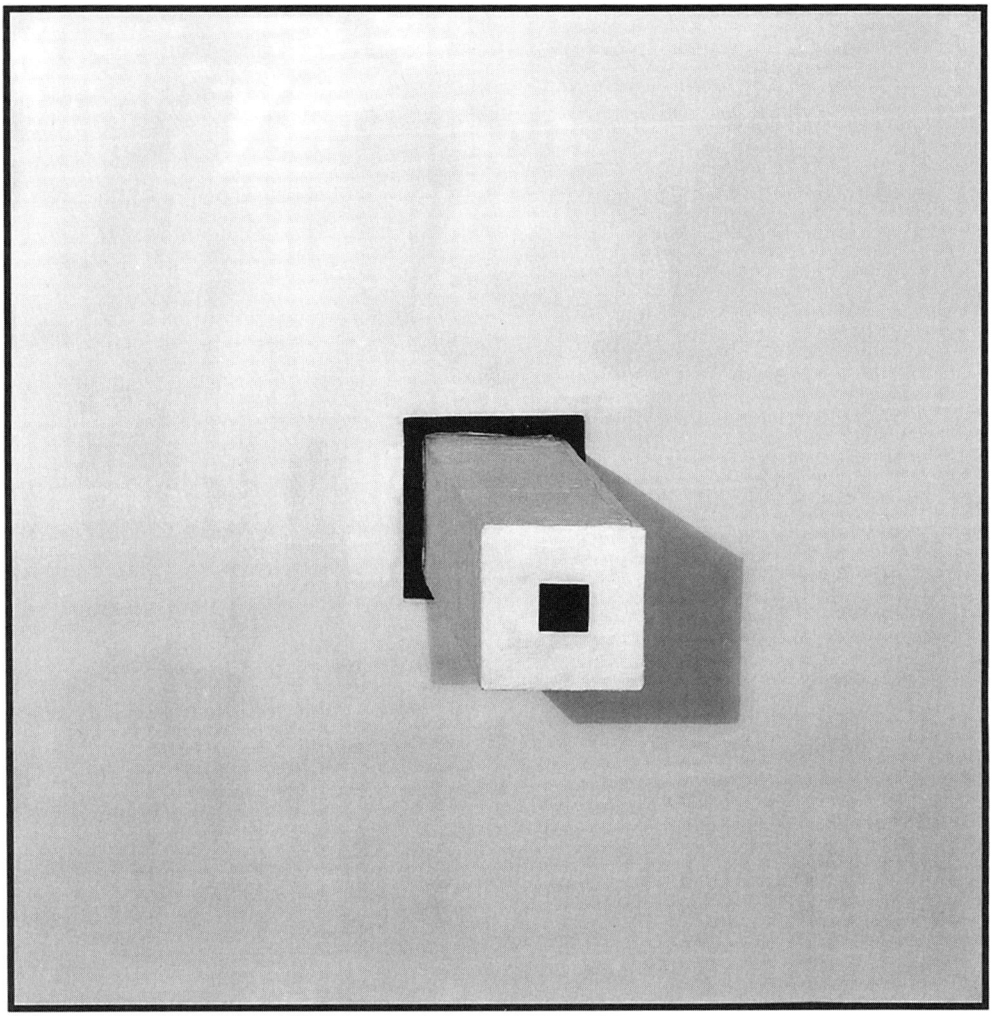

Sol LeWitt, *Wall Structure, White,* 1962. Oil on canvas and wood. 45 × 44½ × 19½ in. The LeWitt Collection, Hartford, Conn. Courtesy of the Wadsworth Atheneum Museum of Art, Hartford, Conn. © 2003 Sol LeWitt / Artists Rights Society (ARS), New York.

ultimately to those developments known collectively as institution critique. Given minimalism's formalist imbrication, then, it is not surprising that artists and critics devoted to minimal art have retained more than a hint of Crehan's and Greenberg's negative evaluation of Rauschenberg as merely recycling the anarchic tendencies of the earlier avant-garde.[17]

The irony to this continued, if surreptitious, judgment of Rauschenberg by standards originally set by formalist modernism is that he had already abandoned his short-lived involvement with such a discourse by 1953, the year of the *White Paintings*' New York exhibition. It is to the context of Rauschenberg's collaborative relationship with John Cage—whom he met in 1951, but would come to know only in the summer of 1952—that we must look to understand this transformation in the discursive framework surrounding the *White Paintings*. That development enabled the work to escape the aporias related to an understanding based on negation and to open up a new path beyond the endpoint of modernist painting represented by the monochrome.[18]

◆

In 1961, the year in which Rauschenberg was being toasted at the Museum of Modern Art's *Art of Assemblage* symposium and a year to which the birthdate of minimalism can plausibly be assigned,[19] Cage made his oft-quoted but little analyzed statement that "The white paintings were airports for the lights, shadows and particles."[20] To date, the most perceptive commentary on Cage's remark may be Louise Lawler's series of photographs, *Shadow Summer, 1987* (1987). Depicting the shadow of *Paris Air* (1919) across the photographs' monochromatic surfaces, Lawler implicitly connects Cage's insight to the example of Marcel Duchamp. Indeed, Rauschenberg's white canvases can be related to Duchamp's *Tu m'* (1918), a painting that includes representations of shadows cast by Duchamp's readymade bicycle wheel, his hatrack, and a corkscrew, along with an actual shadow produced by the protruding bottle brush. Cage's comment that the *White Paintings* were to receive airborne particles also invokes a Duchampian precedent, recalling nothing so much as Man Ray's famous photograph *Dust Breeding* (1920): a close-up depiction of Duchamp's

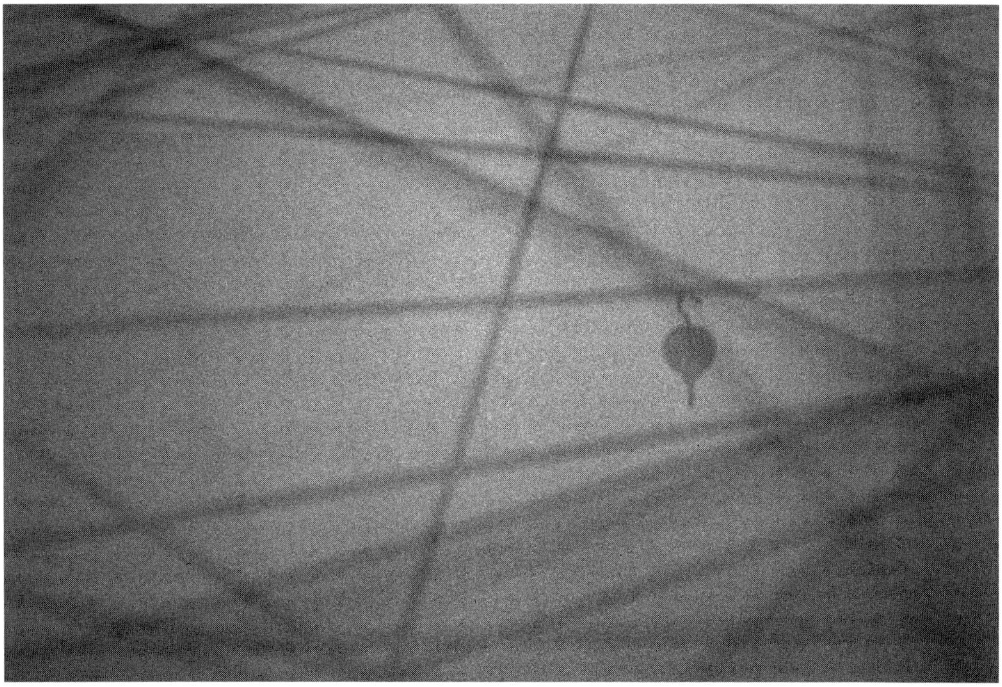

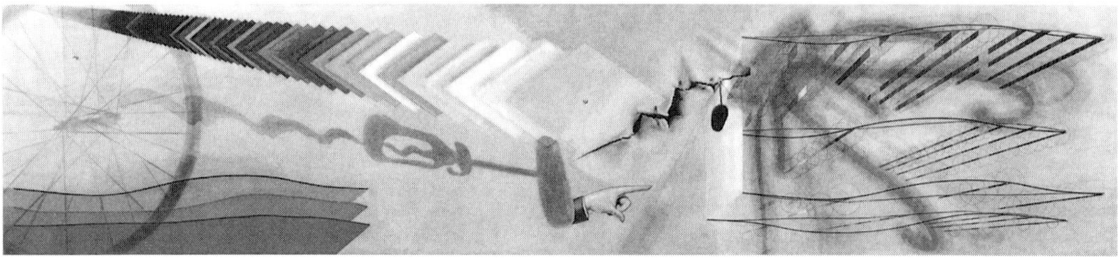

Louise Lawler, *Shadow Summer, 1987 (Gray),* 1987. Cibachrome. 26 × 38¾ in. Courtesy of the artist and Metro Pictures.

Marcel Duchamp, *Tu m',* 1918. Oil on canvas, with bottle brush, three safety pins, and one bolt. 27½ × 119⁵⁄₁₆ in. Yale University Art Gallery. Gift from the Estate of Katherine S. Dreier. © 2003 Artists Rights Society (ARS), New York / ADAGP, Paris / Estate of Marcel Duchamp.

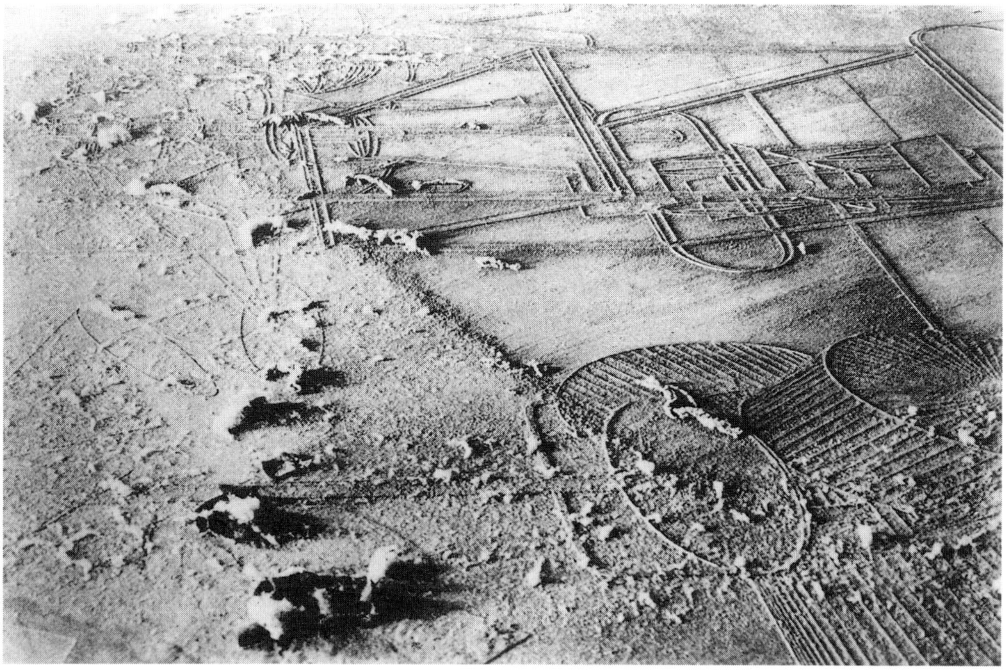

Marcel Duchamp, photographed by Man Ray, *Élevage de Poussière [Dust Breeding]*, 1920, from the *Green Box*. Philadelphia Museum of Art; Arensberg Archives. © 2003 Man Ray Trust / Artists Rights Society (ARS), NY / ADAGP, Paris.

Large Glass (1915–1923) covered with enough dust for it to resemble a miniature landscape. In "On Robert Rauschenberg, Artist, and His Work," Cage suggested that Rauschenberg's panels should be examined in similarly microscopic detail: "The white paintings caught whatever fell on them; why did I not look at them with my magnifying glass? Only because I didn't yet have one?"[21] Even Cage's description of the *White Paintings* as "airports" may have been rooted in this image: in the magazine *Littérature,* the caption beneath Man Ray's photograph reads in part, "view taken from an airplane by Man Ray."[22]

Although Rauschenberg had little or no exposure to Duchamp's work before 1953, Cage had long been familiar with it from visits to the home of Walter and Louise Arensberg in the 1930s.[23] Nevertheless, Cage's understanding of the *White Paintings* seems to have derived not directly from Duchamp but rather from László Moholy-Nagy's *The New Vision,* which Cage cited as "very influential for my thinking."[24] In that book, Moholy-Nagy discusses Kazimir Malevich's *White on White* of 1918.[25] Virtually ignoring the depiction of the square on its surface, Moholy-Nagy described Malevich's painting as "The projection screen"; he explained, "Here is to be found the interpretation of Malevich's last picture—the plain white surface, which constituted an ideal plane for kinetic light and shadow effects which, originating in the surroundings, would fall upon it. In this way, Malevich's picture represented a miniature cinema screen."[26]

This paragraph comes at the end of Moholy-Nagy's account of the history of modern painting, a development he charted through two interrelated factors: the attempt to capture temporal change and the inauguration of a new concept of space. For Moholy-Nagy, the end point of modernist painting was not a self-reflexive flatness but a literal reflectivity. His narration of modern art included such developments as photograms, airbrushing on polished surfaces, and the use of mirrors and transparencies. In a section titled "Neoplasticism; Suprematism; Constructivism," Moholy-Nagy observed:

> These actual reflections and mirrorings bring the surroundings into the picture, attaining through this a pliability of surface which has been striven for ever since the first days of impressionism.

Kazimir Malevich, *Suprematist Composition: White on White*, 1918. Oil on canvas. 31¼ × 31¼ in. The Museum of Modern Art, New York. Acquisition confirmed by agreement with the Estate of Kazimir Malevich and made possible with funds from the Mrs. John Hay Whitney Bequest (by exchange). Photograph © The Museum of Modern Art / Licensed by SCALA / Art Resource, New York.

> The surface becomes part of the atmosphere, of the atmospheric background; it sucks up light phenomena produced outside itself—a vivid contrast to the classical conception of the picture, the illusion of an open window. (p. 39)

In closing the era of perspectival illusion, neoplasticism, suprematism, and constructivism produced a new kind of artistic space: "a new space," Moholy-Nagy explained, "created with light directly, subordinating even paint (pigment)—or at least sublimating it as far as possible." And he concluded, "This stage marks the close of impressionism; it represents the mastery of the surface, not for atmospheric, but for plastic, spatial ends" (pp. 38–39).[27] Figuring as the culmination of Moholy-Nagy's (somewhat chronologically inconsistent) narrative of the development of modern painting, Malevich's white square was "The final simplification of the picture." Not only did it open up a new form of artistic space, it achieved the complete subordination of pigment initiated in the earlier movements Moholy-Nagy had chronicled. About Malevich's work, Moholy-Nagy declared: "It seems—from the standpoint of technical development—that a picture painted by hand is surpassed by the physically pure, 'unblemished,' light projection" (p. 39).

In the remainder of *The New Vision,* Moholy-Nagy follows sculpture and architecture on similar paths. The evolution of sculpture is traced from its inception as a monolithic block through the development of latticed constructions and finally to the invention of kinetic machines. Like painting, therefore, sculpture was presented as progressing from a fixed and static object to one that opens to external events and, finally, incorporates temporal movement. It is in the final section of *The New Vision,* however, that Moholy-Nagy explicitly returned to the discussion of space begun in his consideration of painting. Titled "Space (architecture)," the chapter argued that the truly spatial relations first broached by Malevich's work developed fully only in modern buildings. As opposed to a premodern architecture dealing with circumscribed, enclosed, or neatly divided volumes—what Moholy-Nagy deemed a sculptural sense of space—a "real architectonic conception" entailed the possibility of an open, uninterrupted flow between sections of a building (p. 59).

Importantly, for Moholy-Nagy this uninterrupted physical movement from one area to another within a modern building was conflated with an unimpeded visual perception of different spatial locations. The connection between movement through space and visual transparency becomes explicit in the caption he placed below Lux Feininger's image of the glass curtain wall of Walter Gropius's Dessau Bauhaus building: "Fenestrations produced the inward and outward reflections of the windows. It is no longer possible to keep apart the inside and outside. The mass of the wall, at which all the 'outside' previously stopped, is now dissolved and lets the surroundings flow into the building" (p. 62). At the conclusion of *The New Vision,* Moholy-Nagy brought together the idea of the white projection screen and the transparency of glass in a startling evocation of matter's complete sublimation:

> A white house with great glass windows surrounded by trees becomes almost transparent when the sun shines. The white walls act as projection screens on which shadows multiply the trees, and the glass plates become mirrors in which the trees are repeated. A perfect transparency is the result; the house becomes a part of nature. (pp. 63–64)

It is at this point that Moholy-Nagy's narration of modern art and architecture meets up with Cage's interest in Duchamp, and particularly in the artist's monumental, transparent "painting" *The Bride Stripped Bare by Her Bachelors, Even (The Large Glass).* Although Moholy-Nagy all but ignores Duchamp's example,[28] *The New Vision*—read as stressing the interconnection between space, transparency, and the development of painting—would certainly have informed Cage's understanding of the *Large Glass* as the paradigmatic example of an art that welcomed the intervention of ambient events and blurred the boundaries between interior and exterior. As Cage explained to Moira Roth,

> Looking at the *Large Glass,* the thing that I like so much is that I can focus my attention wherever I wish. It helps me to blur the distinction between art and life and produces a kind of silence in

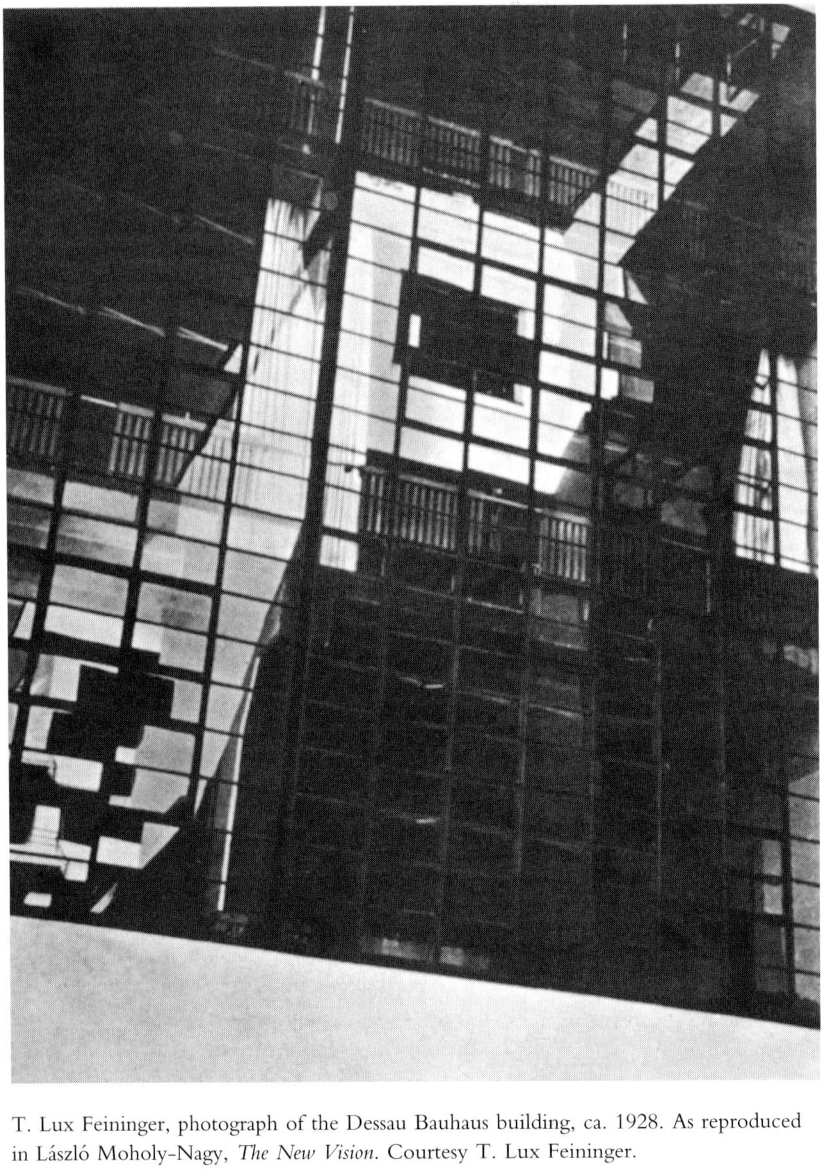

T. Lux Feininger, photograph of the Dessau Bauhaus building, ca. 1928. As reproduced in László Moholy-Nagy, *The New Vision*. Courtesy T. Lux Feininger.

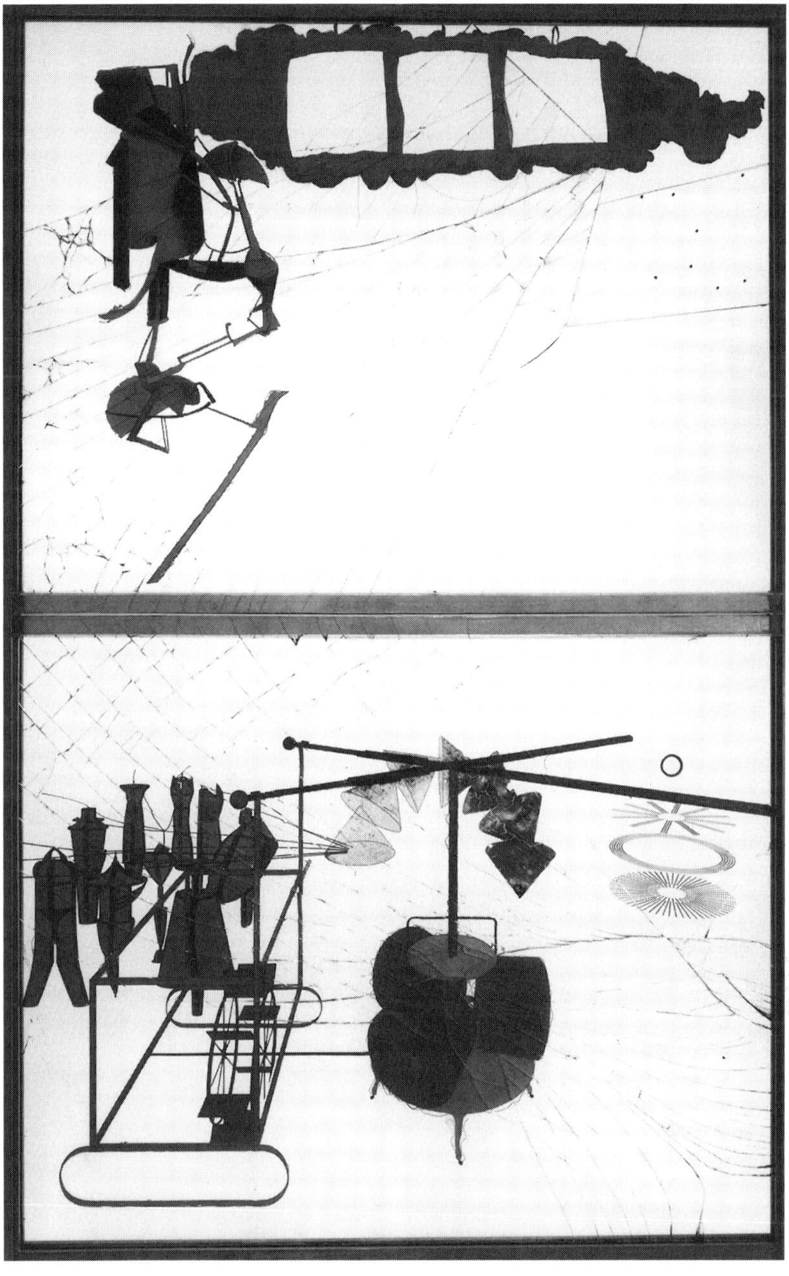

Marcel Duchamp, *The Bride Stripped Bare by Her Bachelors, Even (The Large Glass)*, 1915-1923. Oil and lead wire on glass. 109¼ × 69⅛ in. Philadelphia Museum of Art. Bequest of Katherine S. Dreier. Photograph by Graydon Wood, 1992.

> the work itself. There is nothing in it that requires me to look in one place or another or, in fact, requires me to look at all. I can look through it to the world beyond.[29]

This idea of transparency, of a space or emptiness that allowed the artwork to open up to the environment, played the key role in Cage's understanding of the difference between the historical phase of dada and its neo-dada counterpart. Cage's discussions of the idea of the space that he found in neo-dada always revolved around the interconnected examples of the glass architecture of Mies van der Rohe, the open-lattice sculptures of Richard Lippold, and the works on glass of Duchamp.[30]

When Cage encountered Rauschenberg's *White Paintings,* it would have been easy for him to understand them within the framework set forth by Moholy-Nagy in *The New Vision.* Not only had Rauschenberg created his own versions of Malevich's white square, he had also incorporated mirrors into at least one piece Cage would already have known from the Parsons exhibition.[31] Cage would also undoubtedly have noted the similarities between the blueprint images Rauschenberg had made in collaboration with Susan Weil and the photograms Moholy-Nagy characterized as "a technical first stage" in neoplastic, suprematist, and constructivist practice (p. 39). Seen in this way, Rauschenberg's *White Paintings* occupied exactly the point where Moholy-Nagy's narrative of modern painting left off, surpassing the fixity of pigment in favor of the reception of ambient, temporal events. From this point onward, Cage would adopt Moholy-Nagy's idea that a legitimately "modern" painting had to be capable of incorporating such external, temporal movement. "The way to test a modern painting is this," Cage explained; "If it is not destroyed by the action of shadows it is genuine oil painting."[32]

◆

Cage has always been clear that his infamous *4′33″* of silence was composed after seeing Rauschenberg's *White Paintings.*[33] In this, the most controversial of Cage's works, a performer sits at his or her instrument for the requisite amount of time without sounding a single note, while the audience members are given

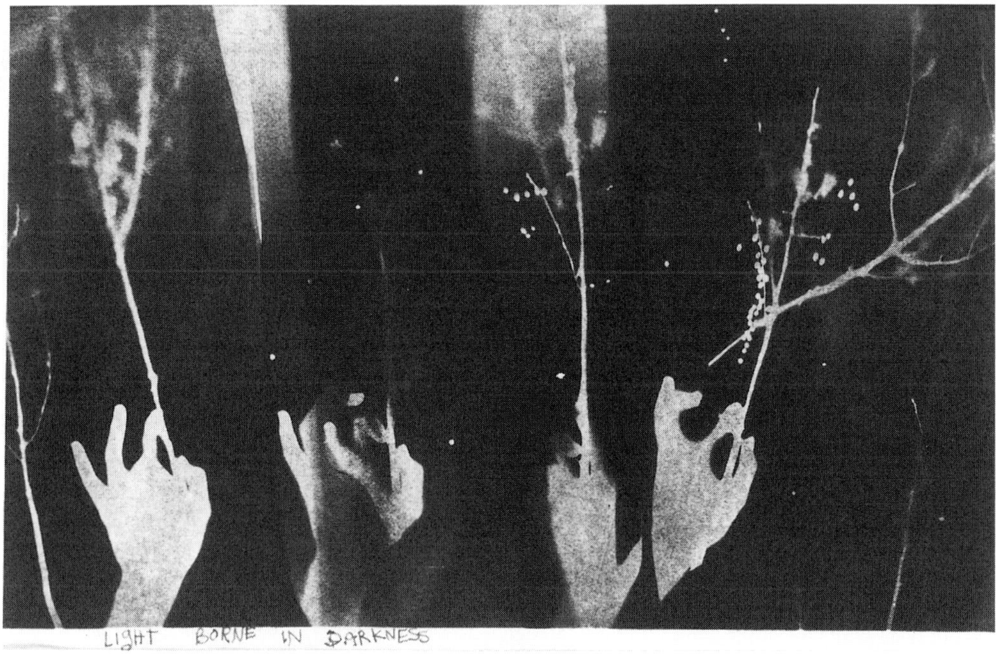

Robert Rauschenberg and Susan Weil, *Light Borne in Darkness,* ca. 1951. Monoprint: exposed blueprint paper. $6\frac{1}{4} \times 9\frac{3}{4}$ in. Milwaukee Art Museum, Milwaukee. Gift of Mr. and Mrs. Irving D. Saltzstein.

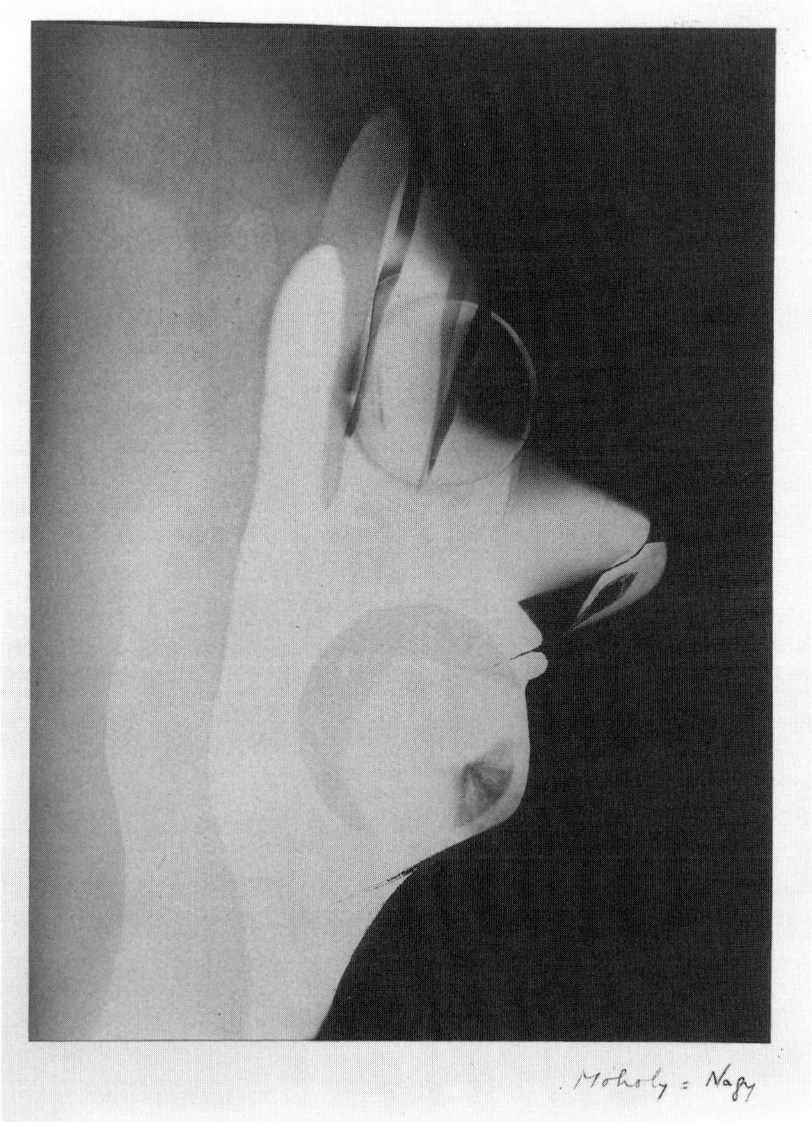

László Moholy-Nagy, *Self-Portrait Lighting a Cigarette,* 1924. Photogram. 14½ × 10¾ in. © 2003 Artists Rights Society (ARS), New York / VG Bild-Kunst, Bonn. Courtesy George Eastman House.

to hear the sounds that occur in their surroundings. Cage would explain that not only did Rauschenberg's *White Paintings* give him the "courage" to compose a piece of such radicality,[34] they made him fear that the development of music had fallen behind that of art. "Oh, yes, I must," Cage recalls thinking, "otherwise I'm lagging, otherwise music is lagging."[35]

Despite Cage's insistence that the *White Paintings* preceded the composition of *4′33″*, historians have been tempted to backdate Cage's silent piece from the summer of 1952 to early 1948.[36] The reason derives from a comment Cage made in the lecture "A Composer's Confessions," delivered at Vassar College in February of that year. Cage explained to his audience that he had "several new desires," the first of which was

> to compose a piece of uninterrupted silence and sell it to Muzak Co. It will be 3 or 4-½ minutes long—those being the standard lengths of "canned" music and its title will be *Silent Prayer*. It will open with a single idea which I will attempt to make as seductive as the color and shape and fragrance of a flower. The ending will approach imperceptibility.[37]

Although *Silent Prayer* undeniably represents an early stage in the development of *4′33″*, the two works—like Rauschenberg's pre- and post-1952 understandings of his *White Paintings*—rightfully belong within separate aesthetic paradigms.

As noted by Eric de Visscher, who has most carefully charted the rapid evolution of Cage's concept of silence during these years, an important component of *Silent Prayer* is its antagonistic relationship to Muzak.[38] Indeed, on one level, *Silent Prayer* appears as nothing more than the abstract negation of the unceasing stream of piped-in, commercial background music. In 1948 Cage had not yet formulated his mature concept of silence, and the "uninterrupted silence" of *Silent Prayer* was still understood in terms of the complete absence of sound. Nevertheless, even at this early stage, Cage's piece was not conceived simply in negative terms and was not intended primarily to shock its audience through musical withdrawal. Instead, with *Silent Prayer* Cage sought to revalue silence as a distinct essence, presenting it with a positivity of its own.[39]

More than being simply the negation of Muzak, *Silent Prayer* was to serve as an acoustical manifestation of a metaphysical concept derived in part from Cage's study of the medieval European mystic Meister Eckhart.[40] His metaphorical description of the piece in terms of "the color and shape and fragrance of a flower" distinctly echoes a line found in Eckhart: "I am come like the fragrance of a flower."[41] In Eckhart, this phrase occurs as one of a series of analogies provided by St. Augustine to describe the manner in which the "eternal Word" can be "uttered in the Person of the Son while remaining God by nature in his nature."[42] Thus, Cage's initial view of his silent piece closely resembled Rauschenberg's earliest understanding of the *White Paintings* in relation to incarnation. Like them, *Silent Prayer* seems to have been conceived as an earthly manifestation of a divine essence, the embodiment of "an organic silence." Indeed, in the immediate context of this quotation, Eckhart describes the indivisible and all-encompassing nature of the divine essence precisely in terms of "absolute stillness" and "silence."[43]

Between 1948 and 1951, however, Cage's idea of silence began to change rapidly and significantly. Instead of seeing sound and silence as opposites, Cage came to understand them as inextricably interrelated. In part, this transformation in Cage's thinking parallels a deeper understanding of Eckhart's theology.[44] For Eckhart, God's divine essence was presented in the form of an all-encompassing and all-supporting "Ground"—"from which," Cage summarized, "all impermanencies flow and to which they return."[45] By 1951, Cage's ideas of sound and silence were further coupled with an emerging interest in Zen Buddhism, which conceived of being and nothingness not as opposed to one another but as necessarily intertwined.[46] But though this understanding of the relationship of sound and silence more completely integrated the existence of one within the other, Cage had not yet overcome the duality between them.[47] While he saw them as more closely interrelated, sound and silence still remained distinct and different—resembling, as he stated in "Lecture on Something," the positive and negative of "an alternating current."[48]

It was Cage's oft-told experience within an anechoic chamber at Harvard in 1951 that enabled him to overcome the remaining distinction between silence and sound. Once inside the room, specially dampened so that no sound could either penetrate the walls or reverberate on the inside, Cage heard not the absolute silence he had been expecting but rather two distinct sounds emanating from his own body: one was the low tone of his blood circulating, the other the high tone of his nervous system.[49] As a result, Cage came to understand the strict impossibility of silence, famously redefining it as the presence of unintentional noises. "The situation one is clearly in," Cage concluded, "is not objective (sound-silence), but rather subjective (sounds only), those intended and those others (so-called silence) not intended."[50]

This event is among the most significant and most frequently recounted in Cage literature. Nevertheless, it seems to have gone unobserved that whatever his actual experience in the anechoic chamber, both Cage's story and the insight derived from it were, in essence, a recasting of Henri Bergson's "The Idea of 'Nothing'" from *Creative Evolution.* In that discussion, with which Cage was familiar, Bergson imagines a scene directly analogous to Cage's within the anechoic chamber in order to demonstrate the futility of attempting to imagine nothing.[51] "I am going to close my eyes, stop my ears, extinguish one by one the sensations that come to me from the outer world," declares Bergson:

> Now it is done; all my perceptions vanish, the material universe sinks into silence and the night.—I subsist, however, and cannot help myself subsisting. I am still there, with the organic sensations which come to me from the surface and from the interior of my body, with the recollections which my past perceptions have left behind them—nay, with the impression, most positive and full, of the void I have just made about me. (p. 278)

Significantly, this section of *Creative Evolution* was devoted to a critique of the reification of the idea of nothing (pp. 295–296)—precisely the type of reification Cage had been attempting in *Silent Prayer*'s elevation of the concept of silence to a substantive essence. Through his demonstration, Bergson sought to prove that such nothingness was in fact devoid of ontological status: it was merely a "pseudo-idea" resulting from confusion within the subject (p. 277). What was perceived as the absence of an object or the negation of an idea actually corresponded only to the finding of one thing while searching for, or expecting, another. It was—to use one of Bergson's examples—like declaring "this is not verse" when, while searching through a bookshelf in order to find verse, one happens upon a book filled with prose (pp. 221, 232).

In the story of the anechoic chamber, Cage imported Bergson's critique of negation from philosophy into music, applying it to sound in specific rather than to being in general; but the conclusion was the same. Indeed, a substitution of the term "sound" for "reality" in Bergson's writing provides Cage's mature understanding of silence exactly. This is Bergson:

> Now the unreality which is here in question is purely relative to the direction in which our attention is engaged, for we are immersed in realities and cannot pass out of them; only, if the present reality is not the one we are seeking, we speak of the *absence* of this sought-for reality wherever we find the *presence* of another. We thus express what we have as a function of what we want. (p. 273)

It is Bergson's critique of negation, expressed in his contention that "there is no absolute void in nature" (p. 281), that ultimately underlies Cage's statement that "There is no such thing as silence," as well as Rauschenberg's later pronouncement that "A canvas is never empty."[52]

Yet, although inextricably related to his understanding of Bergson's critique of negation, Cage's experience in the anechoic chamber was still not, as existing literature would have it, sufficient to produce the understanding of silence showcased in *4′33″*.[53] In the chamber, environmental noises were completely shut out, and what Cage heard was entirely predicated on their exclusion. In *4′33″*, by contrast, the sounds of the environment are allowed to resonate freely within the composition. What connects these two is the idea of transparency developed by Moholy-Nagy in *The New Vision*—hence the profound effect that Rauschenberg's *White Paintings* had on Cage at Black Mountain College. Understood in terms of Moholy-Nagy's incorporation of external events, they indicated to Cage a means of escaping the solipsism of his Harvard experience and revealed to him that music was, as he put it, "behind."[54] With *4′33″*, then, Cage succeeded in moving music into the same "modern" (we would now say "postmodern") paradigm occupied by Rauschenberg. Following on his understanding of the *White Paintings,* Cage's criterion of musical modernity became an acoustical "transparency" to sounds outside the work. As he later noted, "A cough or baby crying will not ruin a good piece of modern music."[55]

In the following year, Cage further clarified the connection between Rauschenberg's *White Paintings* and his *4′33″* in a version of the score dedicated to Irwin Kremin. The original score for *4′33″* was measured out on conventional music paper, with staffs and bar lines but without notes or rests. A second version notated the piece linguistically as "I. Tacet / II. Tacet / III. Tacet." The Kremin version, however, consists of six sheets of entirely blank paper onto which Cage drew six long, vertical lines.[56] Each line represents the beginning or the end of one of the work's three separate movements, which last, respectively, thirty seconds; two minutes, twenty-three seconds; and one minute, forty seconds. Clearly recalling the edges of Rauschenberg's abutted canvases, these lines form the empty structure of *4′33″*. A key provided at the bottom of the page reads "1 page = 7 inches = 56″ [seconds]" and provides the means by which the score can be read horizontally across the page to give the timing of the movements. Visually, the score acts just as does one of Rauschenberg's *White Paintings;* the lights, shadows, and particles falling onto it become analogues of the environmental sounds occurring within the piece when "performed."

◆

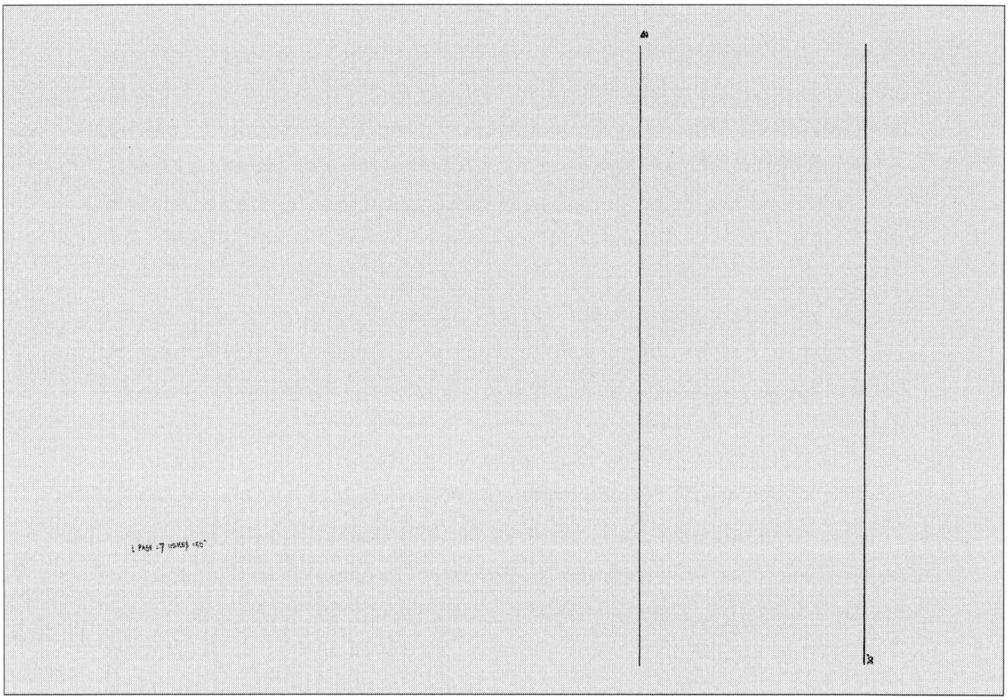

John Cage, *4′33″*, 1952. Score in proportional notation, 1953. Key and first page.

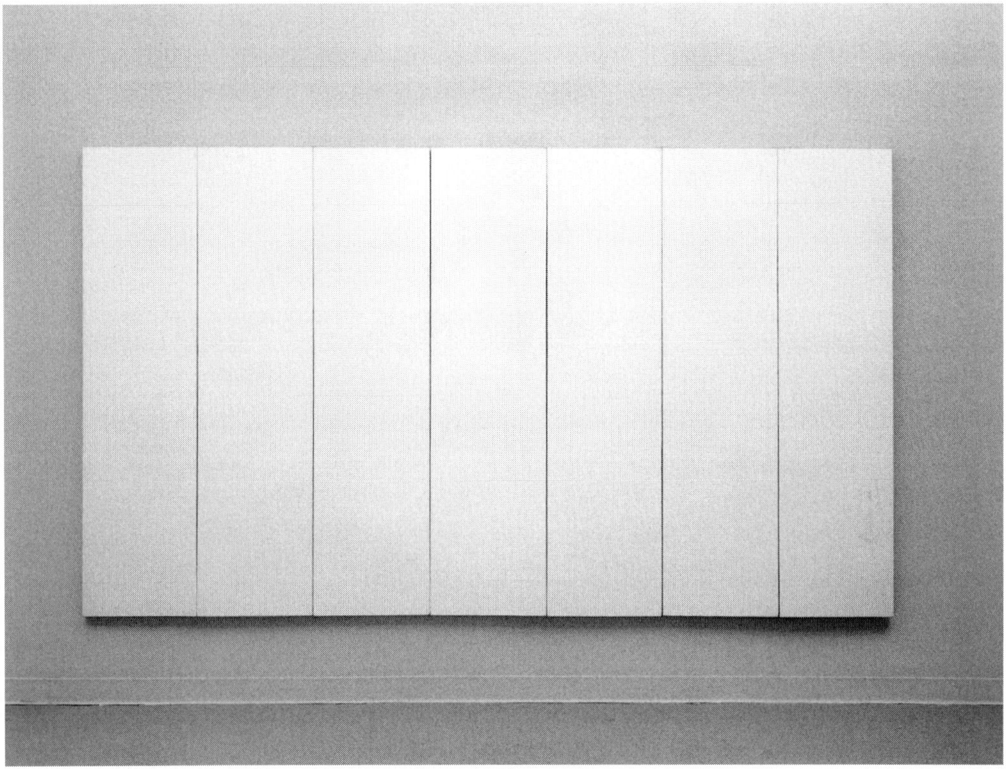

White Painting, 1951. Oil on canvas. Seven panels, 72 × 18 in. each; 72 × 126 in. overall. Collection of the artist, New York.

Cage's assimilation of Moholy-Nagy's ideas to those of Bergson went beyond the deployment of "transparency" to escape the hermeticism of the anechoic chamber. Indeed, Cage's Bergsonism seems to have been particularly profound. While, in *The New Vision,* Moholy-Nagy characterized the concept of transparency as opening the artwork to temporal changes in the surrounding environment and—in his description of the white house with great glass windows—called this environment "nature," it was in Bergson's *Creative Evolution* that Cage (and, through him, Rauschenberg) would find the ideas of nature and temporality (or, more properly, duration) most intricately intertwined.

Since the mid-1940s Cage had adopted the Indian art historian Ananda K. Coomaraswamy's idea that the purpose of art was "the imitation of nature in her manner of operation."[57] Initially, he sought simply to illustrate a cyclical idea of nature, as in the 1947 ballet *The Seasons,* where each movement corresponded to a different time of year. But around 1950, Cage began to espouse a more Bergsonian view of nature as a continual process of creation and change. For Bergson, the ideas of nature and life were characterized not as cyclical recurrence but as "continual *change,*" "perpetual becoming," and the "undivided flux" of creation.[58] Although discussed in terms of what often appears to be an animistic life force—Bergson's famous "élan vital"—this perpetual becoming was ultimately underlain by the incessant, unidirectional flow of time.[59] As Bergson wrote in *Creative Evolution,* "The more we study the nature of time, the more we shall comprehend that duration means invention, the creation of forms, the continual elaboration of the absolutely new" (p. 11). Duration's irreversibility guaranteed that all of creation would necessarily differ from itself, if for no other reason than its existence at a fractionally later moment in time.

Despite existing within this fluid temporal movement, humankind failed to grasp its situation. Bergson argued that perception is filtered through the intellect, which has evolved with a view toward utilizing and manipulating nature to its own benefit.[60] In *Creative Evolution* and elsewhere, however, Bergson was concerned with determining the means by which one might critically mobilize an understanding of reality-in-itself to dislocate those forms of instrumental reason to which the intellect was predisposed. According to Bergson, such dislocation requires a turn away from the intellect, with its focus on intentional action and the associated idea of negation, and toward an identification with nature. This turn Bergson referred to as "intuition," which he understood as the proper substance of philosophy. Bergson summarized the different ontological visions resulting from intellect and intuition thus:

> If we pass (consciously or unconsciously) through the idea of the nought in order to reach that of being, the being to which we come is a logical or mathematical essence, therefore non-temporal. And, consequently, a static conception of the real is forced on us: everything appears given once for all, in eternity. But we must accustom ourselves to think being directly, without making a detour, without first appealing to the phantom of the nought which interposes itself between it and us. We must strive to see in order to see, and no longer to see in order to act. Then the Absolute is revealed very near us and, in a certain measure, in us. It is of psychological and not of mathematical nor logical essence. It lives with us. Like us, but in certain aspects infinitely more concentrated and more gathered up in itself, it *endures*. (pp. 298–299)

For his part, Cage never explicitly echoed Bergson's interest in intuition, nor the typically Bergsonian emphasis on evolution and biology. Combined as they were with his interest in Zen, Cage's borrowings were generally more abstract and less strident than Bergson's *Lebensphilosophie*. Yet Cage did adopt Bergson's ideas of nature as flux in duration, of the role of temporality in the perpetual creation of the new, and of the interrelated functioning of intellect and memory. Like Bergson, Cage saw that to dissociate oneself from the intellect's instrumental predispositions, one had to turn away from the anthropocentric point of view and identify with nature—or, as Cage termed it, the "outside."[61] In the article "Experimental Music," immediately after discussing his experience in the anechoic chamber, Cage observed:

> Until I die there will be sounds. And they will continue following my death. One need not fear about the future of music.
>
> But this fearlessness only follows if, at the parting of the ways, where it is realized that sounds occur whether intended or not, one turns in the direction of those he does not intend. This turning is psychological and seems at first to be a giving up of everything that belongs to humanity—for a musician, the giving up of music. This psychological turning leads to the world of nature, where, gradually or suddenly, one sees that humanity and nature, not separate, are in this world together; that nothing was lost when everything was given away. In fact everything was gained.[62]

In this passage we find Cage echoing not only Bergson's ideas but also his terms. Rather than emphasizing intuition, however, Cage characterized the turn toward nature primarily in terms of the avant-garde strategy of perceptual estrangement. Building on the perspective put forth by Moholy-Nagy, Cage saw the task of the artist as producing works that fostered a more direct perception of duration. Thus he distinguished between a conventional work of art and one that allowed for the perception of temporal events: one was the work as "object," the other the work as "process." As he explained,

> we're no longer making objects but processes and it is easy to see that we are not separate from processes but are in them, so that our feelings are not about but in them. Criticism vanishes. Awareness and use and curiosity enter into making our consciousness. We are glad to see that we are noticing what happens. Asked what happened, we have to say we don't know, or we could say we see more clearly but we can't tell you what we see.[63]

Here, precisely deploying past and present tense, Cage differentiates between intellect (predicated on the grasping of a stable entity) and perception (understood as a nearly pure perception existing within the present). When asked "what *happened*" in the past, Cage does not know; nevertheless, he is "noticing what *happens*" in the present, seeing it more clearly even though it cannot be grasped, cognized, or readily communicated.

On the occasion of Rauschenberg's 1953 exhibition at the Stable Gallery, Cage wrote a statement linking this Bergsonian critique of negation to the *White Paintings*' incorporation of duration. First, he noted the apparent negation of nearly all the artistic features by which the paintings could be grasped:

No subject
No image
No taste
No object
No beauty
No message
No talent
No technique (no why)
No idea
No intention
No art
No feeling
No black
No white (no *and*).

Cage then declared that rather than being empty, these pieces were thereby opened to the temporally changing processes outside themselves: "After careful consideration, I have come to the conclusion that there is nothing in these paintings that could not be changed, that they can be seen in any light and are not destroyed by the action of shadows." Finally Cage exclaimed, in a sort of postscript, "Hallelujah! the blind can see again; the water's fine."[64] In 1961, Cage would elaborate on this final comment, adding the same distinction between perception and recollection noted above: "Blind to what he *has seen* so that seeing this time is as though first seeing."[65]

Such an understanding of the perceptual immersion within duration would have been reinforced by Cage's developing interest in the Zen teachings of Daisetz T. Suzuki. For Cage, Zen represented a philosophy of immanence, a fundamental tenet of which was the rejection of any stable state of transcendence or separation from the actual world. As presented by Cage, the state of Zen enlightenment primarily entailed realizing that transcendence was impossible and that the existence one was in was existence *tout court.* As Cage's own gloss on his oft-quoted remark about the purpose of music—"to quiet the mind thus making it susceptible to divine influences"—would have it: "We learned from Oriental thought, that those divine influences are, in fact, the environment in which we are."[66]

Cage's claim encapsulates the difference between *Silent Prayer* and *4′33″*. The "transparency" of the later work, its openness to the sounds in the environment, is its foregrounding of an immanent existence within the temporality and circumstances of the actual world. After the summer of 1952, Rauschenberg's *White Paintings* had also come to be understood in the same way, losing any residual traces of the divinity or transcendence described to Parsons in favor of concretely embracing the spatiotemporal conditions of their environment.[67]

◆

Rauschenberg's terminology was never as identifiably Bergsonian as Cage's and lacked the composer's relation to Eastern philosophy and religion, but he developed much the same understanding of existence and of the intellect's inevitable arresting of temporal movement. This he was at pains to explain during the *Art of Assemblage* symposium, although lacking their larger context his interjections have remained largely incomprehensible. "Every minute everything is different, everywhere," he declared. "It's all flowing. Where is the basis for criticism, for being right or wrong, without blindly or deliberately assuming or affecting a stop?" With the artwork understood as a means of presenting this ever-changing moment to perception, the question for Rauschenberg in 1961 was still "what should be done to prevent the loss of this moment, to keep this moment from being realized?"[68]

Rauschenberg had already explored temporality in such early works as *This Is the First Half of a Print Designed to Exist in Passing Time* (ca. 1949). By the time of his Stable Gallery exhibition in 1953, he had also come to share Cage's understanding of the *White Paintings* as vehicles for a perception that relativized the atemporal, conceptualizing confines of intellect. He thus declared to Hubert Crehan, "My black paintings and my white paintings are either too full or too empty to be thought—thereby they remain visual experiences. These pictures are not Art."[69] Here, Rauschenberg's assertion that his "pictures are not Art" is of a different order than his earlier claim to Parsons that his "paintings . . . are not Art." Gone is the imbrication with formalist modernism and the attention to medium specificity found in his letter of 1951. The progressive elimination of pictorial elements is no longer conceived as a reduction toward the essence of painting—an aesthetic of negation or, as Crehan termed it, "the purge." Instead, Rauschenberg followed out the implications of the critique of negation; in eliminating artistic elements from his paintings, he was now allowing for incorporation of the temporally changing, non-art realm. By incorporating duration, the *White Paintings* no longer represented a return to the monochrome as degree zero of painting. Rather, they demonstrated that "there is *no* zero," or—as he put it in another statement that met with utter incomprehension from his interlocutors at the *Art of Assemblage* symposium—that within zero, "There must be room for an any way there."[70]

Such declarations enable us to begin to understand how Rauschenberg's *White Paintings* open up a neo-avant-garde paradigm that differs from those of the historical avant-garde as well as formalism and minimalism. For as they came

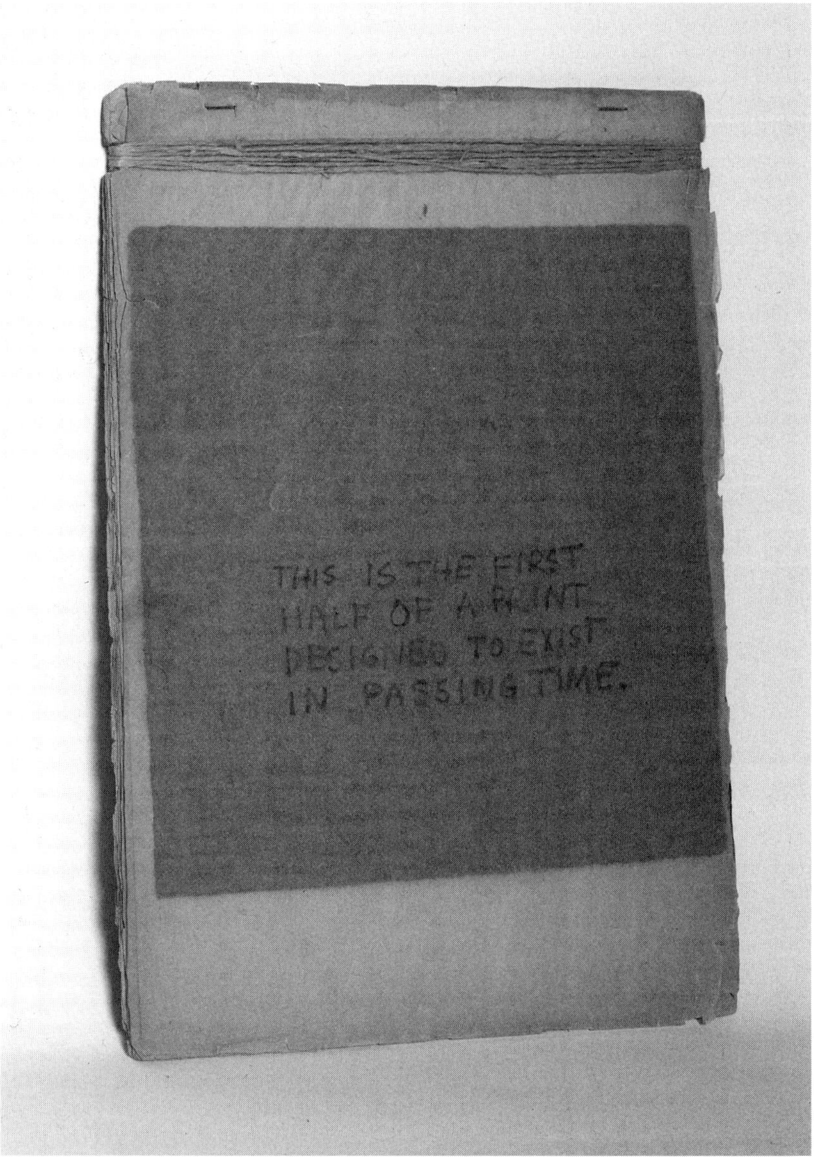
THIS IS THE FIRST
HALF OF A PRINT
DESIGNED TO EXIST
IN PASSING TIME.

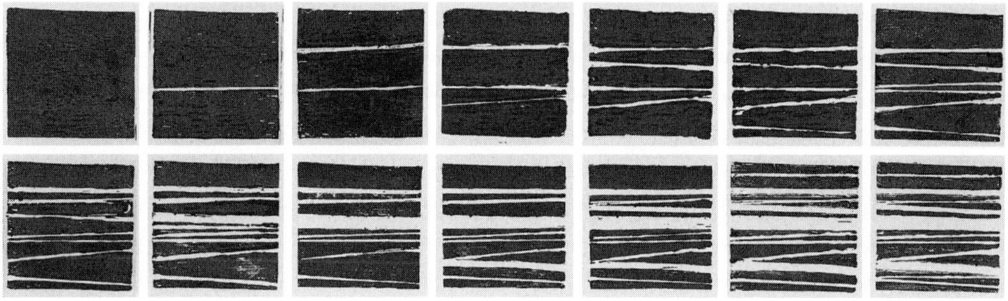

This Is the First Half of a Print Designed to Exist in Passing Time, ca. 1949. Fourteen woodcuts (ink on paper; above) and title page (pencil on tracing paper; opposite) bound at top with twine. $12^{1}/_{8} \times 8^{7}/_{8} \times {}^{1}/_{4}$ in. Collection of the artist, New York.

to be viewed in the summer of 1952, the *White Paintings* no longer figure as either the final products of a determinant negation of artistic conventions or the results of a negation of an abstract or anarchic type. Rather, as Cage's Bergsonism suggests, they had come to be situated at the beginning of an aesthetic paradigm in which difference was conceived as an ontological first principle, the positive and productive motor force driving a dynamic conception of "nature."

◆

Such a reevaluation of difference lends an added dimension to Rauschenberg's production of the early 1950s. It was in the same year as the Stable Gallery exhibition, for instance, that Rauschenberg produced both his *Dirt Paintings* (one of which was dedicated to John Cage) and his *Growing Painting*. When seen from the perspective of a Bergsonian understanding of nature and temporality, these pieces can, like the *White Paintings,* be understood as more than latter-day dadaist critiques of artistic expression. But whereas the *White Paintings* primarily opened themselves to the fleeting contingencies of temporal change, Rauschenberg's dirt and grass paintings turned more clearly toward duration's longer-term effects. "He is not saying; he is painting," Cage observed: "(What is Rauschenberg saying?) The message is conveyed by dirt which, mixed with an adhesive, sticks to itself and to the canvas upon which he places it. Crumbling and responding to changes in weather, the dirt unceasingly does my thinking."[71]

Importantly, the temporality at stake in Rauschenberg's dirt and grass paintings is as far from a minimalist phenomenology, necessarily entwined with the human perceptual apparatus, as it is from a high modernist dream of transcendent or mystical presence. Rather, like Bergson's famous sugar cube that dissolves at its own pace (despite all our impatience), Rauschenberg's dirt and grass paintings appear as attempts to show matter in its own duration: a duration related to the natural creation or deterioration within which humanity exists, but that is not itself dependent on humanity. These works therefore call for the same type of turning sought by Cage—away from an anthropocentric point of view and toward a perceptual identification with life in or as duration. As Cage would write in 1956:

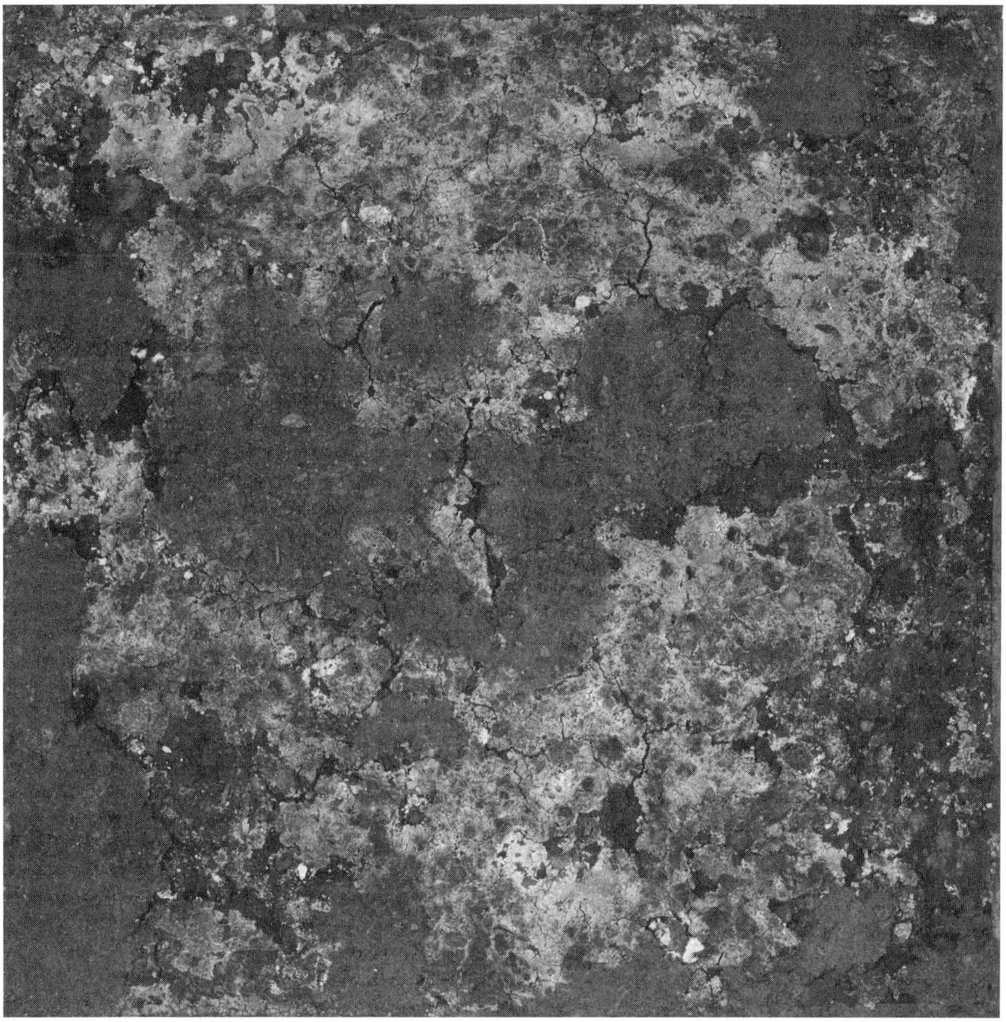

Dirt Painting (for John Cage), ca. 1953. Dirt and mold in wood frame. 15½ × 16 × 2½ in. Collection of the artist, New York.

> For "art" and "music," when anthropocentric (involved in self-expression), seem trivial and lacking in urgency to me. We live in a world where there are things as well as people. Trees, stones, water, everything is expressive. . . . Life goes on very well without me, and that will explain to you my silent piece, *4′33″*.[72]

Here we once again find an echo of that unmediated grasp of existence called for by Bergson in *Creative Evolution.* "Matter or mind," wrote Bergson,

> reality has appeared to us as a perpetual becoming. It makes itself or it unmakes itself, but it is never something made. Such is the intuition that we have of mind when we draw aside the veil which is interposed between our consciousness and ourselves. This, also, is what our intellect and senses themselves would show us of matter, if they could obtain a direct and disinterested idea of it. (p. 272)

Is it not, perhaps, through such a Bergsonian lens that we might begin to approach Rauschenberg's famous, but enigmatic, statement about art and life? "Painting relates to both art and life. Neither can be made. (I try to act in the gap between the two.)"[73] If life cannot be made, that is because it is not contained within the anthropocentric realm, not predicated on intentions of fabrication or manipulation. As interminable flux or perpetual change, life cannot be reproduced or even entirely grasped in its transformations. Art, by contrast, would be understood as referring to the intentional, expressive, and communicative attributes found in, for example, a work of art with a capital A. While all of these are undeniably perceived, the artist nonetheless strictly fails to make them in their entirety; as Cage indicated, "trying to force life into one's own idea of it, of what it should be, is only absurd. The absurdity comes from the artificiality of it, of not living, but of having to have first an idea of how one should do it and then stumblingly trying."[74] The gap between these two poles—of intention and nonintention, object and process, stasis and duration—is not only (as Cage once hinted) the place where every existing thing actually is,[75] it is also where one would situate an art that emulated nature in its manner of operation: purposeless, indeterminate, and ever-changing.

For any perception of duration, however, a certain form of memory is required. This Bergson understood not as a function of dwelling in the past but as a prolongation of the past within the present, a divided and internally fragmented commingling that enables the present to be distinguished from the past. According to Bergson, the past that changes continually also continually builds up, increases as each moment in the present is retired and past piles upon past. This preserved past, which enables the realization of the present, is memory in a nonintentional, nonindividual sense.[76] More than the decay of the *Dirt Paintings* or the growth of the grass painting, it is the accumulation of dust on the *White Paintings*' surfaces that serves as an analogue of this passage of time and storage of the past within the present. The incessant accumulation of dust is what in fact ensures that no two views of a *White Painting* will ever truly be the same no matter how similar the circumstances. Each *White Painting* is like the Heraclitean stream: it is, strictly speaking, impossible to see the same one twice.[77] Moreover, what is seen upon the canvas is itself split between the immediate play of lights and shadows, on the one hand, and the incessant accumulation of dust, on the other. There are thus—as in the "present" moment as theorized by Bergson—two different levels or registers of time that commingle without identity on the surface of each of the *White Paintings*.

This aspect of the *White Paintings* would become clear only in 1953, when Rauschenberg produced his *Erased de Kooning Drawing*. Although the work was described by Calvin Tomkins as a blatantly Freudian symbolic patricide,[78] Rauschenberg has consistently denied any motivation of critique or negation for his provocative action. As he declared bluntly in 1976, "It was nothing destructive. . . . It wasn't a gesture, it had nothing to do with destruction."[79] While not without some measure of aggression, the transformation of the de Kooning into what Rauschenberg called a "monochrome no-image" can be understood from a Bergsonian perspective as the evacuation of intentional imagery and individual expression (i.e., "art") in favor of a receptivity to contingent visual sensations (i.e., "life").[80] Yet, while the nearly imperceptible remnants of

Erased de Kooning Drawing, 1953. Traces of ink and crayon on paper with mat and hand-lettered (ink) label in gold leaf frame. 25¼ × 21¾ in. San Francisco Museum of Modern Art. Purchased through a gift of Phyllis Wattis.

de Kooning's drawing become mere shadows, no longer impeding perception of the actual shadows cast across its surface (and making the drawing, in Cage's terminology, truly "modern"), they were not eradicated entirely. As Thomas Crow has perceptively noted,

> [Rauschenberg's] notorious act of erasing a drawing solicited from Willem de Kooning in no way obliterated its object; instead, with the faint ghost of the heavy original marks still visible after weeks of labor (and *another* drawing showing from the opposite side of the sheet), it made it possible for his white paintings and an autograph piece of de Kooning's art to be apprehended in parallel to one another—the internal contrasts of the latter being diminished to the point that it demanded the same slowed-down, hyper-receptive mode of attention in order to yield up its visual rewards.[81]

Like dust, de Kooning's drawing becomes part of the preserved yet accessible past, as the paper is rendered a palimpsest of two temporalities coexisting in the ineluctably split, dual moment of the present.

To conceptualize the *White Paintings*' reception fully, however, we must also take into account that people have their own particular access to the store of the past that is memory. Each individual's interaction with the past not only is a determining factor in his or her subjectivity but also inheres within the very activity of perception, splitting it among different temporalities as well. This perceptual combination of memory and environmental stimuli further guarantees that every viewer's response to a *White Painting* will differ. Rauschenberg would address such individual reception in the *Art of Assemblage* symposium, proposing it as an inherent, if unrecognized, characteristic of all art. Every viewer, he explained,

> has a different series of experiences to fall back on because all this is about the past. . . . People keep shuffling up to the picture with everything that has happened to them, and they turn to their

> neighbor and tell them that this is what the picture is about. But any two people and any one painting would show that that couldn't possibly be the same reaction every time.[82]

During the course of the symposium, Rauschenberg received support for his position from fellow panelist Duchamp. When asked what type of reaction the readymades were intended to provoke, Duchamp replied that after an initial moment of "disorientation" came an effect of

> connotation—meaning that according to the observer's imagination, he can go into any field or any form of imagination and associations of ideas he wants, depending on his own reactions. In other words, my reactions were not to be his reactions at all. It was a sort of catalytic form in itself, ready to be accepted by everybody, or to be interpreted by the different temperaments of all the spectators.[83]

This impulse to create works that underline such a differential reception, that make each beholder aware of the role played by his or her individual history and subject position, is what forms the crux of the neo-avant-garde project initiated by Rauschenberg and Cage. Their work thus differs from that attributed to the historical avant-garde, for it relinquishes the attempt, common to dada and constructivism, to address or forge a collective political subject based on similarity, commonality, or exchange. For Rauschenberg, as for Cage, any collective subsumption of difference—whether advocated by the Left or the Right, for political mobilization or mass cultural conformity—was suspect. While endorsing a collective agency based on difference, it was precisely on the grounds of a uniform "mass reaction" that Rauschenberg most strenuously objected to the entire notion of shock.[84] This stance also forms an important distinction between Rauschenberg and Cage and their minimalist successors, for their work does not presuppose any common denominator of subjectivity, as in the subject who comes to consciousness of his or her perceptual processes through the phenomenological interaction with the minimalist object.

In this regard, the aesthetic and political position that Rauschenberg and Cage developed can be allied with certain aspects of an identity politics. As Caroline A. Jones and Jonathan D. Katz have argued, "silence," as an artistic strategy, should not be understood as mere apolitical indifference.[85] Rather, it can be conceived as a strategy of resistance—formulated within the context of masculinist abstract expressionism and McCarthyite political repression—that opposes hegemonic cultural values by opening the processes of perception and interpretation to other voices and points of view. To quote from one of Katz's strongest presentations of this position:

> Neither musical nor unmusical, Cage's silence was quite precisely other, escaping the binaries that circumscribed the status quo as the sole arena for contestation. As a result, it managed to be an antiauthoritative mode that was nonetheless not oppositional. Revealing the power of the individual to construct meanings unauthored by, and under the very nose of, the dominant culture, silence was, in a sense, seditious.[86]

Cage and Rauschenberg's antiexpressive, antisubjective, and antiauthoritarian artistic position was clearly in no small part a product of their being positioned beyond the officially sanctioned norms of a heterosexist society. Nevertheless, it would seem difficult to equate their work with any "specifically homosexual aesthetic."[87] Rather, as Katz has recently observed, the radically individualized reception instigated by *4′33″* and the *White Paintings* undermines any form of stable subjective interpellation, leading instead toward a more radical and even utopian queering of sexual relations that can only fully be understood in terms of a post-identity politics.[88] Ultimately, it becomes difficult to limit Rauschenberg and Cage's embrace of differentiation to the realm of sexuality (though I am by no means implying that an analysis on that level is therefore any less valid).[89] For as the following chapters will argue, the indeterminacy initiated in the *White Paintings* and *4′33″* also significantly opposed those forms of individual*ism* characteristic of commercialism, spectacle, and other of the "countless economic interests" that, as Michel Foucault has made clear, ensure and benefit from the very conjunctions of sexuality and power that produce structures of inequality and control.[90] Spectacular reception is, of course, individual—as in the "lonely crowd" of television watchers—but what is given to be seen is either identical to or strictly circumscribed within the limits set by commercial culture. The specificity of the *White Paintings,* by contrast, is that each viewer is continually given to see something different, an experience aimed at subverting any sense of stable or autonomous individuality rather than falsely buttressing it.[91]

Although the *White Paintings* were always nonrepresentational, what changed between 1951 and 1953 was that they came to be understood not as an image of nothing but in terms of a *critique of representation.* Rather than being the product of an arbitrary or anarchic negation, the *White Paintings* and *4′33″* might more properly be understood along the lines of Cage's developing anarch*ism.* For, as the philosopher Todd May has indicated, the critique of representation—on a philosophical as well as a political level—is fundamental to any anarchist position: "What motivates the critique of political representation," writes May, "is the idea that in giving people images of who they are and what they desire, one wrests from them the ability to decide those matters for themselves."[92]

◆

In 1968 Gilles Deleuze (who, like Cage, turned to Bergson in the 1950s) would, in *Difference and Repetition,* formulate his own critique of representation.[93] For Deleuze, as for Rauschenberg and Cage, difference is to be understood as a positive force; and for him, as it was for Bergson, negation is on the order of a pseudo-idea. "Negation is difference," Deleuze explains,

> but difference seen from its underside, seen from below. Seen the right way up, from top to bottom, difference is affirmation. This proposition, however, means many things: that difference is an object of affirmation; that affirmation itself is multiple; that it is creation but also that it must be created, as affirming difference, as

> being difference in itself. It is not the negative which is the motor. Rather, there are positive differential elements which determine the genesis of both the affirmation and the difference affirmed.[94]

Representation, according to Deleuze, serves only to cover over or mask such difference, sheathing it in the conceptual form of the identical and annihilating the function of time. "Representation fails to capture the affirmed world of difference," he declares; "It mediates everything, but mobilises and moves nothing" (pp. 55–56).

It was on the basis of this fundamental affirmation of difference that Deleuze would develop his larger critiques of economic and ideological generality and would begin to formulate a post-identity, "molecular" politics of subjective transformation and a positive conception of desire.[95] But at the heart of Deleuze's project was an idea that was essentially aesthetic: to develop "a theory of thought without image," he maintained, philosophy "needs that revolution which took art from representation to abstraction" (p. 276; see also pp. 56, 68–69).

Such a revolution requires an understanding of "abstraction" that goes beyond those forms of transcendence and idealism so often sought by, or attributed to, high modernism. As the history of the monochrome makes particularly clear, abstract art—although it eliminates illusionistic representation—by no means necessarily eliminates the representational function of the image. From the time of Malevich or Mondrian to that of abstract expressionism, abstract artists have consistently proffered their art as imbued with a subject to which, on some level, it could be subordinated and understood. It is enough, perhaps, to note that the famous club at which the abstract expressionists congregated (and where Cage lectured and Rauschenberg eavesdropped) was initially called "The Subjects of the Artists."[96]

Within this context we can further understand the significance of Rauschenberg's transformed conception of the *White Paintings*. For when viewed as "airports for the lights, shadows and particles," they initiate just such a differential, or "nonrepresentational," abstraction. Allowing the play of temporal change across their surfaces, the *White Paintings* reveal the nonrepresenta-

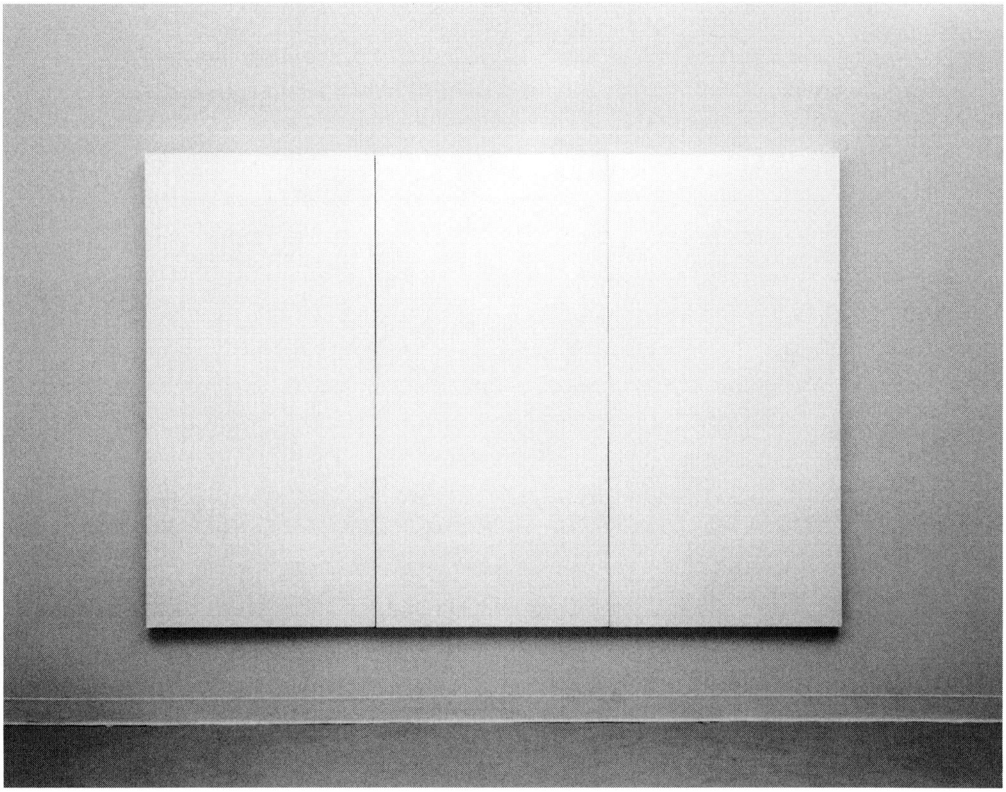

White Painting, 1951. Oil on canvas. Three panels, 72 × 36 in. each; 72 × 108 in. overall. Collection of the artist, New York.

tional forces of difference at work within the image, differences that are shown *differing,* that fracture the totality that is the work of art and approach Deleuze's criterion of finding "the lived reality of a sub-representative domain" (pp. 56, 69). Though they bring together multiple concatenations of perception and temporality, the *White Paintings* perhaps most simply and profoundly exemplify Deleuze's dictum that "The object must therefore be in no way identical, but torn asunder in a difference in which the identity of the object as seen by a subject vanishes" (p. 56). Cage, after all, had already presented this idea in his own discussion of object versus process. "If, at this point," Cage further explained about his revelation within the anechoic chamber, "one says, 'Yes! I do not discriminate between intention and non-intention,' the splits, subject-object, art-life, etc. disappear, an identification has been made with the material, and actions are then those relevant to its nature."[97]

As in Deleuze's philosophy, the full implications of the *White Paintings* and *4′33″* would be worked out only after years of reflection and (artistic) practice. Nevertheless, the critique of representation formulated in the summer of 1952 would serve as the fundamental axiom from which the entirety of Rauschenberg and Cage's multifaceted neo-avant-garde paradigm would develop. Its immediate goals would be twofold: on the one hand, to move beyond the stark (and somewhat passive) manner in which the *White Paintings* had affirmed the forces of difference; on the other, to develop a means of incorporating signification while maintaining a liberated aesthetic reception and a politics of subjective transformation.

Although theirs would be a nearly collaborative project, Rauschenberg and Cage would never entirely agree on the extent of the possible collapse of "art" and "life." As Cage explained much later, his "desire to just erase the difference" between them somewhat opposed Rauschenberg's intention of "working in the gap between the two."[98] It is, of course, Rauschenberg's trajectory that we will primarily follow throughout the remainder of this book. Rauschenberg's development toward the Combine paintings and Combines would quickly bring him up against a series of important limitations, both aesthetic and social, that fundamentally shape any understanding of the stakes of this neo-avant-garde paradigm. It is to this stage of his work that we now turn.

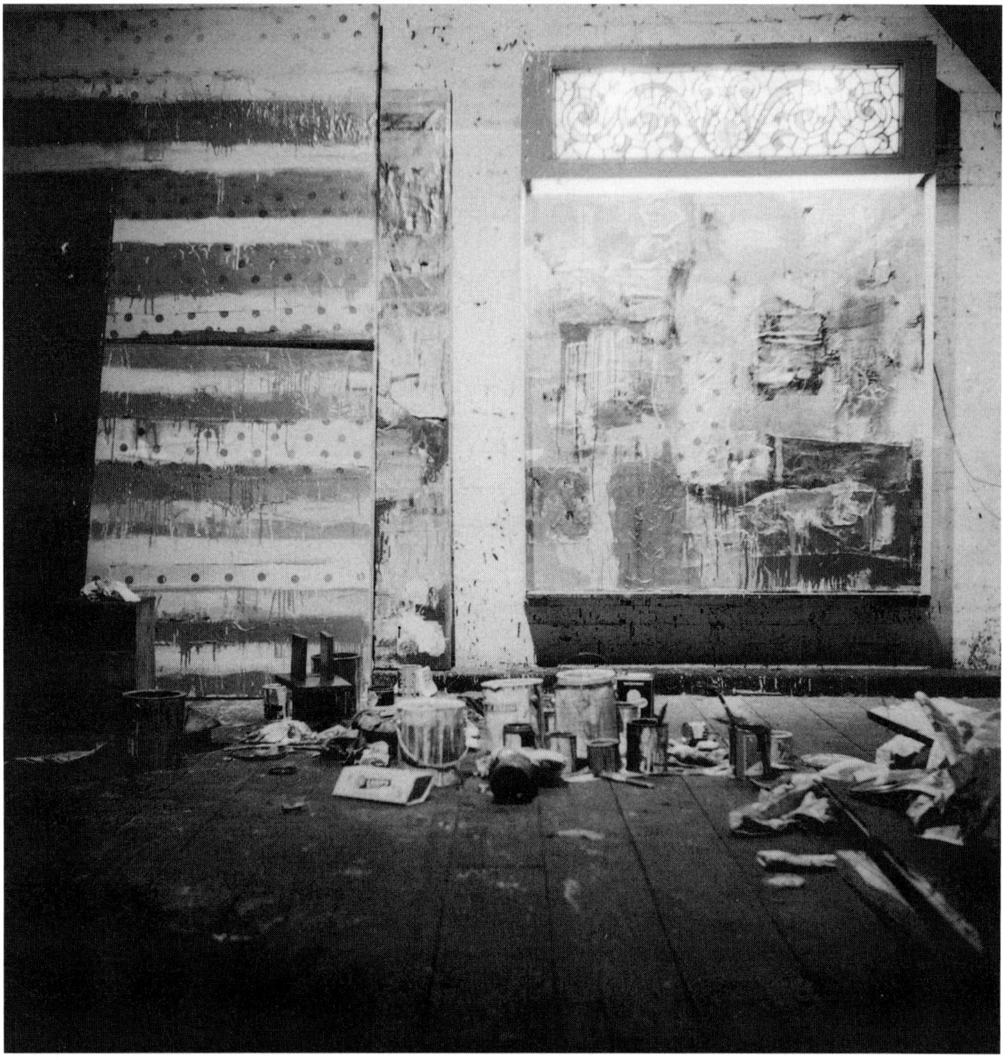

Fulton Street studio, New York, 1954. Photograph by the artist. Works shown (left to right): *Yoicks,* 1954 (detail), unknown painting, ca. 1954 (detail), and Untitled [with shelf and colored glass light box], 1954.

2

Pedestrian Colors

During an interview with Walter Hopps in 1991, Robert Rauschenberg recalled Ellsworth Kelly's first visit to his studio. It was in the summer of 1954, and Kelly—who had only recently returned from France, where he had been living since 1948—was feeling as out of place in his home country as he had felt overseas. "When I left Paris in 1954," Kelly has written, "I saw no art that was being 'made' like mine, and returning to the U.S. I found no one 'making' art that way either."[1] John Cage, whom Kelly had met in Paris several years before, told him where to find Rauschenberg's studio, then housed in a loft building on Fulton Street near the fish market; and Kelly must have been intrigued, perhaps even eager, to meet another artist so near his age that Cage evidently held in such high esteem.

According to Rauschenberg, however, Kelly's initial visit did not go as well as expected. When Kelly caught sight of one of his *White Paintings,* Rauschenberg recalled, "He was furious I had stolen his idea."[2] Kelly would have had legitimate reason to feel defensive. Among the sketchbooks he brought back from France was a project for a series of all-white monochrome polyptychs dating from 1951 to 1952. Kelly's white paintings were to be more systematically involved with seriality and proportion than Rauschenberg's (the widths of Kelly's panels had been calculated so that conjoined they would form a perfect

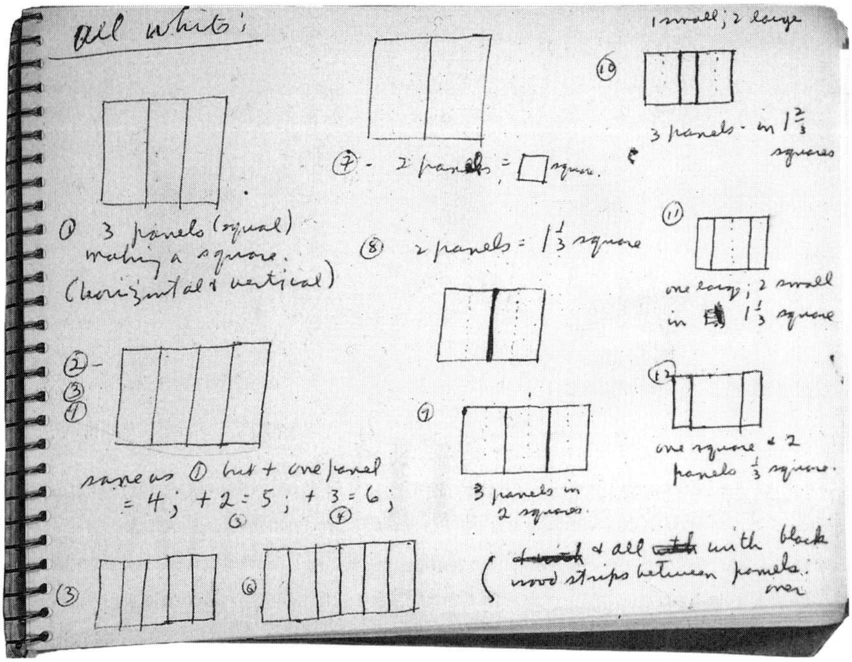

Ellsworth Kelly, page 25 from Sketchbook #15, 1951–1952. Ink on paper. $5\frac{1}{4} \times 7$ in. Private collection. © Ellsworth Kelly.

square, to which further panels would be added in subsequent works), and he foresaw separating certain of the panels with wood strips painted black.[3] Nevertheless, there was an uncanny resemblance between what Kelly had planned and what Rauschenberg had executed, and Kelly must have been startled at the sight. That Rauschenberg had already publicly exhibited his works a year earlier while Kelly's art had yet to be shown in New York would only have deepened whatever frustration or competitive feelings Kelly may have had.

Kelly, perhaps not surprisingly, recalls the encounter differently. Noticing the *White Painting* in the midst of the overwhelming presence of *Red Paintings* and early Combines on which Rauschenberg was just beginning to work, Kelly remembers pointing out the similarity between Rauschenberg's white canvases and the four-panel white painting that his friend Alain Naudé had completed in France in 1952. Naudé's panels, which Kelly photographed at the time, were made of wood covered by multiple layers of white paint that was carefully sanded after each application to give the surface a look of polished marble. Despite noting these differences, it was Rauschenberg, according to Kelly, who seemed nonplussed at the comparison between his work and Naudé's.[4] One thing about the encounter is certain: as E. C. Goosen has related, Kelly left Rauschenberg's studio feeling even more artistically isolated than before.[5]

Regardless of the actual circumstances of their meeting, Kelly's feelings on encountering Rauschenberg's production would certainly have been compounded had he seen the initial state of *Collection* (1954), the Combine painting on which Rauschenberg was working at the time.[6] For as reported by Hopps, far from the layered, multimedia assemblage that it has become, *Collection* began as three conjoined, monochrome panels painted red, yellow, and blue.[7] Although subsequently obscured by the further addition of paint, cloth, newspaper, and other materials (and despite the colors' fading), the bottom third of each panel continues to reflect its original condition: red on the left, now bisected by a deep blue swath of cloth; yellow in the center, now bisected by red; and blue, similarly bisected by red, at the right. In its earliest stage (which could well have been visible in Rauschenberg's studio at the time of Kelly's visit), *Collection* was much closer to Kelly's work than any of Rauschenberg's *White Paintings* had

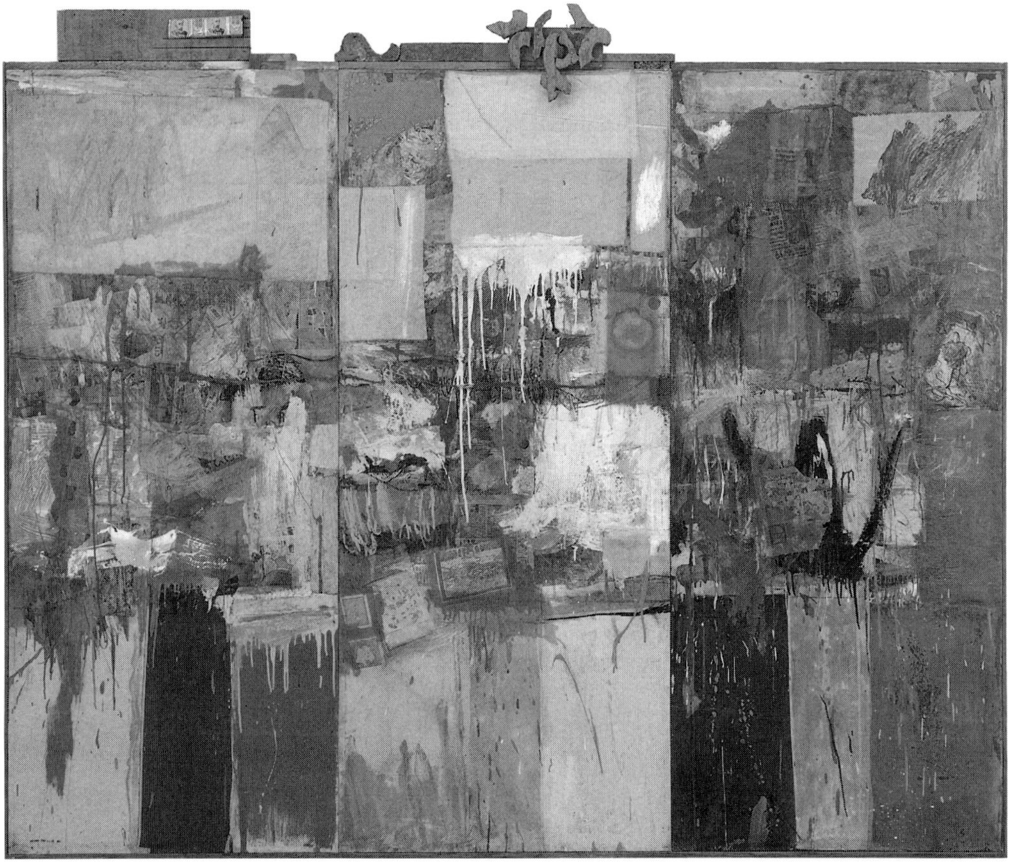

Collection (formerly Untitled), 1954. Combine painting: oil, paper, fabric, and metal on wood. 80 × 96 × 3½ in. San Francisco Museum of Modern Art. Gift of Harry W. and Mary Margaret Anderson.

Ellsworth Kelly, *Red Yellow Blue White and Black,* 1953. Oil on wood, six joined panels. 19¾ × 38⅞ in. Private collection. © Ellsworth Kelly.

been. Indeed, quite unlike the paintings of largely curvilinear forms for which Kelly would initially become known in America, the stock of paintings he brought back from France contained a large number of multicolor, monochrome polyptychs. The first of these, the sixty-four-panel *Colors for a Large Wall,* predated *Collection* by three years. Even more similar, despite the discrepancies in size, would have been Kelly's *Painting for a White Wall* (1952) or, in its invocation of the primary colors, *Red Yellow Blue White and Black* (1953), a work Kelly valued highly enough to send to the Museum of Modern Art later that year.[8]

Although Cage, with whom the painter had corresponded since 1949, had been in possession of Kelly's *La Combe III* since 1951 (the year it was made), there is no evidence that either Rauschenberg or Kelly knew of the other's multipanel paintings prior to the moment of their meeting.[9] In any case, the questions that arise from Kelly's studio visit are not as simple as those of historical priority or the individual property of ideas. Far from vying for a claim of artistic originality, both Kelly's and Rauschenberg's monochromes bring forth now-familiar issues of the neo-avant-garde's repetition of historical avant-garde paradigms. For although neither artist seems to have been aware of it at the time, their multipanel monochrome polyptychs in primary colors invite comparison with Aleksandr Rodchenko's *Pure Red Color, Pure Yellow Color,* and *Pure Blue Color* triptych of 1921.

◆

Rodchenko's goal in organizing the *5 × 5 = 25* exhibition that polemically entered his tricolor monochrome triptych into the history of modern art was nothing less than to lay that history to rest. Eliminating any aspect of specialized skill, subjective expression, or esoteric content, Rodchenko's monochromes sought to replace the individualistic, "creative" model of aesthetic practice derived from the Romantic tradition with an attitude more closely akin to scientific empirio-criticism and an appeal to logical deduction. The result was another apparent end point in the modernist process of aesthetic reduction—a push to the very limits of representation where pigment seeks to escape the

Aleksandr Rodchenko, Untitled (*Pure Red Color, Pure Yellow Color, Pure Blue Color*), 1921. Oil on canvas. Three panels, $24^5/_8 \times 20^3/_4$ in. each. © Rodchenko and Stepanova Archive / RAO, Russia / Licensed by VAGA, New York, NY.

realm of metaphor, signifying only its existence as material and thereby pointing toward the end of painting (as a representational practice) as such. As Rodchenko famously declared in a retrospective assessment of 1939: "I reduced painting to its logical conclusion and exhibited three canvases: red, blue, and yellow. I affirmed: It's all over. Basic colors. Every plane is a plane and there is to be no more representation."[10]

Shortly after *5 × 5 = 25,* the critic Nikolai Tarabukin theorized the utopian dimension of Rodchenko's monochrome painting in "From the Easel to the Machine." For Tarabukin, Rodchenko's achievement of "the last 'picture,'" his evacuation of all aesthetic "content" in favor of the "purely professional exploration of the material elements" of painting, strictly corresponded to the rise of an egalitarian and collective postrevolutionary Soviet society. With the elimination of class divisions and the individual patron or consumer, the easel picture—as an individualistic and ideological representation of bourgeois class interests—had lost all meaning and justification.[11] Rodchenko's monochromes were seen as the very presentation of the easel painting's loss of context and meaning. In a democratic society, Tarabukin argued, the only socially justified "content" of artistic production would be utility, and he called for a transcendence of the regime of representation and an entry into the real world of "production skill" and utilitarian objects: a subsumption of the committed artist into the productive apparatus of the factory in solidarity with the proletariat, from which he or she could no longer legitimately stand apart.[12]

◆

Whereas, as we have seen, Rauschenberg may well have initially understood his *White Paintings* as the final stage on a path of modernist reduction (and thus akin to Rodchenko's monochromes), by 1953 he had come through his association with Cage to regard them as something more: as exemplifications of a positive force of difference made visible through their "transparency" to temporal and environmental factors. In this respect, the utopian dimension of Rauschenberg's neo-avant-garde position both coincided with and diverged from that of his avant-garde predecessor, Rodchenko. While both similarly sought to escape from representation, Rauschenberg aimed not at a productive intervention into culture but at an affirmation of difference attributed (indeed, at that point still too literally attributed) to the natural realm.

In the first stage of Rauschenberg's pursuit of this goal, he seems to have located such difference directly within a "natural," base material, conceived of as entirely external to the subjectivity of the artist.[13] In the black paintings, shown along with the *White Paintings* at the Stable Gallery in 1953, Rauschenberg layered black pigment onto a surface variously more thickly or thinly covered with newspaper and, in at least one instance, fabric.[14] The black paintings mark the first appearance of Rauschenberg's "materialized color," where variation in tone and (later) hue can be attributed to differences in the physical properties of the materials and their interactions, an attribution that problematizes the interpretive move from visual appearance to artistic intention.[15]

Seen from the Bergsonian perspective common to Rauschenberg and Cage, these works may also be understood as another attempt to present matter as immersed in duration: an attempt to overcome the situation of a human perception predisposed, even bound, to the arrest of temporal change and the perception of matter in terms of distinct, static forms. In the majority of Rauschenberg's black canvases, he employed an extremely glossy paint, either alone or in varying mixtures with more matte or even brownish tones. The glossy sheen of the paint, applied at times very thickly, causes the surfaces to reflect light in a pronounced manner, and the texture of the painting further accentuates and refracts this surface shine. Because of the topography formed by the encrusted newspaper, the reflections of light shift markedly in relation to the viewer's position as he or she passes in front of the work. In many of the canvases, the surface encrustations cause dark shadows to form in the folds, and these too shift position according to the changing angles of light.[16] Thus, the black paintings act in much the same way as the *White Paintings* to inscribe the spectator's physical situation into the visual experience of the work.

Yet, whereas the *White Paintings* tend to act as neutral projection screens, "transparent" structures "through" which one is meant to view the world, the black paintings more insistently call attention to their own material existence

Untitled [horizontal black painting], ca. 1953. Oil and newspaper on canvas. 35⅞ × 61⅞ in. Private collection.

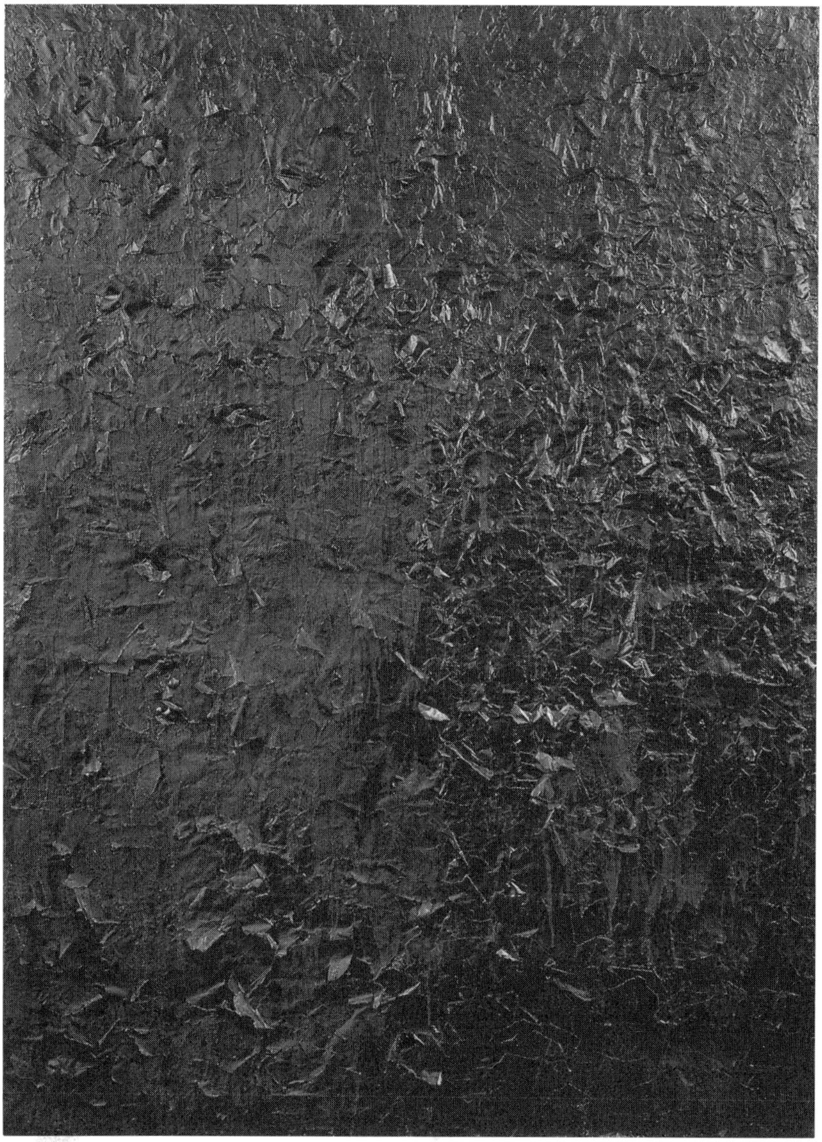

Untitled [glossy black painting], ca. 1951. Oil and paper on canvas. 72½ × 52¾ in. Collection of the artist, New York.

and physical presence. Light falling on the work is more clearly broken up and refracted according to the dictates of the surface texture and the thicknesses and reflective qualities of the paint. The viewer's shadow, for example—although it affects the surface appearance—is subsumed into the shadings created by the painting's own topography. In addition, and also more insistently than in the *White Paintings,* viewing the black paintings brings forth another temporal dimension: the incorporation of time occurs not only as a function of the instantaneous changes in light and shadow, but also through the longer-term deterioration of the collage ground. More readily than traditional archival painting materials (and more visibly than dust accumulation), the newspaper Rauschenberg used so prominently yellows and decays with age. As Dore Ashton noted at the Stable Gallery exhibition: "Beauty is purity, he says, but decay is implicit. Appliquéd newspaper is his disdain of perpetuity."[17]

Though the black paintings did not relinquish the interaction with environmental factors that had characterized the *White Paintings,* their materiality did eliminate the *White Paintings*' last traces of pictorialism (which had led Rauschenberg, at first, to judge the latter as successful paintings),[18] and clearly pushed beyond the boundaries of orthodox formalist modernism.[19] Continuing the critique of representation launched by the *White Paintings,* Rauschenberg regarded the materials in his black paintings as complex but inexpressive, and therefore separate from the anthropocentric realm of metaphorical meaning. For Rauschenberg, an "involve[ment] with the materials separately" was starkly opposed to "arbitrarily designing forms and selecting colors that would achieve some predetermined result"; as he stated, he "didn't have any ideas to support that kind of thing."[20] The black paintings, as Rauschenberg declared, were to be entirely "visual experiences," revealing a multiplicitous and temporal, "natural" materiality as a field of forces apart from metaphorization.[21] He described his black monochromes as foregrounding a "complexity without their revealing anything. The fact that there was lots to see but not much showing."[22]

Although Rauschenberg was opposed to a material's stable ascription of meaning within the general paradigm of representation, his position at the time was specifically aimed against the metaphorization of paintmarks within abstract expressionism. About his suspicion and ultimate rejection of the expressionist paradigm, Rauschenberg has been perfectly clear:

> There was a whole language (used in discussions of the abstract expressionists) that I could never make function for myself: it revolved around words like, "tortured," "struggle," "pain." I don't know whether it was my Albers training or my personal "hang-up" but I could never see those qualities in paint—I could see them in life and in art that illustrates life. But I could not see such conflict in the materials and I knew that it had to be in the attitude of the painter, his interpretation of an attitude that existed separately. In the future, if one were to lose contact with this idea it would be possible to have a completely different attitude about the painting.[23]

Or, as Rauschenberg stated with characteristic brevity and (retrospectively understandable) clarity at the *Art of Assemblage* symposium: "Any material has its content and its independence from meaning. Meaning belongs to people."[24]

Though for Rauschenberg, Cage, and others close to them, Rauschenberg's earliest monochromes succeeded in escaping the representational paradigm, they failed to be similarly received by the critics and the public at large. As we have seen in the typical remarks by Hubert Crehan, they were initially understood in precisely the terms of negation that they refused, held to be abstract negations of artistic expression and akin to dadaism. More troubling to Rauschenberg, however, was an entirely different form of failed reception. As he quickly came to realize, the materials he employed as neutral, reflective screens or brute, material facts nonetheless continued to signify in a conventional, representational manner. If we can judge from the frequency with which he has commented on it, Rauschenberg regarded this form of reception as a significant aesthetic impasse. As he explained to Billy Klüver,

> And then I became disturbed with . . . the outside assumptions, the prejudices about the colors being black or white, and being

> monochrome; the people thought the black was about old and burned and tarred; and they thought the white was about negation, and nothing—some philosophy of nothing. So they [the paintings] were misrepresenting themselves.[25]

Thus, even in attempting to avoid the abstract expressionist metaphorization of paint into terms such as "tortured," "struggle," and "pain," Rauschenberg nonetheless found his work imbued with another set of equally melodramatic significations. "Lots of critics shared with the public a certain reaction," he recalled: "they couldn't see black as a pigment. They moved immediately into association with 'burned-out,' 'tearing,' 'nihilism' and 'destruction.' That began to bother me."[26] By 1954, it had become clear that the paradigm of representational meaning could not be as easily avoided as Rauschenberg might have thought; it seemed that signification would envelop even the most inexpressive of works, making them read against themselves as expression—though perhaps only as an expression of pure negation, nihilism, or dadaist provocation.

◆

Less confrontational than the monochrome paintings, and seemingly more artistic in their juxtapositions of disparate materials, the *Elemental Sculptures* (1953) shown at Rauschenberg's Stable Gallery exhibition have received little in the way of commentary. Despite their more traditional appearance, these sculptural pieces displayed a reliance on materials not unlike the black paintings and seem to have been similarly intended to strain against the limitations of an expressive, representational paradigm. These works were among the earliest of Rauschenberg's pieces to evince his attitude of "collaboration" with materials in which, rather than illustrating an a priori idea, the artist sought to take formative clues from inherent material properties such as mass, weight, gravity, tension, and reflectivity.[27] Hence the sculptures' foregrounding of their components' connective interactions—the way stones hang from ropes, pull against other materials in a demonstration of tension or attachment, or are set within or atop one another.

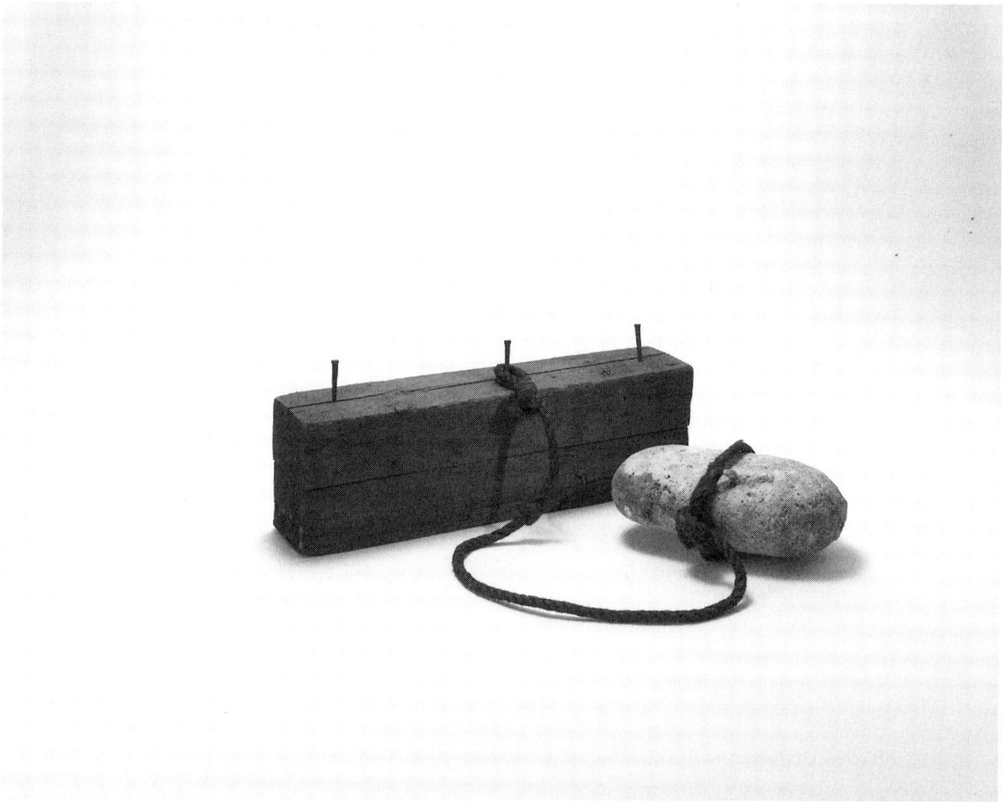

Untitled (*Elemental Sculpture*) [block with tethered stone], 1953. Assemblage: wood block, square-headed nails, rope, and tethered stone. $6^5/_8 \times 17 \times 3^1/_2$ in., block; $3 \times 9 \times 5^1/_8$ in., stone; $29^1/_2$ in. rope (extended). Private collection.

To counteract the more evident compositional aspect of these works—which apparently involved a greater number of artistic decisions in combining their materials than did the *White Paintings* or black paintings—Rauschenberg seems to have relied on audience interaction. No longer merely reflecting the spectators' movements, the *Elemental Sculptures* often called for active physical manipulation or alteration of their components, as in the wrapping and unwrapping of encased objects. Shaking Rauschenberg's wooden *Music Box* sculptures, for example, causes rocks to tumble across the nails protruding on the insides of the work, thereby rearranging the sculpture's parts and producing a clanging, percussive sound. Other works, such as the untitled *Elemental Sculpture* dubbed "block and stones," similarly invited audience members to rearrange the pieces of the work into different configurations. In that particular case, the stones amassed atop the wooden block were to be arrayed by viewers in, to quote the artist, "ways that were not interesting."[28] The *Elemental Sculptures*' visual appearance thus evidently resulted from an interactive process that separated them (to an extent) from the authorial presence and expressive intentions of the artist.

In their openness to chance, their acknowledgment of the audience's role in completing the work of art, and their call to ignore the dictates of taste (as in arranging stones in a manner that was "not interesting"), Rauschenberg's *Elemental Sculptures* attest to one of the earliest stages in his reception of Marcel Duchamp.[29] Although he was undoubtedly introduced to Duchamp's art by Cage, Rauschenberg's first in-depth exposure to the French artist's antiexpressive strategies occurred in late April or early May of 1953 at the Sidney Janis Gallery's important exhibition, *Dada 1916–1923*.[30] Curated in close collaboration with Duchamp himself, the Janis exhibition included twelve of the artist's works, which were shown together in a back room separate from those of the other artists. There, Rauschenberg would have seen *To Be Looked at (from the Other Side of the Glass) with One Eye, Close To, for Almost an Hour* (1918)—a transparent piece related to the *Large Glass* and therefore, however indirectly, to an understanding of Rauschenberg's own *White Paintings*; Duchamp's last "painting," *Tu m'* (1918); and a selection of Duchamp's readymades and assisted readymades, including *Fountain* (1917), *Traveler's Folding Item* (1916), *Paris Air* (1919), *L.H.O.O.Q.* (1919), *Apolinère Enameled* (1916–1917), and *WANTED: $2000 REWARD* (1923).[31]

Rauschenberg's response was immediate and explicit. He has stated that he "was thinking of Duchamp" when he made his two *Music Box* sculptures,[32] pieces that reference the older artist's enigmatic *With Hidden Noise* (1916), which was also on view at the Janis Gallery. The readymade crates that Rauschenberg used to create his *Music Boxes* were closer to detritus than were the ball of twine and bronze plaques employed by Duchamp in *With Hidden Noise* (with the unaltered stenciled words on one of Rauschenberg's pieces replacing the inscription etched into Duchamp's work). Nonetheless, the connection was not lost on Duchamp, who reputedly shook one of the *Music Boxes* at a later group show and remarked, "I think I recognize that tune."[33]

The irony of the public's misreception of Rauschenberg's *White Paintings* and black paintings—the failure to see their refusal of intentional, expressive paradigms—was that it largely repeated his own earlier reception of the anti-expressive strategies of Duchamp. Although Rauschenberg had encountered Duchamp's assisted readymade *Bicycle Wheel* (1913) before the Janis exhibition, he had completely failed to register its transgressive stance toward traditional art, finding it instead "more beautiful than any painting in the exhibition."[34] Similarly, he recalled: "I remember the first Duchamp that I ever saw was *Bicycle Wheel on a Stool,* and I saw it at the same time that I saw a sculpture by Aristide Maillol, in the Museum of Modern Art, and something there by Isamu Noguchi. I saw Noguchi, Duchamp and Maillol, and I didn't see any discrepancy. There was no conflict."[35]

Spurred, perhaps, by the critical response to his Stable Gallery exhibition, Rauschenberg spent the fall of 1953 moving toward an increasingly sophisticated implementation of Duchampian strategies. Rauschenberg's *Automobile Tire Print* (1953) reproduces two of the aesthetic strategies found in *Tu m':* the creation of an indexical mark (the tire track being as causally related to the car's driving as the cast shadow is to the object blocking the light) and the designation of a person other than the artist to perform the mark-making task (Cage's driving

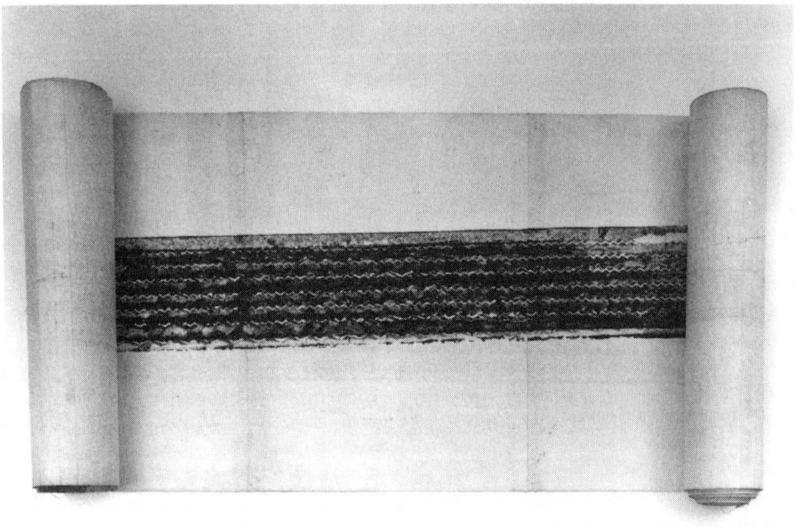

Automobile Tire Print, 1953. Monoprint: oil on paper mounted on fabric. 16½ × 264½ in. (extended). Collection of the artist, New York.

of the car corresponding to Duchamp's employing a commercial sign painter to depict the pointing hand in the center of his canvas).[36] More successfully than any of Rauschenberg's previous paintings or sculptures, *Automobile Tire Print* works to counter subsequent metaphorization with its simplicity and exposure of the process used in its creation.

At around the same time, Rauschenberg deployed an even more sophisticated understanding of Duchampian strategies in the creation of his *Erased de Kooning Drawing*. In it, as Benjamin Buchloh has shown, Rauschenberg implemented an allegorical procedure closely related to certain of the readymades.[37] In a manner akin to Duchamp's use of the *Mona Lisa* in the assisted readymade *L.H.O.O.Q.*, Rauschenberg began by appropriating an existing work of art, although an original in this case rather than a reproduction. He then proceeded to reverse Duchamp's addition of a graffiti-like mustache and goatee to Leonardo's masterpiece by erasing the de Kooning almost entirely.[38] Whether by defacement or effacement, the two works' devaluation of the appropriated representation (an essential factor in the process of allegorization) is equally effective. Rauschenberg's subsequent mounting of the erased sheet of paper within a gold frame, together with the addition of a carefully hand-lettered label with a new authorial attribution, title, and date ("Erased de Kooning Drawing / Robert Rauschenberg / 1953"), simultaneously doubles the visual text with a new signification and calls attention away from the (now depleted) visual aspect of the work and toward the conventional and institutional devices of the work's "framing."[39] In this regard, the Bergsonian dimension of the work explored in the previous chapter, its opening up to temporal and environmental differences, is not inconsequential. For Rauschenberg's *Erased de Kooning Drawing* essentially reenacted the reception of his *White Paintings*: the initial evacuation of expressive or representational meaning in favor of transitional, temporal forces subsequently gave way to a process in which meaning was reattributed to the work from the outside.

Produced at around the same time, the remarkable series of *Elemental Paintings* that Rauschenberg made out of nontraditional materials performed much the same procedure of allegorical appropriation and framing as *Erased de*

Kooning Drawing. Taking dirt, grass, clay, gold leaf, white lead, and tissue paper, Rauschenberg made "paintings" out of them by placing them within a rectangular format and hanging them on the wall.[40] In the finished works, each material emphatically asserts its existence as unaltered stuff. Even the gold leaf, traditionally employed to connote the transcendental realm of the heavens, has been resolutely presented in its substantive form by the foregrounding of the shape and texture of the leaf (which peels at the edges), the tarnish (accentuated by a conspicuously sloppy application of glue), and the differences in the colors of the various types of gold (and in one case silver) that Rauschenberg used. In turning once again toward the use of untransformed materials that had characterized the black paintings, Rauschenberg seems to have wanted to observe the operation, and potentially test the limitations, of the attributions of meaning from the social sphere. If a black painting can be read as burned-out destruction, then what about one made entirely of dirt? or of grass? or of clay? How does white oil paint, which can be read as nihilism or nothing, compare to a thick layer of white lead? Perhaps the clearest test of the meanings that affixed themselves to materials occurred in Rauschenberg's conceptual pairing of the gold leaf paintings with those made out of tissue paper. "For each one I did in gold, I did one [the] approximate same size in toilet paper," he explained to Hopps. "I was testing the market. I knew this. Gold stays and toilet paper gets thrown away."[41] Such an equation of aesthetic quality, taste, or preference with monetary value further explores the precedents set by Duchamp and implemented in such works as the *Tzank Check* of 1919 (also on view at the Janis Gallery in 1953).[42]

In the midst of these experiments with different materials, it must have become clear to Rauschenberg that any attempt to escape from representation and expressive, metaphorical meaning directly into the immediacy of a "natural" field of difference and temporal change was bound to fail. People were not easily going to "lose contact" with the predominant expressive paradigm and adopt the "different attitude about painting" that Rauschenberg initially sought. Despite what must have been a steadily growing realization of this predicament,

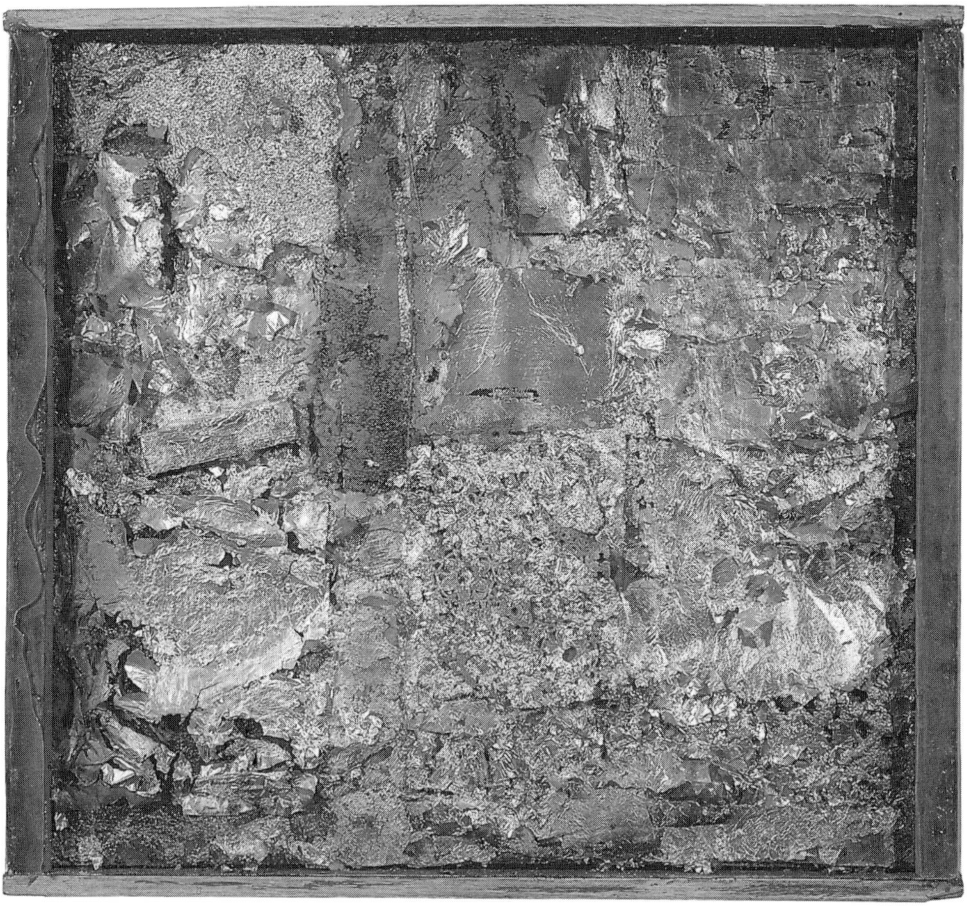

Untitled (*Gold Painting*), ca. 1953. Gold and silver leaf on fabric, newspaper, paint, wood, paper, glue, and nails on wood in wood and glass frame. $10\frac{1}{2} \times 11\frac{1}{2} \times 1\frac{3}{8}$ in. Collection of the artist, New York.

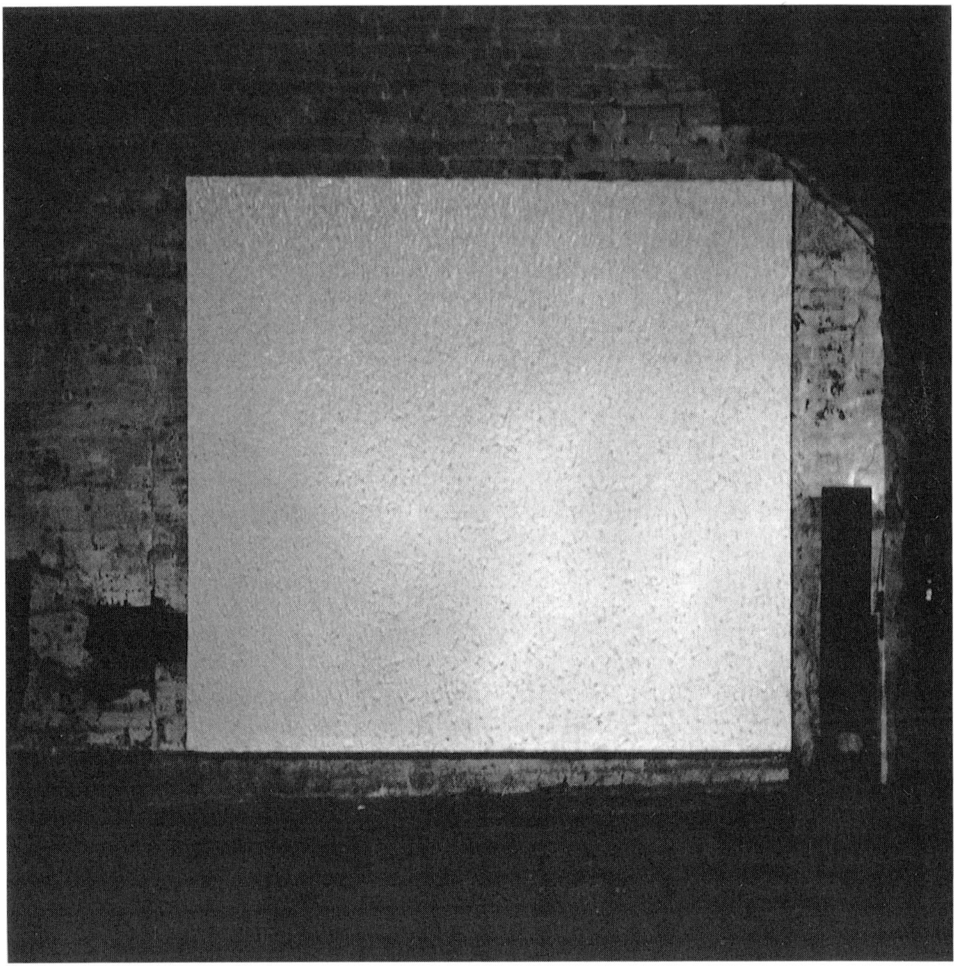

White Lead Painting, 1953–1954. Oil on canvas. Ca. 70 × 72 in. Abandoned. Photograph by the artist.

however, Rauschenberg did not immediately devise a new strategy. The series of all-red paintings that he undertook at the time moved only very tentatively in a new direction. Apparently attempting to choose a color with the same attitude of indifference that Duchamp maintained in choosing a readymade (Rauschenberg recalls that he "picked arbitrarily" the color red),[43] Rauschenberg continued to treat paint largely as an inexpressive material in the manner of the black paintings. Although he learned much from the *Red Paintings,* which culminated in the bichromatic, striped painting *Yoicks* (1954), Rauschenberg ultimately found them no more successful in escaping the representational paradigm than his previous works had been.[44]

Collection, in its inaugural, programmatic presentation of the three primary colors, signaled Rauschenberg's abandonment of the strategy of base materiality in favor of the direct engagement with the problematic of painting and representation that he had avoided since 1951. Yet Rauschenberg did not simply abandon his earlier aspiration to escape representation and affirm nonanthropocentric difference. Rather, he seems to have realized that the path away from representation ran *through* painting, that any escape from the expressive paradigm necessitated a confrontation with painting as such. As we will see, Rauschenberg's turn to painting was neither a cynical, opportunistic retreat from the radicality of his earlier position nor a compromising pictorialization of avant-garde strategies such as the readymade or montage. Whether or not he knew of Rodchenko's monochrome triptych, Rauschenberg was too well aware of the implications of the monochrome as the end point of a reductivist aesthetic of modernist painting to have regarded *Collection* as merely a newfound beginning. More than a simple return to the basic coloristic building blocks of painting, then, *Collection* must be understood as an investigation into the historical conditions of painting after the end of (modernist) painting. Before we proceed with the analysis of this work, however, a detour into Kelly's contemporary investigation of the monochrome will provide a better understanding of the historical conditions that Rauschenberg's postwar avant-garde "painting" confronted.

◆

Although he shared Rauschenberg's ignorance of Rodchenko, Kelly had been introduced to the Marxist critique of easel painting at a 1947 lecture by Herbert Read while he was a student at the Boston Museum School.[45] Read's talk, which Kelly still remembers as a revelation, espoused a position akin to Tarabukin's: the individual expression appropriate to the easel painting was a corollary of a reactionary bourgeois subjectivity. In its stead, he advocated a functionalist vision of the integration of painting and architecture on a monumental scale more appropriate for collective viewing. As James Meyer and Michael Plante have demonstrated, Kelly's interest in and involvement with functionalist aesthetic currents was deep and long-lived, not only deepening throughout his years in France but also surviving for a significant period after his return to the United States.[46] Nowhere was Kelly's adherence to a functionalist aesthetic (his desire, as he put it, "to continue" the "struggle" of his predecessors in the historical avant-garde) more strongly expressed than in his correspondence with Cage.[47] As he wrote in a letter of 4 September 1950:

> I am not interested in painting as it has been accepted for so long—to hang on walls of houses as pictures. To Hell with pictures—they should *be* the wall—even better—on the outside wall—of large buildings.—or stood up outside as billboards or a kind of modern "icon." We must make our art like the Egyptians, the Chinese, and the African and Island primitives—with their relation to life. It should meet the eye—direct.[48]

When Kelly initially met Cage in 1949, he must have found the composer's artistic outlook almost perfectly aligned with his own. Before the 1951–1952 aesthetic and philosophical transformations in Cage's position, both men adhered to a late-functionalist paradigm common to the somewhat institutionalized avant-garde of the forties and fifties: Cage's deriving from László Moholy-Nagy, *transition* magazine, and certain futurist strains in music, and Kelly's from the aforementioned lecture by Read and the modern architectural milieu in

France.[49] Cage, whose advocacy of this position reached its high point in the lecture "Defense of Satie," delivered at Black Mountain College in the summer of 1948, sought the creation of a new, modernist vernacular appropriate to the age. Like Kelly, Cage regarded this new vernacular as necessary for the reconstruction of an integrated, organic community such as those idealistically projected onto non-Western and premodern European cultures. He would thus have well understood Kelly's note that declared, "Even though it is impossible at this time, my intention is that my work should be anonymous. I believe that there should be temples built, and all my effort is toward this building."[50]

Kelly turned toward Romanesque architecture as an anonymous and unified artistic expression of its age, whereas Cage idealized the Gothic for analogous reasons. Yet for both, the individualistic, expressive artwork, whether a musical composition or an easel painting, was seen as appropriate only for an ailing, fragmented, and materialistic bourgeois culture.[51] As Kelly lamented in 1951, "Today, instead of the stained-glass of Chartres, Romanesque frescoes, Byzantine mosaics, Chinese calligraphy, Egyptian reliefs and sculpture, we have cinema, the best-seller magazines and books, the radio and television, produced to 'please,' and for financial profit, not to teach, or to state an absolute truth."[52] Both men's interest in collectivity, in a certain spirituality, and, above all, in an anonymity of production derived from a common desire to overcome the fragmenting and commercially driven individualism of the modern age. "To Hell with exhibitions, galleries, to Hell with money!" Kelly wrote to Cage; "what have these things to do with what must be done?"[53]

As Yve-Alain Bois has demonstrated, Kelly's desire to get rid of the subjective aspects of his art marked most of his French production and led to the simultaneous exploration of a variety of noncompositional procedures, including chance, the grid, and the photograph-like near indexicality of copying that Bois calls the "transfer."[54] In many ways, Kelly's monochrome paintings culminated this noncompositional trajectory. Both the inexpressivity of the single monochrome panel and the paratactic organization of panels within the polyptych seem to abjure the traditional artistic qualities of esoteric, specialized skill in either the conception or execution of the work. To this degree, Kelly's monochromes initially align themselves with those of Rodchenko in underlying motivation as well as overall effect.

Yet even though several of Kelly's early polyptychs limit themselves to the three primary colors (plus black and white), both the derivation and semantic import of Kelly's colors differ from those of his historical avant-garde predecessor. Whereas Rodchenko's monochrome triptych invoked the purportedly universal character of logical deduction as the basis of its appeal to a collective, demythified reception, Kelly never appealed to any such process: not to deductive logic, nor to any ontological priority accorded the primaries as basic or pure, nor to the universal laws of perception or mathematics. (It is enough to recall Kelly's visit to Georges Vantongerloo and his response to the aging Belgian constructivist's lauding of mathematical calculation as a superior basis for artistic production: "He made me understand that *his* kind of painting had to have reasons. I was glad that mine didn't.")[55] Instead, as Bois has pointed out, Kelly's colors were more integrally related to the readymade, utilizing as their starting point the colors of the French schoolchildren's gummed papers found in his collages titled *Spectrum Colors Arranged by Chance I–VIII* (1951); in his book, *Line Form Color* (1951); and in the maquettes produced for his monochrome paintings.[56]

Significantly, in adopting the colors of the commercially manufactured *papiers gommettes* as the underlying palette for his paintings, Kelly—in his quest to erect the universal, "Romanesque" aesthetic of collective viewing that he advocated—seems to have been unable or unwilling to appeal to any foundation or logical bedrock beneath that of the commodity. The absence of such an appeal is evident in Kelly's justly celebrated *Painting for a White Wall,* where the initial maquette's color sequence of a deep (almost black) blue, a pink, an orange, and a white refuses any analysis on the basis of deductive rationality. As Bois has argued, the boldness and idiosyncrasy of the combination of pink and orange, in particular, brings to mind the arbitrary juxtaposition of disconnected commodities, emphasizing that "the polyptych as [Kelly] then conceived it becomes a color chart, like those provided by color merchants."[57]

A similar arbitrariness characterizes not only those collages and paintings owing their composition to chance, such as *Colors for a Large Wall,* but also Kelly's contemporary book project, *Line Form Color.* Although it was to be an "alphabet of plastic pictorial elements" leading to a new form of monumental painting with the ultimate aim of stating, as previously noted, "an absolute truth," Kelly's book lacks any appeal to the kind of deductive rationality that would almost certainly have been required of a historical avant-garde attempt to create an anonymous, universal, pictorial language.[58] Even Kelly's momentary and apparent submission to the "rationality" of the primaries in works such as *Red Yellow Blue White* (1952) and *Red Yellow Blue White and Black* did not entirely mitigate the commercial basis of his colors: red, yellow, and blue were, no less than black, white, or any of the other colors, included in the original set of gummed papers. Indeed, in *Red Yellow Blue White,* Kelly forgoes paint altogether and, in an adoption of a true readymade strategy rare outside of his collages, chose instead industrially dyed fabrics stretched like canvas directly onto their supports. Kelly's use of the same fabric for the dress he designed for his friend Anne Weber only makes the equation between color and commodity in this particular work perfectly clear.[59]

If it had remained at this level, the relationship of Kelly's work to the commodity would have been aligned with the functionalist paradigm that he espoused. As opposed to a modernism predicated on autonomy, in which the encroachments of industry and commercialism are adopted only to be transcended in the process of artistic transformation, the functionalist strain of the avant-garde willingly assimilated the products and productive tenets of industrialization as a means of transcending individual artistic creation. To have adopted his colors readymade would therefore not have been out of line with the historical avant-garde's optimistic, even utopian (though already outmoded) vision of industrialization as an emancipatory force capable of overcoming class and regional distinctions and fostering the universal, collective culture that Kelly desired.

The strength of such an early functionalist position lay in the belief that the representational or Imaginary function of easel painting could be dissolved as the work directly intervened in the transformative re-creation of actual society (the Real).[60] Yet, although Kelly saw his monochrome panels, in their non-illusionistic flatness and materiality, as moving from representational illusion into real space, he never sought to transform the "Real" as did Rodchenko's equally optimistic but more radically productivist program. Aside from brief forays into fabric design (which he does not consider part of his work), Kelly never sought to subsume artistic representation into "production skills," nor to effect a Bauhaus-like intervention into industrial production.

Forming a corollary to Kelly's separation from the productive sphere is the manner in which the visual field figured by his work seems to function at an unbridgeable distance from the natural or material realm. Despite Kelly's goal of an art that would produce "a direct, spontaneous, visual experience," one that would, as he told Cage, "meet the eye—direct,"[61] his artistic vision appears always and everywhere mediated. Opposed to the Imaginary function of the easel painting, and unable or unwilling to fully subsume his art within the natural or productive realm of the Real, Kelly operates on the level of the Symbolic—removed from instantaneous or pure apperception by an intervening, significatory layer, the presence of an Other with which vision is at all times shot through. In addition to the use of store-bought gummed papers, such mediation is particularly evident throughout the artist's early sketchbooks, where the colors of observed motifs are almost never reproduced iconically but are rather notated by descriptions such as "bright orange," "duller orange," "very pale gray yellow," or by the even more abbreviated use of numbers or symbols corresponding to a key.

It is a similarly symbolic, even nominalist, problematic that informs Kelly's monochromes, which he seems to have conceived as "enunciations" of color. Such is the significance of Kelly's story of a child who, on encountering *Painting for a White Wall* hung from a balcony, pointed to the panels in sequence and declared straightforwardly, "black—rose—orange—white—blue—blue—white—orange—rose—black."[62] Although apparently recognizing the symbolic and even linguistic dimension to his work, Kelly, as Bois rightfully points out, sought to instantiate in his monochromes an Edenic dream of a pure,

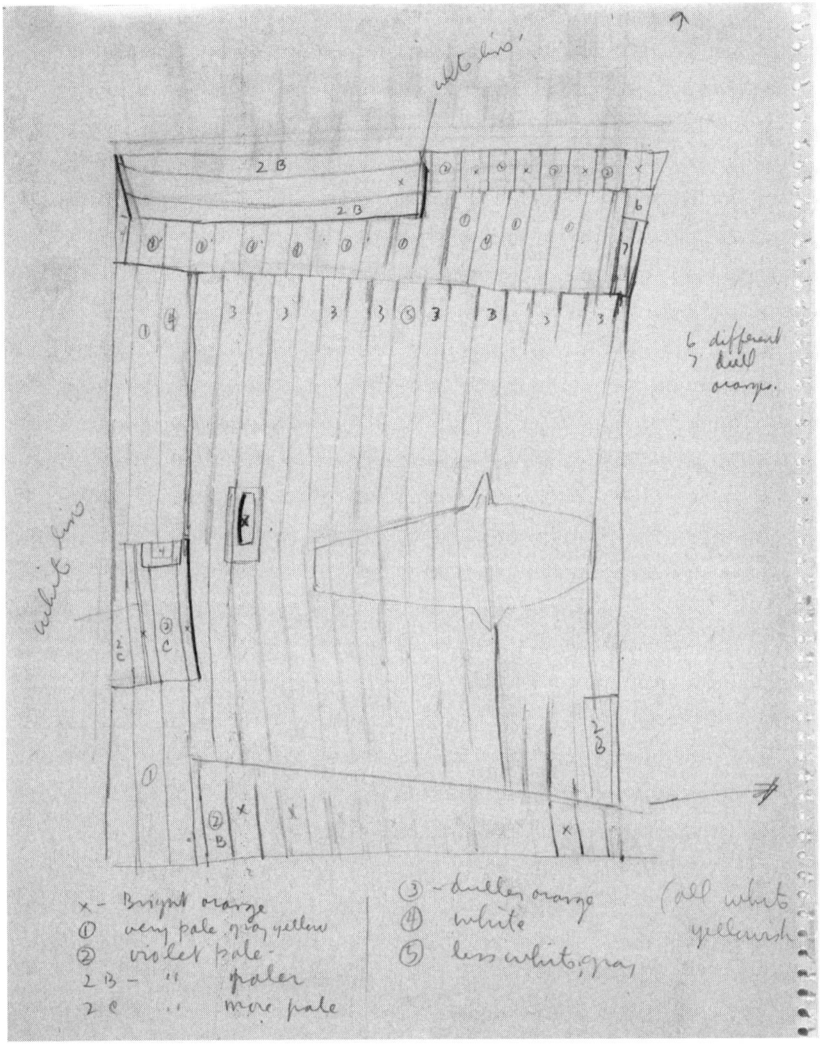

Ellsworth Kelly, *Sketch of a Beach Cabana IV,* 1950. Graphite on paper. 10⅝ × 8¼ in. Courtesy of the Fogg Art Museum, Harvard University Art Museums. Gift of the artist and purchase from the Margaret Fisher Fund and through the generosity of Kenyon C. Bolton III, Agnes Gund and Daniel Shapiro, Richard E. Oldenburg, and Emily Rauh Pulitzer in honor of Neil and Angelica Rudenstein. Photograph by Allan Macintyre. Image © Ellsworth Kelly. Photograph © President and Fellows of Harvard College.

motivated language, one that would overcome the attributes of arbitrariness and mediation foregrounded in his collages. To some extent, this impulse is implied in the very idea of devoting each canvas to a single color: "The monochrome panel as a color sample," Bois declares, "is an index of color as such, designating its own color without transformations."[63] Kelly would ultimately go further, however, by individually and highly specifically mixing each of his colors.[64] While the leftmost panel of *Painting for a White Wall,* for example, approximates the deep black-blue of its colored paper maquette, Kelly admixed it with hints of pink to give it a slightly violet cast. In such an indissoluble anchoring of color as a particular substance to color as its own sign, the Symbolic aspect of Kelly's painting does not disappear but rather strives for the fixity necessary for it to serve as the foundation of a universal art form. Its analogue is a linguistic model in which, as Bois states, "All words are names, all are always singular, and there is no difference between common and proper names."[65]

Starting from the purely paratactic grouping of commercially available colored papers, Kelly's inflection of the panels in *Painting for a White Wall* works to transcend the initial contingency of their organization. Its admixture of pink not only brings the deep blue-black panel on the left-hand side into relation with the pink panel to its right but also seems to have called for the added blue panel at the end, which had not been included in the original maquette. In a subtle yet still impersonal way (being derived from the properties of the initial colors rather than taste), the added blue panel's subliminal, balancing echo—or bracketing, parenthetical punctuation—serves to motivate the work's overall syntactic alignment. Like the poet Mallarmé, to whom he has been compared, Kelly sought to provide a form of necessity that would overcome the arbitrariness of his coloristic "terms" through nearly imperceptible visual assonances and internal rhymes effected on a level that is almost "phonetic."[66]

In so transcending the relation between his colors and the commodity form, Kelly finally proves himself a consummate modernist, reenacting not the death of modernist painting but another stage in its seemingly perpetual rebeginning.[67] For our purposes it is nonetheless important to highlight the particular historical conditions brought to light by his early work. For although Kelly's

Ellsworth Kelly, *Painting for a White Wall,* 1952. Oil on canvas, five joined panels. 23½ × 71¼ in. Private collection. © Ellsworth Kelly.

avowed goal was to continue a certain functionalist avant-garde paradigm of eschewing the easel painting's subsumption to commodity exchange, he ultimately proved unable to find any means of sidestepping a realm of more thoroughgoing and pervasive mediation and commodification. We are not far here from insights that will be gained in pop art, and Kelly's unwillingness to appeal to any "universal" basis other than the thoroughly mediated Symbolic realm brings forth the same specter of a late capitalism now everywhere expanded to preclude direct access to a natural, subjective, logical, or ontological "outside."[68]

◆

Revealed by the relationship between the ubiquitous presence of the commodity and the Symbolic functioning of Kelly's art is a socioeconomic dimension to the situation that Rauschenberg, too, faced in 1954. Although taking a diametrically opposite approach, Rauschenberg's black paintings, *Red Paintings,* and *Elemental Paintings* found it impossible to reach an immediate, natural, or *informe* state beyond symbolic recuperation, thereby revealing a similar condition of foreclosure within a mediated, Symbolic realm. And, as in Kelly's work, it was in the status of color that this foreclosure would be foregrounded and made evident.

Immediately atop *Collection*'s three painted monochrome panels, Rauschenberg applied swatches of industrially produced fabric, equating color with the commodity precisely as Kelly had done in *Red Yellow Blue White.* The conflation of high and low in this near identity of color as artistic material and color as evidently commercial product indicates the closing down of the distance separating art from commercial culture—avant-garde, to use Clement Greenberg's terms, from kitsch.[69] Furthermore, like Kelly's *Line Form Color,* Rauschenberg's *Collection* refuses any recourse to a rational or universal foundation "below" the appropriation of the commodity. The bottom third of *Collection*—in which both the work's original, monochromatic structure and the applied layers of cloth are most evident—initially invokes a rational progression, only to have it immediately undermined. The red panel, bisected by blue, is followed by the yellow panel, bisected by red, and then the blue panel, which is also bisected by red when—if the progression established in the first two panels were followed—it should be bisected by yellow. Likewise, in the red and yellow panels, the more saturated primary color appears on the right, while the final panel reverses the pattern (as was clear even before the panels' fading). Like Kelly, then, Rauschenberg found that conceiving of paint in terms of a commercial color sample leads to an embrace of a certain arbitrariness of combination.

Unlike Kelly, however, whose interactions with color's commodified status had arisen from the complexities inherent in attempting to continue a functionalist aesthetic of the historical avant-garde, Rauschenberg developed these notions in the context of his continuing reception of Duchamp. Indeed, like the more famous rows of colors that run across the center of Rauschenberg's *Rebus* (1955) and *Small Rebus* (1956), the sequence of color blocks along the bottom third of *Collection* appears to reference the trompe-l'oeil succession of color samples in Duchamp's *Tu m'*. As shown by Thierry de Duve, the "pictorial nominalism" of Duchamp's work, his reformulation of painting as a Symbolic procedure, followed precisely from the desublimating recognition that within the modern era the can or tube of paint had long been a readymade, industrially produced commodity like any other.[70] Although, as de Duve notes, this equation was largely unconscious in the 1910s, by the early 1960s Duchamp would come to express the connection clearly; thus, at the *Art of Assemblage* symposium he stated, "Since the tubes of paint used by the artist are manufactured and readymade products, we must conclude that all the paintings in the world are 'Readymades aided'—and also works of assemblage."[71]

Rauschenberg had already begun to emphasize this by-no-means obvious connection in 1954, not only in the interchangeability of painted color with industrially dyed cloth at the bottom of *Collection* but also in the selection of painted colors used above. As we have seen, Rauschenberg had previously attempted to invoke a simple readymade strategy by "arbitrarily" choosing the color for his all-red paintings. With *Collection,* however, he combined an understanding of the Duchampian readymade with the systematicity of Cagean indeterminacy to devise a more sophisticated means of severing any connection between his taste and the colors employed. Rather than choosing a single color, which would not reveal its arbitrary nature, Rauschenberg purchased a number of different paints whose labels had fallen off, and whose contents therefore remained unknown. "At that time surplus paint fit my budget very well," he explained: "It was like ten cents for a quart can downtown, because nobody knew what color it was. I would just go and buy a whole mass of paint, and the only organization, choice, or discipline was that I had to use some of all of it and I wouldn't buy any more paint until I'd used that up."[72] By imposing such a rule of nonexclusion onto each batch of readymade paint he purchased, Rauschenberg guarded against allowing his own taste into the equation after the fact. Regardless of his personal reaction, each color had to make its way into every work.[73]

Similarly, it appears that Rauschenberg also imposed a rule against mixing colors on either the palette or the support, as doing so would both undermine the evidently readymade appearance of the paint and allow taste to return in the choice of which of the infinite range of possible color combinations to pursue. Instead, with rare exceptions, each of *Collection*'s colors recognizably issues directly from the can or tube. The orange that appears as a stroke in the center of the rightmost panel, for example, is also found in daubs on the center panel and again in daubs and splatters on the left. The light blue that appears as a patch just below the horizontal line of red paint on the leftmost panel also peeks out below the yellow that surrounds the circular mirror on the middle panel and recurs both near the bottom and at the top of the panel on the right. This repetition continues throughout the work, with the same colors further recurring recognizably in other pieces of the time such as *Charlene* and *Minutiae* (both 1954).

Even when the colors in *Collection* do encounter one another, they retain a marked separability, as in the red patch applied over the blue paint near the bottom of the panel at the right, or the red-over-orange combination at the same height on the central panel, or the pink and yellow strokes layered over the red patch just to the left on panel one. Even the blue-and-white paintstroke at the top of the third panel (the most clearly mixed of the entire work) fails to fully meld its two components into a single, new color. Across the entire surface of the painting, Rauschenberg's colors do not mix so much as they mingle. Indeed, Rauschenberg described *Collection* and other works of the time as an investigation into "pedestrian color": a strategy inspired by the way that different colors of clothing interacted in a crowded street or room.[74] "Someone might be wearing a very bright tie or green shoes," he explained, "but somehow it was all absorbed because all of these things, even though they were individually brilliant, were accepted in a content [*sic*] that made them both independent and neutral."[75]

Duchamp aptly observed that the production of assemblage was justified by the equation of paint with the readymade, manufactured item. As Rauschenberg matter-of-factly replied when asked why his Combines included so many different objects, "No reason. Painters employ colors that are also manufactured."[76] Because of Rauschenberg's treatment of paint as an industrial product, Duchamp, rather than Kurt Schwitters, provides the key for the development of the Combines. In Schwitters's montage—which Rauschenberg also encountered at the Janis Gallery in 1953, and which was certainly not without impact on his production—scraps of newspaper, ticket stubs, and other refuse of commercial production are primarily used to replace and thereby negate painting's traditional material components. In this deflation of the artwork's pretension to autonomy, however, the negation of paint by collage continues to accord the paint that it banishes from the scene the same preindustrial status that it traditionally enjoys. In Schwitters's work, the more modern form of collage is deployed against the more traditional medium of painting.[77] But in Rauschenberg's work, the collaged and painted passages are treated equally. In *Collection,* the two components do not play off each other with any dialectical tension—alternately reading, for example, as real object and illusory depiction, as flatness and as space. Nor does the materials' disparity produce an impact analogous to that produced by the historical avant-garde strategy of perceptual shock. Rather, the viewer encounters an eminently entropic expanse of materials presented in their virtual identity (an effect even more evident in the heavily collaged sections of *Charlene* and *Minutiae*). Notice, for example, the equivalence of the torn newspaper strip at the left of *Collection*'s first panel with the red paintstroke (now even clearer after the panel's fading) echoing it directly below.[78]

If, as Rauschenberg had discovered in the black paintings and *Red Paintings,* paint could not act as a base material because it was too socially coded, it also could not serve as a legitimate repository of artisanal craftsmanship. As he declared in one of his most celebrated statements, "A pair of socks is no less suitable to make a painting with than wood, nails, turpentine, oil and fabric."[79] No less suitable but, significantly, no *more* suitable either. For by 1954, it had become clear that paint was in "essence" a commodity; therefore any negation of painting by making it confront another mechanically reproduced commodity (with which it could no longer maintain much of a distinction) was as arbitrary and meaningless as continuing to paint in a traditional manner.

This form of the collapse of art and life, the equation of artistic materials with commodities and the effective dissolution of negation, brings forth a nightmare vision of modernism that is the obverse of Kelly's dream of collective anonymity: an annihilation of subjectivity within a late capitalism everywhere colonized by commodification. It is precisely against such a state of de-differentiation that modernist painting had developed since its inception. Yielding as little as possible to industrialization, modernist painting strove to overcome it at every move through an increasing refinement in those areas still available to autonomous, individual manipulation. A high point in the development of this modernist logic had been reached in the work of Jackson Pollock, who, especially in his use of aluminum Duco, had all but conceded the evidently industrial status of paint only to transcend it by his unique form of application (which was itself not free from a certain internalization of mechanization). Indeed, the more that the industrial or commodified nature of the material became undeniable, the more weight was placed on the painter's handling of it until, in Harold Rosenberg's "The American Action Painters" (1952), the work had come to be seen as the residue of a unique event.

◆

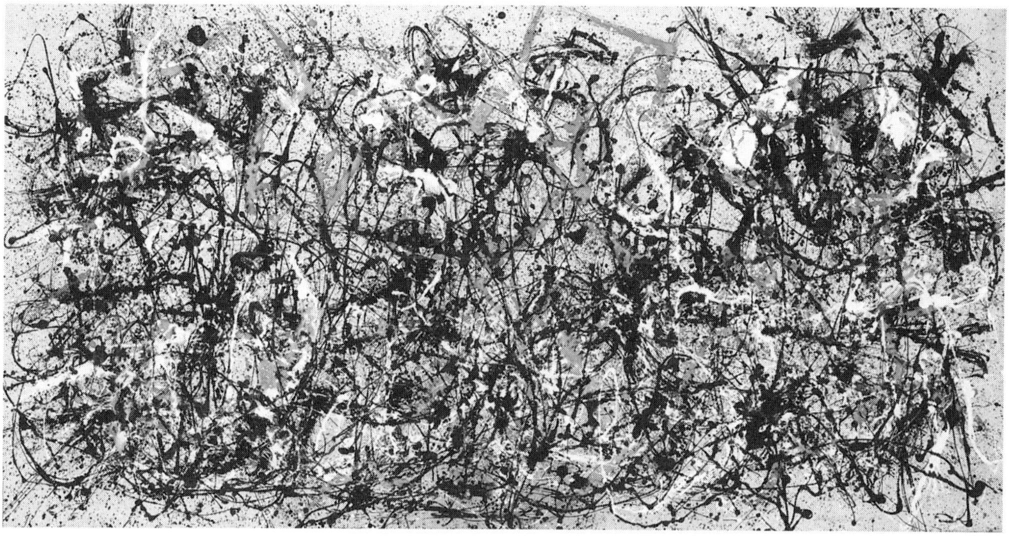

Jackson Pollock, *Autumn Rhythm: Number 30, 1950,* 1950. Oil on canvas. 105 × 207 in. The Metropolitan Museum of Art, George A. Hearn Fund, 1957 (57.92). © 2003 The Pollock-Krasner Foundation / Artists Rights Society (ARS), New York.

Reacting against a rising tide of commercialism in which anything, even a piece of driftwood, could be recuperated as art (precisely the same situation of foreclosure within a capitalist, representational paradigm faced by Rauschenberg),[80] Rosenberg formulated a theory of painterly expression as a moment of pure metaphysical presence. Although in "The American Action Painters" the abstract expressionist painting was understood as "a Sign" (p. 32), it was so only as a derivative, secondary residue of an act of pure autoaffection, a pure ideality where the idea and the expressive action are unified and unique, where "The act-painting is of the same metaphysical substance as the artist's existence" (p. 28). Rosenberg's desire to save the self-presence of the artist from cooptation within consumer society led him to discard from his analysis any communicative aspect or external remnant of the work of art. Representation, aesthetics, form, color, composition, drawing, and all of art's other material components, he argued, "had to go so that nothing would get in the way of the act of painting" (p. 26). The critic's or historian's role was no longer to read the work but to approach or reconstruct the pure presence of the act. This is another version of the dream of art as an Edenic language, a "new plastic language" (p. 34) in which the paintstroke is a mere residue of a pure, enunciative act.

At the top of *Collection,* Rauschenberg seems to refer precisely to such an understanding of the abstract expressionist mark. Each of *Collection*'s panels has been adorned with an expanse of nearly white fabric, atop which are distinct paintmarks but no additional collage. Thus is figured the originary moment of painting: the confrontation of the painter with the blank canvas—the "arena," as Rosenberg had called it, to which the American action painter had taken "as Melville's Ishmael took to the sea" (p. 31). Yet if Rauschenberg is here referencing abstract expressionism, he does so not by reenactment but by citation. The brushstrokes atop these blank canvases—the blue-green scumble on the left and the blue-and-white mixed paintstroke at the far right—appear as quotations or allegorical appropriations of expressive gestures. Indeed, the cobalt blue paintstroke that is placed prominently at the top left of the center panel seems intended for the white fabric to its right (where only a blue line now appears),

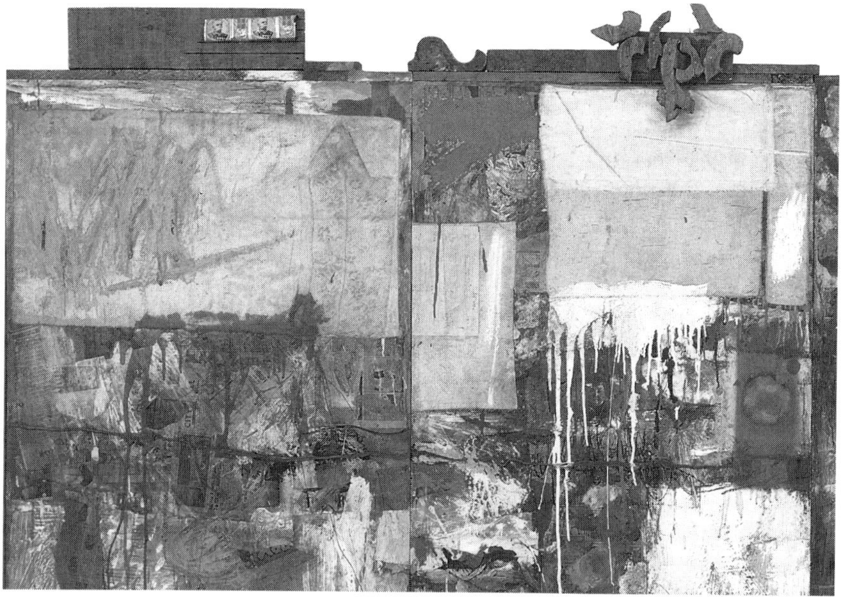

Collection (formerly Untitled), 1954, detail (top of left and center panels).

almost as though it had been detached from its original context and re- or misapplied.

Less obviously, although no less clearly, all of the brushstrokes in *Collection* display similar characteristics. Just as the colors do not mix, so too each brushstroke remains discrete and recognizably distinct or spaced apart from those surrounding it, even if its borders are not precisely defined or are partially obscured by other applications of paint or collage. This is true not only of the last layer of paint applied, like the red stroke just above the blue layer of cloth at the right, but also of earlier marks, like the orange one midway up the rightmost panel that threads its way beneath the green, blue, and brown applied afterward. In this regard, once again, the paints in Rauschenberg's Combine act like elements of collage—separable and detachable, never subsumed within an overall aesthetic construction.

It was precisely the paintmark's appropriability, its ability to be copied apart from the moment of active production ("the revelation contained in the act," pp. 26–27), that had led Rosenberg to demote it to a subordinate status, to see it as inessential in his model of painting as a unique, autoeffective pronouncement of the self—not the empirical self, but an artistic self in the pure presence of self-transformative innovation. In this sense, the paintstroke of Rosenberg's action painter takes on a performative character; it has no referent but rather transforms the subject in the course of its making.[81] As we will see in chapters 3 and 5, neither Rauschenberg nor Cage would be wholly unsympathetic to such an ideal. In *Collection,* however, the brushstroke is not presented as a remnant of an act made in pure self-presence. Following the precedent set by his associate Cy Twombly, who had begun decoding Pollock's drips as graffiti-like inscriptions in 1953, Rauschenberg began to imbue his paintmarks with the constitutive absence of writing.[82] Indeed, at the very center of *Collection,* Rauschenberg uses black crayon to inscribe a distinctly Twomblyesque scrawl. (Later, he would include Twombly's drawings in his untitled Combine of ca. 1954 [commonly called "the man with white shoes"] and in *Rebus,* as if to make his continued relevance clear.)

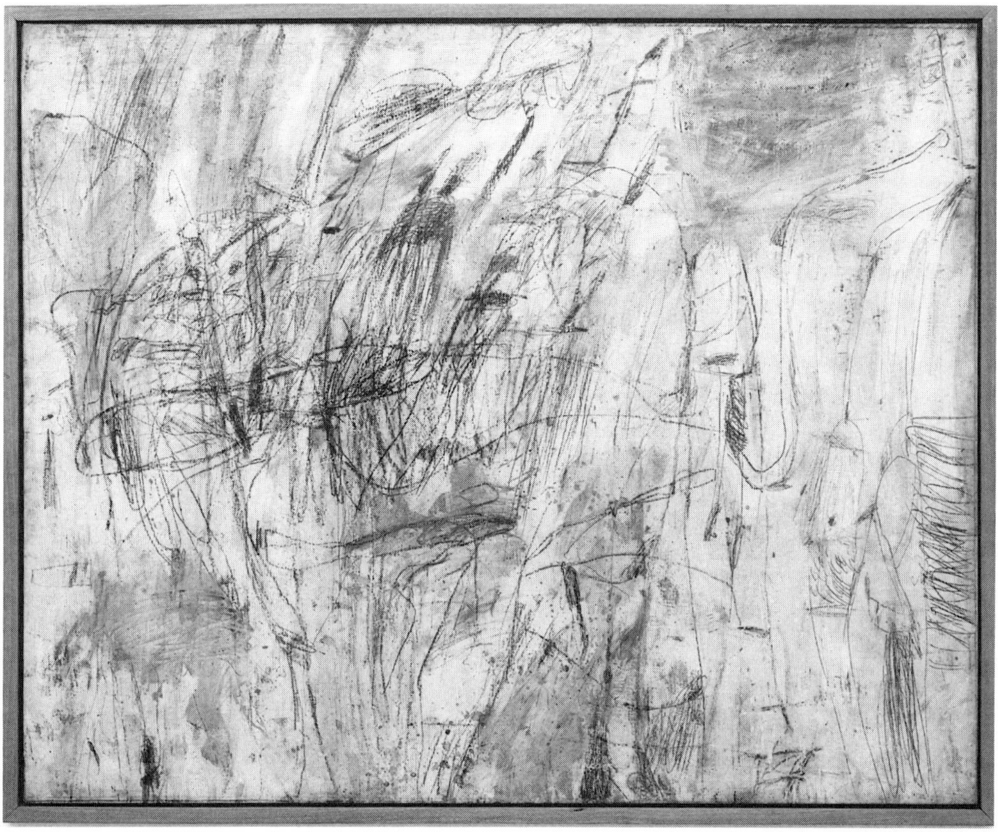

Cy Twombly, Untitled, 1954. House paint, oil/wax crayon, and pencil on canvas. 68¾ × 86 in. Collection of the artist. On loan to the Cy Twombly Gallery, The Menil Collection, Houston. Photograph by Hickey-Robertson, Houston.

But while Twombly emphasized the written mark's quality of defacement, the aggression against the scene of representation that makes the analogy of his work to graffiti so apt, Rauschenberg's "written" paintstroke foregrounded the always open "possibility of disengagement and citational graft which," as Jacques Derrida has shown, "belongs to the structure of every mark."[83] For Rosenberg, it was precisely the production of a mark in the absence of any such transformative intention that led to the creation not of art but of "apocalyptic wallpaper."[84] Yet, as Derrida has never ceased to remind us, a sign such as Rosenberg posits, one that was truly unique and unrepeatable, is not possible—or, at least, would not function as a sign. Iterability, commonly understood as a trait of writing, is in fact proper to the functioning of any sign whatsoever: "This citationality, this duplication or duplicity, this iterability of the mark is neither an accident nor an anomaly, it is that (normal/abnormal) without which a mark could not ever have a function called 'normal.'"[85]

In *Collection,* the iterable nature of the mark is pronounced. It was precisely by foregrounding the repeatability of the paintstroke, its possibility of being copied or counterfeited without the presence of communicative or auto-transformational intent (without the motivation that Rauschenberg could never find "to support that kind of thing"), that Rauschenberg could return to the paradigm of painting. As the same type of stroke is encountered repeatedly across the three panels of *Collection,* any pretense to the paintstroke's uniqueness is belied, and with it the unity and self-presence of the artistic subject that the autographic gesture was to preserve. Regard, for example, how the horizontal, dripping stroke of brown paint overlapping the bottom edge of blank cloth at the top of the first panel is reiterated in white at an analogous spot in panel 2; or how a wet, but less drippy, horizontal stroke repeatedly occurs along the border just above the cloth swatches; or how the Twomblyesque black crayon scribble in the center of the work is echoed by the scribblelike pink paintstroke below it to the left (just above the reproduction of Van Gogh's sunflowers); or how the wispy, dry X in pink just left of center in panel 3 reiterates a similar mark within the square of white paint to its left in panel 2. Such repetition presents a Symbolic functioning of painting that differs not only from Rosenberg's pretension to enunciative self-presence but also from the stability sought by Kelly's nominalist "enunciations" of color as monochrome panels. There is no anchoring of signifier to substance any more than there is a connection to the self-presence of the moment of production. The iterability of Rauschenberg's paintstroke introduces a split or cleft into each one, as its unity is riven by its simultaneous relation both to other marks of the same type and to other appearances of the same color. In the absence of any direct incorporation of time, a nonrecoupable space of difference—a rift or a slippage—is deeply inscribed into the weft of signification.[86]

For Rauschenberg, of course, the paradigm of painting would not have been defined by Rosenberg so much as by Pollock, in whose work could already be seen a negation of the type of subjective presence that Rosenberg's model proposed. In this negation, as T. J. Clark has argued, lies much of the weight of Pollock's abstraction, "its quality of renunciation." All aspects of Pollock's painting, down to the level of handling, work toward undermining a certain form of subjective unity. "The marks in these paintings, as I understand them," writes Clark of Pollock's drip paintings,

> are not meant to be read as consistent trace of a making subject, but rather as a texture of interruptions, gaps, zigzags, a-rhythms and incorrectnesses: all of which signify a making, no doubt, but at the same time the absence of a singular maker—if by that we mean a central, continuous psyche persisting from start to finish.[87]

Yet, as Clark has also been right to insist, Pollock's work, a modernism in extremis, still holds some totalizing force by which the paintmark's incessant negation is recovered as productive of meaning: a meaning issuing from a speaking subject, even if dialogically shot through with other voices and the vicissitudes of the unconscious. Despite all its renunciative fury, there is a positive moment to Pollock's abstraction—"some form of dialectical retrieval," as Clark puts it, "of the word by the speaker."[88] Though infinitely more complex than Rosenberg's argument would have it, Pollock's work nonetheless forges an autonomous, subjective space, a distance set against the encroachments of the commercial world.[89]

This distance—to which Cecil Beaton's famous photographs of fashion models at Pollock's exhibition seemingly give the lie—was one that Rauschenberg and Cage found unconvincing, one that (for reasons we have already investigated) did not succeed in escaping the reification that was its fate in a totalized world.[90] For Cage, Pollock's expressive subjectivity, especially in its striving toward a stereotypical, heterosexual masculinity, lacked any of the spacing found in Rauschenberg and seemed, like the colors on Pollock's canvases, *merely* poured out of a can.[91] Despite Pollock's efforts to put subjective unity into a state of infinite deferral, the will toward expressive totalization, evident even in its negation, was ultimately too much for Cage.[92] Rauschenberg's *White Paintings* had opened toward a form of immanent, temporal differentiation that operated within an infinite totality in which the canvases existed, but which they did not figure or represent (an immanence that paved the way both for the incorporation of the world as untransformed collage and for the violation of the picture plane and framing edge by three-dimensional objects). Pollock's negation did not allow for any such "transparent" opening toward nonanthropocentric difference, even, as Cage noted, when he had attempted painting on glass.[93]

In Rauschenberg's *Collection,* those "events" taking place between the painter and the "blank canvases" at the top of each panel, along with the pretense to originality or autonomy referenced by them, are not negated but are deconstructed in the most literal sense of the term—shaken and undermined by their existence atop a foundation that is shown to consist only of further visual signs: paint, collage, newspaper, art reproductions, and so on. Such an understanding of the paintstroke as inserted into the play of signification (including writing) was not foreign to Rauschenberg's thinking. As he would later explain, "I began using newsprint in my work to activate a ground so that even the first strokes in a painting had its own unique position in a gray map of words."[94] Rauschenberg thus surpassed the purely perceptual understanding of a canvas's never being empty that had informed his *White Paintings* and attained a nearly semiological one. Once "nature" was understood as having been liquidated by the expansion of capital, signification and meaning could not, or could no longer, it seemed, be escaped directly in favor of a base material considered as a form of pure, nonrecoupable difference in itself. Therefore the strategies informing the black paintings and the *Red* and *Elemental Paintings* had to be left behind.

Collection marks a new stage in the process of affirming the nonanthropocentric force of difference that had been "discovered" in the *White Paintings*; rather than being posited as existing beyond the confines of representation, it was now seen as always moving within, between, or underneath the visual field itself. While beginning from an understanding of the effective identity of the artistic realm and that of the commodity, one that seemingly eliminates negation and the pretension to autonomy, *Collection* begins to locate a new form of difference or deferral by which this identity is sundered once again. No longer the pure presence of a difference hypostatized as the natural realm, difference was now presented by Rauschenberg in the form of the deconstructive deferral of meaning within the otherwise totalized social sphere. This presentation requires us to return to Rauschenberg's enigmatic statement concerning the relation of art to life. After the demonic collapse of one into the another had been posited at the bottom of *Collection* (with the equation of color as artistic material and color as manufactured commodity), the deferral of meaning coursing through the work's upper sections begins to open up the "gap" between them anew.[95]

◆

The destabilization of representation first effected within Rauschenberg's *Collection* would help liberate a generation of subsequent artists. Its most immediate and well-known issue would be *Flag* (1954–1955), on which Jasper Johns apparently began work shortly after *Collection*'s completion and which took up, in a characteristically more precise and careful manner, both *Collection*'s nonexpressive, iterated stroke and its relation to collage.[96] A more anarchic and utopian figuration of Rauschenberg's separation of the brushstroke from expression would also arise in such practices as Jean Tinguely's "Meta-Matic" painting

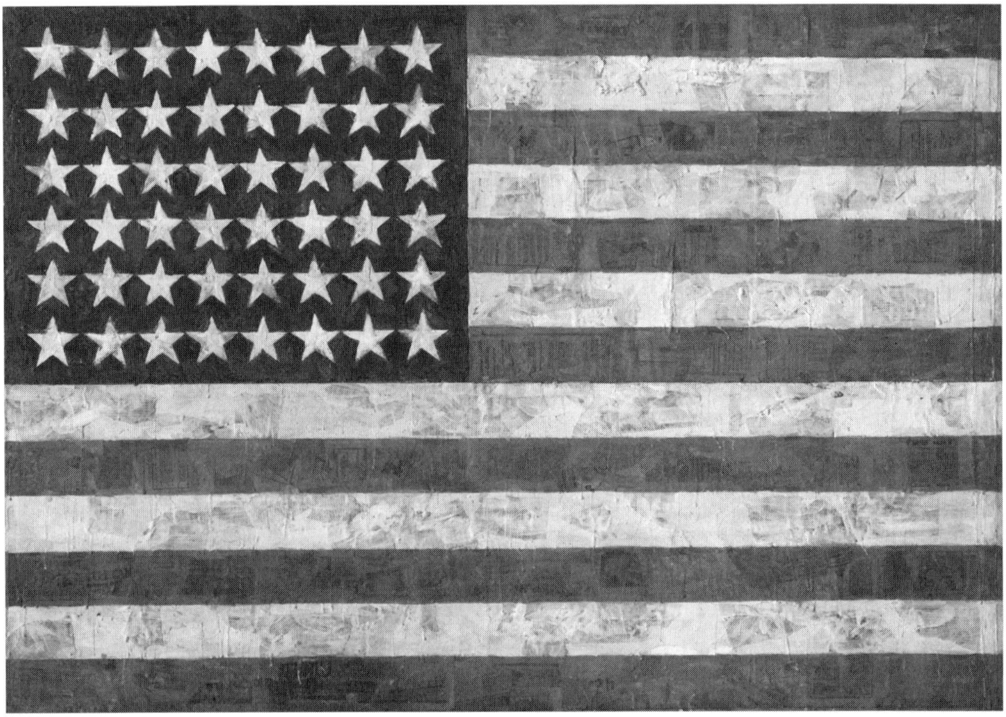

Jasper Johns, *Flag,* 1954–1955; dated on reverse, 1954. Encaustic, oil, and collage on fabric mounted on plywood. 42¼ × 60⅝ in. The Museum of Modern Art, New York. Gift of Philip Johnson in honor of Alfred H. Barr, Jr. (106.1973). © Jasper Johns / Licensed by VAGA, New York, NY. Photograph © The Museum of Modern Art / Licensed by SCALA / Art Resource, New York.

machines and in Niki de Saint Phalle's *Tir* paintings. Despite the seminal nature of Rauschenberg's achievement, however, *Collection* would be for him only a way station, and the techniques pioneered in it would predominate in only a few more works completed within the year. Over the course of the following decade, Rauschenberg would proceed further in the affirmation of difference. The next phase of his artistic development would characterize the Combine paintings proper.

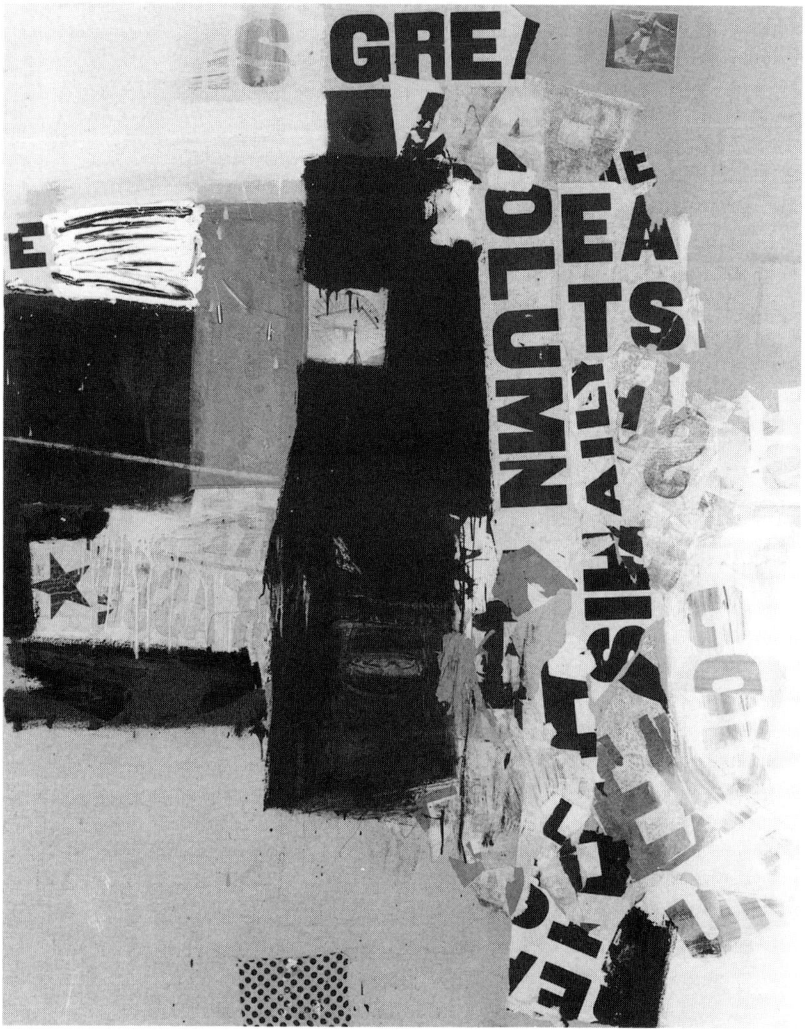

Dam, 1959. Oil, photomechanical reproductions, cloth, and metal object on canvas. 75½ × 61⅝ in. Hirshhorn Museum and Sculpture Garden, Smithsonian Institution. Gift of Joseph H. Hirshhorn, 1966.

3

Mole Archaeology

> Perhaps after all there is no message. In that case one is saved the trouble of having to reply.
>
> —*John Cage, 1961*

Rauschenberg's relationship to the urban environment runs like a leitmotif through the literature on the artist, beginning especially in characterizations of his later Combine paintings and Combines. "If Rauschenberg continues to make found objects precious," writes Irving Sandler, "he treats them less in terms of private sentiments and associations, more in terms of the environment from which they come—the street. The rawness of the city asserts itself increasingly in his work." On the occasion of Rauschenberg's 1963 Jewish Museum retrospective, Alan Solomon observed that from the midpoint of the 1950s the artist's Combines had begun to "reflect the urban environment completely." Dorothy Gees Seckler later noted that the Combines "offered not only objects and fragments that are really present in New York but also a succession of surprising contrasts that are everywhere evident to him in the city."[1] And in "Other Criteria," Leo Steinberg would liken Rauschenberg's silkscreen *Overdraw*

(1963) to "some garbled conflation of controls system and cityscape, suggesting the ceaseless inflow of urban message, stimulus, and impediment." "Rauschenberg's picture plane," he declared, "is for the consciousness immersed in the brain of the city."[2] The artist's own statements have also supported such a position. Rauschenberg explained to Seckler that rather than being "an illustration of my will," he wanted his work to be "more like an unbiased documentation of what I observed. . . . I felt an excitement at being in a city [New York] where you have on one lot a forty-story building and right next to it, you have a little shack. There is this constant irrational juxtaposition of things that one doesn't find in the countryside."[3]

Of all the commentaries focusing on the urban environment, one of the most sophisticated was provided by Brian O'Doherty, who discussed Rauschenberg's art in terms of what he famously called the "vernacular glance." O'Doherty recalled being struck most forcefully by that facet of Rauschenberg's work at the Jewish Museum retrospective. "The work wouldn't let me settle down," he recounted, "and I remember feeling uncomfortable that I'd brought my street reflexes with me. You wanted to look over your shoulder to see if you were going to be run over."[4] The pedestrian's relationship to the urban environment would become the paradigmatic descriptive example of the vernacular glance, an agitated and reactive mode of visual apprehension that, O'Doherty explained, "is what carries us through the city every day—a mode of almost unconscious or at least divided attention" (p. 84). Casual rather than concentrated, the vernacular glance occasioned by Rauschenberg's collage is a look that "tags the unexpected and quickly makes it familiar, filing surplus information into safe categories": "The slight discomfort in perception, refusing to settle, is exactly what deposits the work in its most appropriate context—something that scans, sorts, recognizes, briefly wonders at and moves on" (pp. 84, 85).

Distinguishing it from a mere "careless superficiality" (p. 84), O'Doherty likened the perceptual modality initiated by Rauschenberg's Combines to those of film, television, and advertising. Yet despite his insistence on the vernacular glance's contemporaneity, O'Doherty's discussion actually provided less a new theory of vision than an updating of Walter Benjamin's theory of "distraction." Like O'Doherty's vernacular glance—a perception "so habitual that it is almost disinterested" (p. 84)—Benjaminian distraction was opposed to a fully conscious, contemplative regard, acting instead largely through habit to master the situation with which it was confronted. And also like O'Doherty, Benjamin associated this perceptual mode with a precise urban milieu: not, of course, Rauschenberg's New York, but the Paris of Charles Baudelaire.

In his study "Some Motifs in Baudelaire," Benjamin chronicled the poet's reaction to the enervating effects newly produced by the modern city, the jarring and colliding optical shocks an individual encountered while moving through big-city traffic, where "At dangerous crossings, nervous impulses flow through him in rapid succession, like the energy from a battery."[5] According to Benjamin, it was the motion picture that would most completely take up such shocks as an aesthetic and formal principle, becoming an efficient means of training the human sensory apparatus to withstand their impact. By disarticulating the synthetic integrity of temporal movement, fragmenting place and time through rapidly edited sequences of shot and countershot, film was one of the most effective modern visual forms to disintegrate the "auratic" quality of the traditional, autonomous artwork—the aura being that aspect of perceived distance that separates the viewer from the work of art, a distance Benjamin described in terms of an ineffable sense of life or the feeling that the work was somehow engaged in returning the viewer's gaze.[6]

As Benjamin made clear, the opposition between distraction and the contemplative vision associated with auratic art formed only one aspect of a wider social dialectic. The aura was the aesthetic counterpart or repository of genuine historical experience (*Erfahrung*), and its decay chronicled the extent to which such experience had atrophied with the rise of modernity, to be supplanted by a mere lived-throughness (*Erlebnis*). The latter mode of existence entailed the liquidation of any integral connection to history or memory—a development resulting, in part, from the manner in which stimuli are processed by a subject geared toward cushioning the effects of shock. Somewhat like a photograph, which fixes a moment in time without the photographer's necessarily processing it fully into his or her experience, the "shock defense" of the modern, distracted individual functioned by "assigning to an incident a precise point in time in consciousness at the cost of the integrity of its contents."[7]

As opposed to Baudelaire, whom Benjamin figured as among the last with any hope of salvaging authentic experience from the modern immersion in perceptual shock, the dadaists were described as forging headlong into the aura's willful destruction. In "The Work of Art in the Age of Mechanical Reproduction," Benjamin proposed that by launching an apparently chaotic accumulation of debris at the viewer, the dadaists rendered contemplative immersion impossible and achieved "a relentless destruction of the aura of their creations, which they branded as reproductions with the very means of production."[8] In the "studied degradation" and characteristically heterogeneous juxtapositions of material in dadaist montage, the organic quality of the work disappears and with it the possibility of contemplation.[9] The jarring contrasts of materials crushed together without transition confound traditional modes of perception predicated on an organic unity, and, in that denial, simulate the perceptual effects of shock.[10] As Benjamin Buchloh has argued, in the most relentless and effective of montage practices this shock becomes akin to allegory, producing a distance from the work that promotes a critical consciousness of its structural, historical, or circumstantial preconditions.[11]

Although O'Doherty's characterization of the vernacular glance seems indebted to Benjamin, the Rauschenberg he describes is no dadaist. The relationship O'Doherty sees between Rauschenberg's collage and the urban environment is almost purely mimetic. While a form of perceptual agitation akin to shock may be produced, it bears little resemblance to any type of distanced, critical cognition. Rauschenberg's Combines do not seem capable of mustering enough dialectical force to reveal any of their underlying preconditions.[12] Even where Rauschenberg appears at first to invoke a cubist format (a means by which the viewer could attain an understanding of the work at the level of form or structure), O'Doherty notes that it quickly breaks down, disintegrating "into a kind of additive dementia" (p. 84). Thus any cognitive dimension to the artwork seems similarly destined to dissipate. Toward

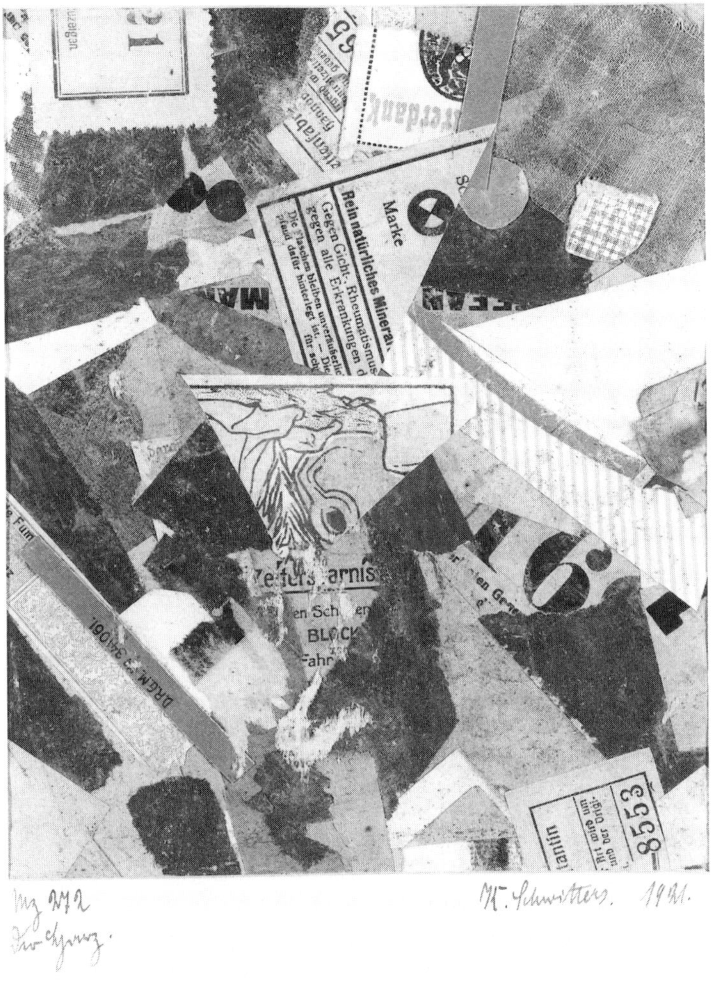

Kurt Schwitters, *Mz 272 Der Harz,* 1921. Collage, cloth, and paper on paper. 7 × 5½ in. © Kupferstichkabinett. Staatliche Museen zu Berlin-Preußischer Kulturbesitz. Photograph by Jörg P. Anders.

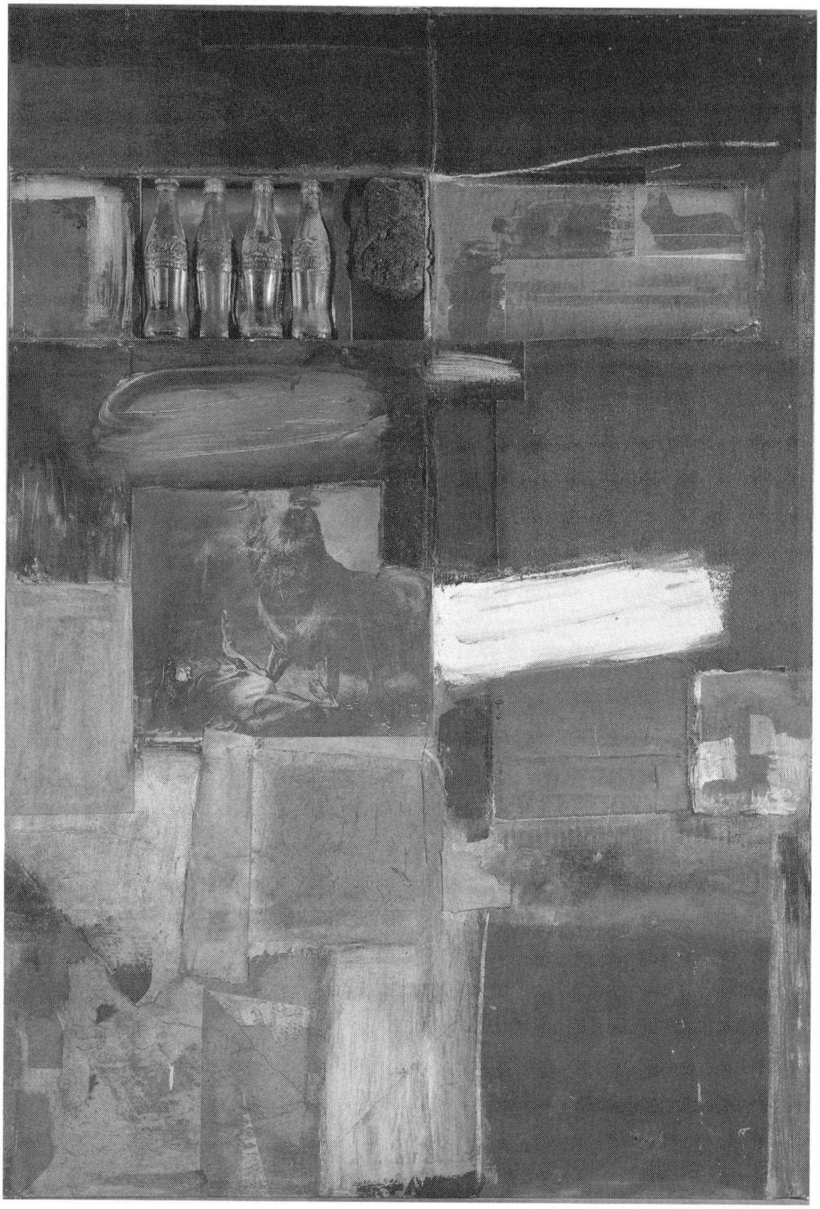

Curfew, 1958. Combine painting: oil, paper, fabric, wood, engraving, printed reproductions, and printed paper on canvas and wood, with four Coca-Cola bottles, bottle cap, and unidentified debris. 56½ × 39½ × 2½ in. Collection of David Geffen, Los Angeles.

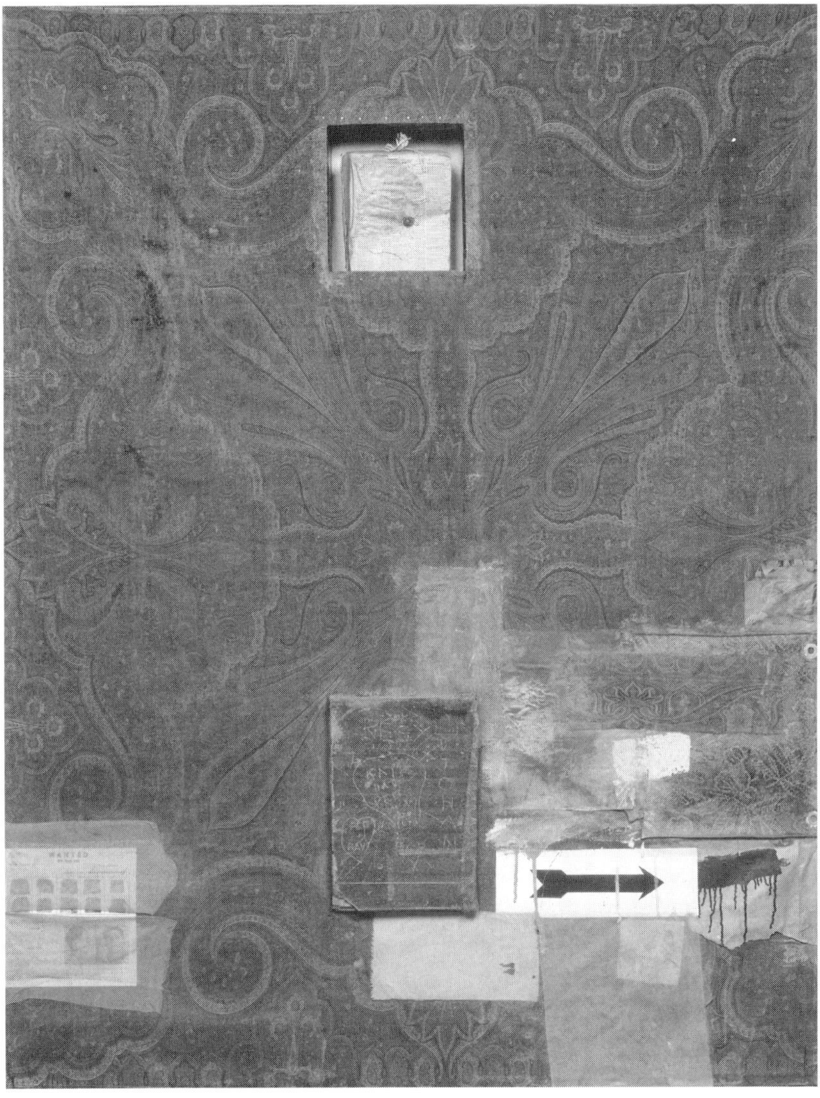

Hymnal, 1955. Combine painting: oil, paper, fabric, printed paper, printed reproductions, and wood on fabric, with telephone directory, metal, and string. Sonnabend Collection. Courtesy Sonnabend Gallery.

the end of his analysis O'Doherty observes that "The images and/or objects [in Rauschenberg's work] do not suggest propositions to be solved, but appear as aspects of process. They contain, or indicate, no solutions, engender no enigmas" (p. 86).

Nor does O'Doherty describe Rauschenberg as a Baudelaire. In Rauschenberg, there is nothing of the composure of Benjamin's poet or the dialectical presence that he, as *flâneur,* maintained to distance himself from the metropolitan crowd even while acting as their "accomplice."[13] Rather, in positing that his work directly reproduces the conditions of the vernacular glance, O'Doherty's characterization of Rauschenberg brings him closer to what Benjamin described as "the man in the crowd": a figure who loses himself among the masses, participating in their manic movements without feeling the horror that still tinged Baudelaire, or the separation that allowed him to understand or judge.[14]

Thus, despite O'Doherty's laudatory intentions, the conclusion to be drawn from his article seems inescapable: relinquishing any claim to, or formal component of, a cognitive structural dimension, Rauschenberg simply and faithfully reproduces contemporary urban shock within a high art format. Forgoing any hope of improvement, transformation, or critique, Rauschenberg's art betrays a reconciliation with, or capitulation to, the contemporary social situation. From this perspective, the challenge posed by the shifting, deconstructive instability of his paintstrokes and collage merely translates the perceptual intensities of a commodity-saturated urban environment. Rauschenberg, whose work O'Doherty compared to "Fifth Avenue window dressing" (p. 84), thus represents an abandonment to the spell of capitalist society, to the auraless eyes that Baudelaire described as "lit up like shop windows."[15] "The vernacular glance," wrote O'Doherty, "sees the world as a supermarket" (p. 84).[16]

•

Despite the long-standing connection critics have drawn between Rauschenberg's work and the experience-dissolving effect of the metropolitan environment, another line of literature asserts his work's integral relation to cultural memory. Rauschenberg's inclusion of artwork reproductions within his Combines has led commentators such as Charles Stuckey and Kenneth Bendiner to claim that, in Stuckey's words, his "interest in the old masters is obvious."[17] More recently, Thomas Crow has endorsed a similar view, arguing that Rauschenberg's Combines evidently and straightforwardly refer to the classical past; in his estimation, such reference "undermines any perception—then or now—that his is a conduit for an undiscriminating 'vernacular glance.'"[18] Indeed, far from having been neglected, Rauschenberg's supposed personal connection to the art of the past has assumed an almost mythical status as explaining the origin of his artistic practice. The story goes that Rauschenberg had no experience of painting apart from seeing reproductions before a visit to the Huntington Art Gallery while on a leave from the navy. There he encountered Thomas Gainsborough's *The Blue Boy* (ca. 1790), Joshua Reynolds's *Portrait of Mrs. Siddons as the Tragic Muse* (1784), and Thomas Lawrence's portrait, *Pinkie* (1794). As Calvin Tomkins recounts,

> He recognized the first two, having seen them in reproduction on the backs of playing cards, but the originals hit him very hard. As he described the experience years later to *Time*'s Robert Hughes, what struck him was "that someone had thought those things out and made them. Behind each of them was a man whose profession it was to make them. That just never occurred to me before."[19]

In this version of the story, it is precisely the auratic qualities of the Huntington artworks—their uniqueness and individual, handcrafted production—that played the defining role in Rauschenberg's response, and those were the qualities to which he would subsequently be seen to be paying homage through the reproductions included in his Combines. It is almost certainly not a coincidence that the statement quoted by Tomkins was first recorded in 1976, the year of Rauschenberg's retrospective at the National Collection of Fine Arts in Washington, an exhibition that marks Rauschenberg's canonization as one of America's own "old masters."[20]

Nearly twenty years earlier, however, in 1958, Rauschenberg provided a much different version of his "discovery" of art. In response to James Schuyler's question, "Is Today's Artist with or against the Past?" Rauschenberg recalled,

> I didn't even know there was art until I left Texas when I was eighteen. The only painting I knew (and I didn't know it was "a painting" until much later) was *Hope*—the woman sitting on a globe with her head in one of those bandage-nooses and I think a lyre? and the water lapping up around her? that green you only get in reproductions!
>
> I think that negates the idea of a painter's relation to official—old master—art. It was neutral ground—that one picture—I responded to visual things, I spent most of my time drawing. *Hope* was just sort of a thing there, not art.[21]

In this account, what is manifest is precisely the loss or impossibility of any direct experience of cultural history, a relation seen to have been severed by the intervention of mechanical reproduction. Here, the green that Rauschenberg first associated with the reproduction of *Hope* interrupts or inhibits any direct reception of the authenticity of the original. Earlier in his response, Rauschenberg had elaborated on this understanding of the distance from cultural memory:

> I don't feel any direct relationship between what I do and existing art. Though there is an unavoidable progression: the things all paintings have in common are paint, and color, and some means of application. With that standard you can make any two pictures appear either alike or different. I don't think whether they're alike or different is really very interesting.
>
> Outside the big idea that there is art I don't think of others' paintings. But I defend the idea of art and know that it is made up of all these paintings. Classic pictures are objects that may or may

not influence what you're doing, just like anything else. Like the radio.[22]

Whereas Rauschenberg distanced his work from an integral relation to history, Rosalind Krauss would be led to liken his collage to a different effect of memory, influenced precisely by the neutrality of the reproductions in his artworks—their quality of being "just sort of a thing there," like *Hope,* without being privileged on account of their history or cultural status, and by their ability to exist on the same plane as any other image or object, "Like the radio." Memory, she wrote in 1974, is a space in which "the image of an actual event we have witnessed, and the image of one we have merely fantasized or dreamed, all *do* possess an equal degree of density."[23] On the evidence of Rauschenberg's Combines, Krauss argued for an inversion of the contemporary idea of memory, changing it from a privileged, internal, subjective connection to the past to a space understood as external. And although Krauss does not specifically mention it, the notion of memory she invokes—one in which all events, whether experienced, fantasized, dreamed, or (we may certainly add) seen in reproduction, coexist to the same degree; in which the recollections are explicitly and fully durational; and in which is found an impersonal or suprapersonal collection of "the shared communality of culture"[24]—is largely Bergsonian.

In the course of his study of Baudelaire, Benjamin posited a specific role for Bergson's philosophy: inadvertently, Bergson's conception of memory presented the conditions of experience in "the inhospitable, blinding age of big-scale industrialism."[25] In the same way, the similarity of Rauschenberg's collage to Bergsonian memory allows for a figuration of memory's more contemporary historical conditions, of the possibility (or impossibility) of an integral, experiential relationship to history or memory in the era of burgeoning late-twentieth-century capitalism.

◆

In the years immediately before the production of his first Combine paintings and Combines, Rauschenberg's meditations on the loss of experiential memory had taken the form of a series of small works produced in Italy. Fabricated away from the stimulating and implicitly demanding atmosphere surrounding Black Mountain College and the beginnings of his collaboration with John Cage, Rauschenberg's Italian works were more closely related to the earlier collages shown at Betty Parsons than to his more recent *White Paintings* and black paintings. Taking the form of intimate, evocative collages; hangings; and oddly precious, boxed collections of miscellany, these works seem like brief, digressive investigations into surrealism. Visiting such old surrealist haunts as used-book stalls and flea markets, Rauschenberg collected old prints and found objects such as a curved horn; a small, skeletal hand; a bird's skull; and a baby figurine. Despite their similar affinity for technical and scientific engravings, however, Rauschenberg's artifacts have a more timeless and less outmoded quality than those typical of surrealism. The bones, beads, skulls, and desiccated insects he collected seem like relics from an archetypal rather than recently fashionable past. Instead of being recovered as dialectically forceful relativizations of the present, Rauschenberg's objects, fostered and protected by the boxes and enigmatic juxtapositions into which he placed them, attempt to retain a certain auratic quality.[26]

This attempt becomes clear in the statement Rauschenberg wrote for the exhibition of his *Scatole e Feticci Personali* (*Personal Boxes and Fetishes*) at the Galleria dell'Obelisco in Rome in 1953:

> The Material used for these Constructions were chosen for either of two reasons: the richness of their past: like bone, hair, faded cloth and photos, broken fixtures, feathers, sticks, rocks, string, and rope; or for their vivid abstract reality: like mirrors, bells, watchparts, bugs, fringe, pearls, glass, and shells. . . . In one case the skull of a bird has been decorated in a rich false history and tassels with a bell on a string attached in reminiscence of her song. A bone on the stage of a box no bigger than a tube of lipstick becomes a miniature monument. . . . Other stringlike totems hang pretentiously boasting of their fictitious past. A contemplative instrument is made with a

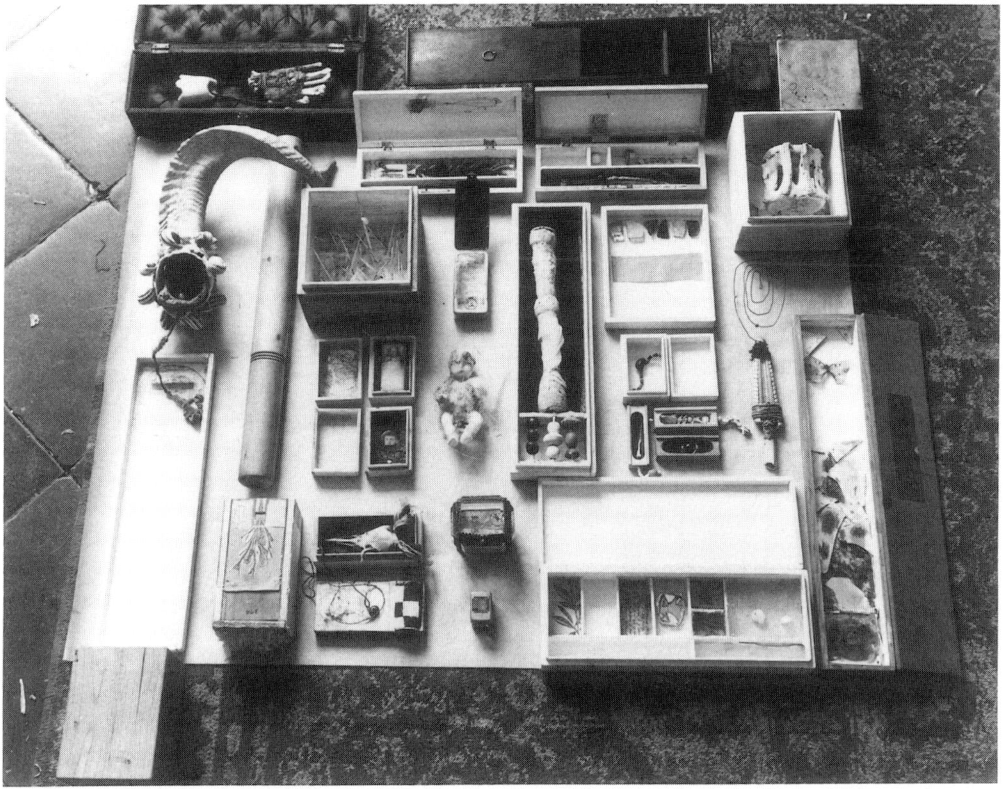

Thirty Scatole Personali, ca. 1952. Arranged and photographed by the artist, floor of Pension Allegi, Rome, 1953. Gelatin silver print.

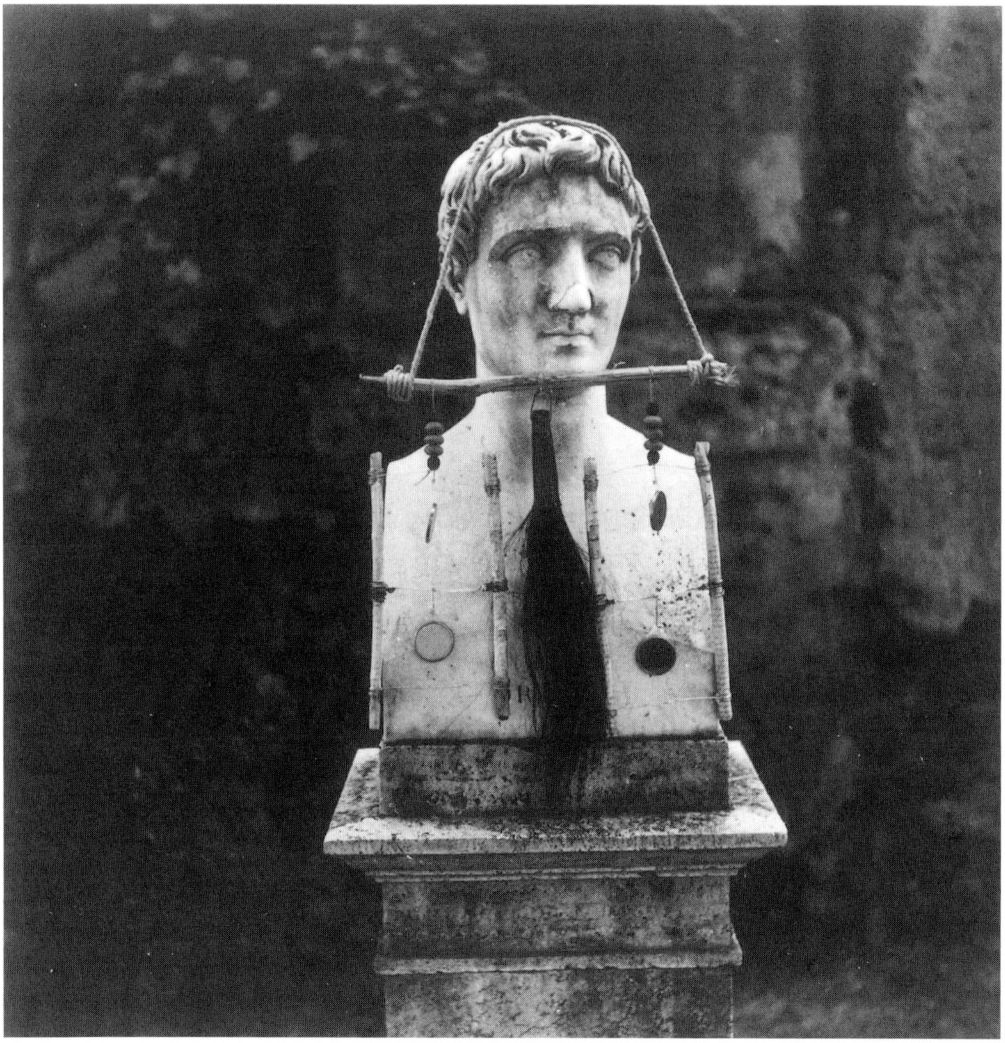

Untitled hanging assemblage from *Feticci Personali* series, ca. 1952. Arranged and photographed by the artist, Pincio Garden, Rome, 1953. Gelatin silver print.

> bead on a coil of wire. You may develop your own ritual about the objects.[27]

In this statement, Rauschenberg characterizes his pieces with all the attributes of Benjaminian aura: availability for contemplation, relationship to ritual, and embeddedness in history. (One work, a dirt-filled box containing a photograph of the artist's eyes looking out from behind a small, plastic lens, seems almost a literalization of Benjamin's description of the auratic artwork's ability to return the viewer's gaze.) But at the same time, Rauschenberg already points to the sense of fraudulence with which these works lay claim to such qualities, indicating the "rich *false* history" of one work and the "pretentious boasting" of another's "*fictitious* past." Their attendant rituals are to be fabricated, not handed down or recovered. The small, almost precious scale of these pieces only serves to attest further to their attenuated figuration of historical experience.

By 1958 Rauschenberg no longer regarded such found objects as imbued with the same relationship to history, whether authentic or specious. Items like those he had collected in Italy were no longer enmeshed within such precious and seemingly personal constructions (though they might eventually make their way into the larger and more impersonal Combines). As he now explained to Schuyler, "They're like an idea: but no specific idea. I have an Etruscan hand that's just that. It's just so literal. It's a fact. A hand."[28] Yet, while Rauschenberg now considered his collected objects devoid of auratic qualities, he did not characterize himself as entirely deprived of access to the past. Instead, once again responding to the question of whether the contemporary artist was "with or against the Past," Rauschenberg described his relationship to history by means of a curious story. "I have a couple of fragments of *the* red and *the* green of Roman frescoes," he began:

> It was one of those places you can go in an afternoon outside Rome. I was among the marble stumps and there was a soft thing, a mole, creeping along. I never saw a mole before. I want beautiful things and he looked so soft and beautiful (but creepy), I could have picked

> him up. I watched him burrow and as he burrowed down he turned over these marvelous fragments. I guess he was an archeologist.[29]

The red and green fresco pieces that Rauschenberg watched the mole exhume would eventually find their place as part of a miniature *Kunstkammer* that gathered on the artist's studio shelf, a direct descendant of his Italian collection of personal boxes and fetishes. As he explained to Schuyler,

> Usually I have a museum-type thing (I just moved my apartment)—they were on a shelf. I rarely touched or looked at them. But I knew they were there: Etruscan votives; a saint's decayed tooth in a frame that looks as though it was hammered out of a license-plate; I used to have two ostrich eggs but I gave one away; an Egyptian Osiris; a faïence sheep: bright blue. I have a prehistoric pot—just a container—it looks like it was made out of chewing gum. I got that in Italy.[30]

On one level, both Rauschenberg's story of the mole and his accumulation of items on the shelf invoke aspects of the allegorical outlook initially theorized by Benjamin and brought to bear on Rauschenberg's work by Craig Owens and Benjamin Buchloh.[31] Like the fragments turned up by the mole, the images within Rauschenberg's Combines are ruins. They have been disembedded from their existence in a particular historical place and time, and as reproductions (or reproductions of reproductions), the images, even those of old master paintings, have been emptied of the integrity of their contents.

Yet the implications of Rauschenberg's story take the analysis of the artist's relationship to the past on a slightly different path. For even though in some ways it is characteristic of an allegorical point of view, largely absent is any overt concern for the redemption of these fragments of the past. Unlike the Benjaminian allegorist with his melancholy gaze, Rauschenberg does not present himself as turned back toward the past. He does not contemplate his museum on a shelf as he had his Italian "fetishes." Although he knows they are

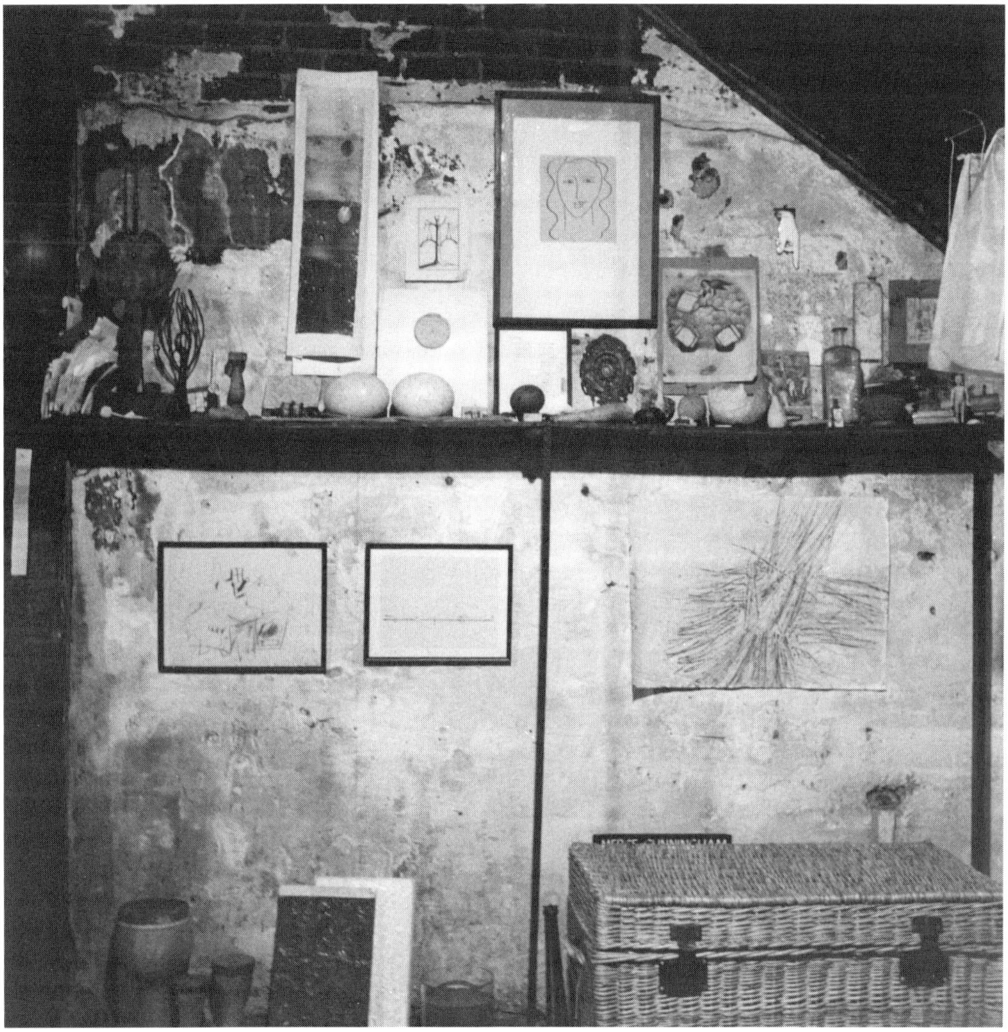

Fulton Street studio view, artist's domestic alcove, ca. 1953. Photograph by the artist. Gelatin silver print.

there, just as he knows the past is "made up of all these paintings," Rauschenberg makes certain to point out to Schuyler that he "rarely touched or looked at" the objects he had gathered. Indeed, in his own presentation of the approach to history, not only does Rauschenberg's archaeologist not look back at the fragments unearthed but, being a mole, it is blind to the objects it encounters, using them only as a means of propelling itself forward. In this figuration, the past is wholly objective: there is between the mole and the frescoes no experiential or integral historical connection.

Like the Benjaminian allegorist, Rauschenberg creates Combines out of the ceaseless piling up of fragments. Like his museum on a shelf, Rauschenberg's Combines are heterogeneous and nonhierarchical, the materials having been accumulated into apparently random or paratactic groupings.[32] Yet diverging from Benjamin's theorization of allegory, Rauschenberg's work, as O'Doherty observed, shows little or no construction of meaning out of the juxtaposition of these parts.[33] Indeed, as Rauschenberg's debate with Roger Shattuck at the *Art of Assemblage* symposium made clear, Rauschenberg forcefully rejected any such constructive quality. He dismissed the historical avant-garde's idea of montage aesthetics as "the most classical form of juxtaposition," uninteresting "because," as he went on to explain, "it's a comparison; it implies the necessity to compare one thing with another."[34]

This lack of a constructive or redemptive dimension to Rauschenberg's art has not gone unnoted in the literature relating his work to allegory. Owens, for example, observed that "By making works which read as *sites* . . . Rauschenberg also seems to be declaring the fragments embedded there to be beyond recuperation, redemption; this is where everything finally comes to rest."[35] Here we come to another of the distinctions between Rauschenberg's Combines and a certain understanding of earlier avant-garde montage. Rather than offering an allegorically redemptive connection to the past, Rauschenberg's work views history in terms of an archive. As Rauschenberg explained to Schuyler, the past ("made up of all these paintings") is, like an archive, known to be there and available for access without its necessarily forming an integral part of one's experience. If the mole in Rauschenberg's story is an archaeologist, then it undertakes its work in a Foucauldian manner, burrowing into a past that is residual without being preserved within the field of memory.[36] Whereas Owens likens allegory to an operation within a contemporary discourse—one that addresses the viewer directly, in the second person—Michel Foucault provides a different model. "The description of the archive," he explains,

> deploys its possibilities (and the mastery of its possibilities) on the basis of the very discourses that *have just ceased to be ours*; its threshold of existence is established by the discontinuity that separates us from what we can no longer say, and from that which falls outside our discursive practice; it begins with the outside of our own language (*langue*); its locus is the gap between our own discursive practices.[37]

◆

Rauschenberg's Combines have a general archival quality that is occasionally foregrounded, whether in such titles as *Collection* (1954) or *Archive* (1963), or as the structuring principle of such works as *Short Circuit* (1955)—which contains a program for a John Cage concert, a Jasper Johns flag painting, and a small oil painting by Susan Weil—or *Black Market* (1961), where a wooden valise connected to the painting by a rope invited viewers to add and subtract objects randomly, provided they leave a visual record of the objects on one of the metal clipboards in the painting's surface. Rauschenberg even described *Rebus* in terms reminiscent of an urban archaeological site, telling Roberta Bernstein that it was "like a concentration of that particular week in that particular neighborhood."[38]

In part, this characterization of Rauschenberg's work in terms of an archive corresponds to Steinberg's famous observations about Rauschenberg's "flatbed picture plane." In "Other Criteria," Steinberg figured the passage from nature to culture in terms of Rauschenberg's seminal transformation of painting from the analogy of a window to that of "any receptor surface on which objects are scattered, on which data is entered, on which information may be received, printed, impressed—whether coherently or in confusion."[39] Yet Steinberg,

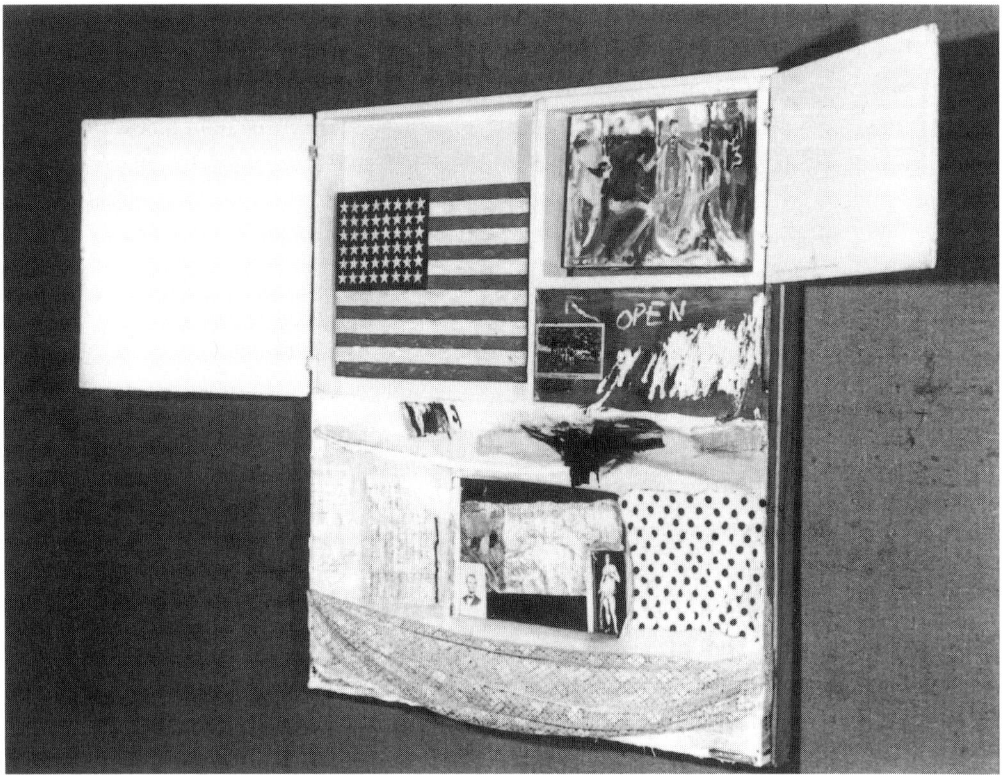

Short Circuit, 1955. Combine painting: oil, fabric, and paper on wood supports and cabinet with two hinged doors. 49¾ × 46½ × 5 in. Collection of the artist, New York.

concerned with the overall nature of this epochal shift, chose not to pay attention to the two more or less distinct phases that define the developing flatbed or archival aspect of Rauschenberg's Combines. As noted by Solomon, O'Doherty, and others, Rauschenberg's earliest Combines are somewhat reminiscent of personal scrapbooks, while in the second phase of their development they come to assume a more impersonal and objective quality.[40]

The Combines of 1953 to 1955 fall within a somewhat nostalgic period in which Rauschenberg's relation to individual memory is most evident, a period that Cage described in passing (and not entirely sympathetically) in terms of cleaning out the family attic.[41] Pieces such as *Red Interior* (ca. 1955) with its appearance of velvet drapery, *Charlene* (1954) with its lace and gaslight-type light fixture, and the early, untitled Combine painting with shelf and colored glass light box (1954) all have the air of recollected domestic interiors. Such materials, as Solomon long ago noted, seem to "refer to life back home. . . . The color reproductions in *Charlene* might be found on a parlor wall in [Rauschenberg's hometown of] Port Arthur; the patches of cloth used for collage recall the country kitchen or attic, fabrics which might be used for housedresses or curtains, doilies, lace, or India prints."[42] Even more explicitly autobiographical is the freestanding untitled Combine known as "the man with white shoes" (ca. 1954). Included in it are newspaper clippings documenting events in the lives of Rauschenberg's family, a photograph of the artist's sister (taken by Rauschenberg), a personal letter, drawings by friends Jack Tworkov and Cy Twombly, and a miniretrospective of Rauschenberg's earlier art, including re-creations of a black painting, a *White Painting,* and a *Dirt Painting.*[43] Although clearly personal in nature, the form of memory conveyed by this piece is already the evidently externalized one discussed by Krauss: Rauschenberg's personal memorabilia are interspersed in a nonprivileged and nonhierarchical manner with other, more random imagery appropriated from the mass media.

In this early period of Rauschenberg's Combines, he primarily adopted a loose, gridlike arrangement of materials. While the grid is a geometrical form both clearly symmetrical and consistent throughout the visual field, it is also a compositional means so immediately evident as not to require any hermeneutic of interpretation or any search for internal motivation—"a symmetry," Cage noted, "so obvious as not to attract interest (nothing special)."[44] The readily understandable nature of Rauschenberg's compositional strategy thus complements on a formal level the other aspects of his work's externalization of personality and personal memory. "For years I've been concerned with the idea of a relaxed symmetry," he explained. "I think of symmetry as a neutral shape as opposed to a form of design."[45]

The self-evidence with which Rauschenberg's compositions are put together—an obviousness seen not only in the loosely stacked grid arrangements of Untitled [the man with white shoes], *Odalisk* (1955–1958), and *Interview* (1955) but also, in a somewhat different manner, in the way in which *Collection, Charlene,* and *Red Interior* are constructed out of separate panels or sections—corresponds to one aspect of Steinberg's conception of the flatbed picture plane. No longer figured as a window, Rauschenberg's work now takes a form closer to "charts [or] bulletin boards . . . on which data is entered."[46] Indeed, as if adhering to a large spreadsheet, the images, paintstrokes, and materials in Rauschenberg's early Combines all seem able to be moved or reconfigured without affecting the overall appearance of the whole.[47] More than the modernist grid, the tabular format noted by Steinberg in this period of Rauschenberg's work makes reference to the compositional layout of the newspaper, whose entirely contingent nature was noted by Cage: "There is no more subject in a *combine* than there is in a page from a newspaper. Each thing that is there is a subject. It is a situation involving multiplicity. (It is no reflection on the weather that such-and-such a government sent a note to another)."[48] Explicitly signaled as early as Untitled [matte black painting with *Asheville Citizen*] of ca. 1952, the affinity between Rauschenberg's work and the newspaper layout further confirms the Combines' relationship to the loss or breakdown of an experiential relation to the world. For as Benjamin observed, it is in the formal makeup of its pages as much as its journalistic style that the newspaper inhibits the reader's assimilation of "the information it supplies as part of his own experience."[49]

◆

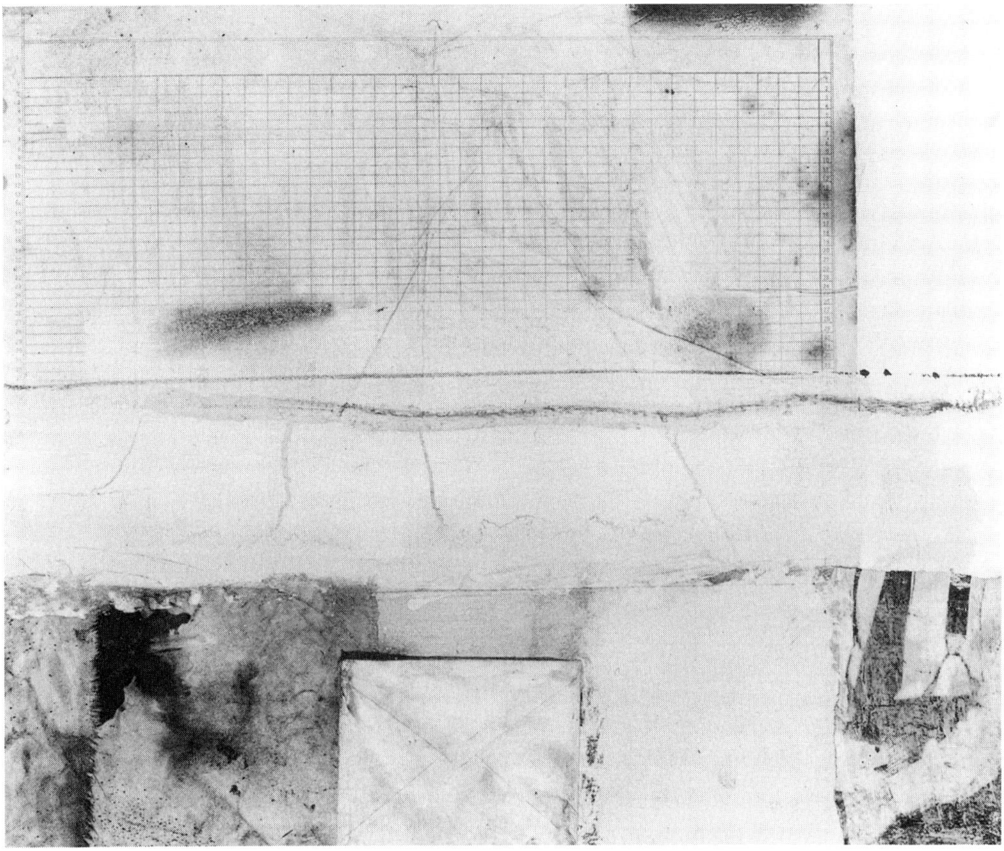

Collage with Letter, 1957. Combine painting: oil, pencil, fabric, and paper on canvas, plus sealed envelope with letter, in wood and glass frame. 16 × 20 in. Photograph by Rudolf Burckhardt. Courtesy The Estate of Rudolf Burckhardt.

Starting around 1955, Rauschenberg began to include graphs, sheets of ledger paper, and calendar grids in his work—references, perhaps, to the chart- or newspaper-column-like quality of his visual information.[50] At the same time, however, Rauschenberg's overall compositional format underwent a change with significant implications for the Combines' figuration of memory. While the Combines' initial developmental phase figured memory and subjectivity as external and thoroughly mediated by the realms of commercialism and mass media, in the second phase of their production even this tenuous remnant of the subject's experiential relationship to the past began to dissolve.

Beginning with *Rebus,* the diarylike or scrapbook quality of Rauschenberg's work disappears. (Rauschenberg described this shift as "trying to kill" the "souvenir quality" of his work.)[51] The fragments or remnants of the past and present—from political posters and newspaper clippings to reproductions of old masterworks—now appear to be further disconnected from Rauschenberg as an individual. It is in this phase of Rauschenberg's work—where, as O'Doherty noted, his material begins "refusing to close the psychological gestalt"[52]—that his Combines more clearly start to assume the archive's functioning as an objective discourse severed from individual experience.

In that shift, *Rebus* is the most important transitional painting. It consists of three panels, clearly bisected by the line of color samples into a six-part grid, but does not have the same sectional quality as earlier works such as *Collection* or *Charlene.* Unlike those pieces, *Rebus*'s images do not seem to have been fitted into gridded sections or newspaper-like columns. Rather, while there is still a vestige of a vertical axis to be found in the rectangle of blue paint and section of white cloth that follow along the division of the two leftmost panels, *Rebus*'s composition has largely devolved from a grid into an arrangement along the central line of color samples.

In his article "On Robert Rauschenberg, Artist, and His Work," Cage devoted his longest description to *Rebus.* Like Steinberg a decade later, Cage observed both the contingency of the assembled materials' arrangement and the horizontality with which the canvas is imbued. After noting the work's two primary axes (the row of colors that laterally traverse the canvas and the vertical

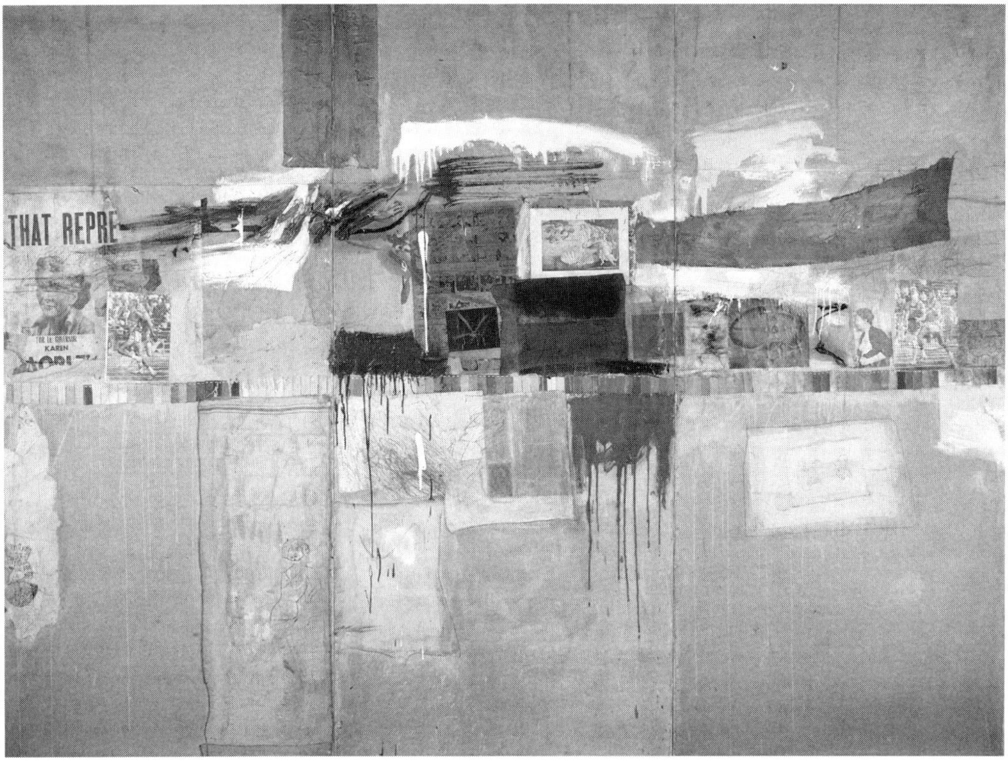

Rebus, 1955. Combine painting: oil, paper, fabric, pencil, crayon, newspaper, and printed reproductions on three canvases. 72 × 70½ in. Private collection.

division of the two canvases on the left-hand side), he wrote: "This is not a composition. It is a place where things are, as on a table or on a town seen from the air: any one of them could be removed and another come into its place through circumstances analogous to birth and death, travel, housecleaning, or cluttering."[53] The most important aspect of this description, as of Steinberg's later and more thoroughly developed consideration of the flatbed picture plane, concerns those materials not connected to the central axis. The large areas of virtually untouched canvas above and below the collaged and painted elements give *Rebus* a feeling of spaciousness and expanse that is distinct from the earlier Combine paintings. These broad areas of uncovered canvas reveal the literality of the support: its straightforward treatment as an actual material existing in the world, and not as a picture plane built up by the effects of interlocking composition.[54]

Although *Rebus*'s canvases do not evidently move out three-dimensionally into the room, Rauschenberg nonetheless treats them more as objects or collage elements than as a theoretical figuration of a pictorial totality or whole.[55] Doing so enables such features as the dripping white paintstroke at the top center and, particularly, the white coloring book image at the lower right to be laid atop the canvas directly, without compositional interconnection to the surrounding materials. The coloring book image, surrounded on all sides by blank space, is entirely detached from the rest of the composition and oriented upside down with reference to it. Cage described this image as "a drawing on a rectangle on a rectangle on a rectangle" (misremembering it as being off to the left- rather than right-hand side of the picture), and he noted, "its situation is that of a farm on the outskirts of a mainstreet town."[56] Relinquished here is any feeling of the need to re-create or justify the picture plane by means of the arrangement of paint or imagery, however loosely applied or heterogeneous. As a result, the materials within *Rebus* appear to be held onto the canvas surface not by means of compositional arrangement but by something more akin to the force of gravity.[57]

Rebus is the most important of Rauschenberg's transitional Combine paintings, but the formal distinction that would come to characterize the second phase of his production seems to have been worked out earlier in a small, untitled piece dated to 1954. Divided vertically by the two adjoining boards, the

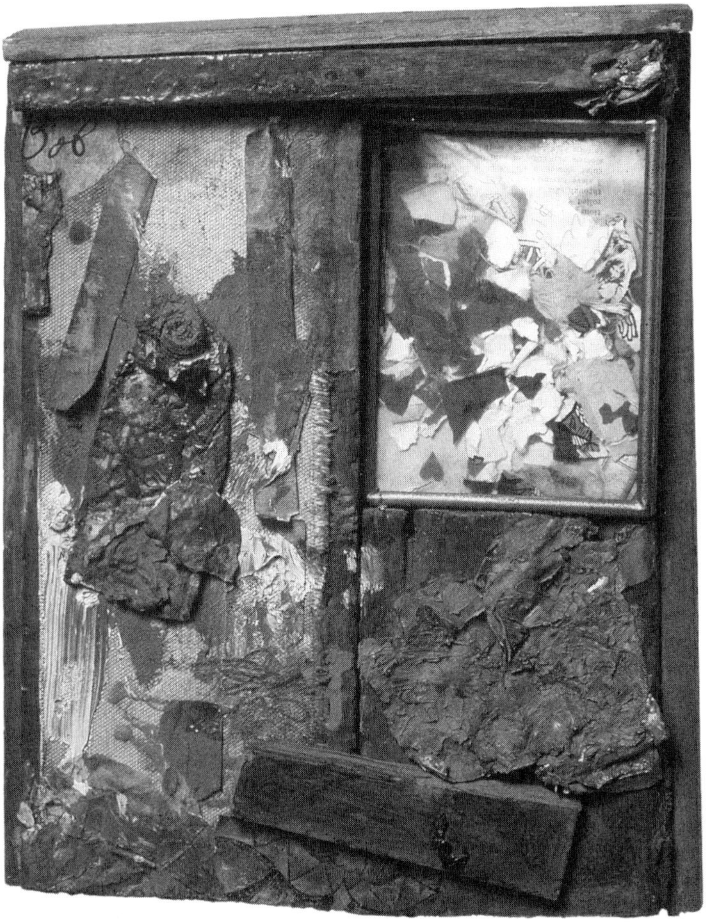

Untitled, ca. 1954. Combine painting: oil, paper, fabric, newspaper, cardboard, wood, paint tube, and glass on wood. 10 × 7¾ in. Collection of Richard and Francine Schapiro.

work's two halves display manifestly different forms of pictorial organization. At the top right is a small gold picture frame, encased inside of which is a jumble of irregularly torn scraps of paper. Held in place by the frame's glass pane, their heterogeneous grouping resembles a Schwitters-like dadaist collage. Parodically mimicking an analytic cubist compositional form, the "picture" seems to build in complexity toward the center and fade off at the edges. In its transitionless juxtapositions and purely aleatory arrangement, this work-within-a-work reprises two of the primary causes of the shock effect engendered by dada. However, by encasing it within a gold frame, Rauschenberg implicitly marked this mode of artistic practice as historical: its former radicality is now a conventionally accepted form of art.

On the left-hand side of the work, Rauschenberg presented a different pictorial model, one that would characterize his work from 1955 forward. Taking a few lengths of tape and a compressed tube of red paint, Rauschenberg laid them onto the canvas without connecting them compositionally to any surrounding element. The flattened tube thus rests within a relatively clear space and, like the coloring book page in *Rebus,* more literally invokes the "horizontality" of the picture plane because it is not held by any scaffolding or compositional arrangement. As though indicating that this would henceforth be his artistic direction, Rauschenberg added to the upper left-hand corner an appropriated scrap of paper with the word "Bob."

In later works such as the untitled Combine painting with toy parachute (ca. 1955) or *Memorandum of Bids* (1956), the "horizontal" aspect of Rauschenberg's flatbed picture plane becomes even clearer. Like the goat that so famously stands in the center of *Monogram* (1955–1959), the collaged materials seem simply to exist on a solidified plane, and therefore they have no need of compositional interconnections of any kind. In works such as *Gloria* (1956), *Factum I* and *II* (1957), or *Painting with Red Letter S* (1957), Rauschenberg's collaged materials seem not so much to come together as to fall apart. *Gloria* and *Painting with Red Letter S* are positively centrifugal, virtually unable even to contain the eye within their canvases' confines, let alone confront it with the configurations that produce effects of shock.[58] By 1961 the disconnected, floor-bound look of

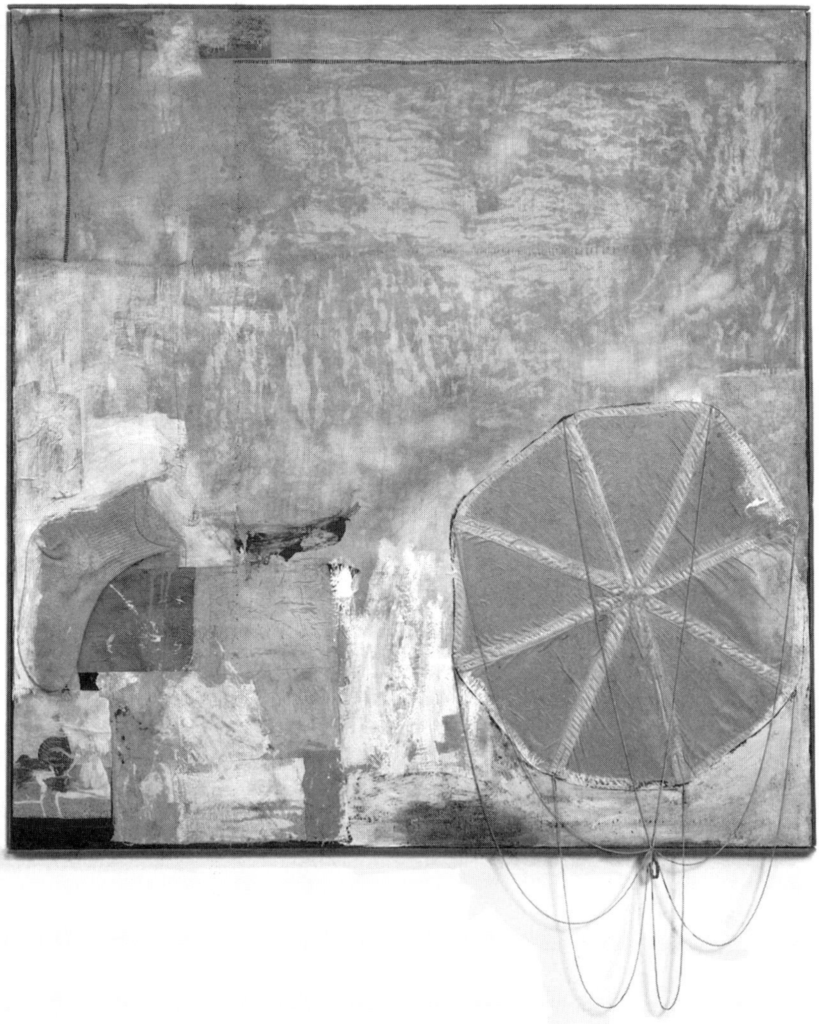

Untitled, ca. 1955. Combine painting: oil, house paint, paper, fabric, and printed reproductions, with sock and parachute. 68 × 55 in. Collection of Stefan T. Edlis.

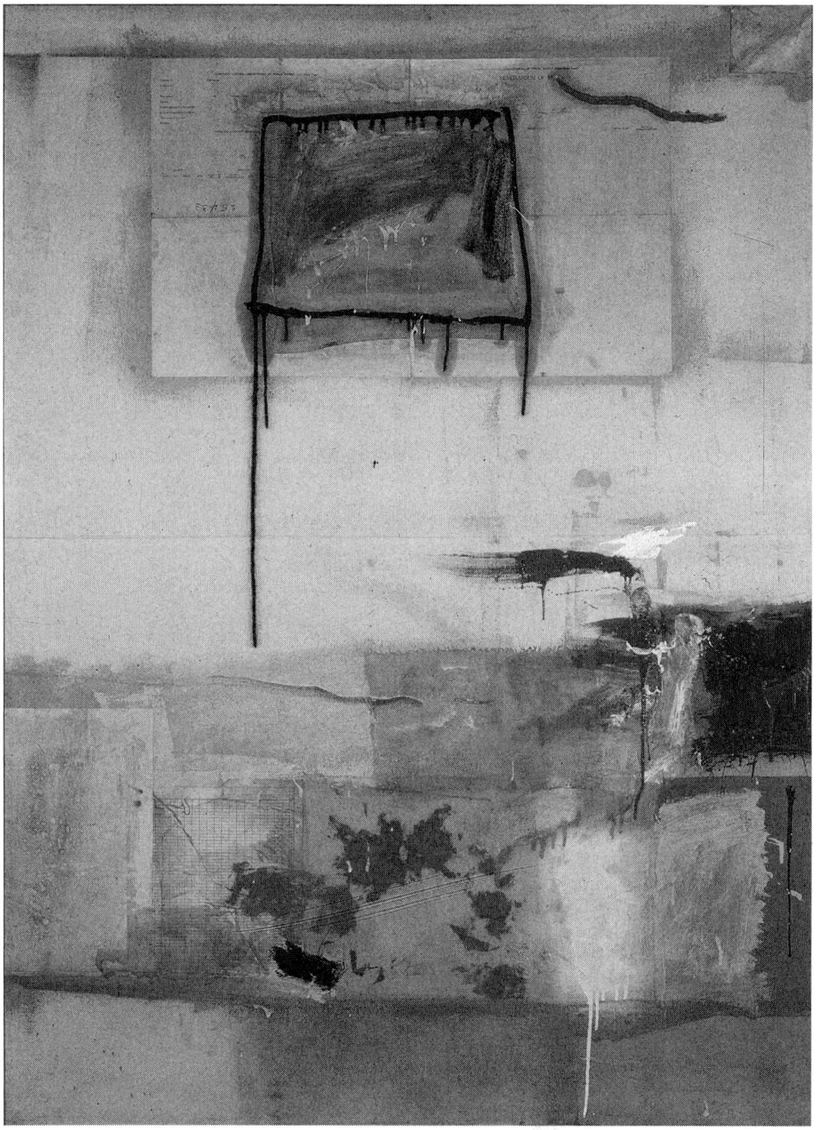

Memorandum of Bids, 1956. Combine painting: oil, pencil, paper, printed paper, and fabric on canvas. 59 × 44½ in. Sonnabend Collection. Courtesy Sonnabend Gallery.

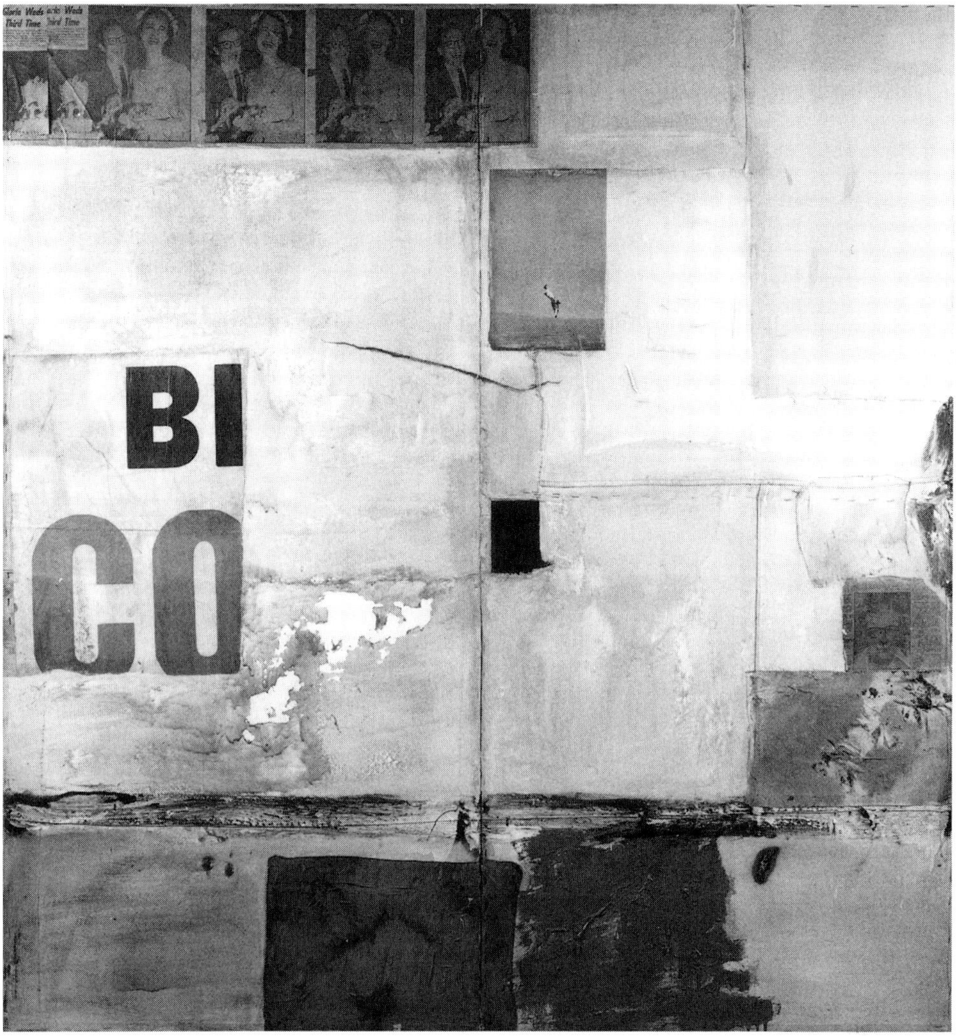

Gloria, 1956. Combine painting: oil and paper collage on canvas. 66¼ × 63¼ in. Photograph © The Cleveland Museum of Art, 2002. Gift of The Cleveland Society of Contemporary Art, 1966.333.

a work such as *Third Time Painting* is clearly no longer following the "classical form of juxtaposition" associated with the historical avant-garde and its "necessity to compare one thing with another" that Rauschenberg opposed at the *Art of Assemblage* symposium.

In this phase of Rauschenberg's work, the disconnection of the materials from one another allows the viewer's eye to wander about more freely, moving from one item to another easily. Connections can be made not just between collage items closest to one another, but also between those related in format, shape, color, material, or subject matter. Yet these connections are no longer the work's primary point, which is rather the circulatory movement across and about the picture's expanse. Even without the evident spacing of a work such as *Painting with Red Letter S,* the eye's chance movement from item to item seems able to continue indefinitely without resolving what is viewed into a comprehensible whole over which the viewer attains sure mastery and without coming to the realization of any underlying structure. Images succeed each other continually and indeterminately. Such was the effect that Rauschenberg's work had on O'Doherty at the Jewish Museum—a feeling of discomfort that he specifically opposed to the contemplative mode of "museum perception."[59]

But while Rauschenberg's flatbed picture plane avoids both the contemplative mode of museum perception and the distracted mode of perceptual shock, it cannot be adequately understood in merely negative terms.[60] Although Rauschenberg stated that "I consider myself successful only when I do something that resembles the lack of order I sense," this *lack of order* still had to be forged within his work.[61] Beginning with the newfound spaciousness of *Rebus,* what Rauschenberg achieved with his flatbed picture plane was akin to what Cage called "the intimacy of multiplicity and emptiness."[62] Like Cage's musical compositions in which "Silence surrounds many of the sounds so that they exist in space unimpeded by one another and yet interpenetrating one another,"[63] the Combines simultaneously separate and interconnect their materials in order to produce more contingent and multiplicitous arrays of interrelations.

Like the reformulation of emptiness accomplished by Rauschenberg's *White Paintings,* this aspect of compositional multiplicity—the "unimpededness

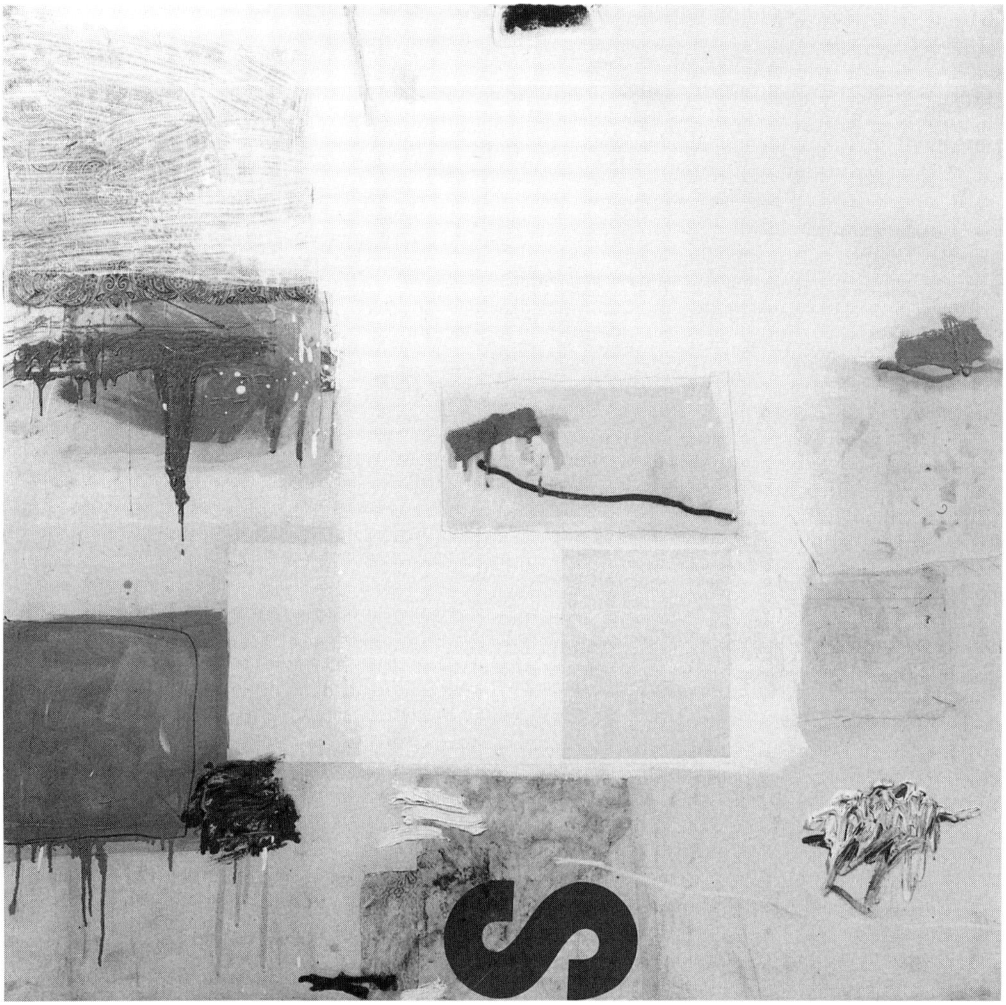

Painting with Red Letter S, 1957. Combine painting: oil and collage on canvas. 50½ × 52 in. Albright-Knox Art Gallery, Buffalo, N.Y., Gift of Seymour H. Knox, Jr., 1959.

and interpenetration" that enables the Combines' materials to form what Cage elsewhere described as "intermittent" "aggregates" or "constellations"[64]—distinguishes Rauschenberg's work from a neo-avant-garde repetition of earlier avant-garde practices and relates it to Cage's idea of neo-dada. For as Cage explained in a different context about the relationship of dada to neo-dada,

> Implicit here, it seems to me, are principles familiar from modern painting and architecture: collage and space. What makes this action like Dada are the underlying philosophical views and the collagelike actions. But what makes this action unlike Dada is the space in it. For it is the space and emptiness that is finally urgently necessary at this point in history (not the sounds that happen in it—or their relationships) (not the stones—thinking of a Japanese stone garden—or their relationships but the emptiness of the sand which needs the stones anywhere in the space in order to be empty).[65]

In this passage, Cage adds a new dimension to the idea of the space that, as seen in the introduction and chapter 1, distinguishes neo-dada from its historical predecessor. Recalling László Moholy-Nagy's descriptions of unimpeded physical motion through a truly "modern" space or his own more general interest in modern buildings, Cage's description evokes an architectural free plan: like the walls, furniture, and people inside a modern building, the materials within a Rauschenberg Combine can be located at any point because of their independence from structural necessity. When not referencing the Ryoanji stone garden, Cage likened this aspect of neo-dada's open space to Mies van der Rohe's Crown Hall at the Illinois Institute of Technology.[66] This separation of structure and content was explicitly found in Cage's own compositions as well. In the score for *Music for Carillon I,* completed shortly after he left Black Mountain College in 1952, Cage laid stenciled dots atop gridded paper in a manner that is entirely independent of the structural quality of the lines. Importantly, however, the architectural space that underlay and enabled the independence of structure and content was also integrally related to the aspect of space that Cage

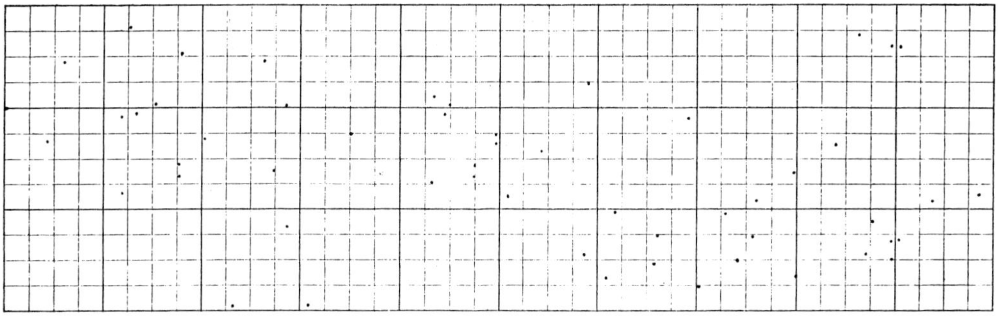

John Cage, excerpt from *Music for Carillon I (Graph) No. 1,* 1952. © 1960 C. F. Peters Corporation. Used by permission. All rights reserved.

understood in terms of transparency: the interpenetration of interior and exterior that characterized equally Rauschenberg's *White Paintings* and Moholy-Nagy's "white house with great glass windows."[67]

Until the 1960s, when Rauschenberg would produce works directly on Plexiglas, such "transparency" was achieved primarily through the use of mirrors, openings in the canvas, or blank spaces that incorporated temporal and environmental change. As much as or more than the movements mechanically or electronically introduced into Combines such as *Reservoir* (1961) and *Third Time Painting,* with their clocks, or *Pantomime* (1961), with its fans, it was this aspect of transparency or "space" that ensured the work's operation as a site of constant transformation. From the mirror and open area in *Charlene,* to the spaced ladder rungs of *Winter Pool* (1959), to the large, blank passages of *Wager* (1957–1959), such openings can be found in nearly all of Rauschenberg's works of the period. Often small, these were nonetheless significant, for, as he insisted,

> Getting the room into the picture was important because I've always felt a little strange about the fixedness of a painting. . . . [A]nd so the use of mirrors and putting open areas in the painting for the wall, which would change from time to time and place to place, to come through and be part of the active image was a way of counteracting that kind of stillness that I found most . . . I didn't find anything in life to relate to that.[68]

"Space," then, is the means by which process enters Rauschenberg's neo-dada collage. External events interpenetrate with the fixed collaged elements already there and thus alter, break up, and recharge the interconnections between them. As the opening of the artwork to process and temporal change, space (rather than negation) is the neo-dada artwork's mechanism of nonidentity. Reactivating the contingent relational arrays between materials, it works to postpone the moment of the artwork's ultimate reification. "The moment a picture begins to look like you think it does," Rauschenberg contended, "it's nearly gone."[69]

Because they are archival repositories of society, made up of the same commercial, mechanically reproduced images that make up the environment, Rauschenberg's Combines do not separate themselves from their milieu by the force of negation. Rather, they interpenetrate it, insistently situating themselves on the same plane and in the same space through the actual, untransposed scale of their materials and the lack of compositional integrity by which they would form an organic (or even inorganic) whole.[70] More explicitly than either the *White Paintings*' dust or the traces left on the *Erased de Kooning Drawing,* the Combines' materials confront the viewer with a certain figuration of memory, or of the past, as evinced most clearly by the inclusion of old master paintings. And inasmuch as it is presented in the form of an archive, this past also figures as accessible from the present.[71] However, these archival remnants, available in the present, are confronted as an objective discourse, a reality of thorough mediation in which the present is no less cut off from integral experience than the past. Yet Rauschenberg's Combines do not simply form mimetic reproductions of the commercially saturated urban environment or its vernacular glance. Rather, the openness of their multiplicitous material constellations seeks a turning similar to that first proposed by the *White Paintings*: away from the increasingly reified and regulated social sphere and toward an immanent, indeterminate force of difference coursing through its interstices.[72] Space, then, in Cage and Rauschenberg's conception of neo-dada, opens onto a difference that while positive (in that it is not, like shock, based on negation) is not affirmative (in the Frankfurt School sense of being identical to the actually existing state of late-capitalist society). Rather than presenting "the world as a supermarket," the artwork's opening to difference provokes a dislocation from the habitual, reified, and uniform perception of the social realm.[73] (This understanding underlay a comment by Cage, who was averse to New York's role as the "marketplace": "With the help, however, of some American paintings, Bob Rauschenberg's particularly, I can pass through Times Square without disgust.")[74]

While Rauschenberg has long described his work as generally "dealing with multiplicity," his later Combines can now be understood as very specifically forming continuous multiplicities—contingent multiplicitous arrangements that shift and change through the nonrepeatable transformations of time.[75] Before a Rauschenberg Combine, and attentive to the changes incorporated into the work's "spaces," the viewer finds him- or herself involved in a process of continually differing perception. Like someone stepping into the Heraclitean stream, once again, an attentive viewer can never see the same Combine twice. As Cage commented, "Over and over again I've found it impossible to memorize Rauschenberg's paintings. I keep asking, 'Have you changed it?' And then noticing while I'm looking it changes."[76]

◆

The questions both of what mode of viewing the Combines call forth and of what relationship they establish with the past are central to the continued debate over the iconographic readings of Rauschenberg's production. In "Reading Rauschenberg," which inaugurated that discussion, Charles Stuckey posited that Rauschenberg's *Odalisk* was a transformative re-creation (or, in his words, a "cockeyed parody") of Ingres's *Grande Odalisque* (1814). He based his analysis on two axiomatic assumptions: first, that Rauschenberg's work conveys a narrative focused on his autobiography; and second, that he is evidently interested in old masters and is attempting to create "modern history paintings."[77] The model being invoked is that of the artist as modern master, one who attempts to rival the old masters and thereby place his own work into the grand artistic canon by updating and transforming their achievements. Its precedent is found in Picasso, who asserted his place in history by revisiting such works as Ingres's *Raphael and the Fornarina* (1814) and Manet's *Le Déjeuner sur l'herbe* (1863).

In his "modernizing" of art-historical sources, Picasso both reveals the traces of his subjective imagination and foregrounds the work of artistic transformation. According to Stuckey, Rauschenberg practiced much the same dual process: "Rauschenberg's visual/verbal plays, like *Rebus,* force an awareness of how we see, by making us share the tangents and confusions, childish, comic and coincidental ones, which he himself endured while facing the abstract problems of making art."[78] For Stuckey, Rauschenberg's Combines were conceived as a form of internal monologue.[79] In this way, the appropriations of mass-media images by which Rauschenberg had figured the subject's externalization are folded back into a traditional communicative paradigm. Stuckey presents Rauschenberg as expressing an inner thought or message, but one now replete with all the "noise" of other thoughts and interferences encountered in the process of expression.[80]

Since the publication of Stuckey's article, Kenneth Bendiner, Roni Feinstein, and others have added Duchamp and Rembrandt to the list of masters to whose work Rauschenberg supposedly refers.[81] Bendiner, for example, finds Rauschenberg's *Canyon* (1959) to be a "witty" though faithful re-creation of Rembrandt's painting *The Rape of Ganymede* (1635).[82] For Bendiner, the stuffed eagle perched atop the cardboard box cantilevering off the painting's surface represents the eagle form assumed by Zeus, while the pillow suspended by a rope is Ganymede, its bisected form representing the boy's buttocks and alluding to the sexual motivation of his abduction. Other elements of the painting are similarly interpreted. The snapshot of Rauschenberg's son Christopher becomes a second representation of the abducted youth, while the photographic depiction of outer space at the painting's right is seen to provide an illustration of "the future residence of Ganymede (Aquarius), a reference to Zeus (Jupiter) and a directional note indicating that Ganymede is being borne up to the heavens."[83]

Yet even as Bendiner amasses a series of such examples, cataloguing the supposed resemblance of *Canyon* to its art-historical model, the cost of fixing the work's meaning becomes clear. In Bendiner's article, it takes visual form as an eleven-point numbered diagram. Unlike Earle Loran's famous formalist illustrations (to which it bears some resemblance), Bendiner's graph does not depict compositional movement or use arrows to show the directional push and pull of the eye through space. Instead, Bendiner bounds and separates *Canyon*'s multiplicitous elements into discrete and determinable signs. The reductive nature of this operation is clearest in area 7, where the busiest part of Rauschenberg's image becomes a single, ragged-edged form. According to Bendiner, this

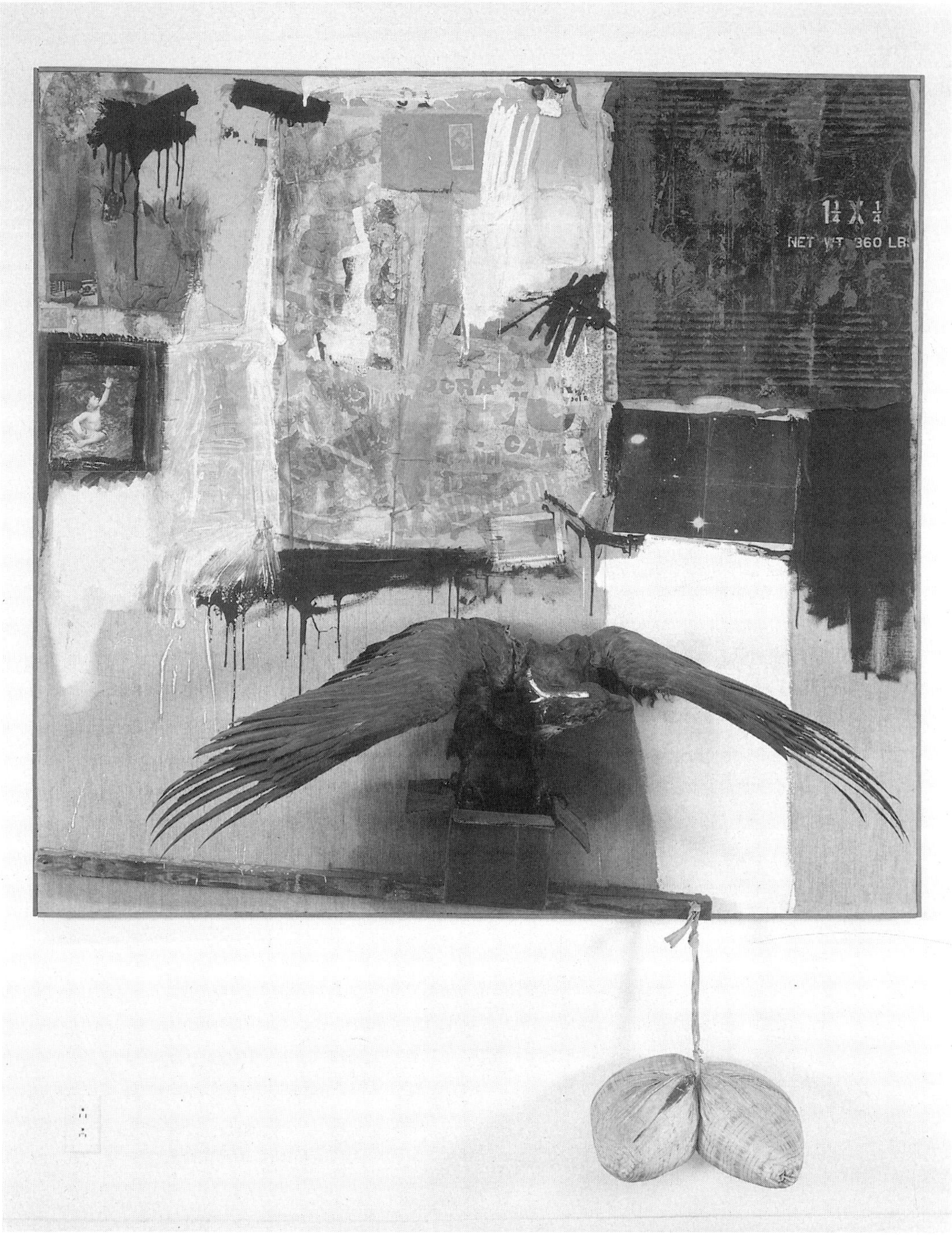

Canyon, 1959. Combine painting: oil, pencil, paper, metal, photograph, fabric, and wood on canvas, plus buttons, mirror, stuffed eagle, cardboard box, pillow, and paint tube. 81¾ × 70 × 24 in. Sonnabend Collection. Courtesy Sonnabend Gallery.

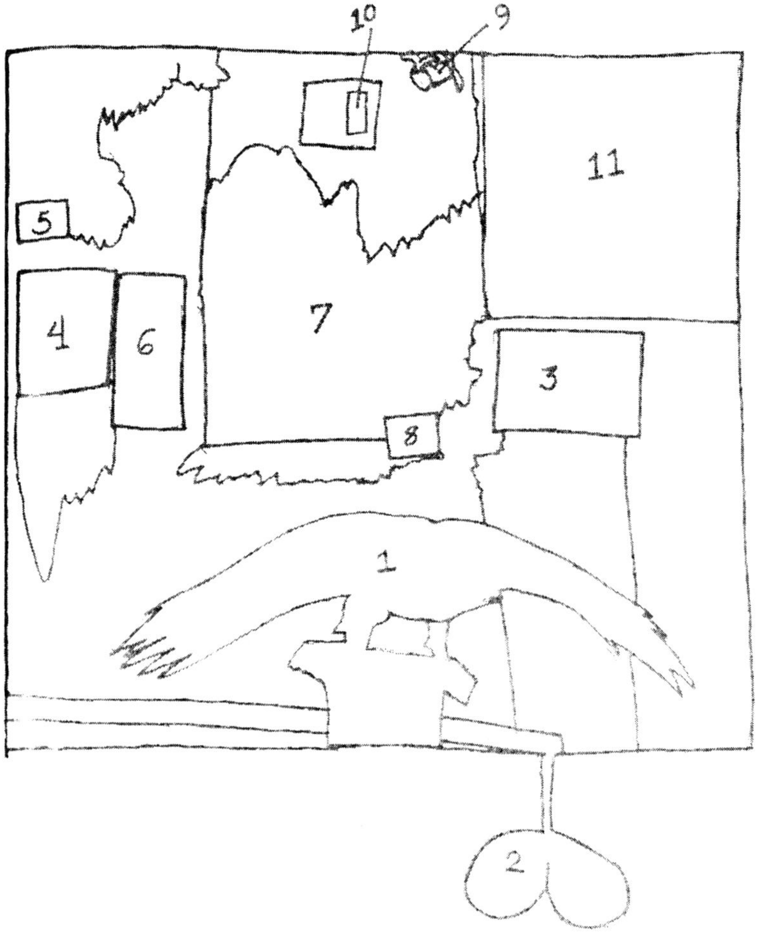

Kenneth Bendiner, diagram of *Canyon*. Courtesy Kenneth Bendiner.

"wild mélange of newspaper and poster headlines, fragmented, cut and disfigured . . . represents the cries of Rembrandt's *Ganymede*."[84]

Bendiner's reading of *Canyon* has subsequently become canonic, sweeping aside other observations and seemingly authorizing other iconographic searches.[85] Such iconographic readings can appear persuasive because the signs selected through the division of signification are actually there. At their level of focus, the interpreters' projected perceptions do match the data before them. Searching for iconography in Rauschenberg is useless not because it cannot exist there but because it can be made to exist anywhere. One only has to choose one's focus and organize, segment, and demarcate the areas analyzed in such a way as to determine it. In that way, as Rauschenberg declared to Schuyler, "you can make any two pictures appear either alike or different."[86]

Although Bendiner's diagram is a too blunt attempt to convert Rauschenberg's Combine into discrete signs, Rauschenberg's collage does traffic in signification. The multiplicities formed by his work are signifying ones, and his "random order" has never escaped the connotational chains that multiply about his materials.[87] As Cage put it, even though Rauschenberg's objects were to be understood as "*fact,* not symbol," they nonetheless mobilized "a poetry of *infinite possibilities*."[88] But this poetry cannot be reduced to Bendiner's stable, visual graph or to a single, written line in the manner of Stuckey's famous deciphering of *Rebus*: "That reproduces sundry cases of childish and comic coincidences to be read by eyes opened finally to a pattern of abstract problems."[89] The distinct but mutually influential realms of words and images in Rauschenberg's work form more unstable relationships: images incite the semantic equivalents of language, and words take on the multidimensionality of images. "When you see an image," Rauschenberg commented, "it almost doesn't exist until you can turn it into a language. When you read something, if you can't see it, you almost can't remember it too, so the words become the images and the images become words."[90] A Combine is not a fixed or univocal arrangement or enchaining of signs, especially if we understand them as referencing a meaning that exists on another plane. Rather, a Combine is a multiplicity and each "reading" is an actualization, a unique, contingent, and changeable act of reception.[91]

◆

Like "Random Order" and the statement he made at the *Art of Assemblage* symposium, Rauschenberg's 1963 "Note on Painting" attempted to translate his visual strategy into text. In it, Rauschenberg interrupted his sentences with words glimpsed from the windows of the Merce Cunningham Dance Company's touring van. It began:

> I find it nearly impossible *free ice* to write about *jeepaxle* my work. The concept I *plantatarium* struggle to deal with *ketchup* is opposed to the logical continuity *lift tab* inherent in language *horses* and communication. My fascination with images *open 24 hrs.* is based on the complex interlocking of disparate visual facts *heated pool* that have no respect for grammar.[92]

Rauschenberg's curious form of writing is not a dadaist "word salad," a pure concatenation of the reified signs of advertising and the commodity.[93] Nor does it mimic an internal monologue, a record of the writer's digressions, false starts, and aimless musings as they intermingle with his more directly formulated thoughts. Rauschenberg's ideas (about the manner in which his work cannot be reduced to linear expression) and the sentences in which they are written are perfectly straightforward. The terms that interrupt them do so as *visual signs,* appearing as such in all their opacity. This text figures a confrontation of sorts between Rauschenberg's reflections and the anonymous, impersonal language of the contemporary environment. It is a confrontation between thinking as a process and language encountered as an archive.

While there is a dimension of signification to be found in Rauschenberg's work, it arises from the *encounter* with this type of anonymous language. The result is that within the Combines, language is no longer stable, its truth waiting to be found and with it that of its utterer, but instead becomes unstable, constantly working to undo its own signification. If Rauschenberg's work has a spatialized linguistic equivalent, it is not that of the diagrammed sentence to which Stuckey referred.[94] Rather, it is akin to the distinctive but equally spatial understanding of language put forward by Foucault in describing the "thought from outside." Arguing against those who understand modern literature in terms of an autonomous self-reflexivity, Foucault declares:

> It is a widely held belief that modern literature is characterized by a doubling back that enables it to designate itself; this self-reference supposedly allows it both to interiorize to the extreme (to state nothing but itself) and to manifest itself in the shimmering sign of its distant existence. In fact, the event that gave rise to what we call "literature" in the strict sense is only superficially an interiorization; it is far more a question of a passage to the "outside": language escapes the mode of being of discourse—in other words the dynasty of representation—and literary speech develops from itself, *forming a network in which each point is distinct, distant from even its closest neighbors, and has a position in relation to every other point in a space that simultaneously holds and separates them all.*[95]

Note how the spatialization of language described here by Foucault strikingly resembles the unimpededness and interpenetration within Rauschenberg's Combines as described by Cage. Like Rauschenberg's collage elements, the points in Foucault's description of language are separated from all others by a space and, like their visual counterparts, they are thus able to form multiplicitous networks that unstitch any linearity.

There is, however, more than a happy coincidence between Rauschenberg's compositional practice and Foucault's evocation of language's "passage to the 'outside.'" To understand this "outside" (which sheds the remaining autonomy of the "natural" materiality that Rauschenberg had earlier pursued), one must understand the larger role it plays in the context of Foucault's two forms of knowledge: the visible and the articulable. Both language and visibilities are external to the subject with which they interact as well as to each other. History, as a set of archives or strata, is constituted out of the remnants of these forms, out of the possible or particular configurations of verbal and visual elements.[96] Yet though it is related to or predicated on the exteriority of language and vision, the "outside" to which Foucault refers is not the same as this exteriority.[97] This point is stressed by Deleuze in *Foucault*: while the dispersion of the verbal and the visual make up two multiplicities different in kind (discursive and nondiscursive), the outside is related to the manner in which these two realms open onto a third—which, unlike them, is not an ordered multiplicity of form but a continuous multiplicity of formation. As Deleuze explains further,

> if the visible and the articulable elements enter into a duel, it is to the extent that their respective forms, as forms of exteriority, dispersion or dissemination, make up two types of "multiplicity," neither of which can be reduced to a unity. . . . And these two multiplicities open up on to a third: a multiplicity of relations between forces, a multiplicity of diffusion which no longer splits into two and is free of any dualizable form.[98]

The outside is thus a complexly interacting field of forces, to which language and visibilities relate as though remnants.[99]

What Rauschenberg sought in his Combines after 1955 was something akin to the passage beyond externality to the outside. It is onto such a transvalued idea of the outside of representation—no longer understood as autonomous from the social or commercial realm—that Rauschenberg's work opens in its unavoidable interimplication of verbal and visual registers, where the verbal and the visual aspects of his Combines do not exactly translate into one another but where the visual incites the verbal, and vice versa. "No competition exists between the physical characterization of the materials and the formation of the signs," wrote Rauschenberg; "Both remain lively impure."[100]

If we understand these Combines as analogous to the type of unstable, continuous multiplicity that Foucault theorized as the outside, and if the outside so conceived is a multiplicity of *forces* rather than *forms,* then the "meaning" of such works (or, rather, their function) is to be found not by any reading of the Combines' arrangements but only in the instability or ungraspability of their arrangements. As the outside of language and of visibility, this third multiplicity is the opening up of formal and signifying complexes to something that is not (in itself) signification: not something that can be captured in a stable and communicable form, but difference as a beyond of signification.[101] It is not "object," to use Cage's terms, but "process." Thus, beyond even the painted and photographed representations of motion in a work such as *Double Feature* (1959), it would be found in the instability that courses through all aspects of Rauschenberg's Combines: the instability, on the one hand, of the visual materials' lack of compositional order—their changeable or contingent nature and the manner in which they refuse to resolve; and, on the other hand, the instability of the words' lack of semantic order—the refusal of their *meanings* to resolve, either in the actual, printed words or in the images' rebuslike incitation of meaning. Above all, however, this outside is approached via the unstable, multiplicitous relationship between the visual and the verbal registers in Rauschenberg's Combines. Such changeability reflects the inability of the mind to close around the Combine as a work of stable signification, the instability that gives rise to the feeling of "dementia" noted by O'Doherty and that undermines memory so that, as Cage observed, the work seems to be changing even when it is not physically altered.

◆

As early as 1972, Steinberg referred to Rauschenberg's picture plane as "post-Modernist," seeing it as "a symptom of changes which go far beyond questions of picture planes, or of painting as such."[102] A decade later, Fredric Jameson

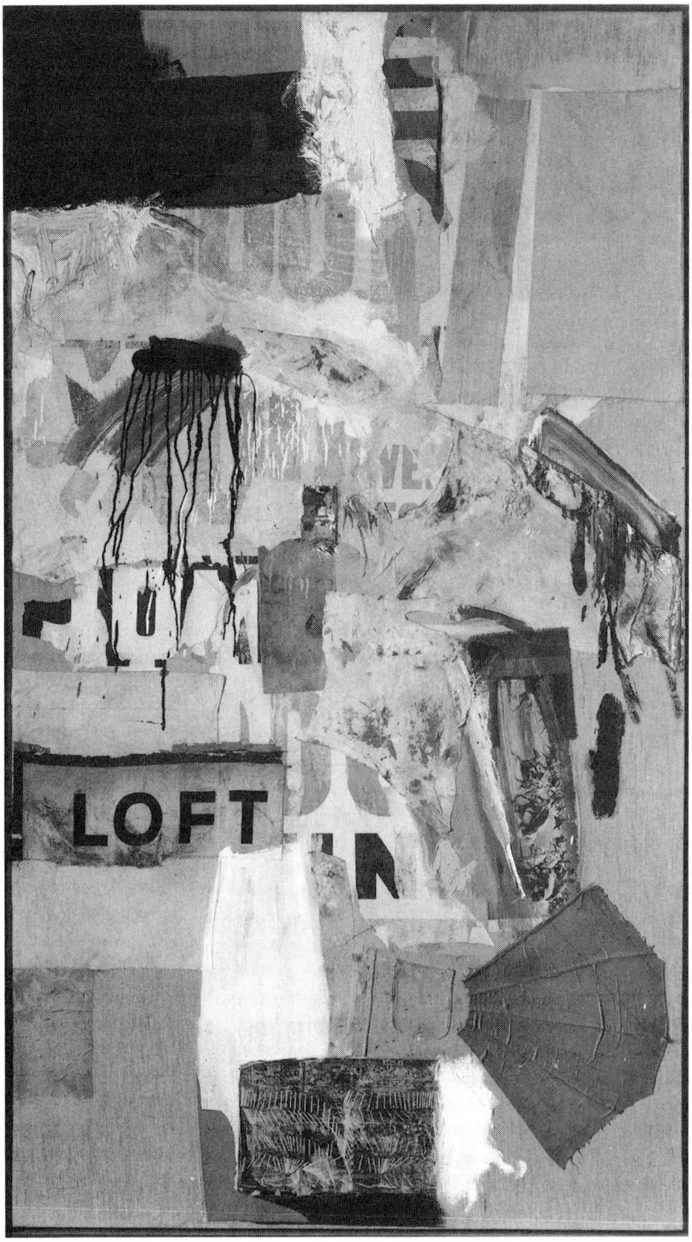

Double Feature, 1959. Combine painting: oil and collage on canvas. $90\frac{3}{4} \times 52$ in. Oeffentliche Kunstsammlung Basel, Kunstmuseum. Permanent loan from the Peter and Irene Ludwig Foundation. Photograph by Martin Bühler, Oeffentliche Kunstsammlung Basel.

linked those changes to the advent of postmodernization: where existence is everywhere reified, where historical memory has been liquidated to an unprecedented degree, and where the globe has been overcome by the forces of multinational capital.[103]

On the one hand, as the previous chapter's discussion of *Collection* suggested, Rauschenberg's Combines are an accurate reflection of the historical situation of a society everywhere totalized by the forces of commodification and mass media. In them, the present and the past are equally cut off from experience, and high art and low are equally mediated by the forces of technological reproduction. Within historical dadaist montage, shock was produced by the juxtaposition of precisely such heterogeneous items from different formal and signifying registers; it arose from such disjunctive collisions as between crafted and manufactured objects, poetic and commercial language, and high art and mass-cultural imagery. In Rauschenberg's Combines, however, such heterogeneity fails to produce any shock at all. And because of this lack of dialectical or allegorical shock effects, Rauschenberg's art has been understood as complicit with the forces of late capitalism.

Yet if signification really is entirely subsumed within a situation of social totalization—if it is, in other words, at this historical moment everywhere reified—then difference can occur only via an opening to the forces of the "outside" and not in the juxtaposition of different registers, however heterogeneous. In this sense, Rauschenberg's aim to open his work up to the multiplicitous and unstable forces of the outside is an attempt to access, from within, the outside of a totalized society. This outside is not so much apart from a reified society as present, virtually, within its interstices, an indeterminate form of difference that evades and thereby relativizes the regulated, cyclical, and territorialized forms of change found in consumer cycles and the temporality of fashion.

Foucault has commented on precisely this relationship between reification and the outside. He notes,

> From the moment discourse ceases to follow the slope of self-interiorizing thought and, addressing the very being of language,

> returns thought to the outside . . . it becomes attentiveness to what in language already exists, has already been said, imprinted, manifested—a listening less to what is articulated in language than to the void circulating between its words, to the murmur that is forever taking it apart; a discourse on the non-discourse of all language; the fiction of the invisible space in which it appears.[104]

It is undoubtedly on account of a similar awareness of social totalization that Cage commented that the space that separated the stones in a Japanese garden and the materials in a Rauschenberg Combine was "urgently necessary *at this point in history*."[105]

◆

Finally, it is important to note that the confrontation of signification with its outside involves forces that act on the subject as well, splitting and dispersing his or her interiority. Such a turn to the outside, in its subjective effect, is less close to dementia than to the "dementation" Cage had learned from Eastern philosophy: the opening up of the mind to changeability.[106] This ability to change one's mind is, as Cage wrote in regard to Rauschenberg, the "switch that distinguishes" humanity.[107] Rauschenberg himself remarked, "If you do not change your mind about something when you confront a picture you have not seen before, you are either a stubborn fool or the painting is not very good."[108]

It is somewhat unfortunate, however, that Charles Stuckey changed his mind about "Reading Rauschenberg," all but repudiating the earlier article in a more recent contribution to the Guggenheim's Rauschenberg retrospective catalogue.[109] In one sense, Stuckey's earlier process of reading proved exemplary. After having succeeded in reducing the multivalence of *Rebus* to a single line, Stuckey chose to pursue his reading further rather than immediately explaining the meaning of his decipherment. Quickly, however, he found himself confronted with a proliferation of associative signifying chains that began to move out beyond his control—"plays within plays," in his terms, that eluded the reduction he had just finished setting forth:

> The "Pogo" [comic strip] episode is about Albert the alligator's bug-like children. The alligator's daughters play to the photo of the flying insect. Its wings rhyme with those of the wind deities in the neighboring Botticelli. The attendant waiting to drape Venus, another bathing beauty, with a red robe or towel, refers both to the red fabric below which covers more photos of insects, and also to the woman with the open blouse at the right. Below here is another pillow case, a *tour de force* by itself: a page from a coloring book with a scene (upside down) from Goldilocks, over which is pasted a piece of white fabric, around all of which a pencil line on the bare canvas makes a pillow shape. The three whites (canvas, fabric and paper) "model" the soft volume of the pillow. Of course, the little bear is a play on the lady with the open blouse, who is also a little bare.[110]

Only after a long string of visual and verbal associations did Stuckey stop and fold the multiplicity he had found back into the mind of the artist, making his analogy between the work's semiotic multivalence and the vicissitudes of an internal monologue. But it is at precisely this point that Stuckey should have continued, following such associative plays until his certainty in recognizing meaning began to falter, until the "plays within plays" of Rauschenberg's *Rebus* began to undermine, unstitch, and disarticulate the self-present manifestation of meaning Stuckey earlier thought he had found.[111]

For Rauschenberg, such an opening up of the subject to a different form of subjectivity was the goal of the postwar neo-avant-garde. As we will come to see in chapter 5, Rauschenberg understood the attempt at subjective mutation, at subjective differentiation and change, to be opposed to those forms of reproduction and standardization of subjectivity effected within a demonically totalized society. Finding that all topoi had been discredited through cooptation, Rauschenberg attempted to use the remaining archival access to the past and present as a means of forging a path into the future. Like the mole archaeologist he had seen in Italy, he found fragments of the past most useful to him as a means of propelling himself forward. For Rauschenberg, this project formed no less than an ethics of continual self-formation. As he explained to André Parinaud, "One must be in a perpetual state of growth in relation to oneself. Continuity itself is an illusion for one must always be against what one has done. When working, the artist must know that he is doing this for the first time. He must shed habits and mannerisms."[112] Or, as he put it more succinctly to Alain Jouffroy, "My morality is not to walk in my own footsteps."[113]

Election, 1960. Solvent transfer on paper, with pencil and watercolor. 23 × 29 in. Private collection.

4

Split Screens

What's a pure medium?

—*Robert Rauschenberg, 1961*

In the fall of 1960, Robert Rauschenberg secluded himself in Treasure Island, Florida, to complete the cycle of Dante Drawings begun two years earlier. On 8 November, however, he interrupted his work to produce *Election,* the only transfer drawing outside the series to feature Rauschenberg's everyman Dante: a nondescript, towel-clad figure appropriated from an advertisement in *Sports Illustrated.* Sitting before the television as the results of the Kennedy-Nixon presidential contest were being broadcast, Rauschenberg employed his signature technique of soaking magazine images in solvent and rubbing them on the back to transfer their ghostly, flickering shadows onto the paper. Alongside Dante, clearly identified in this instance by a large D, *Election* features a smiling image of Jacqueline Kennedy and, above her, oriented inversely, an even larger, more stately image of JFK. In contrast to the prominent, media-friendly faces of the Kennedys, Rauschenberg depicted the defeated Pat and Richard Nixon on a much smaller scale, waving, though barely visible, in the drawing's upper right-hand corner.

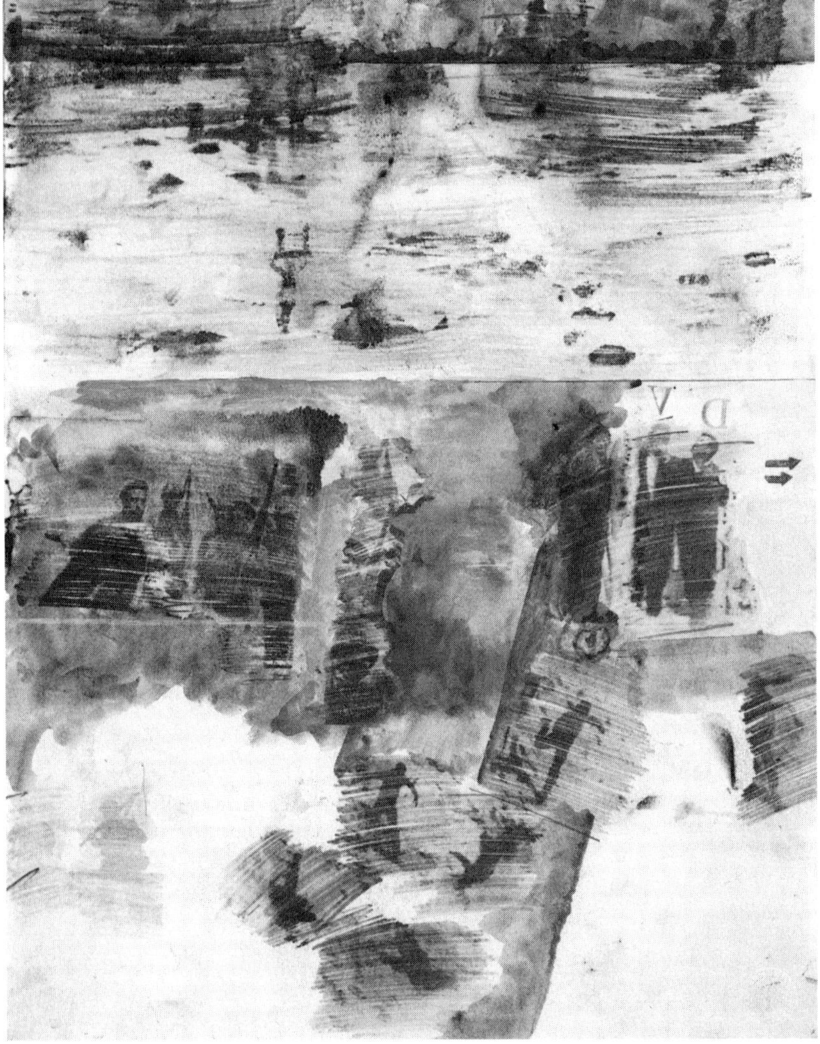

Canto XXII: Circle Eight, Bolgia 5, The Grafters, 1959–1960. Solvent transfer on paper, with pencil, gouache, watercolor, and wash. 14³/₈ × 11¹/₂ in. The Museum of Modern Art, New York. Given anonymously. Photograph © The Museum of Modern Art / Licensed by SCALA / Art Resource, New York.

Emerging out of the contemporary political allusions that had crept into the drawings for Dante's *Cantos XII* and *XXII* (where John Kennedy, Richard Nixon, and Adlai Stevenson all appeared), *Election* formed part of Rauschenberg's self-imposed apprenticeship to narrative illustration. Rauschenberg seems to have regarded this as a specific task, deliberately set against the multiplicitous, nonrepresentational aesthetic characteristic of the Combines. As he explained to Dorothy Seckler, "The problem when I started the Dante illustrations was to see if I was working abstractly because I couldn't work any other way or whether I was doing it by choice. So I insisted on the challenge of being restricted by a particular subject where it meant that I'd have to be involved in symbolism." As opposed to the open-ended actualizations of the visual and verbal contents of a Combine, "An illustration," Rauschenberg insisted, "has to be read; it has to relate to something already in existence and, well, I spent two-and-a-half years deciding that, yes, I could do that."[1]

As has been realized from the moment of their first exhibition, Rauschenberg's drawings succeeded in illustrating the *Divine Comedy* with a particular incisiveness, ingenuity, and care.[2] Generally denser and more hierarchically organized than transfer drawings such as *Cup* (1958) or *Open Season* (1961), the Dante Drawings call attention to narrative and symbolic associations that "funnel inwards" in a manner unlike that seen in their counterparts.[3] The Dante Drawings' explicit sequencing of events, guiding use of directional arrows, and illustrative deployment of words and letters concentrate and channel the viewer's trajectory as markedly as *Course* (1958) (which uses some of the same imagery), *Vacation* (1961), *Fuse* (1961), and other drawings nonhierarchically disperse it throughout the visual field.

Like much of Rauschenberg's subsequent work, *Election* oscillates somewhat precariously between these two poles.[4] Though disposed less hierarchically throughout the page and allowing for a freer, nonnarrative circulation among its visual components, *Election*'s imagery relates thematically to its specific historical context.[5] In the letter accompanying the work's donation to the first family in April 1961, Rauschenberg explained that the presence of the American eagle, the head of a Greek statue, and the countenance of George Washington

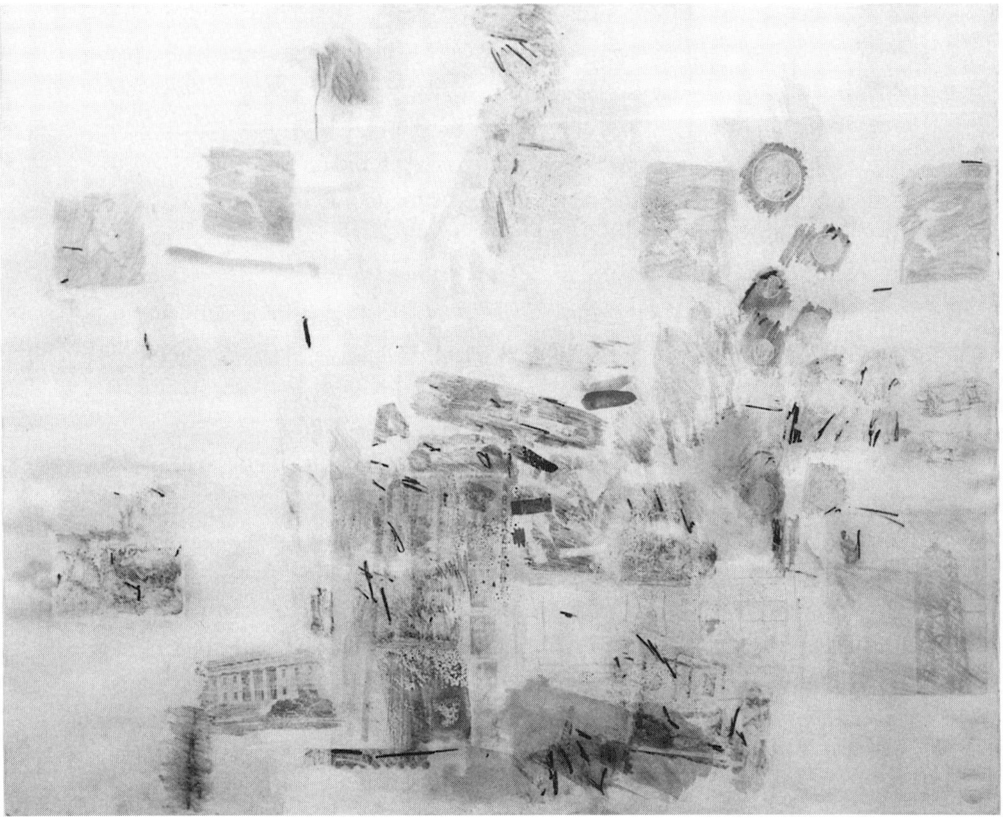

Untitled, 1958. Solvent transfer, watercolor, gouache, colored pencil, and graphite on paper. 22¾ × 29 in. UBS PaineWebber Art Collection.

"reiterates that the content of the drawing is art and politics."[6] Yet even though unrepresented, the circumstances of *Election*'s production—its association with a specific television broadcast—indicate that TV, as much as contemporary politics, also informed the content of the work. In his letter to the White House Rauschenberg made *Election*'s mass-media references clear, describing Jackie Kennedy's color as "headlined, televised, radioed purple."[7]

Earlier that year, John Cage had speculated on the potential connections between the transfer drawings and television. Relating the rapid back-and-forth motion of the artist's stylus to the workings of a cathode-ray tube, Cage noted that "the pencil lines scan the images transferred from photographs" and immediately underscored the connection: "it seems like many television sets working simultaneously all tuned differently."[8] Once made, such an analogy with television seems to encompass nearly all of the transfer drawings' most salient features.[9] In addition to likening the shimmering immateriality of the transferred images to television's (then) low level of resolution, the connection would also account for the drawings' many instances of boxlike framing—both those figurations of individual, technologized vision such as the TVs and astronauts' helmets that proliferate throughout the Dante Drawings and the penciled boxes within which the image scanning often takes place.[10] Moreover, the transfer drawings attain a visual hybridization of flatness and depth in which the three-dimensional space of the photographic source is retained, even as the "scanned" surfaces and surrounding flows of watercolor collapse it onto the support. This fluid slippage between the transfer drawings' various images and the different spatial areas in which they are contained echoes television's ability to subsume and simulate—through entirely different means—distinct historical, dimensional, and perspectival spaces within a continuum where they follow one another without disjunction across the depthless "support-surface" of the television screen.[11] "It's like looking out a window," Cage noted of the transfer drawings, adding parenthetically, "But our windows have become electronic: everything moves through the point where our vision is focused; wait long enough and you'll get the Asiatic panoply."[12]

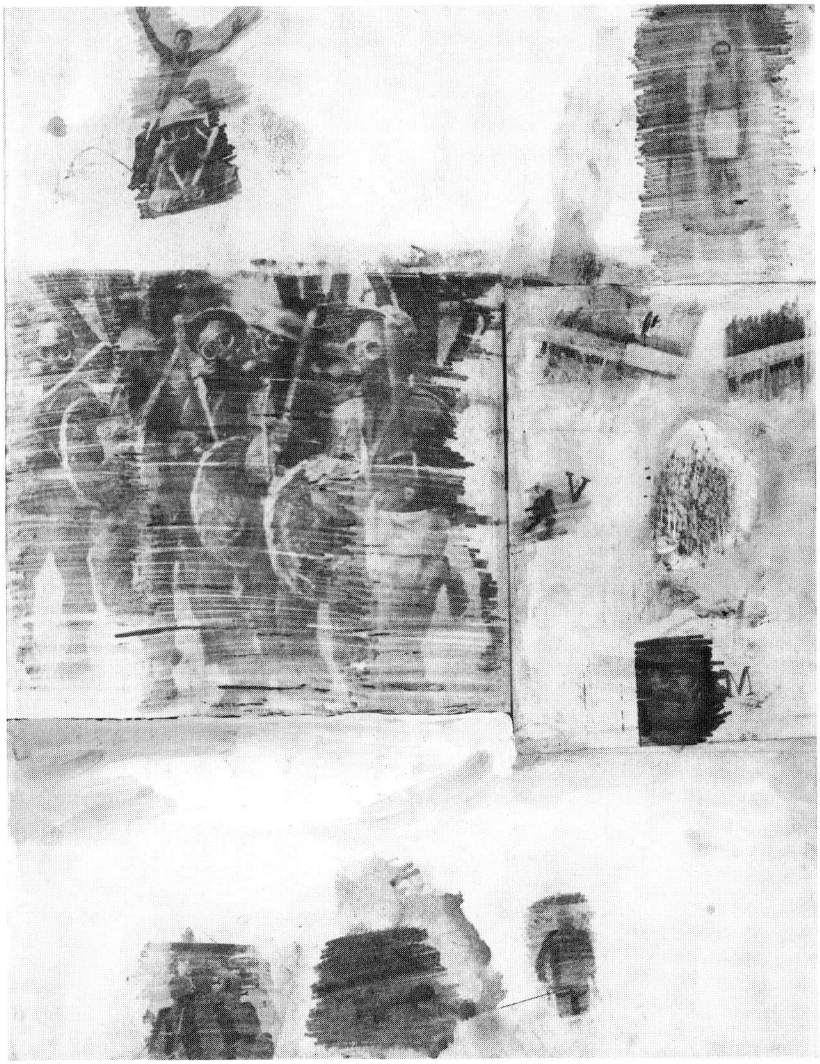

Canto XXI: Circle Eight, Bolgia 5, The Grafters, 1959–1960. Solvent transfer on paper, with gouache, cut-and-pasted paper, pencil, colored pencil, and wash. $14\frac{3}{8} \times 11\frac{1}{2}$ in. The Museum of Modern Art, New York. Given anonymously. Photograph © The Museum of Modern Art / Licensed by SCALA / Art Resource, New York.

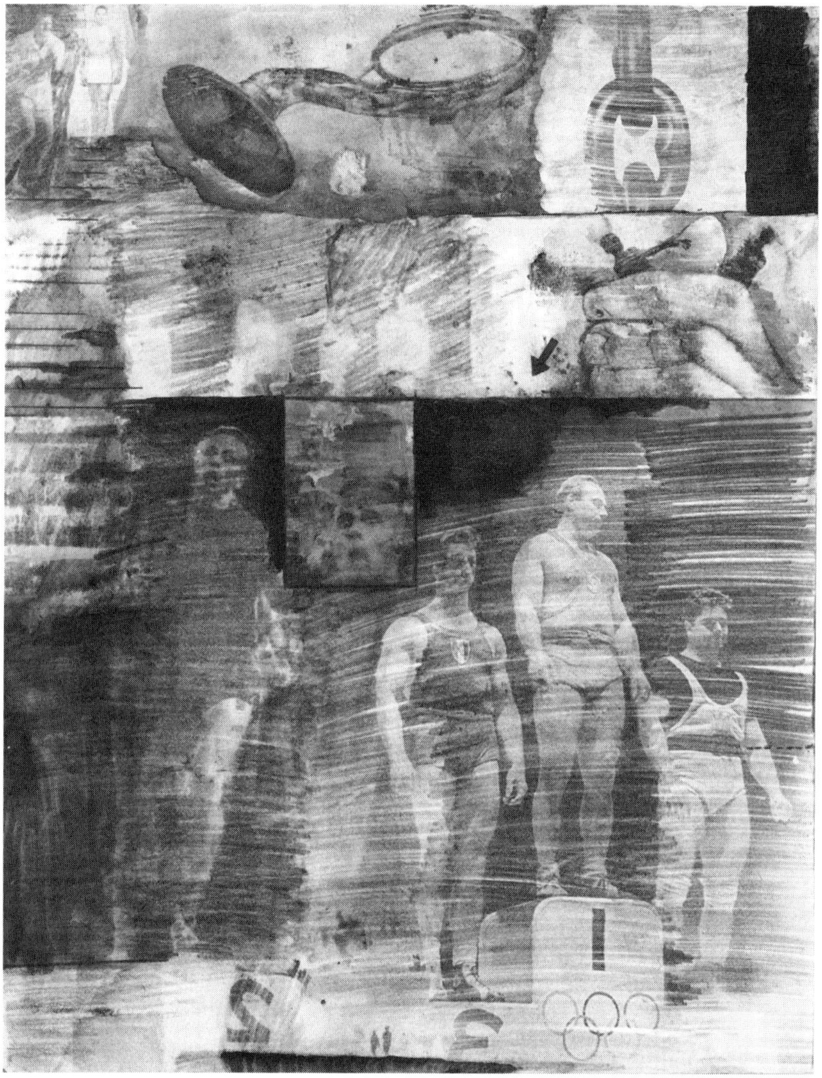

Canto XXXI: The Central Pit of Malebolge, The Giants, 1959–1960. Solvent transfer on paper, with colored pencil, gouache, and pencil. $14^3/_8 \times 11^1/_2$ in. The Museum of Modern Art, New York. Given anonymously. Photograph © The Museum of Modern Art / Licensed by SCALA / Art Resource, New York.

Positing such a relationship between the transfer drawings and television would also illuminate the Dante project's apparently anomalous return to narrative illustration and serial production. Like his incorporation of old master paintings into the Combines, Rauschenberg's turn to Dante has been seen as evidence of his high regard for past culture or an attempt to prove himself a serious artist.[13] Yet just as the relationship of his Combines to the old masters was presented through postcards and other reproductions, so Rauschenberg's relationship to Dante is as strongly marked by the formal evidence of its mediation as by thematic connection to the past. In this regard, Rauschenberg's *Inferno* may actually be less an orthodox illustration of a great book than a project on the order of a made-for-TV miniseries.[14] Such an understanding would be closer to that of Cage, who declared when discussing the Dante Drawings, "As for me, I'm not so inclined to read poetry as I am one way or another to get myself a television set, sitting up nights looking."[15]

In retrospect, Rauschenberg's transfer drawings mark the beginning of a larger aesthetic transformation brought on by the pressures of the media. He later recalled about this period: "I was bombarded with TV sets and magazines, by the refuse, by the excess of the world. . . . I thought that if I could paint or make an honest work, it should incorporate all of these elements, which were and are a reality."[16] What began in 1958 with the transfer drawings appears to have culminated in 1962 with a series of works in which Rauschenberg's discontinuous earlier collage is replaced by a more seamless coincidence of imagery. The developments of that year include the Combine painting *Ace* and the sole example of a "transfer painting," *Calendar;* the adoption of lithography; a failed attempt to photosensitize canvas; and, finally, after Rauschenberg discovered the technique on a visit to Andy Warhol's studio in September, the utilization of silkscreen.[17] That Rauschenberg's desire to, as he told Brian O'Doherty, "get it back flat to see if [he] really did have anything"[18] in the silkscreen paintings and transfer drawings reflects the growing cultural impact of television may seem an art-historical commonplace. Yet television, which appears at first sight a very trivial thing, and easily understood, is in reality (as

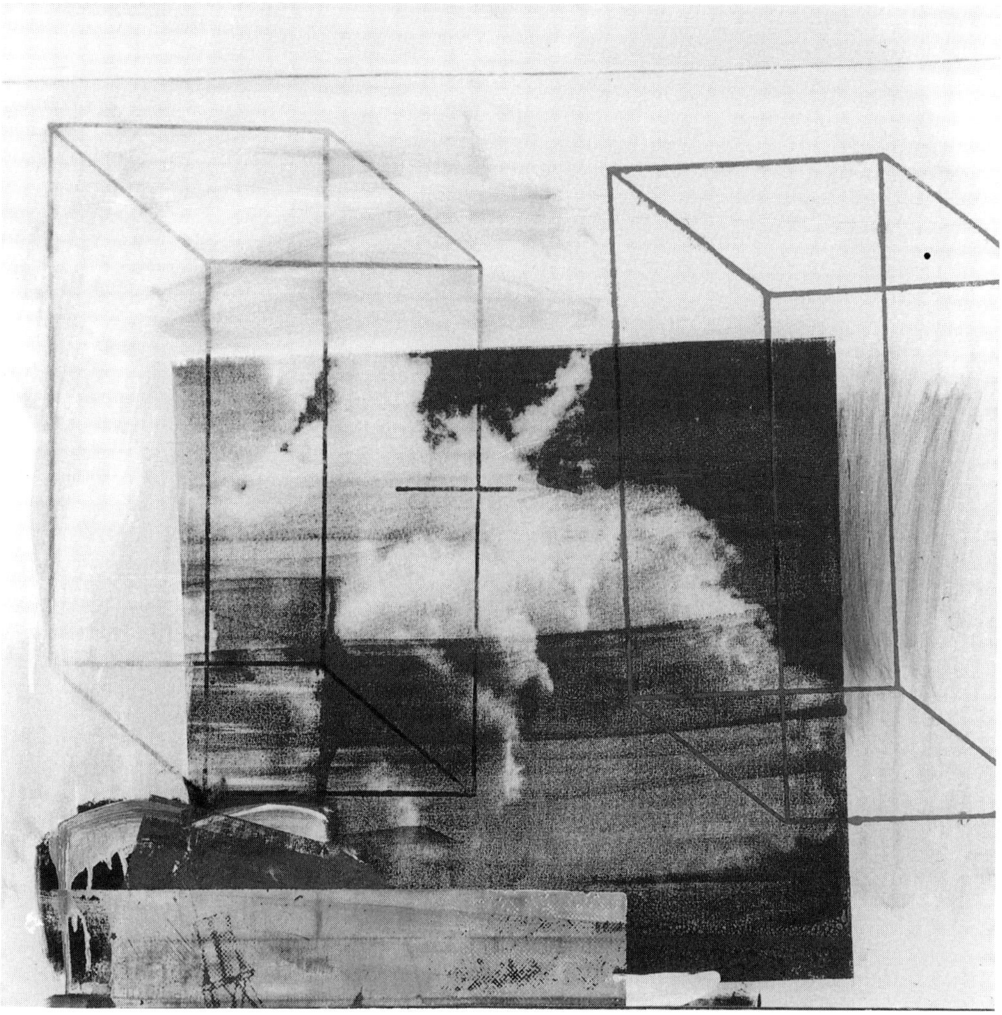

New Painting, 1962. Oil and silkscreen ink on canvas. 36 × 36 in. Collection of Carolyn Brown. Photograph by Rudolf Burckhardt. Courtesy The Estate of Rudolf Burckhardt.

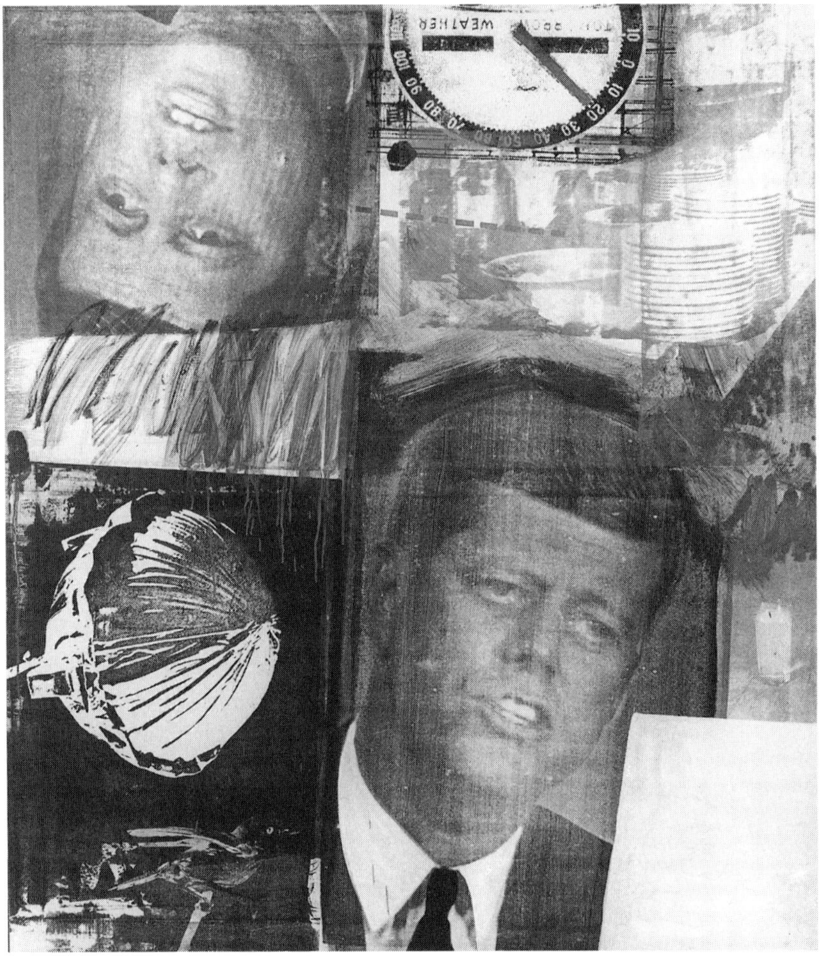

Untitled, 1964. Oil and silkscreen ink on canvas, 58 × 50 in. Collection of Janet and Robert Kardon. Photograph by Rudolf Burckhardt. Courtesy The Estate of Rudolf Burckhardt.

Marx said in another context) a very odd thing, abounding in metaphysical subtleties.

◆

Perhaps the dominant critical understanding of television is as an instrument or agent of spectacle, that replacement of the perceptible world where, as Guy Debord has declared, "the commodity contemplates itself in a world of its own making."[19] As Rauschenberg moves from the objectified, materialized imagery of his Combines to the relatively substanceless images in his Dante Drawings (literally peeling the images off their supports and further divesting them of their original contexts), he seems almost necessarily to be delivering the intimate spaces of reading, drawing, and perhaps even desire to the order of spectacle.[20] More recently, however, the direct association of television with spectacle has been both strengthened and problematized by the work of Jonathan Crary. Responding to a remark in Debord's *Comments on the Society of the Spectacle* (that in 1967 the spectacle "had barely forty years behind it"),[21] Crary has noted the coincidental historical emergence of spectacle and the perfection of television technology. More than simply the substanceless visuality offered by television—which, by entering directly into people's homes, made visual representation more extensive, continuous, and atomized than ever before—spectacle, Crary argues, developed primarily from the synchronous conjugation of sound and vision introduced nearly simultaneously by television and the sound film.[22] The effect was a new form of subjective perceptual training, the transformation, in Debord's words, of images into "tangible figments which are the efficient motor of trancelike behavior."[23] "Spectacular power," Crary observes,

> cannot be reduced to an optical model but is inseparable from a larger organization of perceptual consumption. Sound had of course been part of cinema in various additive forms from the beginning, but the introduction of sync sound transformed the nature of *attention* that was demanded of a viewer. Possibly it is a break that makes previous forms of cinema actually closer to the optical devices of

> the late nineteenth century. The full coincidence of sound with image, of voice with figure, not only was a crucial new way of organizing space, time, and narrative, but it instituted a more commanding authority over the observer, enforcing a new kind of attention.[24]

But at the same time that he reinforces the connection between television and spectacle, Crary warns against the critical traps of either ontologizing television as a singular, distinct entity or medium (when, in fact, it is a disparate aggregate of technical, economic, and perceptual forces) or of totalizing it—whether pessimistically, as in Debord's "society of the spectacle," or optimistically, as the imminent utopia of Marshall McLuhan's "global village."[25] "Of course," writes Crary,

> television is a global tracery of linkages that produces truth and that increasingly dominates the arena of the lived; but, at the same time, as with any deployment of power, the surface that television mobilizes also encompasses barely visible alcoves, striations, and folds. . . . These, then, are the overlapping spaces to be comprehended: a circuit of power that can be uniform and seamless as a macrophenomenon, but that is broken, diversified, and never fully controllable in its local usage.[26]

From this perspective, spectacle is only one particular, though predominant, manifestation of the technological, perceptual, and economic functions that come to make up television; it is not identical with the totality of those functions.

Crary proceeds to specify two of the primary features of television's spectacular operation. The first is that focusing of and hold over an individual's attention established with the development of synchronized sound; the second is a particular modality of representation in which the visual field is organized into a unified form—a stability of visual appearance or a "redundancy of representation" on which formations of signification and power can be erected.[27]

In 1959, a year after starting work on the Dante Drawings, Rauschenberg began to investigate the connection of sound and vision by embedding three radios beneath the surface of the Combine painting *Broadcast*.[28] Given Crary's characterization of the stability of spectacular representation, it is no doubt significant that Rauschenberg also initially sought to accompany *Broadcast*'s sonic dimension with a more uniform and seamless visual appearance than that which had characterized his earlier work. As Gene Swenson reported, *Broadcast* was originally much bolder and more broadly and flatly painted with imagery that, according to Rauschenberg, "you could see from across the room."[29] Yet even while courting the audiovisual functioning of spectacle, Rauschenberg worked to counteract its unitary perceptual focus. Although the audience was invited to turn the knobs on the surface of the painting, the radios could not be controlled directly or independently. The two knobs on the painting's surface—one for volume and one for frequency band—manipulated all three radios at once, and by setting them all differently Rauschenberg rigged it so that no two radios would ever play the same station or at the same volume.[30] *Broadcast* thus works to fragment the audience's attention across three asynchronous and interfering channels, creating, in effect, a miniature version of Cage's four-minute aleatory composition "Imaginary Landscape #4" (1951), in which twelve radios were "played" by twenty-four performers.

The visual appearance of *Broadcast* underwent a similar transformation. Although explicitly pursuing a more homogeneous visual surface, Rauschenberg found that the addition of sound rendered the original state of the painting too flat and one-dimensional. He recalled that "The painting went dead," with a "superficial" and "static" look, "like a poster." "I realized," he told Swenson, "that the details should not be taken in at one glance, that you should be able to look from place to place without feeling the bigger image. I had to make a surface which invited a constant change of focus and an examination of detail. Listening happens in time. Looking also had to happen in time."[31]

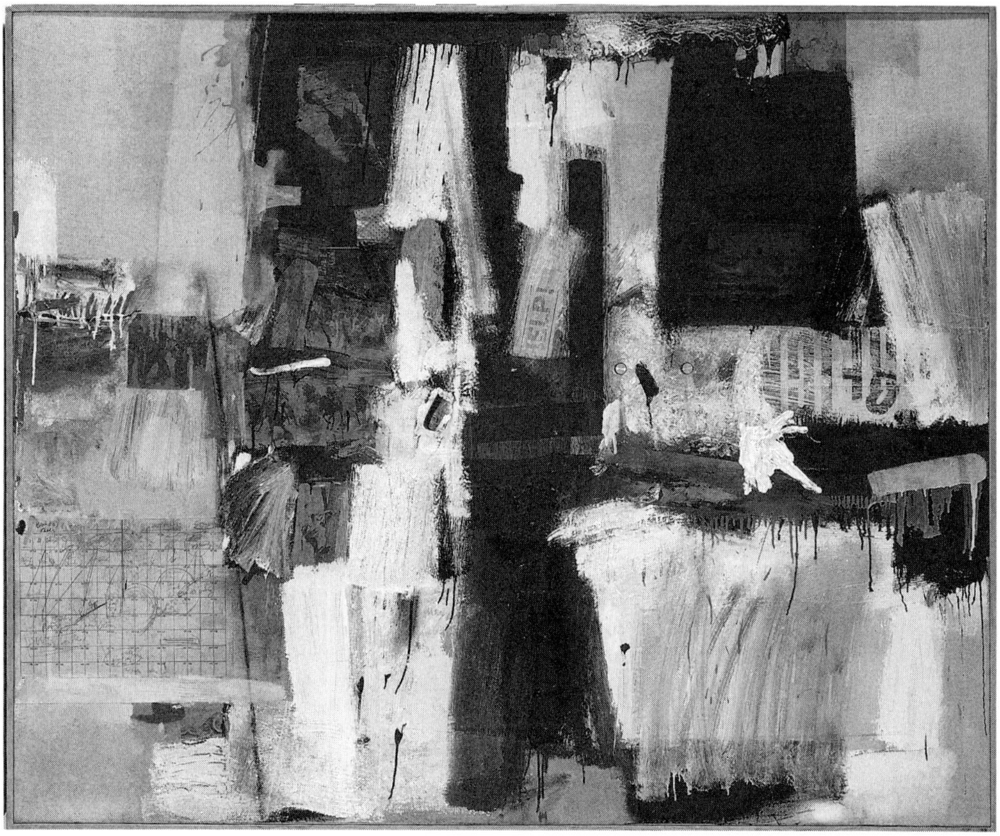

Broadcast, 1959. Combine painting: oil, pencil, paper, fabric, newspaper, printed paper, printed reproductions, and plastic comb on canvas, with three concealed radios. 61 × 75 × 5 in. Collection of Kimiko Powers. Courtesy of Gagosian Gallery.

Thus, in *Broadcast*'s final state Rauschenberg fell back on the chance, time-bound, part-by-part perception that had characterized his earlier work. Interspersed within a field of evident and expressionless brushstrokes, *Broadcast*'s collage elements—including a broken comb; newsprint images of a horse race, a submarine, and a cityscape; and printed words such as "Help!" and ". . . REIGN"—solicit the meandering, aleatory form of looking that had long been a hallmark of his Combines. What Rauschenberg had been seeking, however, was a more unified and easily recognizable appearance, one in which *Broadcast*'s details would exist within a single depth of field, but which would avoid flattening into an overly static subordination of its component parts. In works such as *Trophy II (For Teeny and Marcel Duchamp)* (1961) and, particularly, *Ace*—originally intended to house five radios—Rauschenberg returned to this pursuit of a more consistent and quickly perceived visual field.[32]

Ace marks a departure for Rauschenberg, not only because it was flatter than most of his earlier work—a feature emphasized by the broad, rectangular areas of light blue and green paint at the right and, further, by the two cardboard boxes pressed flat against the surface of the canvas—but also, and more important, because it attained a visual homogeneity that eliminates what he had called "changes of focus."[33] This is noticeable both in Rauschenberg's covering of the printing on the box at the lower left, a move that forecloses any impetus to approach and decipher it, and in the manner in which all the visible letters, including Rauschenberg's stenciled "signature" at the lower right, are of a size that can be read easily "from across the room." It was no doubt to complement this effect that Rauschenberg insisted on housing *Ace*'s proposed radio control panel in a separate console at some distance from the painting. In this way, there would be no need, as had been the case in *Broadcast,* for the spectator to approach the painting in order to manipulate its sound.[34]

The silkscreen paintings of the next two years follow *Ace*'s lead in getting rid of the "changes of focus" that characterized Rauschenberg's earlier work. Although the paintings did not entirely eliminate the temporality of viewing (as in the panorama-like *Barge* [1962–1963], which is physically too large to be

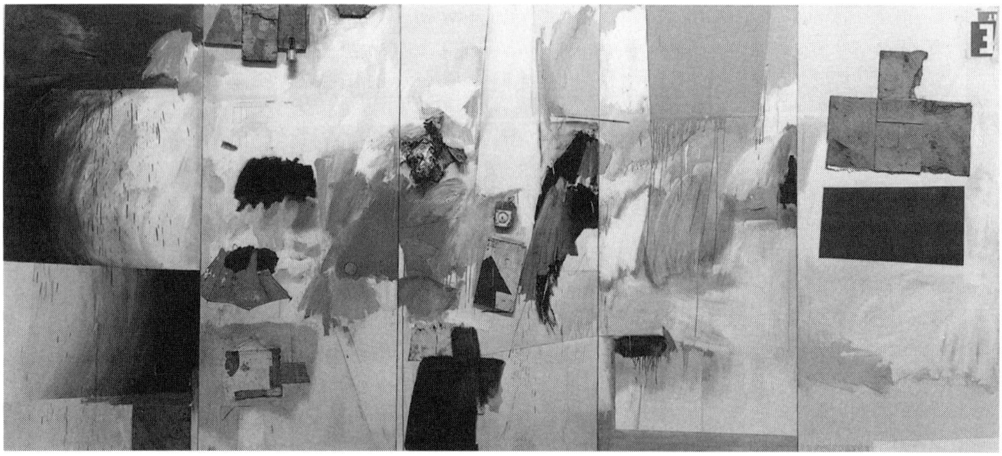

Ace, 1962. Combine painting: oil, cardboard, wood, and metal on canvas. 108 × 240 in. Albright-Knox Art Gallery, Buffalo, N.Y. Gift of Seymour H. Knox, Jr., 1963.

taken in at a glance), the relative insubstantiality of the silkscreen imagery no longer rewards an in-depth, readinglike scrutiny.[35] Instead, it calls for a scanning of the canvas from a single distance, an effect O'Doherty found characteristic of the "vernacular glance" and, once again, likened to watching TV.[36]

◆

Like Crary, Samuel Weber has also warned against ontologizing television. He points not to a unifying conception of television as a medium but to the three aspects of production, transmission, and reception as the three distinct "places" (or "times") in which television operates and by which it is internally divided. "The unity of television as a medium of presentation," Weber writes,

> thus involves a *simultaneity* that is highly ambivalent. It overcomes spatial distance but only by *splitting the unity of place* and with it the unity of everything that defines its identity with respect to place: events, bodies, subjects. The unity of place is split because the "act" of viewing television does not "take place" simply *in front* of the television set, as it might were it simply to involve the viewing of *images*. . . . As the name of the medium says very precisely, one looks at *a certain kind of vision*. And that vision is taking place not simply on the screen but simultaneously—or rather, quasi-simultaneously, since there is always a time-lag—somewhere *else*.[37]

In Weber's analysis, the primary component of television's spectacular operation derives from the apparent unity and insistent self-presence of the televised image that serves to cover over such constitutive internal differences. "If," he continues,

> television is both here *and* there *at the same time,* then, according to traditional notions of space, time and body, it can be *neither fully there nor entirely here.* What it sets before us, in and as the television

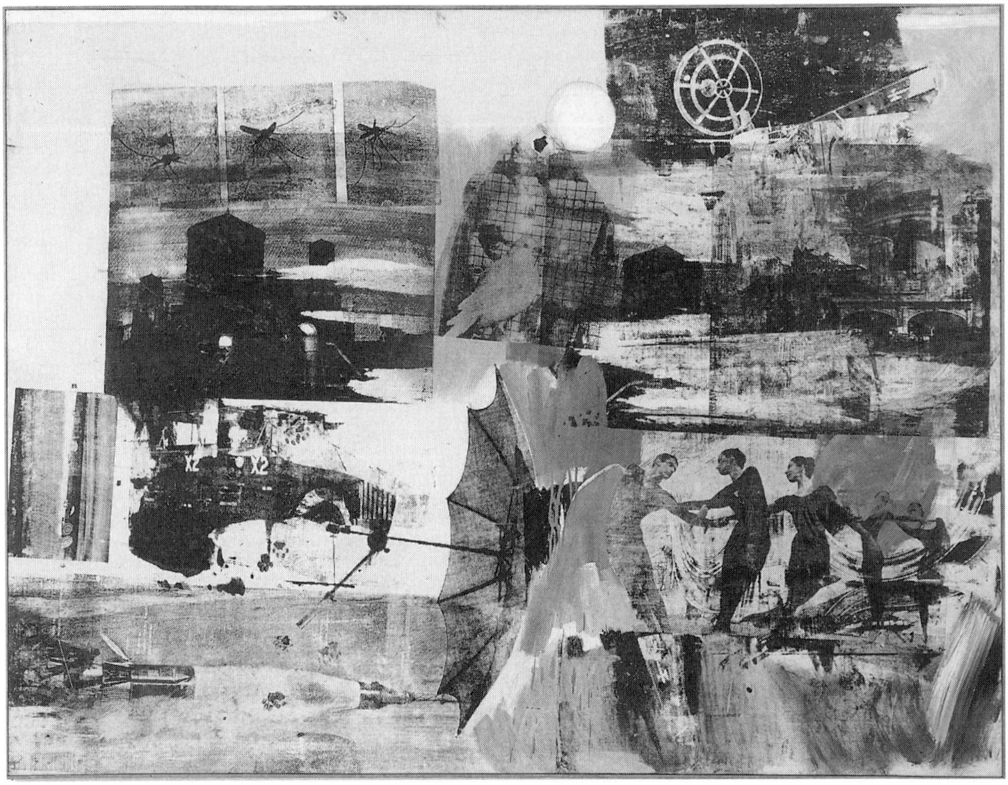

Scanning, 1963. Oil and silkscreen ink on canvas. 55¾ × 73 in. San Francisco Museum of Modern Art. Fractional and promised gift of an anonymous donor.

set, is therefore split, or rather, it is a *split* or a *separation* that camouflages itself by taking the form of a visible *image*.[38]

If Rauschenberg's silkscreens manage to defeat or avoid a spectacular representational presence, it is not through any temporality of perceptual scanning, which, as O'Doherty indicated, is entirely consistent with television viewing. Rather, it is through the manner in which the iteration of the silkscreen images—both within and between canvases—institutes a split or fissure within the very unity of the work itself. Drawing on insights found initially in the brushstrokes of *Collection,* Rauschenberg seems to have translated the simultaneous and differential here *and* there of the televised image into a similarly undecidable here and there of silkscreen imagery repeated across more than one canvas at a time.

Such a diffraction of the individual work had already been pioneered in Rauschenberg's *Factum I* and *II* of 1957. Viewed as a parodic attack on abstract expressionism's pretensions to originality, the *Factums* are commonly understood as the painstaking duplication of one apparently spontaneous work by another.[39] Despite the enumeration in the titles, however, Rauschenberg actually worked on both canvases simultaneously—sometimes adding to one and then the other, and sometimes the reverse—so that, to quote Rauschenberg, "neither one of these paintings was an imitation of the other."[40] Talking to Emile de Antonio, he noted, "I painted two identical pictures, but only identical to the limits of the eye, the hand, the materials adjusting to the differences from one canvas to another. Neither one was painted first to compensate for that."[41] As this quote suggests, at issue for Rauschenberg was not the exactness of reproduction but the difference within repetition. "I was interested in the role that accident played in my work," he explained to Richard Kostelanetz. "I wanted to see how different, and in what way, would be two different paintings that looked that much alike."[42]

When comparing the two works side by side, slight but noticeable differences quickly begin to emerge: the placement of the red letter T, a few inches

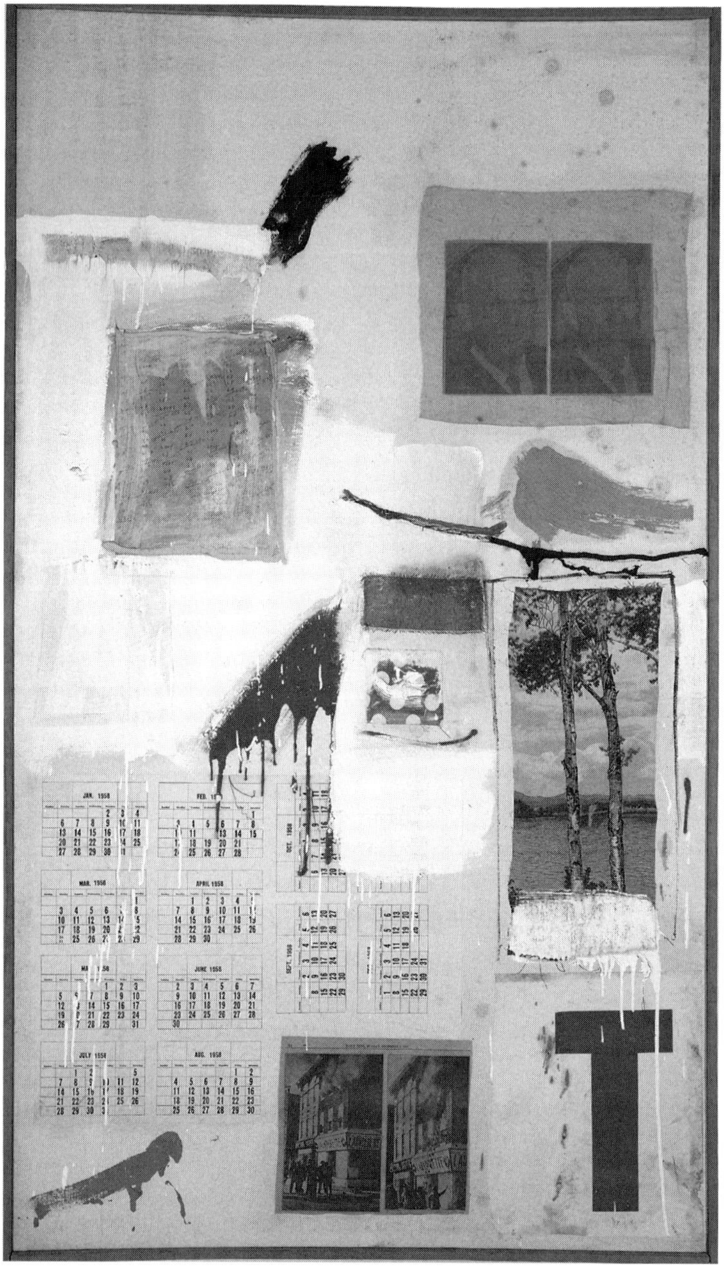

Factum I, 1957. Combine painting: oil, ink, pencil, crayon, paper, fabric, newspaper, printed reproductions, and printed paper on canvas. 62 × 35½ in. The Museum of Contemporary Art, Los Angeles. The Panza Collection.

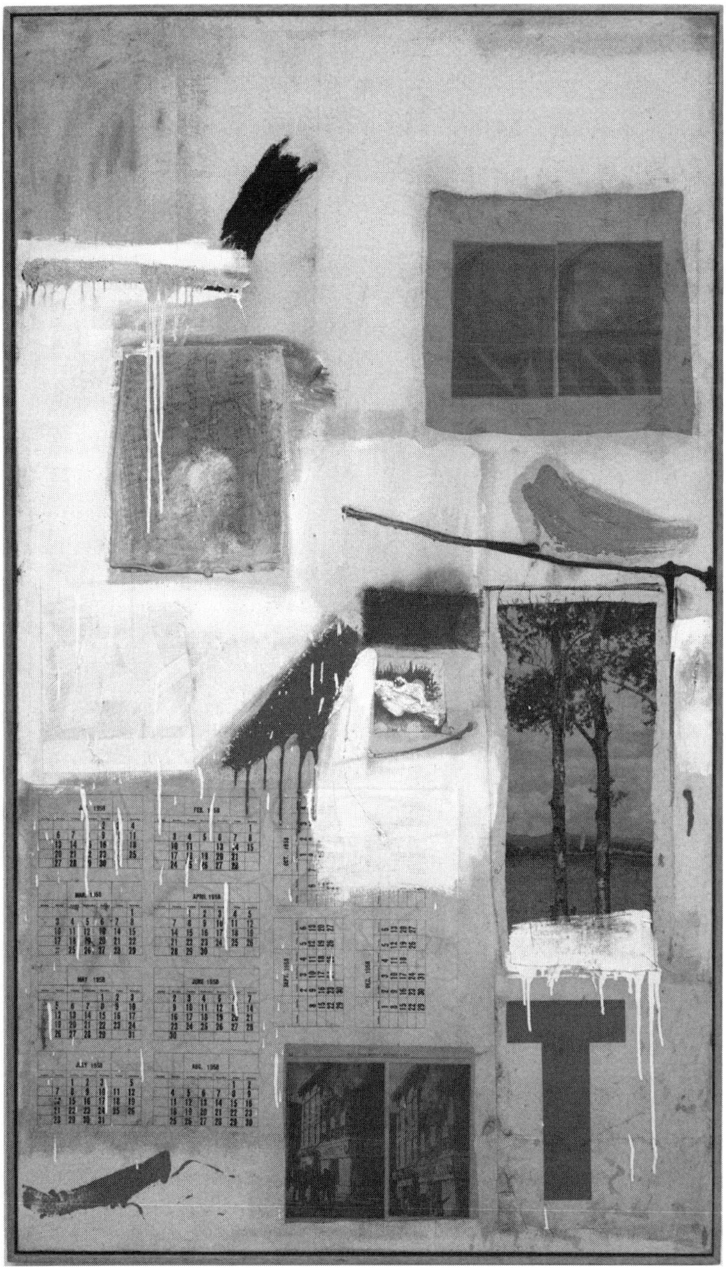

Factum II, 1957. Combine painting: oil, ink, pencil, crayon, paper, fabric, newspaper, printed reproductions, and printed paper on canvas. 62 × 35½ in. The Museum of Modern Art, New York. Purchase and an anonymous gift and Louise Reinhardt Smith Bequest (both by exchange). Photograph © The Museum of Modern Art / Licensed by SCALA / Art Resource, New York.

further from the corner in *Factum II* than in *Factum I;* the remnant of text barely visible at the bottom of the *Daily News* clipping in *Factum II;* the slightly different sizes and shapes of the polka-dot fabric at the center of the two canvases; the red and yellow brushstrokes that are larger in *I* than in *II,* whereas the white brushstroke beneath the trees has more drips in *II* than in *I;* and so on . . . even down to the two canvases' different patterns of discoloration.

A further layer of difference arises out of the works' internal repetitions. The two trees on the piece of cloth at the right, for instance, while twins, subtly diverge from one another in the disposition of their leaves and branches.[43] Both images from the *Daily News* at the bottom of the canvas depict the same burning building, but from slightly different distances and at slightly different moments in time. Even the misprinted calendars on the left-hand side take the form of a repeated array of grids, differentiated by the arrangement of numbers within. The most prominent of *Factums*' paired images, however, are the two Eisenhower portraits at the upper right. Although they initially read as exact reproductions, the absolute identity of the two images is ultimately unclear; and even studying the work at close range only gives rise to increasing doubts. Is the head on the left turned ever so slightly more forward than its counterpart? Does the bordered white triangle in the corner extend further into the picture at the right? Are they in fact two separate photographs taken at the same sitting? or, perhaps, two images of the same photograph as printed in separate newspapers?[44] or a slightly different registration of the image during the course of the same paper's print run? or simply two images cut from the newspaper slightly differently? Or do the differences between them arise from Rauschenberg's addition of the layer of translucent scrim or the faint markings of blue paint applied to the images on the right?[45]

In 1961 Cage described the ability of the repetitions in and of the *Factums* to release a proliferating series of differences:

> Hallelujah! The blind can see again. Blind to what he has seen so that seeing this time is as though first seeing. How is it that one experiences this, for example, with the two Eisenhower pictures

> which for all intents and purposes are the same? (A duplication containing duplications.) Everything is so much the same, one becomes acutely aware of the differences, and quickly. And where, as here, the intention is unchanging, it is clear that the differences are unintentional, as unintended as they were in the white paintings where nothing was done.[46]

Cage's link of *Factum I* and *II* back to Rauschenberg's *White Paintings,* though seemingly offhand, is important. For like the *White Paintings,* which revealed the temporal effects of lights and shadows, the *Factums* contain repetitions that are not static but work to reveal the effects of a positive, nonanthropocentric force of difference. Rather than collapsing in on themselves in a fixed and exchangeable identity, Rauschenberg's repetitions form resonating sequences of differences that proliferate throughout each work and into one another. "All it means," Cage wrote about Rauschenberg's "duplication of images," "is that, looking closely, we see as it was everything is in chaos still."[47]

Although readily perceptible when one looks directly at the two canvases, the differences between the *Factums* prove nearly impossible to recall in their absence. Thus, while undoubtedly present, the differences found in the works' painted and collaged areas remain at an elusive, a-signifying, and preconceptual level capable of subverting the dictates of memorization. In this regard, *Factum I* and *II* exemplify an ideal that Marcel Duchamp put forth in the *Green Box* and that Cage would cite frequently throughout the 1960s: "*To lose* the po*ssibility of* ***recognizing*** [Identifying] 2 *similar objects*—2 colors, 2 laces, 2 hats, 2 forms whatsoever to reach the Impossibility of sufficient *visual* memory, to transfer from one like object to another the *memory* imprint."[48]

Yet even though the differences between Rauschenberg's two *Factums* thwart the viewer's mnemonic capacities, they do not simply disappear in the observation of one canvas alone. Rather, they continue to haunt each individual work, rendering it incomplete and defeating any claim to full self-presence.[49] Thus neither canvas can any longer attain the solidity and self-identity that can privilege it as an original against which the other can be judged as a copy.

Almost a decade later, Gilles Deleuze would theorize precisely this effect in terms of simulacra. "By simulacrum," he wrote in *Difference and Repetition,*

> we should not understand a simple imitation but rather the act by which the very idea of a model or privileged position is challenged and overturned. The simulacrum is the instance which includes a difference within itself, such as (at least) two divergent series on which it plays, all resemblance abolished so that one can no longer point to the existence of an original and a copy. It is in this direction that we must look for the conditions, not of possible experience, but of real experience (selection, repetition, etc.). It is here that we find the lived reality of a sub-representative domain.[50]

It became a pressing project for Rauschenberg to explore the subversion of representational self-presence in *Factum I* and *II,* but his intent was not primarily to prolong the aesthetic or artistic life of the paintings, nor even to reveal an underlying ontological condition conceived as chaos. Rather, his undermining of representational fixity ultimately opposed the dictates of a generality that subsumed and neutralized perceptible differences so as to render them available to the abstract mechanisms of exchange.[51] Setting perception against conceptualization in precisely this way, Cage asked of the *Factums*, "And is this a poetry in which Eisenhower could have disappeared and the Mona Lisa taken his place? I *think* so but I do not *see* so."[52]

Rauschenberg consistently voiced his position as opposition to the "idea," which he regarded as a debilitating fixation of meaning and therefore akin to "commercial art." He had explained this (in a characteristically obscure manner) during the *Art of Assemblage* symposium, where he dismissively described "understanding" as "a product of good marketing, a general agreement that disposal is necessary," and "an economical way to feel."[53] Rauschenberg broached the issue more clearly and explicitly in describing his insistence on using live radios in works such as *Ace* and *Broadcast:* "To have used a tape" to produce the radio sounds, he explained, "would have been like commercial art in the sense that it would be a rendering of the idea. I'd like for the sound to be as fresh as the daily fall of dust and rust that accumulates. . . . This insistence on the piece operating in the time situation it was observed in, is another one of the ways of trying to put off the death of the work."[54]

Several months before Rauschenberg made these comments to Dorothy Seckler, Cage had similarly articulated the stakes involved in Rauschenberg's position. Responding to questions after a lecture at Yale University in December 1965, Cage declared: "The place where we most run into this thing of relationships is at the single point where we have what appears to be repetition." After citing René Char's statement that "Each act, even the repeated one, is virgin" and Duchamp's observations about the "impossibility of sufficient visual memory," Cage proceeded to explain that

> if we take the path of looking for relationships, we will slip over experience-wise all those things that are obvious, like repetition, and we will go where Schoenberg wanted us to go to far-reaching variation. But, if we take[,] if we change our mind and turn utterly around and refuse this business of relationship, to use Duchamp in our own experience, we will be able to see that those things that we thought were the same are in fact not the same. And this is very useful in our lives, which are more and more going to have what appears to be repetition. . . . Now, in a world like that, the perceiving of difference in the repeated, mass-produced items is going to be of the greatest concern to us.[55]

◆

At the end of *Difference and Repetition,* in an uncanny recollection of Cage's comments, Deleuze proposed that

> there is no other aesthetic problem than that of the insertion of art into everyday life. The more our daily life appears standardized, stereotyped and subject to an accelerated reproduction of objects

> of consumption, the more art must be injected into it in order to extract from it that little difference which plays simultaneously between other levels of repetition.[56]

But writing nearly twenty years later, with the rise of an information economy, Deleuze saw that the standardization of the commodity had become less important, superseded by television's equally repetitive and stereotyped subsumption of perception into a single, characteristic "medium shot" or "middle ground" view.[57] In that form, entirely co-opted by its spectacular function, television represented a wholly technologically and sociologically mediated vision without artistic or critical remainder. Thus "the encyclopedia of the world and the pedagogy of perception" that Deleuze found in postwar cinema "collapse to make way for a professional training of the eye, a world of controllers and controlled communing in their admiration for technology, mere technology." "TV," he continues, "is, in its present form, the ultimate consensus: it's direct social engineering, leaving no gap at all between itself and the social sphere, it's social engineering in its purest form."[58]

For Deleuze, the ascendance of television in the 1960s formed part of an epochal shift in the development of capital and power. This was not simply a transformation to a later stage of capitalism (although it was that as well). Rather, it was primarily marked by the demise of what Michel Foucault's analysis had labeled disciplinary regimes and by the advent of "the new social power of the postwar period, one of surveillance or control."[59] Whereas the "principal technology" of disciplinary societies was spatial confinement—first within the family, and then in an enfilade of schools, barracks, factories, hospitals, and prisons—the "control societies" of the postwar era saw such autonomous institutions gradually replaced by more open-ended, continuous forms of domination. Taking advantage of rapid telecommunication technologies, this new form of control operates across unbounded territories; and because of their capacity to track individuals unobtrusively, the electronic tag and the remote video camera have become its signal technologies. Yet in its function of breaking through spatial confinements—its apparent capacity to be simultaneously present in two places at once, to bring "the Asiatic panoply" into Cage's front room—it was actually television that served as the most ubiquitous instigator of the breakdown of all "interiors."[60]

Television thereby effected a certain liberation from the sites of disciplinary confinement, but its spectacular operation—its institution of a hermetic perceptual training and its camouflaging of any gap or fissure within the image produced—marks it as an instrument of control; "television," as Deleuze wrote to Serge Daney, "is the form in which the new powers of 'control' become immediate and direct."[61] Faced with this alteration in the regime of power, Deleuze would recast the "sole aesthetic problem" he articulated in *Difference and Repetition* in terms of extracting from television certain "noncommunicative supplement[s]," differences that play among its unacknowledged folds, or "circuit breakers" that can interrupt the viewer's inexorable perceptual training.[62]

Keeping in mind the ubiquitous and deterritorialized expansion of television in the 1960s, we can perhaps begin to open up the full implications of Rauschenberg's silkscreens. For despite their strict unlocatability, the differences between *Factum I* and *II* remain physical. Revealed in the comparison of the two works are the "accidents" that have befallen each material—the individual history of each item of collage or application of paint as it, to quote Rauschenberg, "adjust[ed] to the differences from one canvas to another." By contrast, as noted above, the relative immateriality of the silkscreens' imagery does not convey the same specificity of existence at a particular place and time.

Yet, while the silkscreens bring about a decrease in the material distinctions between the images, they effect a corresponding increase in the immaterial haunting of difference internal to each. No longer attributable to a material given, nor shown in action as in the fleeting shadows that play across the *White Paintings'* surfaces or the mirrors and open spaces of the Combines, difference is revealed in the silkscreens primarily as an ungraspable, spectral negativity, an absence inhering within the very heart of the image. In this way, Rauschenberg's silkscreen images are split internally, divided like the recurrent image of Venus at her mirror (sometimes heightened by the impression of a stretcher bar

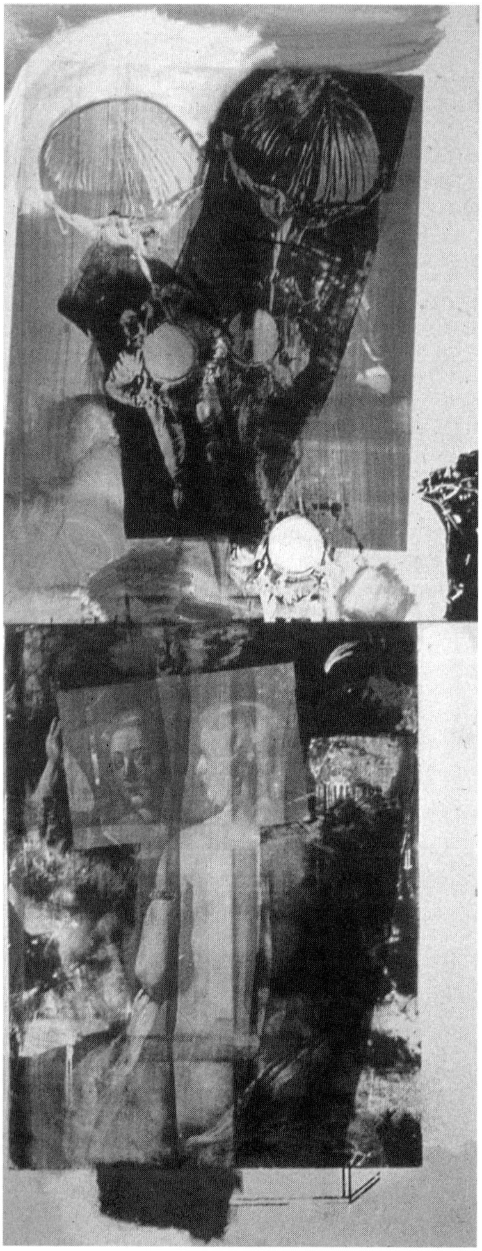

Trapeze, 1964. Oil and silkscreen ink on canvas. 120 × 48 in. Private collection. Photograph courtesy of Leo Castelli Gallery.

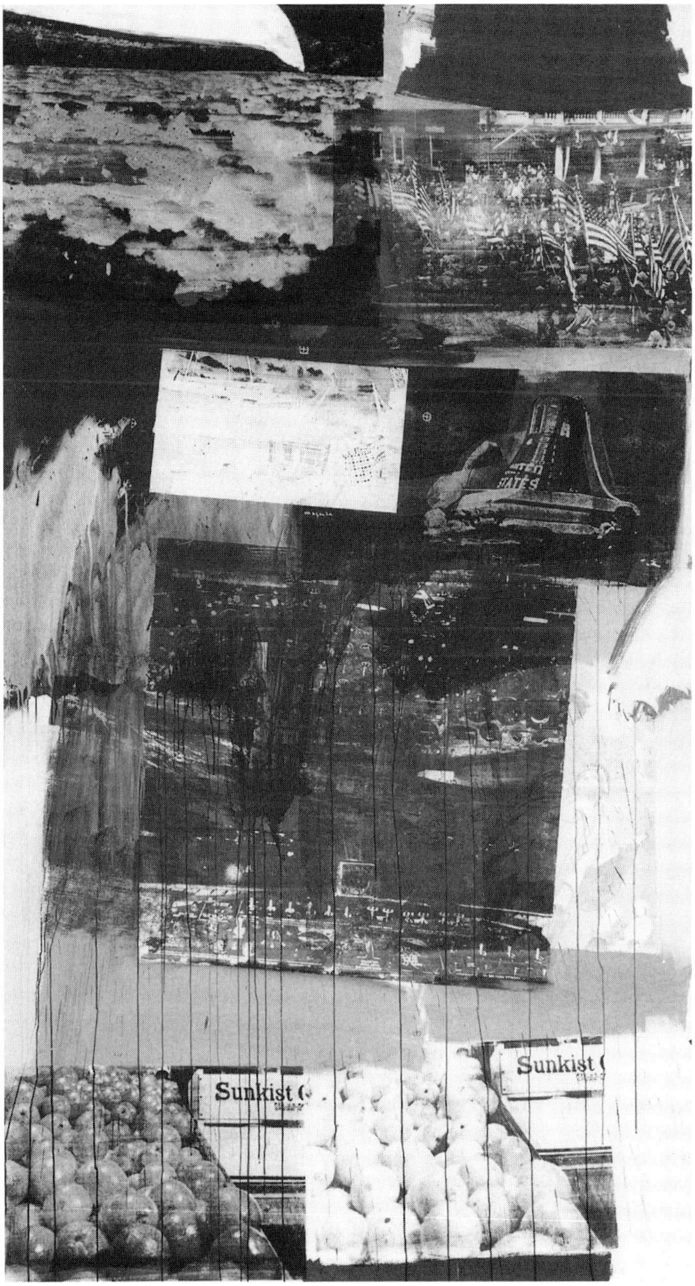

Whale, 1964. Oil and silkscreen ink on canvas. 108 × 59¾ in. Hirshhorn Museum and Sculpture Garden, Smithsonian Institution. Gift of Joseph H. Hirshhorn, 1972. Photograph by Lee Stalsworth.

or a seam caused by the screen's double registration) or like the astronaut at the top of *Trapeze* (1964)—multiplied and pulled apart into a series of repetitions. Indeed, such internal bifurcations proliferate throughout the silkscreen series, appearing, for instance, in the doubled Sunkist orange crates at the bottom of *Whale* (1964), the TV-like sequences of the landing space capsule in *Die Hard* (1963), or the multiplied views of beach umbrellas in *Archive* (1963). As uncanny as the differences found in *Factum I* and *II,* the silkscreens' repetitions lack their materiality to such an extent that, in the comparison of two canvases such as *Retroactive I* and *II* (both 1963), the astronaut or the pointing figure of JFK appears not so much as one image repeated by another as the *same* image simultaneously visible in two different places at once (and thus, as Weber reminds us, not entirely present in either one). At this point, we come to understand more fully the transformation caused by the silkscreen paintings, as Rauschenberg passes from a method reminiscent of mechanical reproduction—physical, separable repetitions, produced one after the other like two copies of the newspaper—to a method closer to optoelectronic transmission—simultaneous and split simulacra, like an image broadcast on two different television screens at once.

According to Debord, spectacle renders "everything that in human activity exists in a fluid state" into "image-objects"; these circulate within a regulated "pseudo-cyclical time" that "is in fact merely the *consumable disguise* of the time-as-commodity of the production system, and exhibits the essential traits of that time: homogeneous and exchangeable units, and the suppression of any qualitative dimension."[63] Such, of course, is precisely the temporal experience that characterizes TV watching—an experience in which, as Warhol once observed, one encounters "the same plots and the same shots and the same cuts over and over again."[64] Yet such a generalized and indifferent exchange between spectacular images and moments is possible only through the congealed covering over of difference within the units to be exchanged, the "exclusively quantitative" "self-equivalence" that also characterizes the commodity form (even if this, in turn, is covered by a no less exchangeable form of pseudo-differentiation).[65] In the simulacral split of repeated images, however, Rauschenberg produces differences that are unquantifiable and unexchangeable and that work to

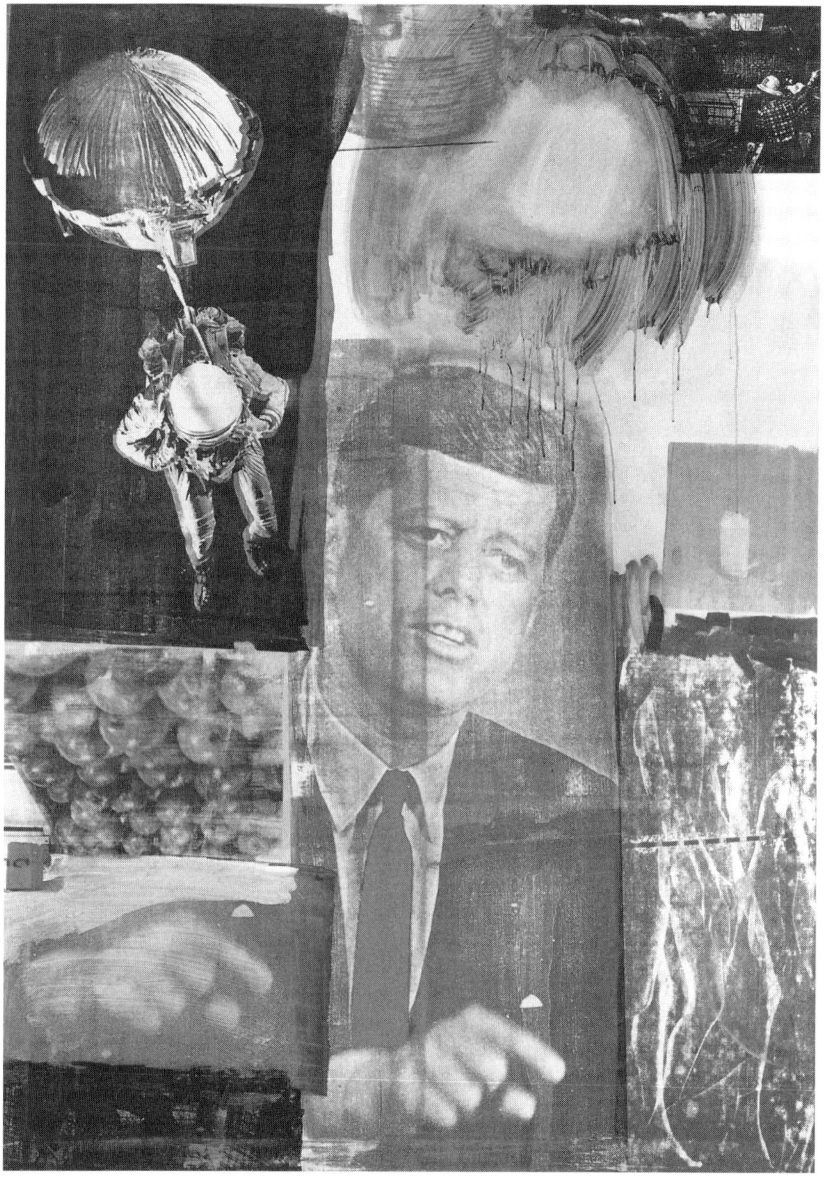

Retroactive I, 1963. Oil and silkscreen ink on canvas. 84 × 60 in. The Wadsworth Atheneum Museum of Art, Hartford, Conn. Gift of Susan Morse Hilles.

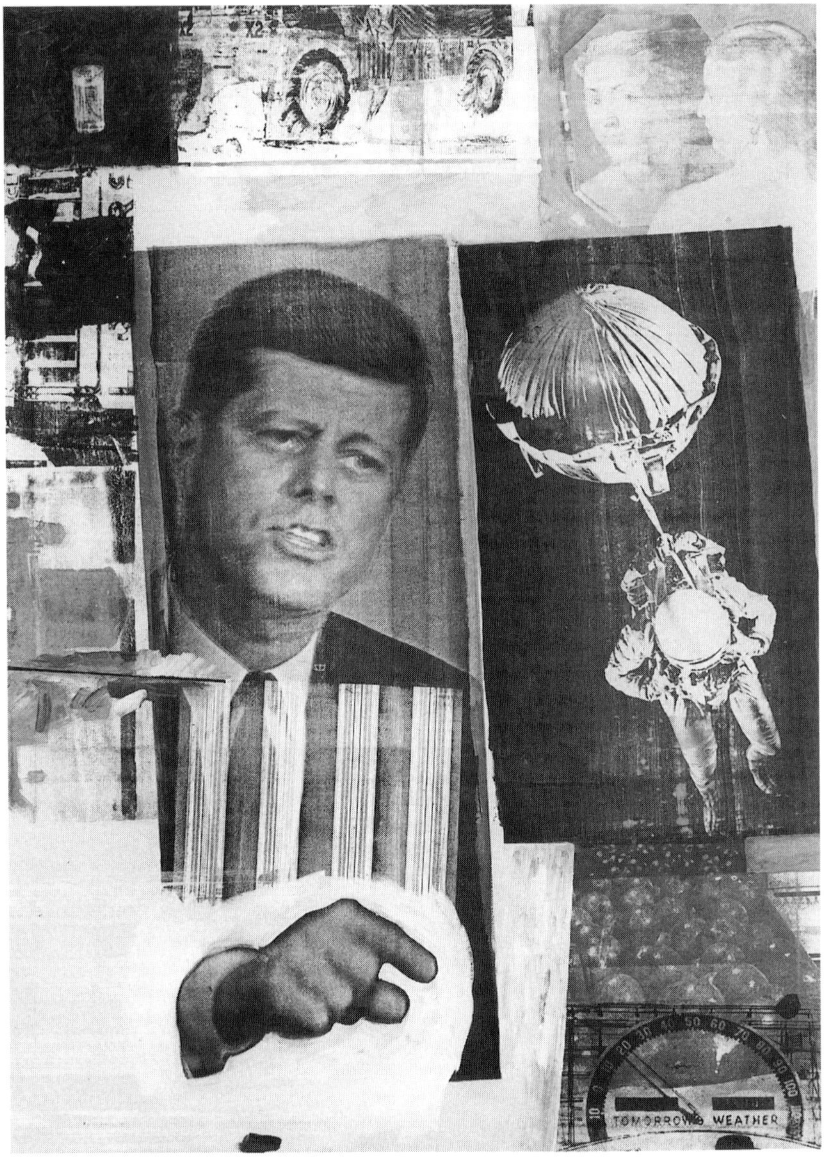

Retroactive II, 1963. Oil and silkscreen ink on canvas. 84 × 60 in. Collection of Stefan T. Edlis. Photograph by Rudolf Burckhardt. Courtesy The Estate of Rudolf Burckhardt.

undo the generalizable forms of recognition or "visual memory" necessary for spectacular consumption.[66] In freeing perceptible differences from the rule of abstract conceptualization and exchange, Rauschenberg's silkscreens uncover differences that the spectacular image works to conceal, revealing what Crary calls the "barely visible alcoves, striations, and folds" underneath representation.

◆

In 1967 (the year *The Society of the Spectacle* was published and *Difference and Repetition* was going to press), Michael Fried addressed the stakes involved in the competing perceptual models advanced by contemporary art. In "Art and Objecthood," Fried famously defended as "presentness" an instantaneous form of visual apprehension that he found synonymous with aesthetic quality. Before a convincing late-modernist artwork, he proposed, "It is as though one's experience . . . *has no* duration—not because one *in fact* experiences a picture by Noland or Olitski or a sculpture by David Smith or Caro in no time at all, but because *at every moment the work itself is wholly manifest.*"[67] The culminating development of Clement Greenberg's formalist aesthetics, Fried's proposition of the image's manifest self-presence was to serve the interrelated functions of safeguarding art from the debasement of commercial culture, or kitsch, and guaranteeing the unitary and transcendent status, however fleeting, of its viewing subject.[68] And as the perceptual hypostatization of modern art's claim to autonomy, Fried's metaphysic of artistic presence was as dependent on the exclusionary, institutional confines of the museum as it was on a certain discourse of formalist art history.[69] Fried therefore rightfully understood that the art he was defending was "at war" with those currents that were developing within minimalism.[70] For the minimalist object not only opposed "presentness" with a mundane perceptual temporality that Fried likened to theater, but it also led the viewing subject to become aware of the phenomenological aspects of his or her perceptual activity and, eventually, to recognize the institutional and even disciplinary constraints on that activity as well.[71]

Less remarked than Fried's polemic against minimalism is the ad hominem attack of "Art and Objecthood" on Rauschenberg and Cage, both of whom were made to represent the degeneration of artistic standards. "A failure to register the enormous difference in quality between, say, the music of Carter and that of Cage or between the paintings of Louis and those of Rauschenberg," Fried maintained,

> means that the real distinctions—between music and theatre in the first instance and between painting and theatre in the second—are displaced by the illusion that the barriers between the arts are in the process of crumbling (Cage and Rauschenberg being seen, correctly, as similar) and that the arts themselves are at last sliding towards some kind of final, implosive, hugely desirable synthesis.[72]

Although Fried singled out Susan Sontag as having promoted this vision of synthesis out of a mistaken trust in her own "theatrical" sensibility,[73] the dissolution of the distinctions between media that he describes would seem better understood as a local manifestation of the larger breakdown of all interiors heralded by television. Thus, Debord rather than Fried most clearly presented the socioeconomic significance of such developments. Despite its pretensions to autonomy and regardless of its genre, art in the modern period had become "subject, as one instance among others, to the movement governing the history of the whole of culture as a separated realm"[74]—that is, it was subject to the pressures of spectacle. In their uniform recourse to a strategy of interchangeable serial production, the abstract artists championed by Fried were no freer of the stigma of this condition than any others.[75]

To the two more well-known formalist and minimalist models of aesthetic perception that "Art and Objecthood" discussed, Rauschenberg adds a third, one that was as opposed as minimalism to the false claims of self-presence which, far from protecting art from commercialism, served only to reproduce or guarantee spectacle's function. Rather than proffering a claim to manifest presence, Rauschenberg's silkscreens are fractured among different places and times and solicit a form of perception that (unlike both Friedian transcendentalism and minimalist phenomenology) is internally split and haunted by difference. Rauschenberg would ultimately prove as uninterested in postminimalist institution critique as in formalist modernism. This testifies, perhaps, to the fact that he was no longer focused on the confines of disciplinary institutions but was already, as indicated by his attraction to television, considering the mediatized, technological spaces of control.

Such an analysis necessarily invokes Rauschenberg's more general relationship to technology. Although he was undoubtedly a technological optimist,[76] he was not content by any means with the actually existing conditions of technology. It is in the performances and work with "art and technology" to which Rauschenberg increasingly devoted himself throughout the remainder of the 1960s that the insights initially gained in the silkscreens would be developed most extensively. We now turn to this little-examined aspect of Rauschenberg's endeavors.

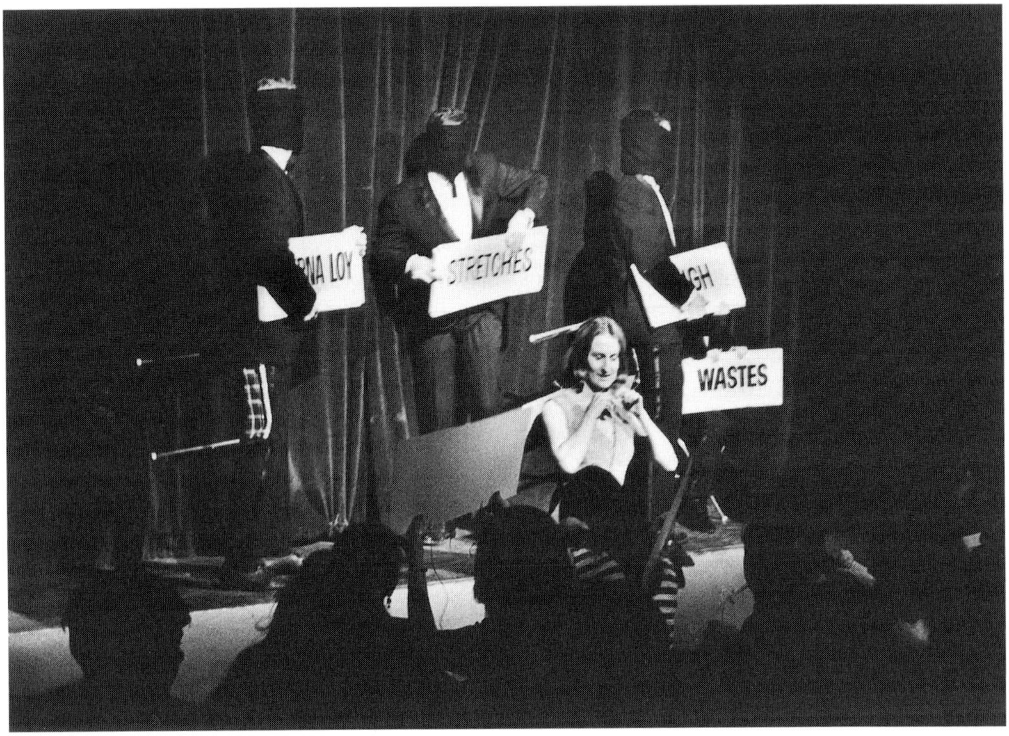

Map Room II, 1965. Expanded Cinema Festival, Film-Makers' Cinematheque, Forty-first Street Theater, New York, 2 December 1965. Pictured: Trisha Brown and members of the ensemble. Photograph by Peter Moore. © Estate of Peter Moore / VAGA, New York.

5

Moving Images

The conditions of a true critique and a true creation are the same: the destruction of an image of thought which presupposes itself and the genesis of the act of thinking in thought itself.

Something in the world forces us to think. This something is an object not of recognition but of a fundamental *encounter*. What is encountered may be Socrates, a temple or a demon. It may be grasped in a range of affective tones: wonder, love, hatred, suffering. In whichever tone, its primary characteristic is that it can only be sensed. In this sense it is opposed to recognition.

—*Gilles Deleuze, 1968*

The action begins before the curtain is drawn. Such an opening, while unconventional, is not entirely unexpected as this is the "Expanded Cinema Festival" at the Film-Makers' Cinematheque, and Robert Rauschenberg's Map Room II *is only one of a number of performances determined to transgress every convention of the movie theater.*[1] *Wearing tuxedos and large black blindfolds that cover almost the entirety of their faces, the four performers—Rauschenberg, Steve Paxton, and Deborah and Alex Hay—enter the scene on the stage in front of the curtain. To complete their unusual guise, each is outfitted with a camping stool attached to the seat of his or her pants. Sitting in a line, each performer holds a stack of one-by-two-foot white cards with words in clearly legible black lettering. The phrases they form, while grammatically correct, are nonsensical. "Myrna Loy stretches high wastes." "Schielman counts complex bayous." After each phrase the performers shuffle their cards and switch positions. Moving blindly from one place to another, each member of this unwieldy chorus carefully but fumblingly passes off his or her cards each time so that the stacks remain in the same position despite the movements of the individuals. "Grieg standardizes canned geysers." "St. John is tacky bayous."*

A proper and somewhat official looking woman, Trisha Brown, enters in front of the stage and faces the audience. Holding up a square white card with a string on it in the manner of an airline hostess demonstrating the use of a life vest, she politely instructs those audience members who have been furnished with similar cards: "Take this string on the card. Put it around your neck and hang the card behind your seat."[2] While the audience complies, the tuxedoed performers finish the last of their permutations. "Dirksen is complex slicks." "Myrna Loy chairs canned passes." Brown then leaves the scene.

Unbeknownst to the audience, Brown's exit is the cue for the first sequence to stop. The blindfolded performers exit as the lights dim and a film projector in the back of the auditorium starts up. It begins to project a travelogue about Austria, not onto a screen behind the curtain but onto the sea of white cards hanging on the backs of the first five rows of the audience. The cards, as Steve Paxton recalled, "provided enough overall surface so that from the back of the house the film could be recognized, barely, though it was chopped into small bits of images and sound. The words of the hearty voice accompanying the film had been scrambled, along with the frenetic efforts of an orchestra."[3] At this point the curtain finally rises to reveal Rauschenberg on stage wiping what appears to be a large, dirty wall with Noxon metal polish. As he does so it becomes clear that the surface is reflective, a mirror; a slide projection of Mount Rushmore tilted on its side is slowly revealed, its reflection cast back onto the other side of the auditorium.

As Rauschenberg leaves, Deborah Hay enters the stage wearing a dress over which hangs a cylindrical cage made out of chicken wire. Inside it, on perches, are three live white doves, which flutter at each disturbance caused by her movements. "She appeared before the audience, moving her hands at the wrist, her expression solemn, her eyes wide,

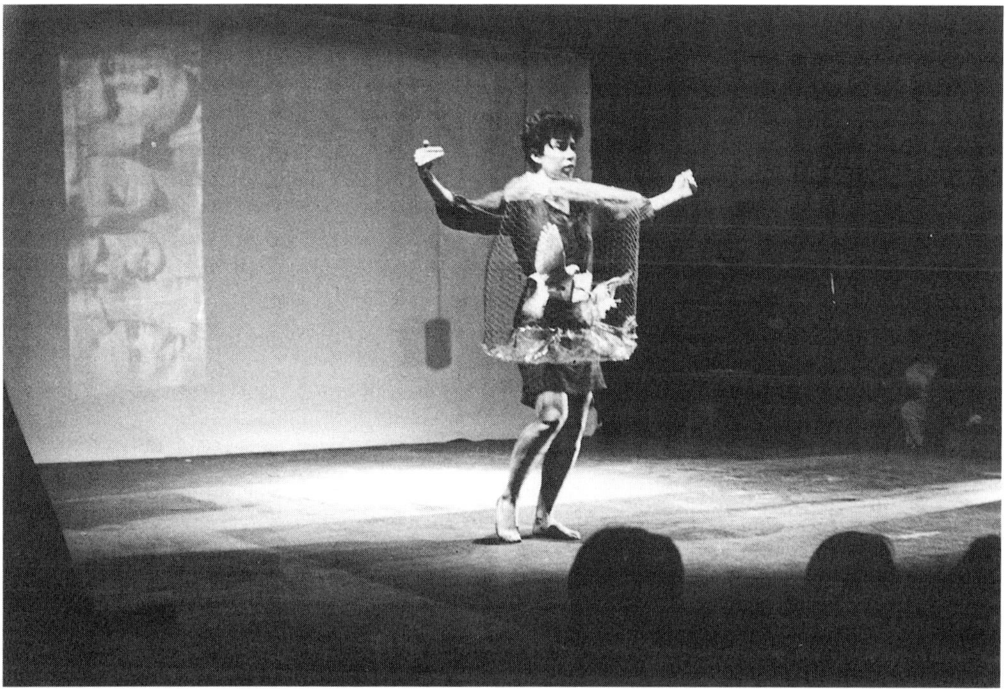

Map Room II, 1965. Expanded Cinema Festival, Film-Makers' Cinematheque, Forty-first Street Theater, New York, 17 December 1965. Pictured: Deborah Hay. Photograph by Peter Moore. © Estate of Peter Moore / VAGA, New York.

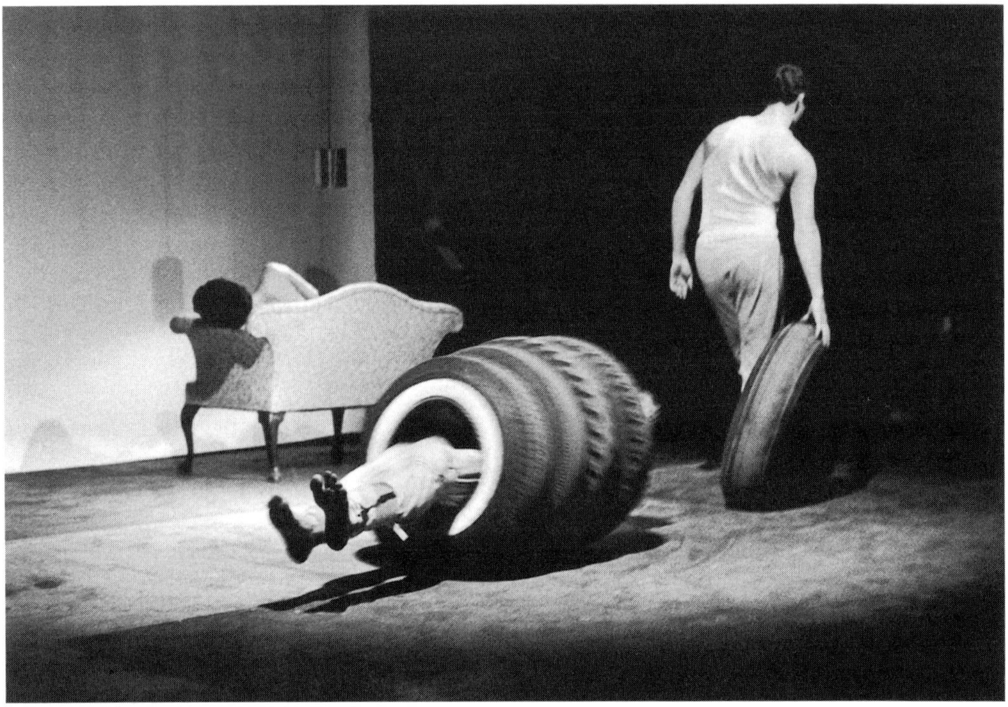

Map Room II, 1965. Expanded Cinema Festival, Film-Makers' Cinematheque, Forty-first Street Theater, New York, 2 December 1965. Pictured: Deborah Hay, Alex Hay, and Steve Paxton. Photograph by Peter Moore. © Estate of Peter Moore / VAGA, New York.

moving gently, slowly across the stage, because she was rather afraid of birds and did not wish to excite the doves. . . . Slowly, tentatively, almost mincingly she moved."[4]

There then begins a long sequence of performers interacting with tires. First, perhaps, is Trisha Brown's "tire solo." Crouching in an awkward position inside a single tire so that her backside protruded out in one direction, she rolls (or is rolled by Rauschenberg) to the center of the stage. Steve Paxton and Alex Hay also come onstage at this point, having traded their tuxedos for sweatsuits and T-shirts. They move with a tire on each foot, stepping awkwardly and wrestling with their cumbersome footwear. They sit close to the ground, rolling over backward with the tires still on their feet. At one point, Alex Hay crawls into a single tire, thrusting his arms out to the side like oars and propelling himself forward. At another moment, he crawls lengthwise into four tires as if he were an axle, rolling quickly across the floor while Paxton travels, somewhat less briskly, across the stage with both feet in a single tire, helping it along with his right hand. The longest of these sequences consists of Paxton and Hay, both standing upright with tires on each foot, moving atop a mattressless bedspring outfitted with contact microphones that are amplified through a Wollensak tape recorder. The sounds, cacophonous and metallic, echo throughout the auditorium, overlapping with the fractured sounds of the movie being projected (which, according to some accounts, only comes on at this time).

It is during this part of the performance that an antique beige sofa is brought onto the stage and placed beneath a light that hangs from the ceiling. Deborah Hay, now dressed in a "flesh-colored" leotard that closely matches the color of the sofa, quickly moves across the stage, switches on the light, and climbs onto the couch, which faces upstage. While Alex Hay, Paxton, and Brown are rolling about the stage in various interactions with the tires, Deborah Hay, just visible over the back of the sofa, makes slow, languid and somewhat suggestive movements, appearing to blend with the furniture as a sort of "couch sculpture."

As all of this is going on, Rauschenberg slowly enters from the right-hand side of the stage. Deborah Hay stays on the couch, but Alex Hay, Paxton, and Brown amble or roll offstage in their tires. Rauschenberg is a striking presence, taller than the other performers by dint of the foot-high plastic platforms into which the sculptor Arman has encased his white buck shoes. Struggling with their nearly twenty pounds of weight, Rauschenberg clunks across the stage. Arms swinging with the effort, he carries in his

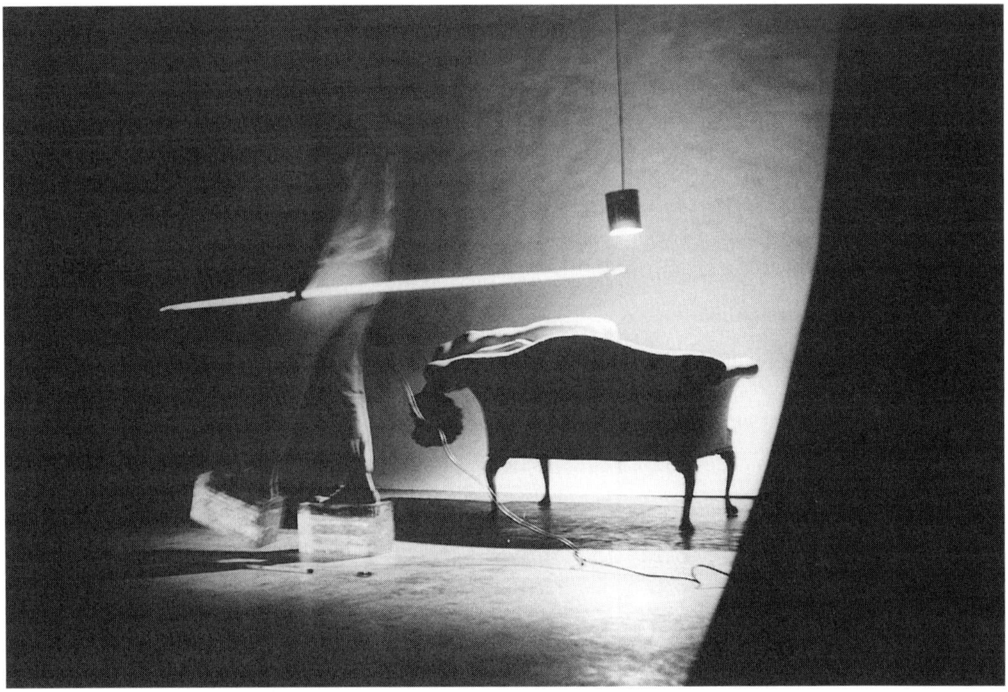

Map Room II, 1965. Expanded Cinema Festival, Film-Makers' Cinematheque, Forty-first Street Theater, New York, December 1965. Pictured: Rauschenberg and Deborah Hay. Photograph by Robert R. McElroy. © Robert R. McElroy / Licensed by VAGA, New York.

hands a red and a multicolored, rainbowlike neon tube; each is lit by the power produced by a Tessler coil, whose electrical current is running directly through his body. When he lays the tubes down, they go out, lighting up again when he grasps them before taking another few heavy steps. The stage lights now slowly dim to total darkness, leaving Rauschenberg to generate his own light, accompanied only by the lamp hanging above the sofa behind him. He bends down to the floor with the lit tubes in his hands, allowing the neon to shine through the clear plastic platforms of his shoes. At that point, Map Room II *comes to an end.*

In an incident that has become famous in the literature on the artist, Robert Rauschenberg, having won the Grand Prize at the 1964 Venice Biennial, telephoned a friend in New York and asked that his existing cache of silkscreens be cut from their frames and destroyed. As Calvin Tomkins has noted, this act, for an artist of Rauschenberg's then undeniable currency, represented a squandering of considerable resources and future financial returns.[5] From that moment and throughout the following decade, Rauschenberg would largely abandon painting and devote himself to theater pieces and works incorporating "art and technology."

To date, these two strains of Rauschenberg's mid-1960s production have been regarded as entirely separate categories or genres, even though they were pursued coterminously and often, as in *Map Room II* (1965), coincided and overlapped.[6] In part this view reflects the differing critical receptions accorded these two facets of his work. Although they were closely interrelated, Rauschenberg's theater events, in which the aesthetic of his Combines was extended to the interaction of performers and props, were more easily categorized, more successful, and apparently more understandable than his exclusively technological productions. Rauschenberg's first choreographed performance, *Pelican* (1963), seems to have become an immediate hit; two years later, when the work was reprised at the First New York Theater Rally, the critic Erica Abeel lauded it as the most successful of all the entries. In her oft-cited review, "Daedalus at the Rollerdome," Abeel noted that "Rauschenberg is already the master of the new medium . . . the Theater Piece's best bet for a long and happy life."[7]

On one level, *Pelican* was all about movement, the possibilities and juxtapositions of different types of locomotion. It functioned by contrasting the graceful movements of the Merce Cunningham dancer Carolyn Brown—walking on her hands in a circle, executing a forward roll, pirouetting masterfully toward the back of the arena—with the somewhat comic, though not ungraceful, movements of Rauschenberg and Per Uvelt (or, in later performances, Alex Hay) on roller skates.[8] After making their entry kneeling on a pole suspended between two bicycle wheels, Rauschenberg and his partner spun in circles with multicolored parachute-like contraptions on their backs. Then, skating in arcing patterns around the pirouetting Brown, they joined to turn her around, on pointe, in a series of poses in which their actions were both equated and juxtaposed with hers. "In *Pelican*," declared Abeel, "Rauschenberg breaks down the distinction between the scenic element and the dancer, merging the two in a sort of locomotive human combine. The dancer functions as a vital center, generating a complex wing-and-wheels contraption."[9]

Though movement was, in large part, the work's "theme," it was only one component of its aesthetic effect. As seemingly captured in the memorable photographs of the swooping, skate-clad Rauschenberg (later included in the third panel of his monumental print, *Autobiography* [1968]), *Pelican's* impact also arose from the production of more or less distinct visual images, the "Mesozoic apparitions" and "hybrid monsters" (in Abeel's description) formed by Rauschenberg and Hay.[10] This aspect of Rauschenberg's performances has been duly noted by later commentators as well. According to Nina Sundell, for instance, "Photographs of Rauschenberg's theater pieces reveal the same kind of mysterious and powerful images that he was able to create with similarly ill-assorted objects in his Combines."[11] More recently, Steve Paxton, one of the most frequent performers in Rauschenberg's theater events, observed, "Movement can be generated in a variety of ways, and he [Rauschenberg] generated his by couching people within images and then allowing these images to coexist, collide, or follow one another." Paxton added, "In his choreography, he animated people with tasks within images: the task of the men in *Pelican*, for example, was to wear the animating parachutes and skates and to kneel and wheel."[12]

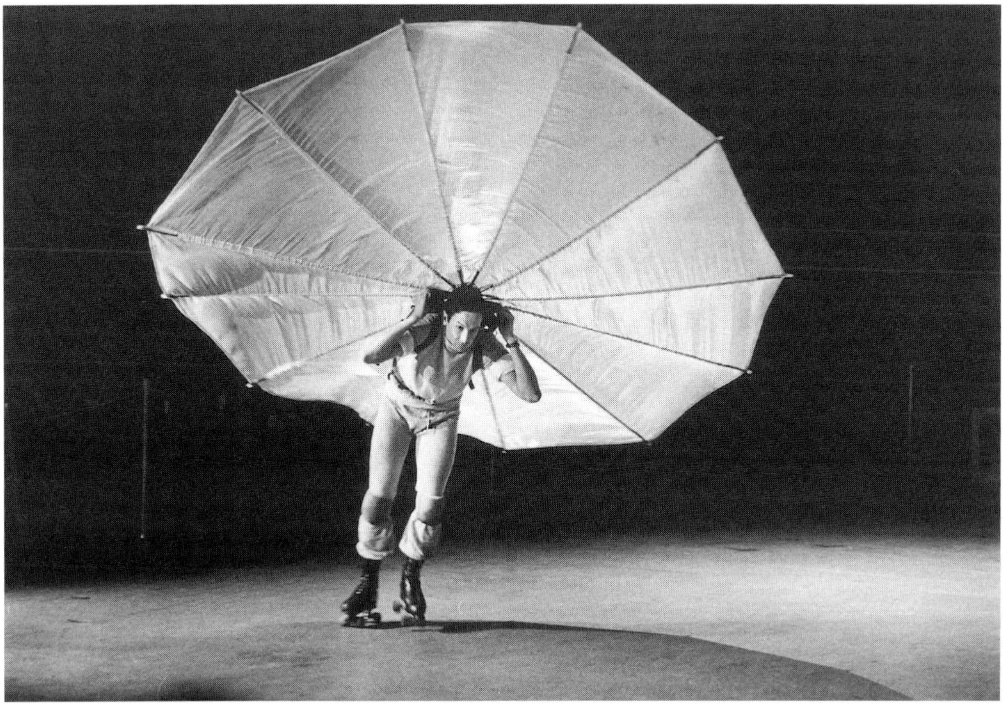

Pelican, 1963. First New York Theater Rally, abandoned television studio, Broadway and Eighty-first Street, New York, May 1965. Pictured: Rauschenberg. Photograph by Peter Moore. © Estate of Peter Moore / VAGA, New York.

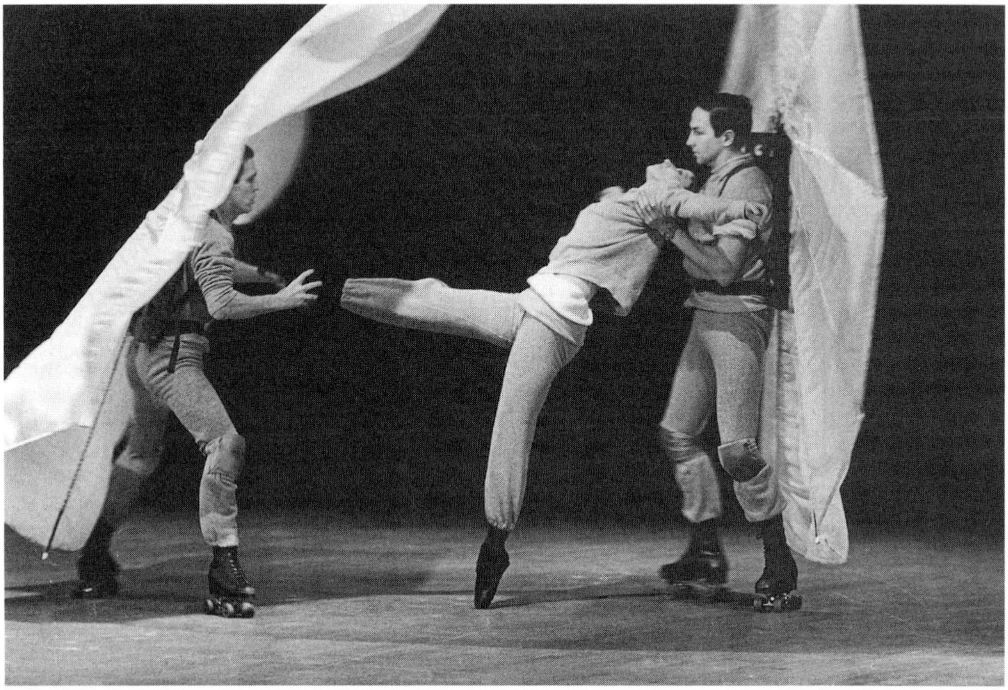

Pelican, 1963. Pictured: Alex Hay, Carolyn Brown, and Rauschenberg. Photograph by Peter Moore. © Estate of Peter Moore / VAGA, New York.

Paxton's and Sundell's references to the different sections or segments of Rauschenberg's performances as "images" faithfully echo the artist's own descriptions. Throughout his lengthy 1968 conversation with Richard Kostelanetz, Rauschenberg repeatedly called the various parts of his performances "images." Deborah Hay's appearance in a wire mesh birdcage and again on the couch in *Map Room II,* Trisha Brown's interactions with the tire in the same performance, the turtles with flashlights strapped to their shells in *Spring Training* (1965), and Steve Paxton's appearance on a wheeled platform with live chickens in *Linoleum* (1966) are all described in this way. "I didn't want the audience to be involved with who it was that was in the tire and what the person looked like," said Rauschenberg of Trisha Brown's tire solo. "What I wanted was *the most abstract image* at that particular moment."[13]

Each of these "images," and others such as the blindfolded chorus with words at the outset of *Map Room II* and Rauschenberg walking across the stage with plastic shoes and lit neon tubes, serve as momentary focal points within the performances, isolable segments in which performer and prop interact with some closeness. Although inextricably interwoven with other movements and activities, these images call attention to themselves as discrete units that leave an impression on the spectator and call for interpretation. They appear as significant, as signifying—indeed, in a manner that remains to be determined, as signs—but not as either images or signification are habitually understood. They are not, despite their subsequent descriptions, essentially of the same order as the photographs by which they are now primarily known. Rather, they put the status of both image and signification into question, and it is in the relationship between Rauschenberg's performance "images" and the movements that animate and run through them that we will have to seek the specificity of his theater events.

I. Although initially sparked by his longstanding association with the Merce Cunningham Dance Company, for which he provided sets, costumes, and lighting, Rauschenberg's own performance aesthetic developed mainly within the context of the Judson Dance Theater.[14] Because the group embraced untrained performers, Rauschenberg was able to participate in the Judson circle more integrally as a dancer and a choreographer than Cunningham's more virtuoso aesthetic would allow. Indeed, after the Cunningham Dance Company's 1964 world tour ended with a break that left Rauschenberg, on the one hand, and Cunningham and John Cage, on the other, on less than harmonious terms, the Judson dancers would assume the role of Rauschenberg's closest artistic collaborators.[15]

While he participated in the activities of the fledgling Judson Dance Theater from the beginning, visiting and taking part in Robert Dunn's seminal choreography workshop from which it arose,[16] Rauschenberg's initial public role was that of lighting designer. One of Rauschenberg's first appearances in that capacity (if not the first) was at the premiere of Yvonne Rainer's *Terrain*, which was held at the Judson Memorial Church on 28 and 29 April 1963; he lit it with the same bright and even style that he had developed for Cunningham.[17] To a certain extent, the evening-length *Terrain* was the culmination of Rainer's early aesthetic, incorporating influences ranging from childhood reminiscences to her studies with Dunn, Ann Halprin, and fellow Judson dancer Simone Forti.[18] Overall, the choreography had a certain "pop" feel to it, as movements and stances were appropriated from classical, modern and popular dance forms, nondance quotidian tasks, and even film.[19] At the same time, however, *Terrain* also clearly pointed toward the minimalist dance aesthetic that Rainer would come to pursue in such works as *Parts of Some Sextets* (1964–1965), a piece in which Rauschenberg would later perform.[20]

In retrospect, the definition of Rainer's then-emerging minimalist position was clearly signaled in the juxtaposition of the first and second sections of *Terrain: Diagonal* and *Duet. Diagonal* was preceded by a sort of prologue in which the entire group of dancers walked in a "clump," following a predetermined pattern from point to point about the performance area and pausing at certain moments before changing direction. Like another dance of 1963, *We Shall Run* (in which Rauschenberg would also perform),[21] *Terrain*'s opening foregrounded unexpressive, everyday movements without any recognizable relationship to traditional dance forms. It was followed by the *Diagonal* section proper in which

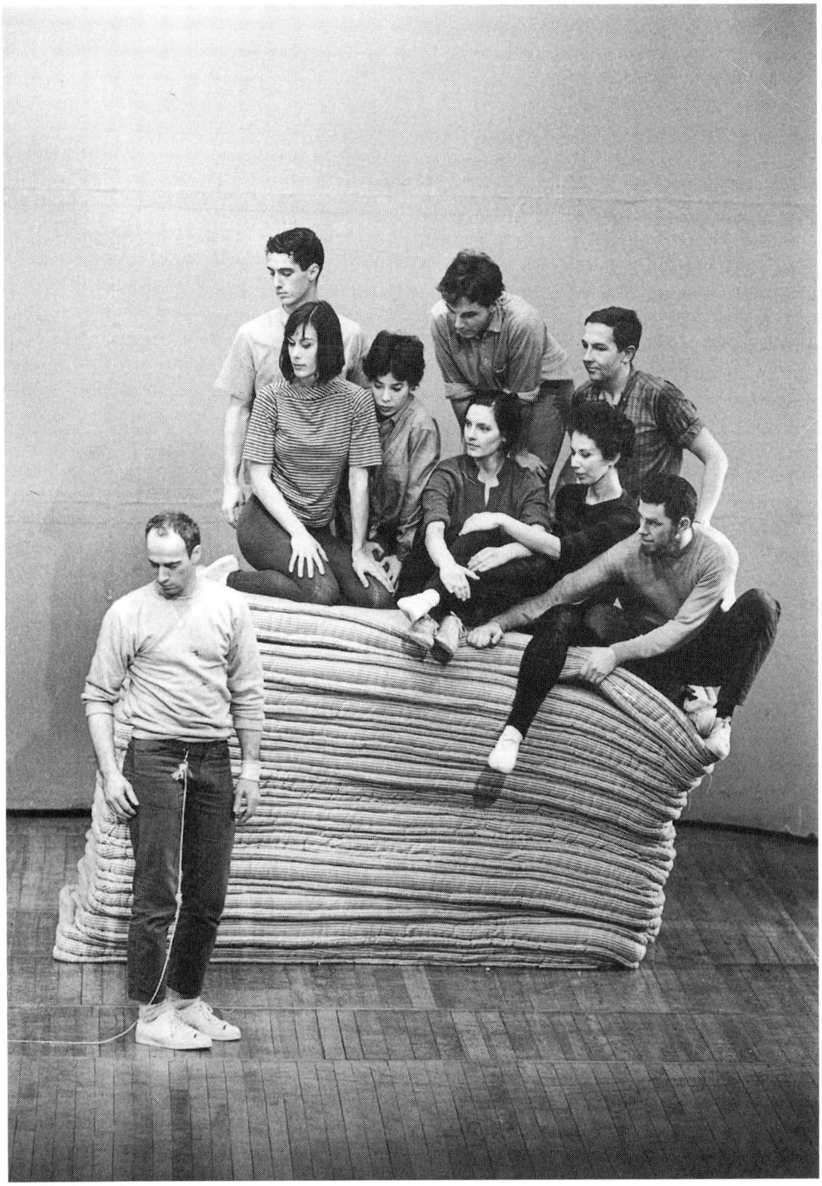

Yvonne Rainer, *Parts of Some Sextets,* 1965. Avery Theater, Wadsworth Atheneum, Hartford, Conn., 7 March 1965. Pictured: Robert Morris, Steve Paxton, Rainer, Deborah Hay, Tony Holder, Sally Gross, Judith Dunn, Rauschenberg, and Joseph Schlichter. Photograph by Peter Moore. © Estate of Peter Moore / VAGA, New York.

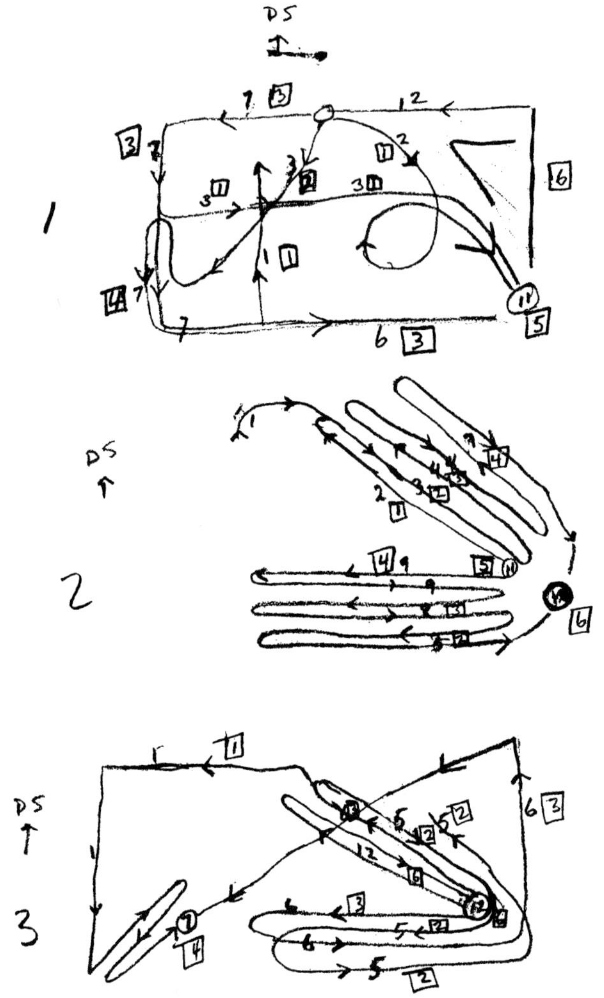

Yvonne Rainer, dance notes for *We Shall Run,* 1963, from *Notes and Drawings.* Pen and pencil on paper. 8 × 5 in., on a page 11 × 8½ in. Courtesy of the artist.

the dancers traversed the stage on the diagonals drawn from corner to corner, performing a series of ten traveling movements whose sequence was determined by a set of improvisational choices structured by rules as in a game. These movements ranged from the mundane ("Walk," "Run," "Crawl-straight legs"), to the idiosyncratic ("Straight-leg waddle—arms high doing small windmill"), to those appropriated from various sources (a "Triplet run" from dance class, and what Rainer called the "Movie death run" taken from the end of Godard's *Breathless*); all were interspersed with another "game" involving quotidian movements that was called "Passing and Jostling."[22] While not as concise or doctrinaire as some of Rainer's other, more minimalist, dance pieces, the montagelike opening sections of *Terrain* nonetheless eschewed or negated the illusionistic virtuosity of both traditional and modern dance; in its prologue, especially, it foregrounded the obdurate materiality of the dancer's body and a sort of degree zero of movement.

Rainer's position with regard to the traditional illusionism common to both ballet and modern dance was made clear, in an almost didactic fashion, in *Duet*, the second section of *Terrain*.[23] In it, Rainer and Trisha Brown performed in black stockings and lace push-up bras: Rainer executed an adagio she had learned in ballet class, Brown, a combination of ballet postures and raunchy burlesque dance motions. Then, as a not-so-subtle commentary on their respective movements, both dancers struck a series of still poses that recalled the conventions of pinup photography. Although it had been performed as an autonomous dance the previous February,[24] *Duet*'s full implications became clear only here, when it was juxtaposed with the previous section of *Terrain*. It left no doubt that Rainer's aesthetic classed such forms of traditional choreographed movement as part of the degraded and co-opted realm of commercial representation and spectacle.[25]

Rauschenberg would have found much to admire in *Terrain* and the many other examples of Rainer's choreography that he saw or in which he participated. His own performances displayed a similar interest in nonhierarchical composition, a certain found or quotidian movement, and an interaction with props akin to the task or tasklike performance practices of Rainer and others within the Judson set.[26] And yet at the same time, precisely because of their commonalities, Rauschenberg could hardly have failed to recognize Rainer's developing aesthetic of negation, what would soon become her profound and resonant minimalist "NO" ("NO to spectacle no to virtuosity no to transformations and magic and make-believe no to the glamour and transcendency of the star image no to the heroic no to the antiheroic . . . ").[27] Since his own artistic project had, for more than a decade, been engaged in problematizing such a direct form of aesthetic negation—instead positing difference on the unstable edge between a spectral, shifting negation and an affirmation of difference as a positive force—it is tempting to read Rauschenberg's *Pelican*, which premiered at the Pop Festival in Washington, D.C., a mere two weeks after *Terrain*'s debut, as a response to Judson's developing minimalist aesthetic. As opposed to Rainer's *Duet* (which had been performed earlier that evening) with its scathing critique of dance imagery and illusionism, Rauschenberg's *Pelican* incorporated his own and Uvelt's movements not to negate the balletic movements of Carolyn Brown but to articulate them within a new complex of performers and props and to multiply the "images" that they formed.

Although Rauschenberg's next two performances, *Shot Put* and *Elgin Tie* (both 1964), lacked *Pelican*'s subtlety and effectiveness, they continued to explore the interaction of performance and image production. In *Shot Put*, Rauschenberg danced in total darkness with a flashlight strapped to his ankle. Through a series of somewhat awkward movements—"Jerk rt leg up, open and close knee / Pull forward then do convulsive roll / Turning into *arabesque* position and *turning slowly*. . ."[28]—he left a trail of ephemeral traces in light, a sort of fleeting, abstract line-drawing. Though it recalled the more famous films and photographs that had captured Picasso's use of light to sketch such figures as a running man or a bull, Rauschenberg's performance eschewed any such pictorial aims, striving instead, it seems, for a more direct presentation of movement itself.[29]

In contrast, *Elgin Tie,* which Rauschenberg performed later that year at the Moderna Museet in Stockholm (following a reprise of *Shot Put*), apparently took a diametrically opposite approach, with a more explicitly imagistic or even iconographic intention. Reportedly inspired by the centaurs on the Elgin Marbles he had recently seen in London—"that fantastic combination of men and animals"—Rauschenberg originally hoped to create a similar hybrid image by dousing his body with flour while riding on the back of a cow.[30] But he quickly abandoned any such parodic or illustrational strategy; the performance of *Elgin Tie* was more closely related to the multiplicitous aesthetic of Rauschenberg's Combines than to any motif on the Parthenon frieze. Beginning by climbing through a hole in the roof and down a rope, and outfitted with various objects—a sandwich (which he ate), a plastic bag filled with water, a burlap sack, a ball of string (which he unraveled), and so on—Rauschenberg ended up in a metal barrel filled with water. After emerging from the barrel soaking wet, he stepped into a pair of sneakers that had been firmly affixed to the wooden cart on which he and the barrel stood; he then leaned forward and commenced to knot, unknot, and reknot a necktie drawn from his pocket. Ultimately, the cow's role was reduced to entering the performance area from one side and leading the cart with Rauschenberg and the barrel still on it out a doorway on the other. In its final version, *Elgin Tie* lost any iconographic resonance and was instead largely dominated by the Combine-like structure on and around which its activities took place. Although Rauschenberg included the movement of two living beings, the result was less performance art than a mobile, as the actions of both Rauschenberg and the cow failed to become more than what was, essentially, a moving sculpture.

•

Leaving behind the strict relationship to the aesthetic of his Combines seen in *Elgin Tie,* the theater events that Rauschenberg would stage over the next two years—*Spring Training, Map Room I, Map Room II,* and *Linoleum*—more successfully brought together performers and props in various, loosely assembled, overlapping segments that resolved into intersecting, but nonetheless isolable, moving images. These heterogeneous amalgams of beings and materials eschewed both the subject-object separation characteristic of the performer's traditional relationship to decor (and maintained to a large extent even in the performer-prop interactions of Judson's minimalist choreographers) and the metaphorical fusion with or cloaking of the subject accomplished by traditional costuming.[31] Refusing any such metaphorical displacement or transformation, Rauschenberg's images are created from the physical confrontation of their component parts. In *Map Room II,* for instance, Alex Hay, Steve Paxton, and Trisha Brown do not act like, or move like, wheels or automobiles: they undertake and react to the task of moving with tires. Deborah Hay does not look like, or perform like, a dove, but moves in physical combination with the doves in the cage about her midsection. "In each case," Rauschenberg explained of Hay's living dovecote in *Map Room II* and the human chicken-coop device performed by Paxton in *Linoleum,* "I wanted the actual object of the bird, rather than just bird-like activity. I liked the combination of two independent elements being forced to operate as a single image."[32]

Far from being occasional, such combinations of performers and props actually served as Rauschenberg's primary means of organizing and choreographing theater events. As Nancy Spector notes in the Guggenheim's retrospective catalogue, Rauschenberg's performance "scores" consist almost entirely of lists of components to be joined together. Consider, for instance, his notes for *Map Room II,* which clearly mark out each of the images to which he would refer:

in front:	tuxs + words + masks + stools
open [curtain]	
Mt Rush:	slide + proj + noxon + mirror + *Bob*
Birds:	*Deb* + 3 doves + cage + dress + pack belt
trisha solo:	*Trisha* + tire
duet tire:	*Alex* + *Steve* + 4 tires springs + contacts + wollensak on

trish roll thru:	*trisha* + tire
Steve big tire roll:	*steve* + 2 big tires springs + contacts + wollensak off
Steve 1 tire:	*Steve* + tire + *Alex* + 4 tires *Deb* + couch
	light on
alex 1 tire:	*alex* + tire
neon:	Bob + shoes + 2 tubes + buzzzz[33]

But despite the impression left by such notations, Rauschenberg's performance images do not derive from an act of addition; their components do not simply coalesce to form a new totality. While he was interested in attaining a certain amount of cohesion among the separate parts that make up each image—"so that integration would happen as easily as possible—so that there would be as little separation as possible"—their differences were never to be fully subordinated within a new whole.[34] Rather, Rauschenberg was interested, as he put it, in "a kind of combined coexistence to make a single image."[35] Inverting, in a sense, the operation of the silkscreen paintings, where an unstable split haunts the work of art even when the viewer confronts a single canvas, Rauschenberg's hybrid performance images bring together two or more components without extinguishing the fault line of difference that runs between them. "It's like adding two and two," Rauschenberg explained at the time, "and not getting four *or* five."[36]

The components within Rauschenberg's performances are added, not as numbers or objects, but as vectors: their combination represents two or more forces that come together to produce a force with a different magnitude and direction. The performer who comes into contact with a prop encounters it not simply as an inert object but as a conduit or repository of forces that react against or upon those exerted by the performer. In *Map Room II,* Steve Paxton and Alex Hay, attempting to perform a certain motion—walking "in a more or less normal fashion"[37]—find their movements diverted by the tires. Film of the performance reveals the men and the tires in a sort of struggle; the men grapple with the forms of the tires and the tires exert forces that alter the movements of the performers, deflecting them from their path and causing them to move in a different manner, at a different speed, or in a different direction. At times, Paxton and Hay gain command and dominate the tires: "moving," as Rauschenberg put it, "with the attitude that feet had the ability to roll,"[38] they cause their unwieldy accoutrements to do what they want for a step or two or three. At other moments the forces exerted by the tires overpower the performers, as the tires stop, fall over, or roll too far forward or back. Everything at this point in the performance happens slowly, on a small, almost microscopic scale; the scene reveals itself as a painstaking examination of the interaction of forces and forms.

The other images in *Map Room II* are likewise produced out of such performer-prop interactions. In the case of Trisha Brown's crouching movement within one of the tires, her actions are not so much opposed as they are governed by the particular capacities, propensities, or resistances of the tire's form. "Her method of moving was actually determined by her position" within the tire, Rauschenberg would maintain, controlling "how you can move and what sorts of things you can do."[39] Here, the differential between active and reactive forces is not the same as in the case of Paxton and Hay; the forces exerted by the tire are relatively greater, with two results: not only are Brown's motions less normal or habitually human ones, but her own form is affected. "I have photographs of it," Rauschenberg told Kostelanetz, "and I find it hard to recognize as a human body."[40] In Deborah Hay's performance with the small brown settee, the interaction of performer and prop is less integral; Rauschenberg merely instructed her to "Move from position to position on the couch, always considering the couch as *part of your image.*"[41] Less directly exerting an influence on Hay's movements, the couch acts as a locale that exudes a certain

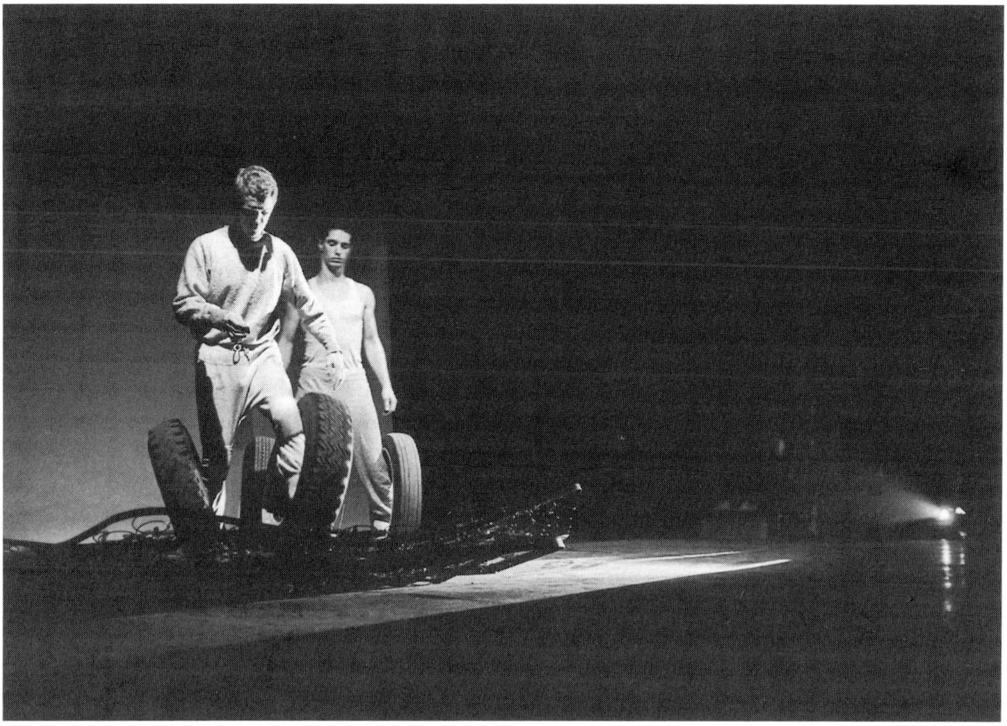

Map Room II, 1965. Expanded Cinema Festival, Film-Makers' Cinematheque, Forty-first Street Theater, New York, 2 December 1965. Pictured: Alex Hay and Steve Paxton. Photograph by Peter Moore. © Estate of Peter Moore / VAGA, New York.

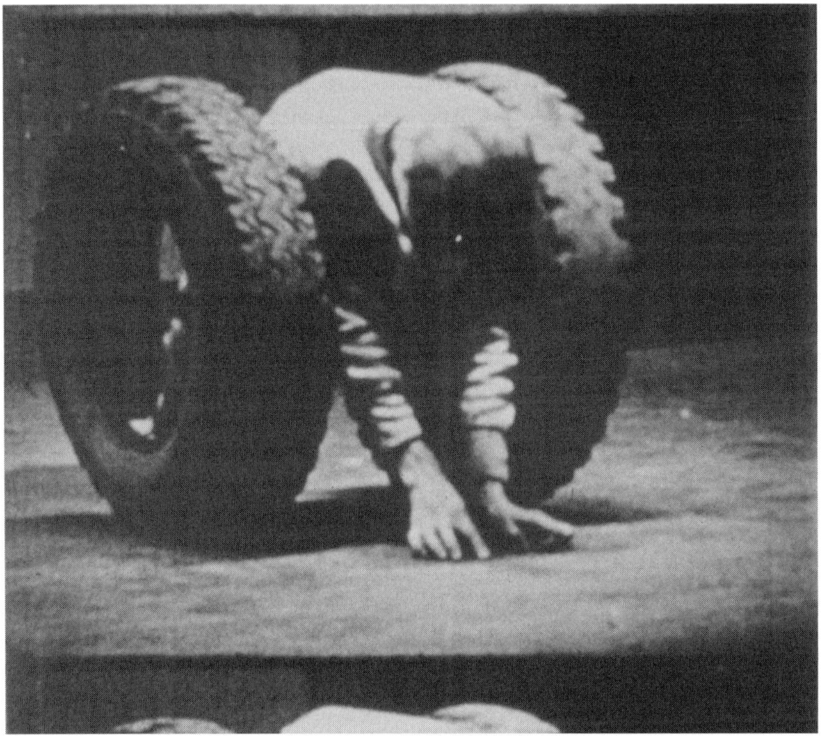

Map Room II, 1965. Film still. Pictured: Steve Paxton.

immaterial pull, bending or directing her activities toward it: "Never once did she just stand up and be a person standing on a couch." The result, once again, was a certain alteration of form: "The image," according to Rauschenberg, "wasn't couch and wasn't person."[42]

The forces and forms at play within Rauschenberg's performances are not limited to the physical: they can be auditory, as in the amplified sounds emitted by the bedsprings rolled over by Paxton and Hay; visual, as in the gradually revealed projection of Mount Rushmore or the cut-up travelogue; electric, as in the energy of the Tessler coil that runs through Rauschenberg's body and lights the neon tubes; or animate, as are the cows, doves, chickens, turtles, or other humans with which the performers interact. In each case, force is manifested as movement and transformation over time, the refusal to allow the forms to settle or resolve. The components within each performative amalgam interact in a mutual disarticulation and defamiliarization, bringing forth a multiplicity of unstable and continually transforming "images." As in the case of Trisha Brown, Steve Paxton, and Alex Hay in *Map Room II,* where the tires defamiliarize the movements of human bodies and they, in turn, defamiliarize the habitual functions and properties of the tires, the components of Rauschenberg's performance images continually exchange their determinations until they become virtually unrecognizable.

II. Although Marcel Duchamp was present at the performance of *Map Room II* at the Film-Makers' Cinematheque (attending in the company of Cage), no phase of Rauschenberg's work initially appears less connected to the elder dadaist's example than his activities in performance.[43] Rauschenberg himself seems to have sought a link between the two when he agreed to reprise Duchamp's role as Adam from Francis Picabia's *Cinésketch* in Elaine Sturtevant's *Relâche* of 1967.[44] A more convincing, if less direct, connection between Rauschenberg's performances and the work of Duchamp, however, is suggested by the idiosyncratic reception of the *Large Glass* proposed in the mid-1950s by the French critic Michel Carrouges, who saw in that work the formation of an important type of hybrid, dynamic "system of images."[45]

Focusing particularly on the unconsummated sexual act figured within Duchamp's *The Bride Stripped Bare by Her Bachelors, Even,* Carrouges came to characterize what he would call a "celibate" or "bachelor machine." Carrouges took the term from Duchamp's notes for the *Green Box,* in which the "machine célibataire" designated a segment of the lower mechanism of the *Large Glass* that the artist depicted very precisely in both elevation and plan. According to Carrouges, however, it was Duchamp's *Large Glass* in its entirety that formed the bachelor machine. Moreover, Duchamp's contraption was only one, if one of the most privileged, of a larger class of fantastic literary or artistic devices that included constructions by Franz Kafka—the disciplinary machine in *In the Penal Colony* and Gregor Samsa's room in *The Metamorphosis*—as well as various examples in the work of Raymond Roussel, Alfred Jarry, and Michel Leiris, among others.

For Carrouges, all such bachelor assemblages had a certain similarity of mechano-morphic operation. In the *Large Glass,* this aspect was signaled overtly through its concatenation of "draft pistons," "water mills," and "chocolate grinders," as well as the device that Duchamp had specifically called the "bachelor machine." However, as Carrouges made clear, these were only representations of the bachelor machine's functioning, and as such they were somewhat deceptive. He was at pains to point out that his idea was not essentially on the order of representation: not every mechanical appearance was necessarily a bachelor machine, nor did every such machine necessarily appear. In his words: "Unlike real machines and even the majority of imaginary but rational, useful machines like Jules Verne's *Nautilus* or the rockets of science fiction, the bachelor machine appears first of all as an impossible, useless, incomprehensible, delirious machine. It may even not appear at all, depending on how far it blends into the landscape around it."[46]

Not identifiable by appearance alone, a bachelor machine can be determined only by a certain functional isomorphism, "the presence of a series of exactly comparable gears, dependent in a parallel fashion on one another and through which a similar process takes place."[47] These gears reveal the second, determinate aspect of the bachelor machine: an internal bifurcation or opposi-

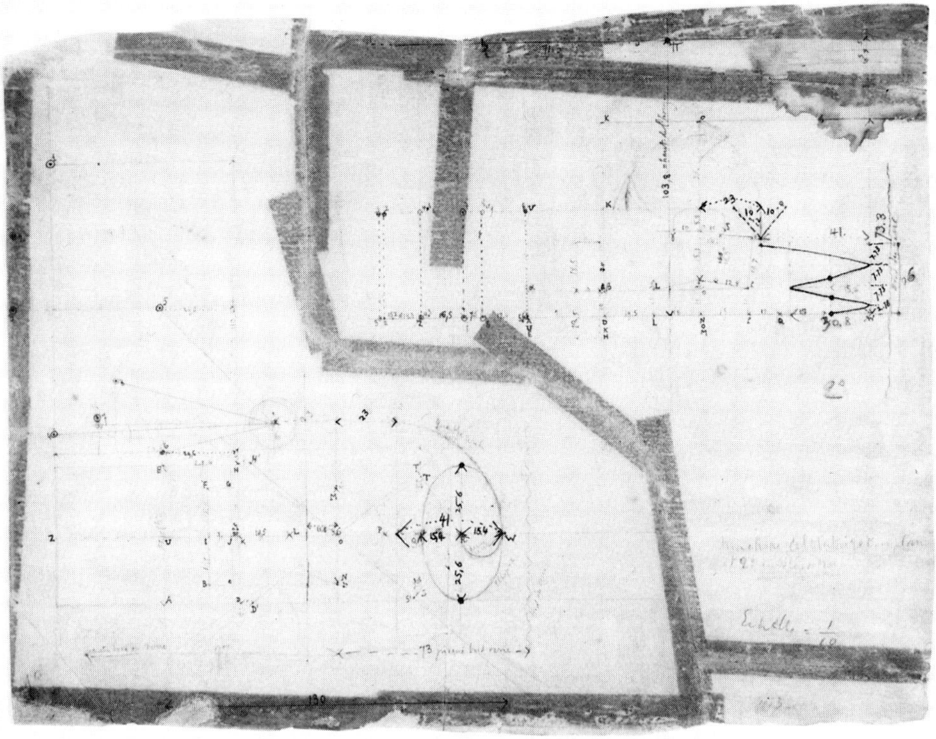

Marcel Duchamp, *Machine célibataire 1° en plan et 2° en élévation (Bachelor Apparatus, 1. Plan and 2. Elevation),* 1913. Red, purple, black, and blue ink and graphite with red crayon notations on paper, cut into 2 pieces and later rejoined. $10\frac{1}{2} \times 13\frac{7}{8}$ in. Philadelphia Museum of Art: Bequest of Alexina Duchamp. © 2003 Artists Rights Society (ARS), New York / ADAGP, Paris / Estate of Marcel Duchamp.

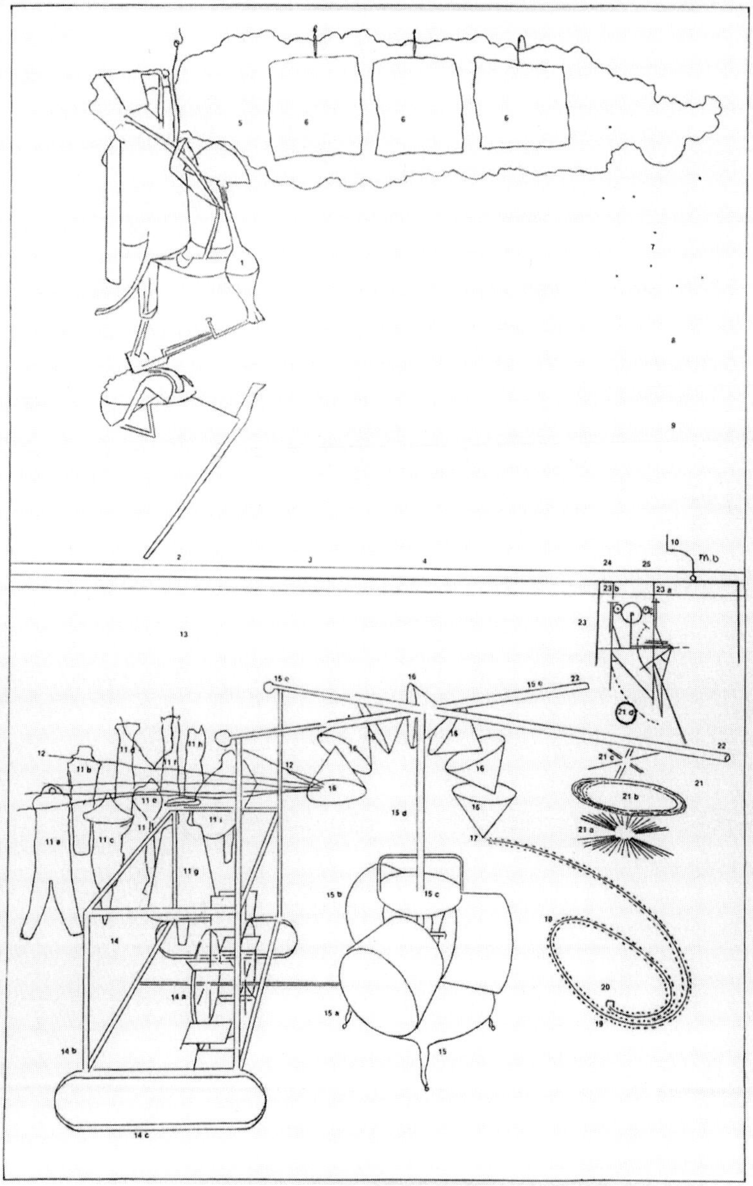

Marcel Duchamp, *The Large Glass Completed,* from *The Large Glass and Related Works,* published by Arturo Schwartz, 1968. Etching on handmade paper. Philadelphia Museum of Art. © 2003 Artists Rights Society (ARS), New York / ADAGP, Paris / Estate of Marcel Duchamp.

tion between forms, a construction in which the components of the machine are united without losing the element of difference that runs between them. Such an opposed yet intertwined relationship appears once again overtly in Duchamp's *Large Glass*—this time as a division between the sexes, reinforced by the vertical partitioning of the bachelors and the bride within different domains. Indeed, in one of the notes dedicated to the bachelor machine, Duchamp details the peculiar divided connection between them:

> The desire motor is the last part of the bachelor machine. Far from being in direct contact with the Bride, the desire motor is separated by an air cooler (or water).
>
> This cooler (graphically) to express the fact that the bride, instead of being merely an asensual icicle, warmly rejects (not chastely) the bachelors' brusque offer. This cooler will be in transparent glass. Several plates of glass one above the other.
>
> In spite of this cooler, there is no discontinuity [*solution de continuité*] between the bachelor machine and the Bride. But the connections will be *electrical* and will thus express the stripping: an alternating process.[48]

At another level, it is this crucial determinant of the bachelor machine, the opposition within the connection between its component parts, that, according to Carrouges, "expresses the bachelor machine's specific function, which is solitude and death." Once again, he finds this function conveyed overtly in the *Large Glass*, through the bride's appearance as what Duchamp referred to as a "skeleton" and the bachelors' inhabitation of what was termed "the cemetery of uniforms and liveries."[49] Yet this aspect of the *Large Glass* as a bachelor machine was also and more fundamentally embodied by the unconsummated erotic interaction figured therein, the reproductive failure of the jointly sexual and mechanical device that leaves the bride and bachelors without progeny, the "definitively unfinished" state of the *Large Glass* that fails to fulfill its initial animating narrative.[50]

In their mobile interrelation of different components (as gears or levers that exert forces on one another) and in their failure or refusal to meld into a totality (their continued internal bifurcation and opposition), Rauschenberg's performance images operate according to the strict functional tenets of Carrouges's celibate machines. The figure of death that signals the bachelor machine's "specific function" even arises at certain points within Rauschenberg's performances as well: in the eggs dropped from the rafters and smashed on the ground in *Spring Training,* for example; or, in *Linoleum,* in Steve Paxton's biting into fried chicken while part of an assemblage wheeling around six live hens. But like the figures in Duchamp's *Large Glass,* these are only reminders or signs of the function of which they are a part. The intimate relationship of the bachelor machine to death and nonreproduction—what Carrouges termed its conjunction of "Eros and Malthus"—begins to take on its full implications only within the perspective of a "general economy" as theorized at the same time by Georges Bataille.[51]

In *The Accursed Share,* Bataille explained that our habitual outlook is conditioned by the capitalist imperative to accumulate wealth by means of efficient production. A premium is therefore put on the economic and mechanical principles of energy conservation and mass productivity that allow for the greatest accumulation at the lowest cost, and any deviation from that norm is viewed only as an unfortunate and undesirable waste of resources. Entirely reversing such presuppositions, in his "general economy" Bataille predicated his analysis on a consideration of totality as infinite or absolute. From this perspective—which took in the whole of the natural and cultural worlds, including the realms of the sacred and the profane—it was clear to Bataille that there was always an energy surplus (powered ultimately by the sun) that constantly needed to be expended. Thus, he argued, consumption (as *consummation,* the destruction or waste of resources), not production, was the fundamental underlying problem of economics on a universal scale, as was witnessed periodically in moments of vast, unproductive expenditure of resources and energy without reserve. His example, famously, was the potlatch of the Native Americans on the coast of the Pacific Northwest—a ritual by which each leader tried to top the other

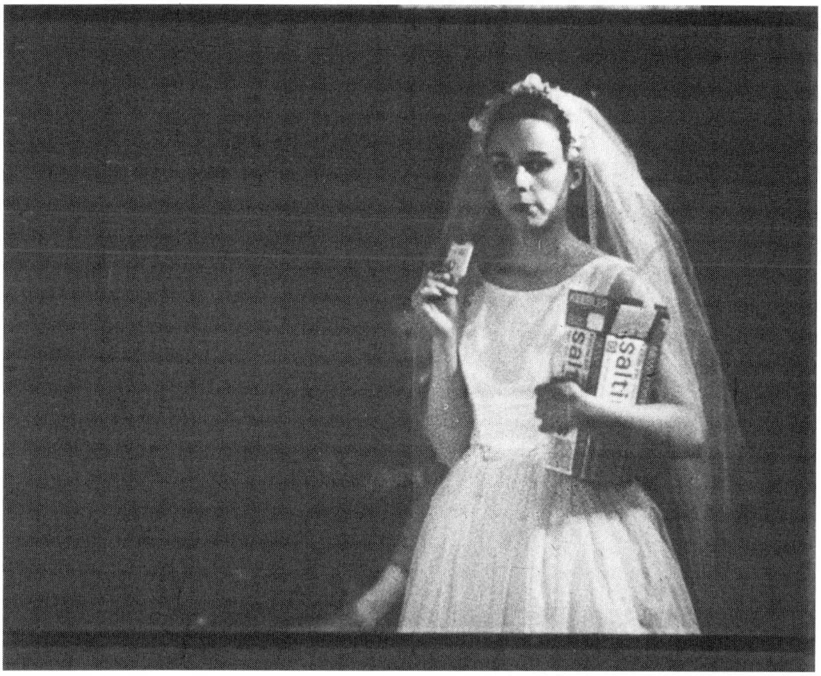

Spring Training, 1965. Film still. Pictured: Barbara (Dilley) Lloyd.

through spectacular displays of the destruction of wealth.[52] Incomprehensible and literally meaningless from the limited viewpoint of a restricted economy, such incidents of a-signifying waste were actually the moments at which a restricted everyday existence opened up to its beyond.[53] Thus, the analysis in Bataille's "book of political economy"[54] went far beyond the realm of purely financial or monetary transactions. From the perspective set forth in his general economy, the habitual subordination of cause to effect, resource to production, present expenditure to future accumulation, and expression to a priori meaning and interpretation all give way to a sovereignty of existence that would no longer be ruled by calculated ends.[55]

Carrouges drew explicitly on Bataille and saw the bachelor machine's refusal or inability to engage in sexual reproduction, its celibate function, as being at one with a contestation of the rule of efficient production. Resolutely opposed to the restricted industrial regulations of utility, energy efficiency, and exchange, the bachelor machine is a device that operates only by breaking down; it manifests itself most explicitly in its propensity for a form of mechanical failure that is at the same time a spectacular (in the sense of extravagant) self-consumption.[56] The bachelor machine is thus an antiproductive and antireproductive device—or, rather, it is a mechanism that produces only a form of nonreproduction, a moment of nonidentity beyond the mechanical production of the self-same and a momentary opening up of the restricted economy to its beyond. "The eruption of death" in the bachelor machine, writes Carrouges, "far from being terminal, affirms itself as the entry into inaccessible domains."[57] Thus, while from a teleological point of view—of mechanical production, sexual reproduction, or thematic or iconographic meaning—the bachelor machine must be judged a failure, it enters into another realm, one of extravagant waste or destruction, polymorphous sexuality, and semiotic excess. From this standpoint, the bachelor machine is an immensely productive device, a creator of disorderly signifying dissemination.[58]

Rauschenberg's performance images are like Carrouges's bachelor machines in that they too operate only by breaking down. The level of concern here is not that of the performers' actions (though a failure to accomplish their requisite tasks can always occur).[59] Rather, the breakdown in Rauschenberg's theater events occurs in the register of a recognizable semiotics or semantics. Although Rauschenberg's performances create and convey a plethora of images, they nonetheless fail to signify clearly or efficiently. Multitudes of images appear and call for interpretation without producing readily legible and comprehensible signs, overwhelming and thereby jamming the efficient functioning of the interpretive mechanism. To the degree that they solicit and call forth the attention of the spectators, the performance images signify; but because the movements of the performers and props mutually disarticulate one another, these "signs" fail to achieve the stability by which they can enter into the normal interpretive hermeneutic, the exchange from signifier to signifier or signifier to signified. Such failure is clear not only from the almost total nonexistence of interpretive critical literature on Rauschenberg's performances, but also from writers' consistent recourse to unstable linguistic hybrids to describe the works: Abeel's "Mesozoic apparitions," "hybrid monsters," and "composite torso-head-wing structures," for instance, or the "modern centaurs—half men, half autos" of Steve Paxton. Refusing to negate performative imagery, as done by Rainer's minimalist dance, and refusing as well any return to purportedly universal symbolism, such as that employed in the happenings of Allan Kaprow,[60] Rauschenberg's performances exhaust themselves in a virtual potlatch of signifying production, a vast semantic expenditure of imagery that is nonetheless useless within the confines of the restricted economy of recognition and interpretation.[61]

III. Although Rauschenberg had been familiar with the *Large Glass* since at least 1954,[62] he probably was not exposed to any such decoding of the Duchampian aesthetic until 1960, when he encountered Jean Tinguely's *Homage to New York,* the large mechanical assemblage that spectacularly self-destructed in the garden of the Museum of Modern Art on 17 March of that year. Upon their initial meeting, Tinguely invited Rauschenberg to contribute a component to his *Homage to New York,* and Rauschenberg produced what he referred to as the work's "mascot," a small electrical device titled *Money Thrower.* When

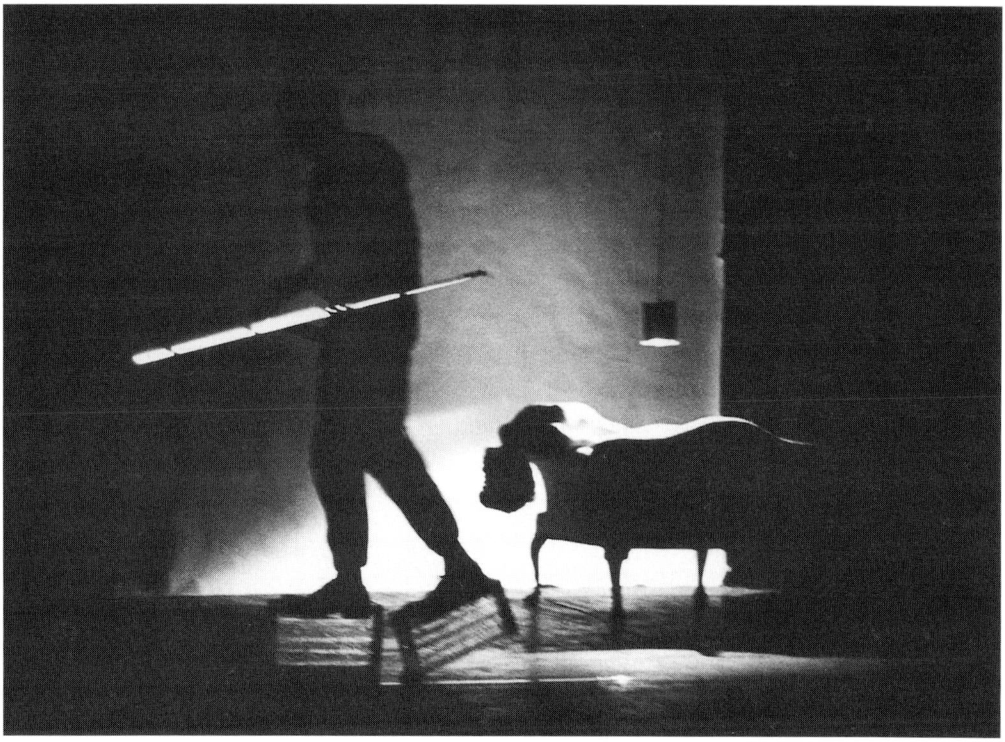

Map Room II, 1965. Expanded Cinema Festival, Film-Makers' Cinematheque, Forty-first Street Theater, New York, 17 December 1965. Pictured: Rauschenberg and Deborah Hay. Photograph by Peter Moore. © Estate of Peter Moore / VAGA, New York.

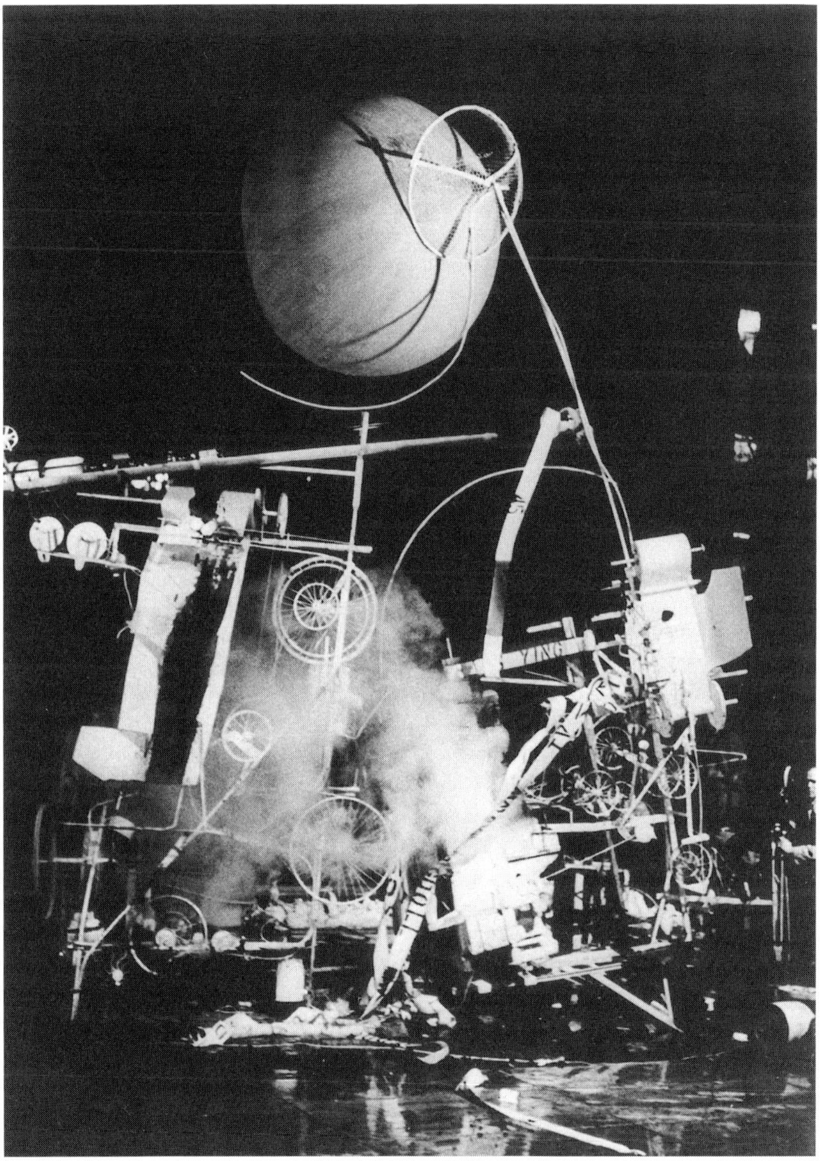

Jean Tinguely, *Homage to New York,* 1960. The Museum of Modern Art Sculpture Garden, New York, 17 March 1960. Photograph © David Gahr.

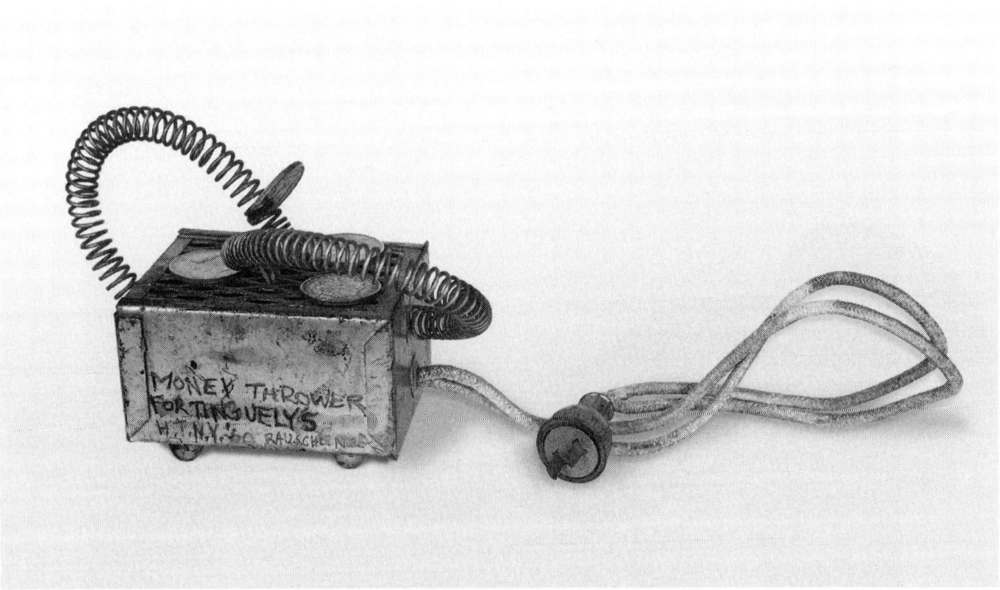

Money Thrower for Tinguely's H.T.N.Y., 1960. Electric heater with gun powder, metal springs, twine, and silver dollars. 6¾ × 22½ × 4 in. Collection of Pontus Hultén.

activated by Tinguely's machine, heater coils on the box ignited a small amount of gunpowder, releasing a spring and randomly catapulting a dozen silver dollars into the audience. Besides adding to the general chaos of the event, Rauschenberg's *Money Thrower* succinctly demonstrated his understanding of the stakes involved in Tinguely's bachelor machine: it was unconcerned with well-functioning, efficient production and sought instead to enact a wild, unproductive expenditure.

Rauschenberg's attraction to Tinguely and artists associated with him such as Niki de Saint Phalle was immediate. In 1961 he would dedicate one of his few "Trophy" Combines to Tinguely and soon after collaborated with the Swiss kinetic sculptor on several occasions, ranging from the performances of *Homage to David Tudor* (1961) and *The Construction of Boston* (1962) to the troubled exhibition *Dylaby,* or "Dynamic Labyrinth," at the Stedelijk Museum in Amsterdam (1962). More important, Rauschenberg's enthusiastic response to *Homage to New York* seems to have been the primary impetus behind his decade-long and increasingly elaborate interactions with technology. Indeed, it was through meeting Tinguely that Rauschenberg became acquainted with Billy Klüver, the Bell Labs engineer who had helped the Swiss artist gather and assemble the materials to construct his suicidal sculptural machine.[63]

Almost immediately, Rauschenberg began to collaborate with Klüver on what would eventually become the multipart, multisensory sculptural ensemble *Oracle* (1962–1965). Both a continuation and a transformation of the aesthetic forged in the Combines, *Oracle* consists of a heterogeneous array of appropriated, cast-off items, including a window frame, a car door, a washtub, metal ductwork, and various types of wheels. As was his usual practice when embarking on a substantially new series of production, Rauschenberg chose to work in a largely monochrome "palette," carefully stripping most of the paint from the acquired pieces.[64] While a concealed mechanical pump transformed one of the sculptures into a fountain that circulated water from a stove pipe into a trough, *Oracle*'s primary technological element (directly descended from the Combine painting *Broadcast* and the first idea for *Ace*) consisted of five remote-controlled radios that were secreted into all but one of its six sculptural

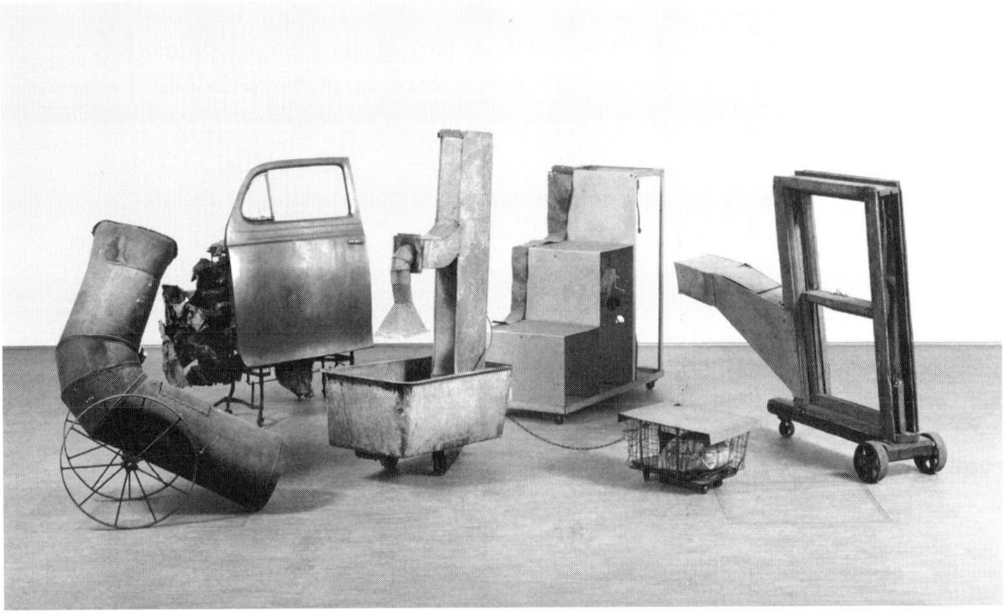

Oracle, 1962–1965. Five-part found metal assemblage with five concealed radios: ventilation duct; automobile door on typewriter table, with crushed metal; ventilation duct in washtub and water, with wire basket; constructed staircase control unit housing batteries and electronic components; and wood frame with ventilation duct. Installation dimensions variable. Musée National d'Art Moderne, Centre Georges Pompidou, Paris. Gift of São and Pierre Schlumberger.

components. Through the efforts of Klüver and his associates, these were made to scan the frequency spectrum at differing rates by the use of small, variable-speed motors that could be adjusted but, like the radios in *Broadcast,* not directly controlled by the audience's manipulation of dials fitted into the staircase-like unit of the work.[65]

As we have seen, Rauschenberg's Combines brought together images and words, visibilities and articulabilities, or what was seen and what was read, in such a manner that they produced a proliferating instability of signification; they thereby opened up—in the fleeting, temporally changing connections and juxtapositions between their elements—a third register that could be understood as the continuous multiplicity or plane of organization of that changeability itself, an "outside" that was on the order of a force of differentiation, instability, and change (see chapter 3). In *Oracle,* Rauschenberg attempted to expand the relatively limited role played within such an operation by the "transparent" openings or moving devices by which literal change was incorporated into the Combines. "I think that one of my chief struggles now," he declared to Kostelanetz, "is to make something that can be as changeable and varied and alive as the audience. I don't want to do works where one has to impose liveliness or plastic flexibility or change but a work where change would be dealt with literally."[66] As it more directly presented difference, movement, and changeability, the active technological component in *Oracle* was not only integrally related to the movement found in Rauschenberg's performances but also harked back once again to the *White Paintings*' fleeting incorporation of changes in light, shadows, and particles of dust. He told Dorothy Seckler about *Oracle,* "I'd like for the sound to be as fresh as the daily fall of dust and rust that accumulates—that doesn't mean that from time to time one doesn't clean it off."[67]

◆

In *Oracle*'s predecessor, *Broadcast,* Rauschenberg had ultimately "objected to the fact that one had to be standing so close to the picture that the sound didn't seem to be using the space the way the images were reacting to each other."[68] Yet even though *Oracle* produced a more active and encompassing audiovisual experience, one through which the visitor could literally pass, its realization paled in comparison with Rauschenberg's original plans for the incorporation of technology. During his initial discussion with Klüver about potential collaborations, Rauschenberg inquired into the viability of creating a fully enveloping, reactive, and multisensory technological apparatus. "He asked me," Klüver recalled, "if it was possible to make an interactive environment where the temperature, sound, smell, lights, etc., could be affected by the person who moved through it."[69]

Rauschenberg would not relinquish this idea for nearly a decade, and each of his major technological projects of the 1960s initially began as an attempt to realize it. Talking to Seckler in December 1965, after he had finished *Oracle* (and during the time he was forming a conception of "9 Evenings: Theatre and Engineering"), Rauschenberg reiterated and expanded on this goal:

> I have been thinking about a group of independent sculptural units that will form a single unit when combined. They will be sensitive to the proximity of the spectator—responding even to his body temperature—and they will be so delicately controlled by circumstance that two people viewing these forms will see something different from what is seen by either a crowd or one person. They will be responsive also to forces outside the jurisdiction of the viewer—to weather and passing traffic. Viewing of the work will not be completely dependent on seeing and the attention and desires of the viewer will be modified by circumstance.[70]

In October 1967, after having exhibited the *Revolvers* (1967) and as he was beginning his work on *Soundings* (1968), Rauschenberg explained to a reporter from the *New York Times* that despite being unable yet to solve all the technical problems, he still conceived of an environment "that would be responsive to weather, to people viewing it, to traffic, noise and light."[71]

Closer to the end of the decade, when starting on what would ultimately become his last major technological work, *Mud Muse* (1968–1971), Rauschenberg extended his thinking even further to include the possibility of reacting to the spectators' moods, thoughts, and brain waves. Lewis Ellmore, one of the engineers from Teledyne Corporation who helped undertake the project, recalled:

> Fundamentally, Bob wanted to escape from the limitations of two dimensions and to couple the work, in a way yet to be defined to the observer.
>
> . . . We thought about the types and forms of energy, which could be sensed and used to activate and regulate the dynamics of the work. Again, everything from deliberate and direct observer control [of the environment] to purely random processes. We included sound, light, motion, odor, etc., etc. At one time we looked into actually being able to sense the mental state of the observer, but while theoretically possible, it seemed to be a bit advanced in terms of actually implementing it.
>
> We went on to explore ways of stimulating the observer, not only visually, but with both audible and non-audible sounds, pressure differentials and so on. Finally, we looked into means of selectively creating emotional responses in an observer and, in fact, of using these emotions to further modify the art.[72]

Beyond representing an overly optimistic projection of the capabilities of technology, Rauschenberg's vast, multimedia environment was largely a hypostatization of the force of change evident in the unstable imbrication of words and images in the Combines; in the manifold significatory instability created by *Broadcast*'s and *Oracle*'s multiple, overlapping radio broadcasts; and in the disarticulatory movements of performers and props within his theater pieces. In this case, however, Rauschenberg aimed not only at giving his work the effectiveness of an actual force but also at ensuring that it have a more direct impact on the spectator in order to modify his or her perceptual, and ultimately subjective, capacities. In discussions of the work with Frank LaHaye of Teledyne, this goal gave rise to the idea of spectators exiting an environment of imperceptible subsonic vibrations in a state of literal disorientation. ("It gets in harmony with the natural beat of the human body and can produce psychedelic effects," LaHaye explained of such vibration. "The idea didn't fly with either Teledyne or the museum. They didn't want to risk the consequences of people coming out of the tunnel stoned.")[73] Even the much more rudimentary technology incorporated into the earlier *Pantomime* (1961), a work consisting of two electric fans plugged into an outlet in the canvas, came to be similarly understood by Rauschenberg. Although it appeared to present a Jasper Johns–like parody of the abstract expressionist brushstroke—somewhat like Tinguely's "meta-matic" devices that mime the artist's anguished confrontation with the canvas—Rauschenberg described the piece in 1966 in terms of the perceptual change resulting from the forces exerted by the air currents:

> I thought of it as a kind of an air relief. Any physical situation is an influence on not only how you see if you look but also what you think when you see it. I just knew that if you were standing in a strong breeze, which was part of the painting, that something different would happen. If I did make a point, it is that even the air around you is an influence.[74]

Ultimately, the impetus behind all of Rauschenberg's work with technology was to produce a direct and palpable force that would change the spectators on a sub- or nonrepresentational level. Speaking once again with Kostelanetz, he elaborated on the effect he hoped his technological (and performance) pieces would produce by likening it to the force of law. To the question of whether he had "a moral objection . . . to those dimensions of life that force us to be more specialized than we should be," Rauschenberg replied,

> I do, because I think we have this capacity I'm talking about. You find, for example, that an extremely squeamish person can perform fantastic deeds because it is an emergency. If the laws have a positive

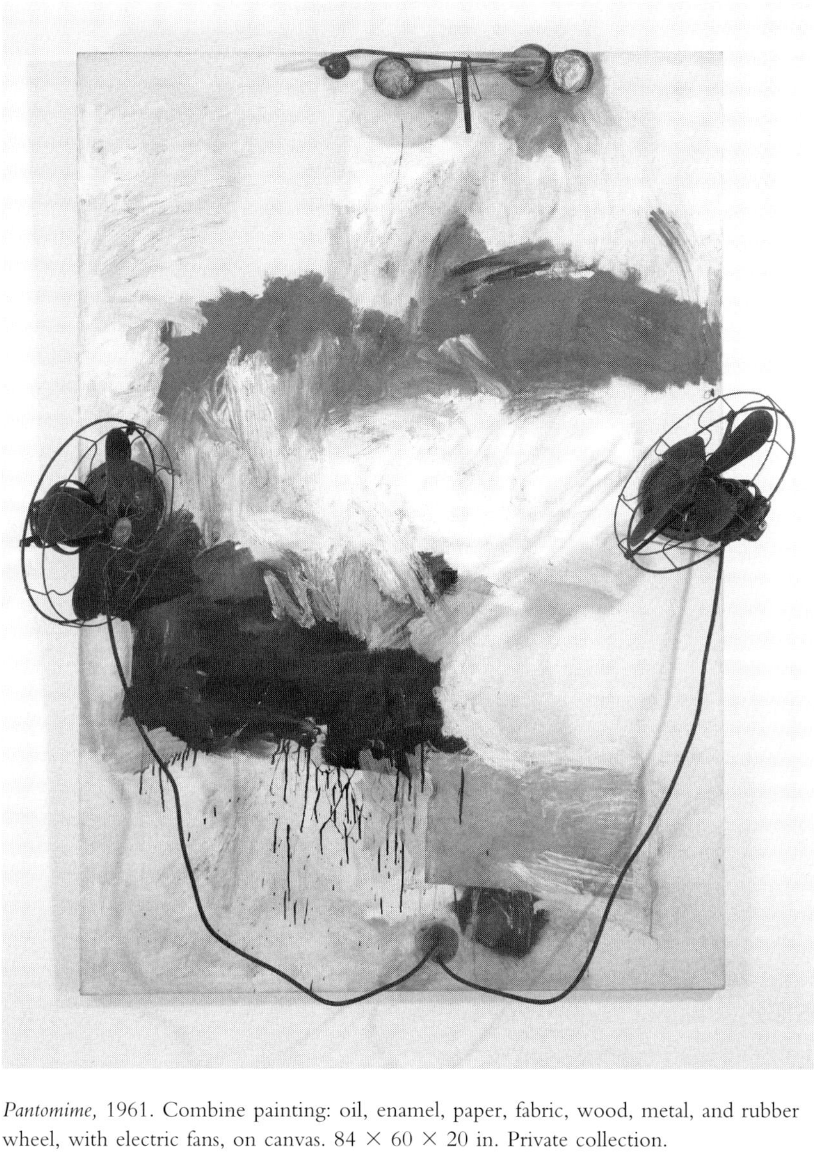

Pantomime, 1961. Combine painting: oil, enamel, paper, fabric, wood, metal, and rubber wheel, with electric fans, on canvas. 84 × 60 × 20 in. Private collection.

> function, if they could have, it might be just that—to force someone to behave in a way they have not behaved before, using the faculties he was actually born with. Growing up in a world where multiple distractions are the only constant, he would be able to cope with new situations.[75]

◆

Beyond functioning as the ideal behind nearly all of Rauschenberg's technological pursuits, this vast, dreamed-of-but-never-realized machine is significant because it served as a countermodel to the "mega-machine" of postwar society.[76] In discussing his interactions with technology—which to his mind remained neutral—Rauschenberg posited an opposition between the two poles of "industry" and "humanism."[77] The term "industry" as used by Rauschenberg was not confined to the assembly line or manufacturing plant; instead, it represented the whole of the social apparatus connecting people and technology to (1) *capitalism*—"The thrill of making another dollar has carried us so far out of our lives and any real sense of what technology is about and what it does mean to us"; (2) *enlightenment*—"We are so busy progressing that we have lost any realistic sense or even need for it [technology]"; and (3) *bureaucracy*—"it is about the middle-management guy who is afraid even though the boss has told him that we are doing this. . . . The research people immediately get interested . . . but the problem is the middle-man."[78] It was this industrial complex, according to Rauschenberg, that overwhelmingly dictated the terms on which most artistic collaborations were forced to proceed. "The temptation for industry is to take the artist in superficially as the artist is appearing to them," he explained. "If they can get just a little company color out of the collaboration, that is all they want really in most cases. They would do it rather than recognize this [broader] collaboration that Frank La Haye [*sic*] has talked about, where it is essential that humanities are considered in industry."[79]

Against this embeddedness of technology within the restricted economy of mass production and capitalist accumulation, Rauschenberg opposed a "humanism" predicated not on any static and universal conception of the subject but on his own ethos of self-transformation—his "morality," as he had put it, of not walking in his own footsteps (see chapter 3). As Rauschenberg commented to Kostelanetz, "Being a complex human organ, we are capable of many different things; we can do so much. The big fear is that we don't do enough with our senses, with our activities, with our areas of consideration; and these have got to get bigger year after year." Within everyday situations, Rauschenberg went on to elaborate, such self-transformation was far from the norm. Although he contended that subjective change could on rare occasions be brought about by encounters in daily life, the result was usually temporary; for once people were "out of these extraordinary situations, they reverted to the same kind of thinking as before."[80]

In this reversion to preestablished modes of thinking, Rauschenberg came up against the debilitating and ideological function of representation within the self-reinforcing mechanisms of the industrial mega-machine. Industries' propensity to treat the artist as he or she "is appearing to them"—that is, in a static, status quo representation—was only a more specific and benign aspect of the more general repressive functioning of spectacle. In the process of ensuring the reproduction of the materials necessary to continue current socioeconomic relations, the overall industrial apparatus went beyond manufacturing identical products to reproduce desired forms of consciousness within individuals themselves.[81] This reproduction occurred via the spectacular expropriation of the subject's lived experience into a fixed representation to which he or she henceforth conformed; subjective change was resisted, Rauschenberg lamented, because alienated individuals operate on a transcendent rather than immanent level, as though "it is somebody else's life that they're functioning in, instead of recognizing the fact that it is still just them and the things they are surrounded by."[82]

As we have seen in the previous chapter, beginning as early as 1961, Rauschenberg had connected such an expropriation of life within the image and deadening of thought within the idea (the reduction of art's role to "carrying out an idea rather than witnessing an unknown idea taking shape") to the realm of "commercial art."[83] The "understanding" that such conceptual knowledge afforded, and that led to "disposal" rather than confrontation, was, as he stated at the *Art of Assemblage* symposium, "an economical way to feel."[84] "When you just illustrate your feeling about something self-consciously—" he noted again in 1965, "that is for me almost a commercial attitude."[85] Apparently the acute sense of closure, or foreclosure, of representation that Rauschenberg found in "industry" had developed out of the ever-increasing pressures of television, illustrated magazines, and other forms of standardized spectacle; for Rauschenberg, these had become "a reality" that he increasingly felt his work had to address (see chapter 4). The result of such pressures, or so Rauschenberg feared, would ultimately be a universal leveling and conformity, an annulling of the differences in individual subjectivity. Thus, it would seem that Rauschenberg's concern for the future of humanity under "industry" has remained constant since the 1960s. As he explained recently:

> We're going to end up with a generic world. Where everybody is going to be exactly the same. It doesn't matter about changing colors or anything. Even Africa is becoming like that. . . . I'm not going to live that long, but for me seeing everything leveled down to the same attitude is going to be the most depressing. I look forward to the differences. I need them, I respect them.[86]

At his most ambitious, Rauschenberg hoped technology would allow him to create a machine on the order of Tinguely's *Homage to New York* that would more explicitly integrate the spectators into its functioning, both as motors—their actions and reactions, in large part, setting the device into motion—and as products, for they would emerge in some sense transformed. Amplifying and indeterminately processing all the subrepresentational, individual, subjective, and environmental contingencies that are habitually screened out in the daily industrial routine—random thoughts or changes in mood, as well as such external factors as traffic and weather—Rauschenberg's work would provide a constantly changing, individualizing experience in which "no two people will ever see the same thing."[87] His aim was to create a disarticulatory type of (anti)feedback that could dissolve the limiting and self-reinforcing circuits of thought and behavior. The "public" that Rauschenberg found "predictable" would thereby be "educated to risk."[88]

Rauschenberg explicitly extended such considerations into the realm of sexuality in the *Carnal Clocks* (1969), which he undertook in reaction to the "boring and obvious" depictions of eroticism in the newly emerging realm of commercial pornography.[89] Apparently anomalous works within Rauschenberg's oeuvre, these partially reflective, silkscreened boxes depicting a variety of genitalia and other sexualized body parts derive from the same impulse as all his technological endeavors.[90] In them, pornographically explicit close-ups (of cocks, cunts, anuses, testicles, and male and female breasts, along with more metaphorically sexualized flowers, drainpipes, the eye of a buffalo, and other images) are sequentially made visible by a series of timed electric bulbs that circle the work's inside borders. The two rows of lights—one of which changes every two and a half minutes, the other every half hour—cause the assortment of disparate part objects to appear in all possible combinations: penis with vagina or anus, but also with hand, breast, flower, and so on. The result is a twenty-four-hour circuit that resembles nothing so much as the vertiginous "image system" of Bataille's similarly pornographic *Story of the Eye,* in which, as Roland Barthes described it, each in a metonymic series of terms (eye, egg, testicle, etc.) follows the other "without our ever being able to stop the chain."[91] A certain scopic desire thus becomes the force by which the viewer is induced to interact with Rauschenberg's machine. As he commented, with characteristic obscurity, about the *Carnal Clocks* in 1969, "Forces have to be felt and real, or absent."[92] Each *Carnal Clock* therefore works like the larger technological machine that Rauschenberg had dreamed of: the "desires of the viewer," who is reflected in the mirrored surface, are to be "modified," deterritorialized from their habitual trajectories and expanded into a more polymorphous series of interactions.[93]

IV. In his synthetic historical discussion "Periodizing the 60s," Fredric Jameson posited as one of the defining characteristics of the decade the incipient looming up of the "Institution" in the popular and resistant social consciousness.

Driven largely by "the tremendous expansion of the media apparatus and the culture of consumerism" that came together in spectacle, there arose, according to Jameson,

> the discovery, within a hitherto antagonistic and "transparent" political praxis, of the opacity of the Institution itself as the radically transindividual, with its own inner dynamic and laws, which are not those of individual human action or intention, something which Sartre theorized in the *Critique* as the "practico-inert," and which will take the definitive form, in competing "structuralism," of "structure" or "synchronic system," a realm of impersonal logic in terms of which human consciousness is itself little more than an "effect of structure."[94]

The artists associated with minimalism reacted to this discovery (understood not solely through the ahistorical lens of structuralism but also through the Marxist dialectics of Herbert Marcuse)[95] initially by taking up an oppositional practice of negating all those artistic conventions that had seemingly been coopted—whether of painting, sculpture, dance, or music—and eventually, as Hal Foster and others have shown, by confronting and testing the institutional limits and frameworks of the arts, their "discursive rules and institutional regulations."[96] This was very much the trajectory followed, for instance, by Yvonne Rainer. From the staunchly oppositional "NO" presented by her early minimalist dances, beginning perhaps with *Terrain,* she moved through a more properly minimal or object-oriented practice—as in *Parts of Some Sextets,* in which she "created 'theater-objects' that don't 'look back' at the audience (therefore making 'excessive' demands on them)."[97] By the end of the decade, she had evolved an explicit testing of institutional boundaries, most notably in works such as *Performance Demonstration* (1968) that questioned the separation of instruction from performance in a public meditation on artistic process.[98]

Arising at precisely the same historical moment, Rauschenberg's engagement with "industry" was undoubtedly produced by his similar recognition of the opacity caused by late-capitalist expansion. Yet as he sought to forge a certain type of resistance to the demonic totalization of the sphere of representation attendant on "industry" or spectacle, his guide would be neither structuralism nor Marcuse but the decidedly more anarchistic example of Antonin Artaud.

◆

Artaud stood behind not only Rauschenberg's theater events but nearly the whole of the postwar development of artistic performance. Indeed, the impact of the dissident surrealist playwright on those active in the 1950s and '60s was so great that his work should be counted as one of the central neo-avant-garde artistic recoveries of the time.[99] Of all the voices of the historical avant-garde that called for the destruction of art and the exaltation of life, Artaud's was one of the most uncompromising, his vehemence making it easy for some to dismiss his legacy as mere unbridled, anarchistic destruction. In reality, however, the specific form of art that Artaud decried—what he considered a false, European view of art and of the theater—was limited to mere "artistic dallying with forms": a symbolic understanding of art in which it was subservient to, and illustrative of, some a priori artistic intention or text.[100]

Art, in this sense, was for Artaud only one particular moment within representation's larger expropriation of life, which he referred to as "the second phase of Creation, that of difficulty and the Double."[101] Within this phase, which to his mind encompassed the whole of Western civilization and metaphysics itself, life too, in its readily observable, everyday appearance, was assimilated to and contemplated as mere form. This idea of life as form was precisely *not* what Artaud exalted above all else: "Furthermore, when we speak the word 'life,'" he declared in the preface to *The Theater and Its Double,* "it must be understood we are not referring to life as we know it from its surface of fact, but to that fragile, fluctuating center which forms never reach" (p. 13).

Thus life as it habitually appeared—a false, European view of life—was already one with the false, European form of art that Artaud so passionately deplored. "True" life, as the statement above makes clear, was that which did not and could not appear within the realm of the Double, that which eluded representational form. This life, as the "fluctuating center" beyond representation, the "underlying menace of a chaos" sensed beyond the confines of intellectual ideas and artistic forms (p. 51), was on the side of *force;* it was, according to Artaud, the unique affliction of Occidental civilization to have traded the one for the other, traded force for form, in its ideas of both life and of art. "If our life lacks brimstone, i.e., a constant magic, it is because we chose to observe our acts and lose ourselves in considerations of their imagined form instead of being impelled by their force," wrote Artaud: "True culture operates by exaltation and force, while the European ideal of art attempts to cast the mind into an attitude distinct from force but addicted to exaltation. It is a lazy, unserviceable notion which engenders an imminent death" (pp. 8, 10).

Found within Artaud is a vision of totality as a constraint and of representation as a fraud or stealing away of the true existence of life (force) by its duplication; in that duplication, movement, energy, time, change, growth, becoming, and all other ineffable characteristics of existence are fixed, congealed, and covered over by what Bataille called the "frock coat" of representational form.[102] Totality is a theater, and theater is already totality: in its classical form, it performs the duplicity and replication of all aspects of life in their subservience to representation, in the dissimulation of the unrepresentability of the living present.[103]

Although no aspect of this expropriated world of form escaped his attack, Artaud was most vehement in his denunciation of language. Language—written language foremost, but also speech or action subservient to it—was little more than the stultification of thought. "It must be admitted," he contended,

> even from the Occidental point of view that speech becomes ossified and that words, all words, are frozen and cramped in their meanings, in a restricted schematic terminology. . . . Everything concerning the particular enunciation of the word and the vibration it can set up escapes them, and consequently, everything that it is capable of adding to the thought. A word thus understood has little

> more than a discursive, i.e., elucidative, value. And it is not an exaggeration to say that in view of its very definite and limited terminology the word is used only to sidestep thought; it encircles it, but terminates it; it is only a conclusion. (pp. 117–118)

"The Occidental theater," he insisted, "employs speech not as an active force springing out of the destruction of appearances in order to reach the mind itself, but on the contrary as a completed stage of thought which is lost at the moment of its own exteriorization" (p. 70). Thought, therefore, if it is to be a truly living thought—"the power," as Artaud put it, "not to define thoughts but *to cause thinking*" (p. 69)—cannot satisfy itself with merely recognizing and reproducing linguistic definitions or, what amounts to the same thing, surface forms. It needs, rather, like life, to attain the mobility of a force. Otherwise, as Artaud lamented, we are no longer thinking beings but must be content to "remain mere recording organisms" (p. 13).

Despite Artaud's ceaseless affirmation of "life," the theatrical and artistic revolution that he proposes, while total, does not amount to a call for pure presence, the utter collapse of art and life, or the simple exaltation of life over art. Artaud's "Theater of Cruelty" is not so much willfully anarchic as it is, as Derrida has persuasively argued, properly deconstructive.[104] For Artaud, perhaps lamentably, the world of form and representation is not simply to be wished away or avoided in favor of a supposedly pure energetics of force; rather, it is to be shaken or displaced so as to reveal—as a negative, as an incorporeal "shadow"—the force that is concealed by it. "But the true theater," he argued,

> because it moves and makes use of living instruments, continues to stir up shadows where life has never ceased to grope its way. The actor does not make the same gestures twice, but he makes gestures, he moves; and although he brutalizes forms, nevertheless behind them and through their destruction he rejoins that which outlives forms and produces their continuation. (p. 12)

Artaud proposes the deployment of gesture, movement, vocalization, mise-en-scène—anything that does not reduce itself to language, imitation, or the illustration of a priori symbols or intentions—not to escape form but to deform and "brutalize" it. It is thus from a vantage point not *beyond* but irredeemably *within* the system of representation that Artaud's affirmation of life as a force escaping or existing beyond it takes on a value: a value not of mystification or the harmless formulations of magic, but of a certain type of nondialectical negation. Within a world everywhere subsumed by the Double, by the negation of life, such an affirmation functions as an anti-Hegelian negation of that negation, the revelation of the shadow or outside of the restricted totality that representation purports itself to be.

◆

Because Rauschenberg was present at Black Mountain College in the summer of 1952 when M. C. Richards translated and discussed *The Theater and Its Double,* he had been exposed to Artaud much earlier and much more thoroughly than most of his peers in the world of postwar performance.[105] During that time, the approach taken to Artaud's work by David Tudor and John Cage was particularly disciplined and precise, as they investigated the effectiveness of the nonhierarchical, indeterminate, and hence nonexpressive performative syntax that Artaud discussed.[106] It was, in part, in order to put these aspects of Artaud's work into practice that Cage organized an untitled performance that summer which came to be known as *Theater Piece #1* or the *Black Mountain College Event.* Widely regarded as the first postwar "happening," Cage's performance took place around and among the audience. Each participant engaged in an activity unrelated to the others, in a sequence of independent and overlapping time allotments: Tudor played Cage's *Water Music,* Merce Cunningham improvised a dance through the aisles, Nick Cernovich projected a series of slides, and Cage, Richards, and the poet Charles Olson all read from atop ladders situated throughout the audience. Rauschenberg, whose *White Paintings* were hung from the ceiling in formation, occupied his time by playing old records on a Victrola in the corner.[107]

Along with Bergson, and no doubt equally transmitted through Cage, Artaud would have been an important touchstone for Rauschenberg's aesthetic transformation during that time. No doubt, an Artaudian opposition of force and form played a significant role in Rauschenberg's long-standing emphasis on process over product—in, as Cage put it in 1961, his "regre[t] that we do not see the paint while it's dripping."[108] In Rauschenberg's statements of that time and later, wet paint, as matter in movement and still visible alteration, was (in the wake of Jackson Pollock) code for force. "And getting the room into the picture was important," he explained to Billy Klüver in 1963, "because I've always felt a little strange about the fixedness of a painting, like that after the paint has stopped running, and the canvas is dry, that the only changes are really very subtle and they are not perceptible unless you have known the picture before."[109] Other facets of Rauschenberg's work, such as his refusal to sketch his pieces beforehand (as doing so would render them illustrations of a priori ideas) and his continual seeking of various means to put off the death of the work, to keep the forces of change somehow in action after the work has been completed, can be understood from a perspective akin to (though partially inverting) Artaud's resistance to having his production spirited away from him by the realm of representational appropriation.[110]

Although undoubtedly present since the early 1950s, Rauschenberg's interest in and attraction to Artaud seems to have grown in direct proportion to his feeling of late-capitalist foreclosure within the spectacle's restricted economy. Not only was Rauschenberg's final theater piece, *Urban Round* (1967), his most explicit return to an Artaudian mise-en-scène,[111] but by the end of the decade he had come to be almost paraphrasing passages from Artaud. Regard, for instance, Rauschenberg's explanation of his aesthetic outlook to Suzi Gablik in 1968:

> When you do away with genius, you also do away with quality. At that point life became very immediate and personal. I would not describe success as the goal, or even making the best picture, but using your sensibility and the materials in your life (objects and

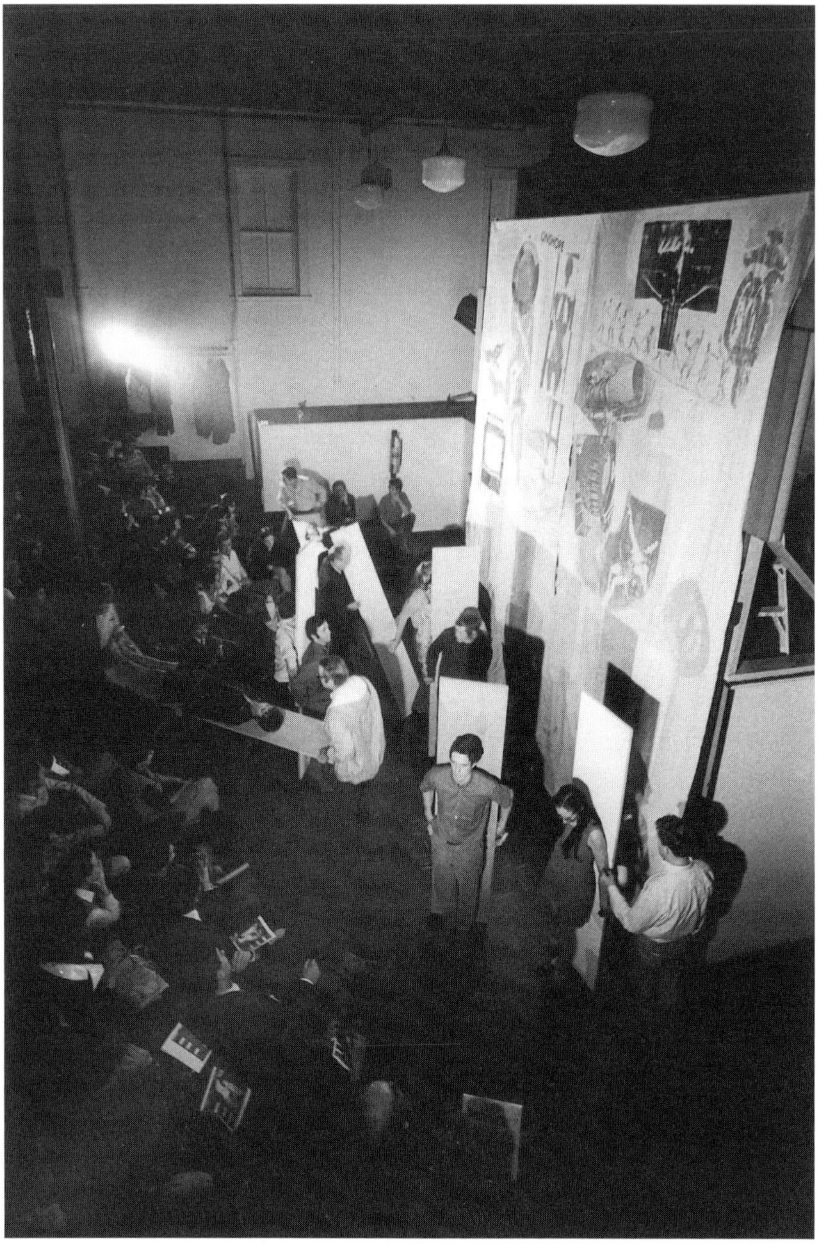

Urban Round, 1967. Fall Gallery Concerts, School of Visual Arts, New York, 19 November 1967. Photograph by Peter Moore. © Estate of Peter Moore / VAGA, New York.

> thoughts) as thoroughly as you can. I don't like saying it for two reasons: (1) defining this particular area tends to destroy it, or at least to damage it, and (2) language tends to be fixed, and what I'm describing is a mobility. I told a newspaper man the other day that I thought we were moving into an area now which had as its uniqueness that what a man thinks is less and less important than his way of moving from thought to thought. So that I think eventually we'll give up thoughts, and there will be a constant flow of concern. Thoughts then would only exist when you were faltering, or ineffective. By thoughts I mean particular ideas.[112]

This passage contains reminiscences of Artaud's positions on the fixity of language and the stultifying effect of definition, the immediacy of life (in opposition to success, teleology, genius, or quality), and the necessary mobility of a true thinking. Likening thinking and artistic production to one another, Rauschenberg describes both in terms of a *force* that surpasses in intensity and effort the "particular ideas" that are weak, ineffectual, and static *forms*.

Seen from within the "self-movement of the spectacle" as the negation of life, Rauschenberg's increasing emphasis on keeping the artwork alive—open to the living, temporal forces of change and thereby subverting appropriation within the dead realm of representation—is the strict analogue of Artaud's opposition to the deadening extinction of force in form.[113] Indeed, the realm of representation and "the Double" as described by Artaud would receive no better or more concise characterization than Rauschenberg's reference to the artwork's transformation into "a facsimile of itself":

> When someone close to you has been away it's only in about the first fifteen minutes that you're back together that you notice how he has changed from the idea you have of the way he looks. The same thing happens to a painting: when it becomes so familiar that one recognizes it without looking at it, the work has turned into a facsimile of itself. If you do work with known quantities—making

> puns or dealing symbolically with your material—you are shortening the life of the work. It is already leading someone else's life instead of its own.[114]

Later in the same interview, Rauschenberg continued to expand this highly Artaudian position, opposing the expropriation of the forces of a particular moment and their subsumption within a space "organized from the vantage of an absent [or autonomous] site, an illocality or invisible utopia"[115] beyond the spatiotemporal existent. Thus, as he went on to explain, "Consistently there has been an attempt to use the very last minute in my life and the particular location as a source of energy and inspiration rather than retiring into some other time or dream or idealism. I think that cultivated protest is just as dreamlike as idealism."[116] Rauschenberg, like Artaud, therefore called for a theater in which movement and image, force and form, had not yet been separated within the realm of representation. In that sense, Rauschenberg's performances were indeed like his Combine paintings and Combines, but only in their unfinished state: "You see," Rauschenberg explained to Kostelanetz, "there is really very little difference between the action of paint and the action of people, except that paint is a nuisance because it keeps drying and setting."[117]

And strictly like Artaud, Rauschenberg in his nonrepresentational theater did not simply oppose life to art or foresee the collapse of the two. The representational realm of signification was not to be avoided in the pursuit of any supposed or mystical immersion within force. It is enough to recall, once again, Rauschenberg's famous formulation about art and life. "Painting," he said, "relates to both art and life": it relates, that is, to both form and force, but in itself is neither fully one nor the other ("Neither can be made").[118] Rauschenberg's work—which acts "in the gap between the two"—thus operates at the limit of the realm of representation and that which is its shadow or other, the nonrepresentational diagram of forces, differences, and temporal movement.[119] *At the limit:* but Rauschenberg has the same understanding as Artaud that one could not simply move outside or exist simply within either realm. "You can't make it if you are outside art and you can't make it if you are in it."[120]

Rauschenberg's theater events perform the same type of deconstructive operation: art and life, forms and forces, objects and movements are revealed to be in a state of active, mutual disarticulation. If, as Rauschenberg maintained, there was in theater "no separation of life and work," he was in no way positing their simple identity but was referring instead to the continual brutalization of forms by forces, of props and performers by movement and disarticulatory interactions.[121] We thus see, in one sense, the significance of Rauschenberg's insistence that his performances formed "images": it is an acknowledgment, of sorts, that they could not avoid but rather continued to exist within the realm of representation—and perhaps even spectacle. Yet Rauschenberg's performance images were not identical to the spectacular images or photographs of them that remain, cut off from movement in space and time, mere facsimiles of the works themselves. Rauschenberg's performance images do not (as does the photograph that remains) refer to any prior image, whether physical or mental: they do not, in this sense, re-present. But his approach manifestly differs from the minimalist strategy of seeking to avoid as much as possible the production of images altogether, reducing art or performance to a degree zero by which spectacle could be avoided or annulled. Rather than relying on such an oppositional negation, Rauschenberg's critique of spectacle multiplies "images"—precipitating one against the other, confronting one against the other, one within the other—in an interpenetration of forces whose only value is in affirming the play outside meaning. Rauschenberg's strategy is not a reserve or withdrawal, not the "next to nothing" of a "blank form" sculpture or a neutral "theater object" erasing the traces of a co-opted culture, but a kind of potlatch of unstable, moving images that burns, consumes, and wastes images in the bachelor affirmation of death: not a negation, but a sacrifice and a challenge.[122]

V. It thus becomes clear that the vast, kinetic machine that Rauschenberg pursued for more than a decade was none other than the dream of a Combine in which the paint would never dry, a mechanical Theater of Cruelty that, as a veritable instantiation of the nonrepeating, nonreproductive force of change, would never confront the viewer in the same way twice. Compared to the potentials of the technological artwork that Rauschenberg envisioned but could never achieve—an all-encompassing environmental machine—all the pieces he actually produced during what he came to call his "'blowing fuses' period" seem like small parts or pale shadows.[123] The interactivity of a work such as *Dry Cell* (1963), for example—a tentative piece made up of a metal armature supporting a clear Plexiglas sheet silkscreened with the image of a military helicopter—is confined to the small, sound-activated motor that spins in reaction to stimuli from the spectator or the room. Although this was undoubtedly on the order of a "study," neither the later *Revolvers* nor *Soundings* represents much of an advance; both ultimately amounted to little more than animated silkscreen paintings controlled by push buttons or sound-activated switches. The larger *Solstice* (1968), which manages to envelop the viewer inside a passage of transparent sliding doors, also remains a disappointingly far cry from the synaesthetic technological environment that Rauschenberg had in mind. Even the *Carnal Clocks* ultimately confined their figuration of polymorphous desire to a two-dimensional, square surface area.

Although he did not consider them equal, Rauschenberg understood his performances of the period to be pursuing the same goals as the grand technological achievements he envisioned. Immediately after having expressed to Kostelanetz his desire to produce "a work where change would be dealt with literally," Rauschenberg confided that "It's very possible that my interest in theatre, which now is so consuming, may be the most primitive way of accomplishing this, and I may just be working already with what I would like to make."[124]

Rauschenberg's performances modeled the type of subject set forth by his vast technological machine. No more of a complete and unchangeable object than the props within his theater pieces, Rauschenberg's performing subject was also revealed as a set or multiplicity of forces capable of entering into various alternating and provisional assemblages with the other forces manifest around it.[125] Pushing beyond the limiting and self-reinforcing confines of the "ego" that obtains even within supposedly free improvisation, Rauschenberg's subject was to be in transformation, in continuous confrontation or collaboration with the objects and forces coming from the outside.[126] "I am mostly involved in

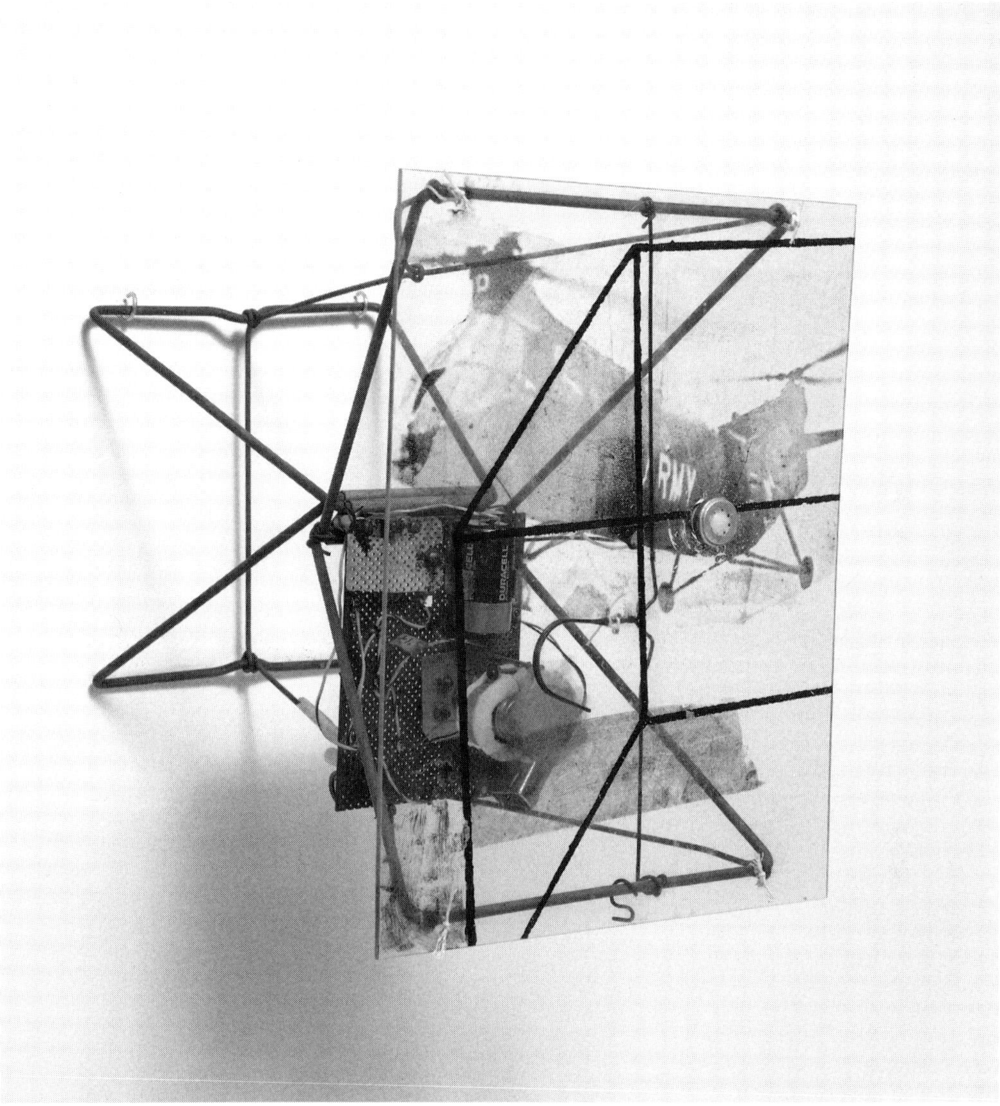

Dry Cell, 1963. Silkscreened ink and oil on Plexiglas, with metal coat hanger, wire, string, sound transmitter, circuit board, and battery-powered motor, on metal folding camp stool. 15 × 12 × 15⅜ in. Collection of the artist, New York.

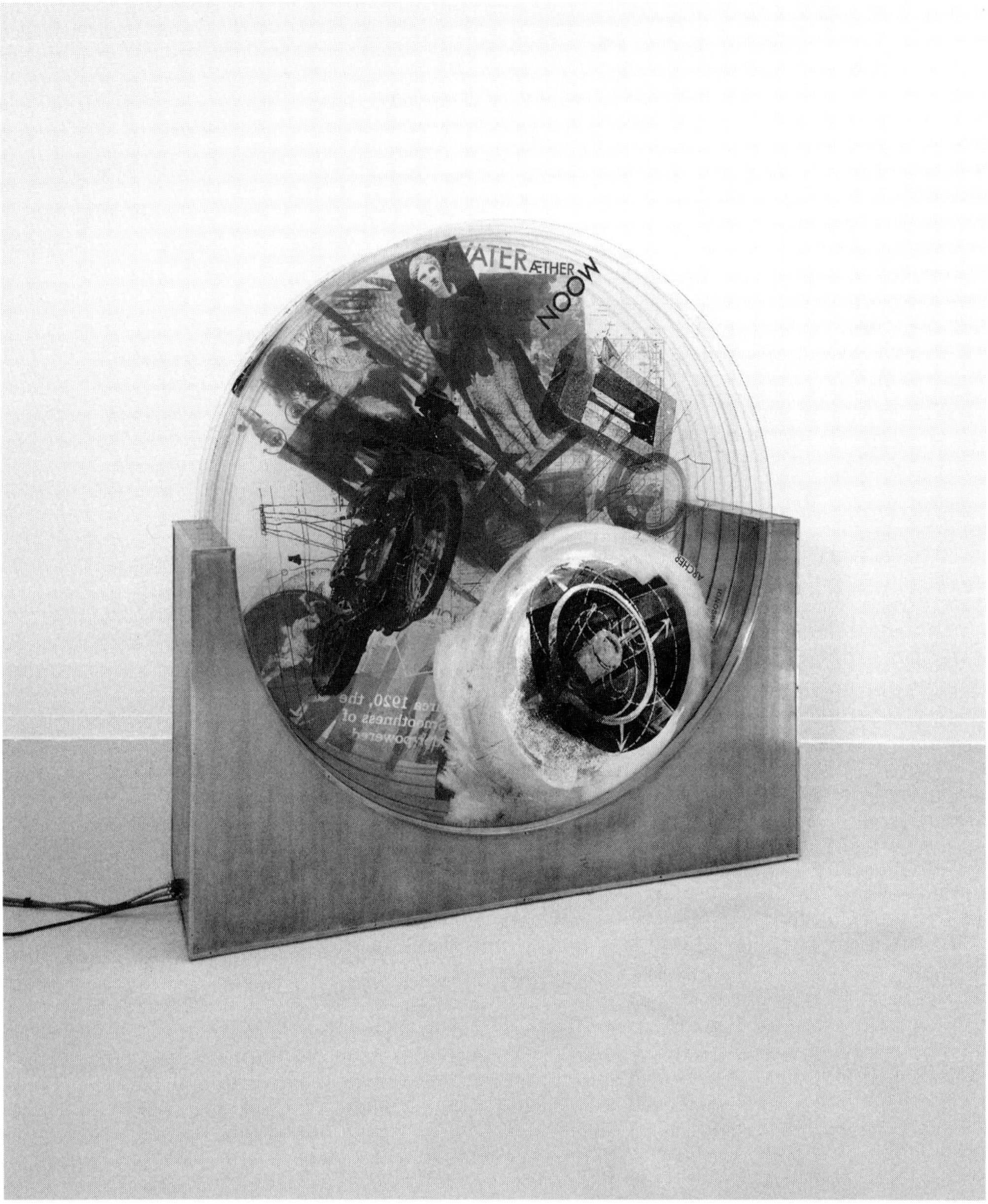

Revolver, 1967. Silkscreened ink on five rotating Plexiglas discs in metal base, with electric motors and control box. 78 × 79 × 24½ in. Collection of the artist, New York.

changing what I am doing," Rauschenberg recounted in the 1970s; "And sometimes it has been quite a strain. I got into both technology and theater and printing because I don't like the single ego. . . . I just don't want to have one. It might be good for some other artist, but for me some kind of self-assurance would be death."[127]

Yet if Rauschenberg's performances are to be analogues—even primitive analogues—of his hoped-for technological machine, he could not be content with their mere modeling of the subject, even if it was a temporal, moving one; they would, rather, have to move beyond the *representation* of subjective change. Nor could they simply signal the impotence of language and representation;[128] they would have to be demonstrations. For in Rauschenberg's vast, technological artwork, spectators were to be confronted not primarily with representational forms, but with an array of nonrepeating, individualized, affective forces by which to put into question their very identity. What was to be challenged was precisely the submission to any a priori model or ideal with which the spectators could identify or conform. To be successful, therefore, Rauschenberg's performances would have to instigate a new mode of reception, a different means by which the relatively isolable, bachelor images within them could invoke or compel interpretation. Like Artaud's performative gestures, Rauschenberg's moving images would have to confront the mind through some sort of "direct pressure on the senses" and thereby effect some form of "dissociative and vibratory action upon the sensibility."[129]

♦

Such a new form of artistic reception had been Rauschenberg's goal since he reconceived the importance of the *White Paintings* in 1952 and had been his expressed purpose since at least 1961. In that year, when answering André Parinaud's question of what he was "trying to communicate through a picture," Rauschenberg explained: "The effort of the concentration of my energy on a message would limit me, and I prefer to go toward the unknown." He later elaborated, "If there was a specific message, I would be limited by my means, my ideas, my prejudices. What interests me is a *contact;* it is not to express a message."[130] More than likely, Rauschenberg had borrowed the term "contact" from Duchamp, who had stated three years earlier in his famous lecture "The Creative Act": "All in all, the creative act is not performed by the artist alone; the spectator brings the work *in contact* with the external world by deciphering and interpreting its inner qualifications and thus adds his contribution to the creative act."[131] Indeed, in the interview with Parinaud, Rauschenberg endorsed precisely such a turn from the expressive paradigm and the supposed plenitude of the art object to a mode of reception that made room for a differential and individualized response. "In what concerns me," he declared, "I deliberately seek to surpass the message and to go beyond. I would like to make a painting creating a situation which leaves as much of a place for the viewer as for the artist."[132]

It would be on this point of individualized reception, we should recall, that Rauschenberg and Duchamp found themselves in agreement later that year during the *Art of Assemblage* symposium (see the introduction). Yet the calculation that Duchamp proposed in "The Creative Act"—his famous determination of an "art coefficient" as the difference between the "unexpressed but intended" meaning of the artist and the "unintentionally expressed" meanings that the beholders nonetheless perceive[133]—was not the same as Rauschenberg's form of addition in which two plus two does not equal four or five. What Duchamp was describing was the unavoidable semiosis that occurs in any form of signification, the ability of the work to produce differential receptions that necessarily exceed the grasp and control of the issuing subject.[134] This was celebrated by both Duchamp and Rauschenberg as the artwork's capacity for "connotation," able to enter into different fields of signification "interpreted by the different temperaments of all the spectators."[135]

Yet what Rauschenberg had accepted, even promoted, at the beginning of the decade as a form of liberation seems later, with the evident rise of spectacle and the ensuing sense of representational foreclosure, to have begun to strike him as a sort of prison house. The unintended, "connotative" meanings generated by the work appeared unable to escape a stereotypical and restrained realm of signification. As Rauschenberg had found in the reception of each series of his production from the *White Paintings* to the Combines, all his artworks fell prey, more or less rapidly, to the attribution or imposition of preset, static, interpretive meanings. In one form or another, iconography, as the science or technique of subsuming all meaning to the recognition of what had gone before, always returned.[136] Every attempt to push the viewer into the unknown, into realms of dynamic thought, had been (or would be) more or less quickly brought back into the realm of the already known, explained in terms of the artist's sexual orientation, his dyslexia, his childhood, art-historical precedent, or eternal symbolism. Eventually, Rauschenberg came to feel that the best that one could hope for with a static work of art was that it would generate at least one new signification upon the extinction of its initial, multiplicitous effect—that its "form" would be "second hand to nothing" and would "have a chance to become," as he put it, "its own cliché."[137]

By the midpoint of the 1960s, however, what Rauschenberg sought was an artwork that would be more dynamic and could therefore avoid "the inevitable fate of any inanimate object,"[138] the petrifying attribution of stable representational meaning (such as that which had led him, so long before, to view Duchamp's readymade as a mere sculpture). Thus his interest in performance: for it seemed to Rauschenberg that the only way to animate artistic components as forces and to keep them from congealing into set forms onto which facile forms of recognition would come into play was through perpetual motion. "I learned that a work of art—say, a painting or a piece of sculpture, is an elusive quantity—that is, the fact that it's *concrete* makes it elusive," is how Rauschenberg would explain to John Gruen this propensity for static pieces to accumulate set meanings: "The dance, on the other hand—and the fluid relationship between dancer and audience—is *really* concrete, not elusive at all." And this concreteness, once again, entailed a new relationship to the spectator. As he elaborated, "My relationship to dance is . . . directly responsible for my new interest in the spectator's active role. . . . You see, both parties are in a critical relationship in terms of immediacy and spontaneity. They combine to create a living, palpable *force of contact.*"[139]

◆

In 1961, the same year that Rauschenberg first mentioned the idea of "contact" to Parinaud, Cage described a similar aspect of Rauschenberg's work in terms of "encounter." "There is, in Rauschenberg," he wrote, "between him and what he picks up to use, the quality of encounter. For the first time."[140] In this instance, Cage used the word to characterize Rauschenberg's productive procedure, his attempt to "collaborate" with his materials, to be unfamiliar with what he is doing in order to avoid the dictates of taste and a priori intention or expression.[141] In focusing on production, Cage echoed what was undoubtedly one of the sources of his terminology, Harold Rosenberg's "The American Action Painters." "The painter no longer approached his easel with an image in his mind," Rosenberg proposed;

> he went up to it with material in his hand to do something to that other piece of material in front of him. The image would be the result of this encounter.
>
> . . . If [a representation of] Lucrece should come out she will be among us for the first time—a surprise.[142]

Within Rosenberg's article, as we have already seen, this observation formed part of an expressive artistic paradigm, though a paradigm strained to its breaking point—for, as Rosenberg contended, the abstract expressionist artist had nothing to express.[143] Despite his allusion, Cage would certainly have rejected Rosenberg's emphasis on the creative subject and the necessary relationship he posited between the artwork and the artist's biography. Rather than embodying the idea that "A painting that is an act is inseparable from the biography of the artist,"[144] Rauschenberg's *White Paintings* and Cage's *4′33″* had demonstrated in the year of Rosenberg's essay that the force of an encounter derived from its contact with the forces of the "outside." Nevertheless, Cage was undoubtedly interested in Rosenberg's description of the almost physical confrontation between artist and materials and in his attempt to theorize an aesthetic of artistic production that went beyond the confines of representation, that sought to produce new forms, images, and significations rather than to recognize the old.

Cage had already brought up the notion of an "encounter" several years before applying it to Rauschenberg's production. In his 1957 article "Experimental Music," Cage related it to the "new hearing" that would arise when the listener was introduced to the sounds of an experimental composition; there he presented the encounter primarily as an aspect of artistic reception. Once liberated from the dictates of representation and the illustration of authorial messages, sounds were to be "themselves rather than vehicles for man-made theories or expressions of human sentiments."[145] Such a conception did not suppose that the sounds, the artistic materials, were unmediated facts, displaying an inertness understood to resist the attribution of meaning.[146] Rather, in a manner analogous to Rauschenberg's performances, Cage's experimental music was to release a plethora of stimuli (here auditory rather than visual). Meanings would still be attributed and elicited, but they would be indeterminate—the interpretations would not be determined by the prior existence of their interpretand. Cage proposed that the process of interpretation would give way to what he called "response ability"—the arousal of individual emotions, affects, or thoughts within the spectator. "This project [of freeing sound from intention] will seem fearsome to many," he observed, "but on examination it gives no cause for alarm. Hearing sounds which are just sounds immediately sets the theorizing mind to theorizing, and the emotions of human beings are continually aroused by encounters with nature." He underscored the role of each listener: "These responses to nature are mine and will not necessarily correspond with another's. Emotion takes place in the person who has it."[147]

Thus, one year before the lecture "The Creative Act" was delivered, Cage had proposed much the same turning as Duchamp: to compensate for the art object's lack of plenitude by embracing the viewers' subjective responses and accepting the uncontrollability of semiosis as a liberatory revelation. As always, however, Cage's reference to nature is crucial within this context. For as we saw in chapter 1, nature, within Cage's Bergsonian conception of it, was not a repository of archetypal or motivated meaning but rather a state of continual, nonanthropomorphic difference and temporal change.[148] Thus, in addition to leading to an undetermined and individual response, an encounter must necessarily be an encounter with difference. It is always, as Cage put it with regard to Rauschenberg, "For the first time"—that is, without presupposition, recognition, or the facile forms of understanding that such modes of reception encourage. (Recall that in his 1961 interview with Parinaud, Rauschenberg had similarly declared, "One must be in a perpetual state of growth in relation to oneself. . . . When working the artist must know he is doing this for the first time. He must shed habits and mannerisms.")[149]

Like Cage's notion of the encounter made possible by experimental music, the "force of contact" incarnated by Rauschenberg's performances and the "images" to which they give rise oppose any interpretation understood as a mere recognition of the work's preestablished meaning.[150] But even more strenuously do they eschew the mere refusal of meaning, of thought, or of interpretation, a refusal that favors a quietistic acceptance of life as it exists. Rauschenberg's performances and the images they produce—having little of the natural or quotidian about them—strongly resist any such reading. Rather, these encounters, as Cage noted, "set the theorizing mind to theorizing." Meaning and intelligence come into play in the interpretation that Rauschenberg's performance images, as signs, call forth, but they do not do so from *before;* they do not rely on the realms where signification has already been determined, within the already existent, co-opted, and restricted economy of totalized representation. Instead, they come into play only *after*—after they have been opened to the outside by the contact or encounter with difference. It is from the perspective of a totalized, late-capitalist social sphere ruled over by preset, commodified pseudo-difference that the impulse of an encounter that forces a creative thinking—a mobile "act of thinking"—becomes the basis of a profound critique.[151]

VI. The radicality of Carrouges's analysis of the bachelor machine is to be found in his discussion of its (non)functioning, in his description of the machine's disarticulation of the reproductive circuits of established meaning and its relation to a nonproductive expenditure of signification that opens out beyond the realm of the restricted economy. Nonetheless, as evidenced in Carrouges's own writings, this analysis continually threatens to fall back into a mere surrealist thematics of eroticism and death. For both Rauschenberg and Cage, surrealism was anathema; its trust in an objective chance that fell back on the pathways of the unconscious and free association was understood as limiting possibility and restricting signification within the confines of the individual subject—if not of the ego, then the subconscious. "My heart didn't go out to Surrealism at all," Cage explained in 1966; "Automatic art, in fact, has never interested me, because it is a way of falling back, resting on one's memories and feelings subconsciously, is it not? And I have done my utmost to free people from that."[152] Rauschenberg had been even more blunt on the subject a year before: "I hate Surrealism," he told Brian O'Doherty, and he explained to Dorothy Seckler his distance from the exaltation of objective chance:

> I don't mess around with my subconscious. I try to keep wide-awake. If I see any superficial subconscious relationships that I'm familiar with—clichés of association—I change the picture. I always have a good reason for taking something out but never have one for putting something in. I don't want to—because that means that the picture is being painted predigested.[153]

As he had informed Parinaud a few years earlier, "I didn't see any difference between automatic painting and the other kind."[154]

Although in performances such as *Spring Training* and *Map Room II* Rauschenberg had largely been successful in avoiding such forms of association, *Linoleum,* which was captured on film during a performance in the WNET studios (and distributed as part of *Aspen* magazine),[155] resembles nothing so much as a surrealist-inspired dream. In part, this impression arises because here Rauschenberg more explicitly trafficked in images with a symbolic content, perhaps thereby upping the ante in (or the difficulty of) disarticulating representational and metaphorical meaning. Nevertheless, the evocative appearances of the nineteenth-century dress worn by Simone Forti, the chicken-coop bachelor machine of Steve Paxton, the elongated American flag (pure surrealism) that Rauschenberg cut to size, Robert Breer's movable sculptures, and the

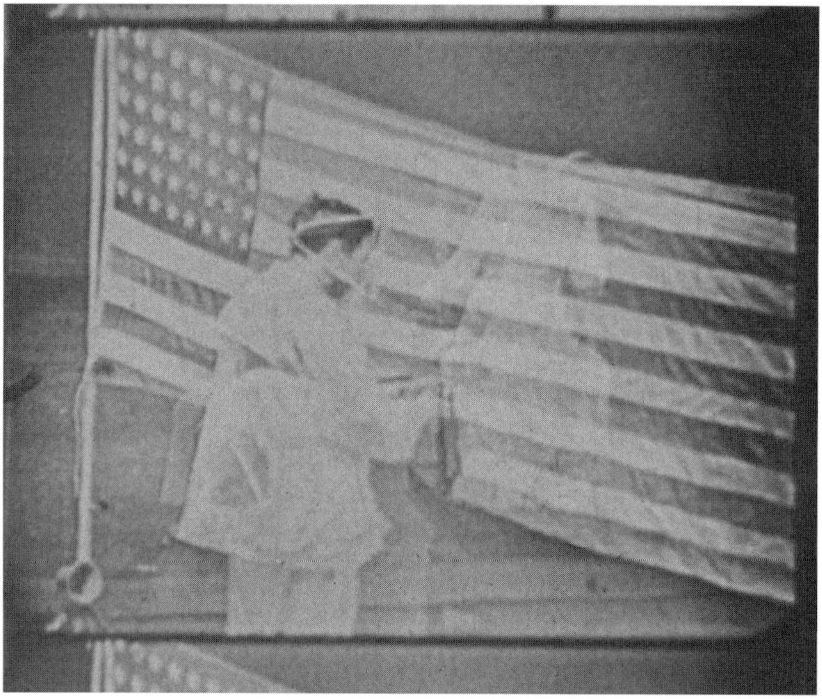

Linoleum, 1966. Film still. Pictured: Rauschenberg and Trisha Brown.

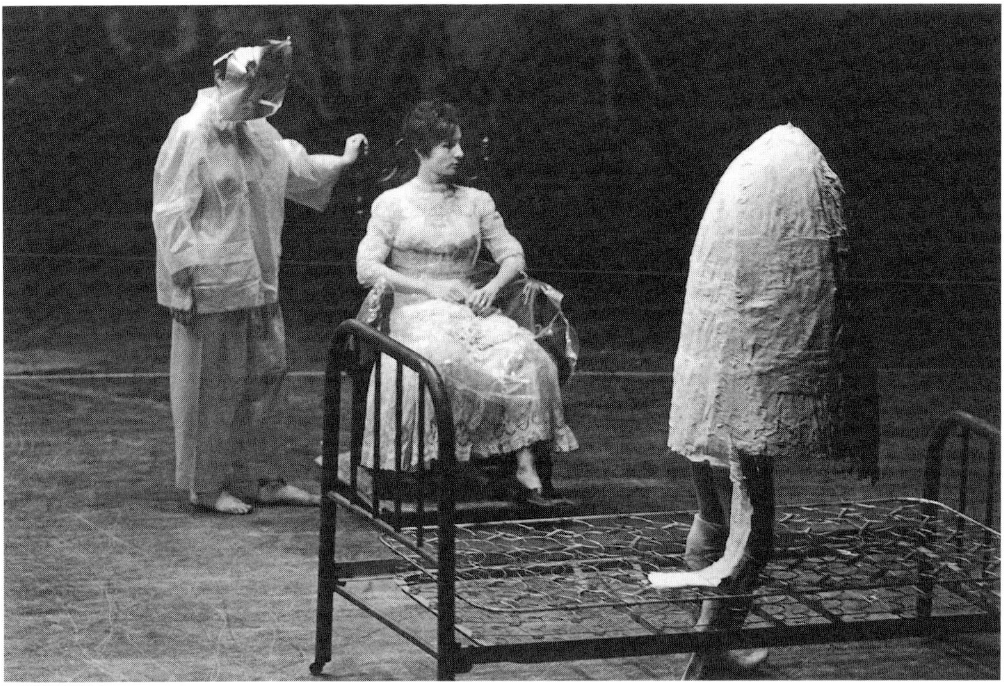

Linoleum, 1966. NOW Festival. Pictured: Deborah Hay, Simone (Whitman) Forti, and Alex Hay. Photograph by Peter Moore. © Estate of Peter Moore / VAGA, New York.

uncanniness of Alex Hay's actual fusion into a hybrid form (through the bed-spring on his legs and the plaster eggshell-like costume that he wore) all bring into play the familiar associative traps of surrealism. To use Rauschenberg's terminology, they lack the "immediacy" of an encounter and instead have a certain unmistakable "souvenir quality."[156]

Beyond the associative capacity of the props and costumes, however, *Linoleum*'s surrealistic air seems to be an effect of the film itself—its condensation of the time and space of the performance. *Linoleum* had first been seen at the NOW Festival in Washington D.C. In the film, the expanse of the large roller skating rink, where the audience's focus was dispersed among activities taking place far apart and viewed in the round, was replaced not only by the smaller space of the studio but also by the viewpoint of the camera, which imposes a unity of focus and narrative sequencing onto the various proceedings. As a result, *Linoleum* enters the space of image, representation, and associational sequencing (emphasized by the film's superimposition of images) that makes its diversity appear dreamlike. The camera reterritorializes representation and restricts the open-ended *contact* of performers and objects and of spectators and performance images. And in the repetition and finality that the performance attains on film, *Linoleum* is transformed from a bachelor machine of semiotic expenditure into a machine that works well, in that the recording allows it to be conserved and run through the same paces again and again.[157]

To a large extent, the same failing affected the technological works Rauschenberg actually managed to execute in the 1960s: the *Revolvers, Soundings, Solstice,* and the *Carnal Clocks*. Each is able, perhaps, to produce a large or even infinite number of visual combinations in the overlapping or selective lighting of their transparent planes. Yet each of these superimpositions, every degree of visual diversification, is nonetheless restricted and restrained within a mechanism intended to work well. One glance at any of these pieces is enough to see almost instantly all the images in their full number of combinations—or at least the limited totality of the mechanism within which they are all contained. What was to be a process of encounter between subject and image has become only a more complicated (and, in fact, not that much more complicated) mechanism of sterile variations. And the force that was to contact the subject within Rauschenberg's imagined synaesthetic, reactive, technological machine becomes the effect of a finger on a switch, the ticking of a clock, an impulse in an auditory sensor, or the optical triggering of a sliding door.[158]

In retrospect, Rauschenberg's aims for technology seem to have been realized most effectively in his final and least typical technological work of the era, the colossal and apparently anomalous *Mud Muse* created in collaboration with Teledyne Corporation as part of the Los Angeles County Museum of Art's "Art and Technology" program. Although Rauschenberg began with the same dream that had guided him for more than a decade—that of an entirely reactive technological environment capable of processing the spectators' movements, body temperatures, brain waves, and thought patterns—he ended up with a nine-by-twelve-foot rectangular vat of bubbling drillers' mud. The ambitious interactive component he had envisioned was first reduced to an audio sensing device that would use the sounds of the environment to trigger the pressurized, bubble-producing air valves; then, for technical reasons, it was eliminated altogether.[159] Yet as *Mud Muse*'s interactive force diminished, its character as an immense, wasteful expenditure became more readily and unavoidably apparent. "Pure waste, sensualism, utilizing a pretty sophisticated technology," was how Rauschenberg described it:

> I think you immediately get involved with *Mud-Muse* on a really physical, basic, sensual level as opposed to its illustrating an interesting idea, either successfully or unsuccessfully, because the level of the piece, on the grounds of an idea, is pretty low. . . . There is no lesson there. . . . It was to exhibit the fact that technology is not for learning lessons but is to be experienced.[160]

In the end, *Mud Muse* reproduced the action of Rauschenberg's *Money Thrower* for Tinguely's *Homage to New York* on a larger scale. It was above all a wasteful expenditure of vast amounts of money and resources of the multinational conglomerate that was his partner.

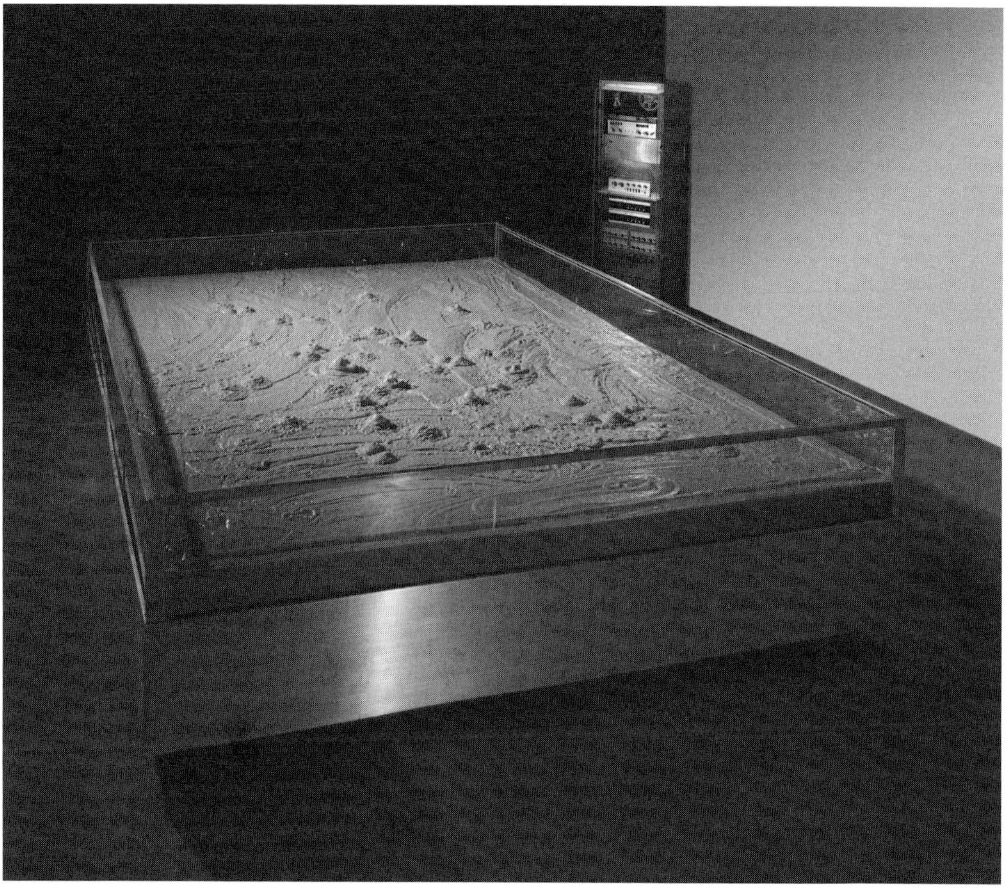

Mud Muse, 1968–1971. Bentonite mixed with water in aluminum-and-glass vat, with sound-activated compressed-air system and control console. 33 × 108 × 144 in. Moderna Museet, Stockholm. Gift of the New York Collection, 1973.

Rauschenberg's ambition was much larger, of course, and his years spent pursuing technological collaborations, his cofounding of Experiments in Art and Technology (E.A.T.), and other such activities can be understood only in light of it. He intended nothing less than to introduce a bachelor machine into the mega-machine of late capitalism, to disarticulate the social mechanism of "industry" by means of the bachelor machine's function of nonreproductive breaking down, to cause the social mega-machine to be incapable of reproduction (of the status quo), and thereby to make it produce something else.

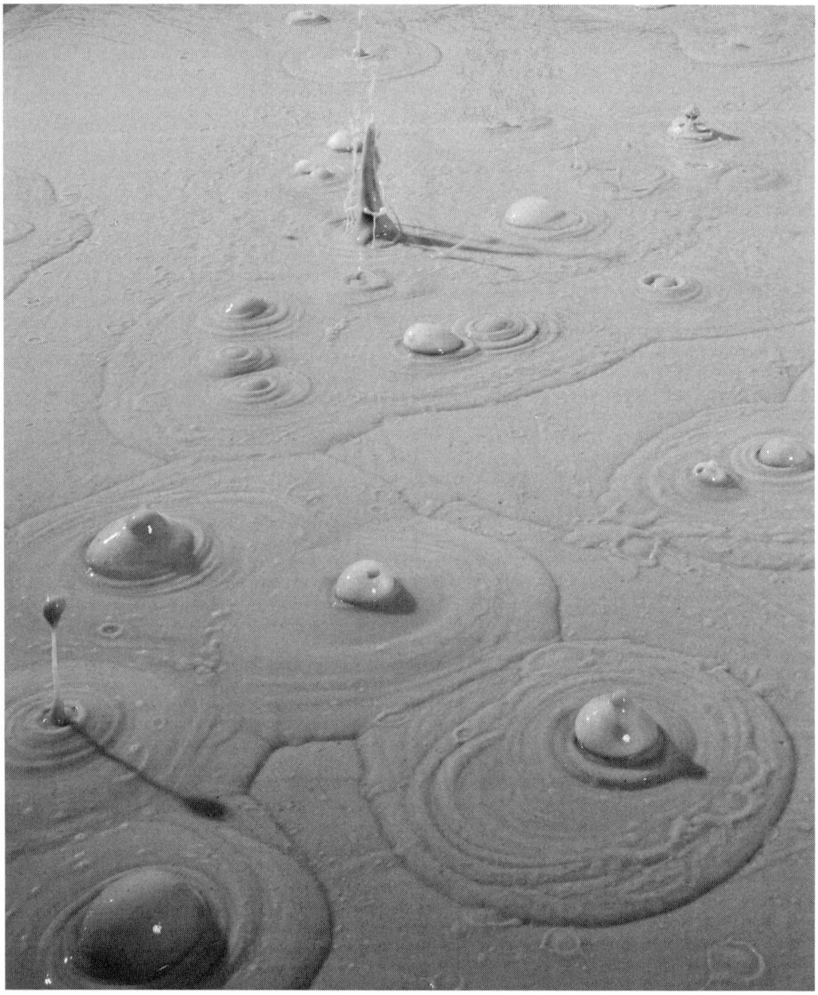

Mud Muse, 1968–1971, detail.

Conclusion

Mud Muse was not only Rauschenberg's last major technological undertaking, it arguably signaled the end of an era in his artistic production. With remarkable consistency for almost two decades, Rauschenberg pursued an artistic project of opening perception to difference. Whether approaching it through painting, modernism, spectacle, or subjectivity, Rauschenberg sought to open a limited and increasingly foreclosed realm of representation to forces of the "outside." To a certain degree, the denouement of this project followed the general historical trajectory of the 1960s: from a period of escalating hope in the ability to transform society (through art, through performance, through technology) to a period of growing disillusionment. By the end of the decade, Rauschenberg's works would reflect this disenchantment. The *Currents* print series of 1970, for example, attempts no longer to open out from the confines of spectacle but rather to preserve, or even embalm, a moment of it. Made up entirely of newspaper articles and headlines, *Currents* forms a sort of time capsule from the end of the "Great Society," buried so that future observers would know how it ended: in escalating violence, warfare, political backlash, and police repression.[1] The contrast with the optimism of the immediately preceding *Stoned Moon* lithographs (1969–1970), which Rauschenberg made in the context of the space program, could not be more telling.

Throughout the 1970s, Rauschenberg could increasingly be found in his retreat on Captiva Island, Florida, where his first non–New York area pieces, the *Cardboards,* were completed in 1971. A few years later, his second major American retrospective was staged at the National Collection of Fine Arts in Washington, D.C. Whether intentionally or not, this exhibition, timed to coincide with the United States' bicentennial, enshrined Rauschenberg as America's contemporary old master. It was a mantle he would be less and less able or inclined to resist, although it is perhaps only recently that he has come to embrace it fully.[2] Rauschenberg has, of course, never ceased making art and has always been capable of producing works of undeniable beauty.[3] Yet from the end of the sixties on, the pretense of working in the gap between art and life would progressively disappear. Eventually, even Rauschenberg would be forced to admit that there was little possibility of maintaining any reception of his works as other than "Art" of a traditional kind. As he put it to Calvin Tomkins, "I think the shadow of the escape has cut me off at the pass."[4]

Rauschenberg's neo-avant-garde artistic project came to an end with the sixties not merely because of his personal disillusionment with political events or professional submission to art world pressures. From our perspective, more than thirty years on, it is possible to see that Rauschenberg's early endeavors came up against certain historical limitations that affected his implicit conceptions of both power and liberation. These were at least twofold. In the first place, despite his characterization of the mega-machine of corporate "industry," Rauschenberg seems ultimately to have regarded representation as part of a hierarchical, top-down form of oppression, a state or sovereign form of power. In so doing, he failed to take into account the extent to which "liberation" onto a plane of immanence would necessarily entail encounters with new forms of power that also operated within such an immanent realm.[5] In the second place, Rauschenberg's neo-avant-garde project never entirely escaped an economic perspective tied to mass production and consumption. Arising out of concerns initially formulated in the 1940s, Rauschenberg's outlook seems always to have been directed chiefly against the types of leveling conformity decried by the leftist thinkers of that time.[6]

At the beginning of the twenty-first century, however, it has become clear that capital no longer needs a mass, or even a lonely crowd, but is instead quite capable of casting the unique individual as its model consumer. As we have become well aware, the Internet makes a certain individuated and interactive experience the norm for consumption (in the process both extracting information and giving back an individuated product). From this point of view, the subject sought by Rauschenberg's unrealized technological machine, one who can readily react, adapt, and transform to different situations, appears less the model of a wholly liberated individual than an avatar of the perpetually educated worker of the information economy: one who is required to move quickly from position to position within an era of ever more rapidly shifting capitalism. In this regard, the postmodernization heralded by Rauschenberg's neo-avant-garde project appears to have anticipated certain historical transformations as much as it challenged them.[7]

Yet some such activity of prefiguration is perhaps all that the avant-garde can be expected to do. To see in Rauschenberg's project only failure when it is judged against its most utopian intentions is almost certainly disingenuous. Indeed, every avant-garde project, viewed from such a perspective, has similarly failed. But as Michel Foucault has argued, it is only through such moments of attempted resistance that new formations of power are made to reveal their contours.[8] Indeed, to serve as one of the means by which newly emerging formations of power are brought to light in order to be confronted might more plausibly be considered the role of the artistic avant-garde. In this manner, and despite Rauschenberg's own particular version of avant-garde "failure," his postwar artistic production remains valuable for the new perspectives, practices, outlooks, and points of application that it helped foreground. Born from a vision of the increasingly stringent commodification encompassing all of life's dimensions, Rauschenberg's attempts to relate representation to an "outside" broached issues whose relevance is perhaps only now becoming clear: issues of postspectacular society, posthuman subjectivity, and a neo-avant-garde (or perhaps still oppositional post-avant-garde) adapted to them.

For this reason, as I have argued throughout this volume, it is less Peter Bürger who most appositely characterized Rauschenberg's avant-garde repetitions than Gilles Deleuze. For Bürger, the history of the avant-garde played out Marx's famous observation from *The Eighteenth Brumaire of Louis Napoleon*. Its historical period ended in tragic failure, and its neo-avant-garde revival was little more than farce.[9] Yet playing on the term "repetition," which in French also has the meaning of "rehearsal," Deleuze provided a much different reading of Marx's famous passage. As he wrote in *Difference and Repetition:*

> When Marx also criticizes the abstract false movement or mediation of the Hegelians, he finds himself drawn to an idea, which he indicates rather than develops, an essentially "theatrical" idea: to the extent that history is theatre, then repetition, along with the tragic and the comic within repetition, forms a condition of movement under which the "actors" or the "heroes" produce something effectively new in history.

He then declared, "The theatre of repetition is opposed to the theatre of representation, just as movement is opposed to the concept and to representation which refers it back to the concept."[10]

Deleuze's final observation contains what I have argued to be a central component of Rauschenberg's overall artistic strategy: the refusal to put a stop to movement, the opposition to subsuming art beneath the concept or "idea," and the attempt to postpone a work's becoming "a facsimile of itself" in which its particularity, impact, and challenge can be contained and ultimately disposed of. In Rauschenberg's case, what he feared happening to individual works has happened to an entire era of his production. Whether his works are understood as a mere repetition of dada or through the most traditional ideas of signification, the predominant strains of Rauschenberg's reception have worked together to stifle the challenges that his art initially posed.

As befits the artist under discussion, however, I will risk ending this book on an optimistic note. For there nevertheless remains Rauschenberg's palpable and widespread impact on contemporary forms of oppositional aesthetic practice. Rauschenberg's was a position with which artists across the board were confronted and to which they almost necessarily had to respond: from minimalism to pop, happenings to fluxus, arte povera to nouveau realism to capitalist realism. Some (such as Allan Kaprow or Andy Warhol) developed aspects of Rauschenberg's production further; others (such as nearly all the minimalists) rejected it almost entirely. But in either case—indeed, in both cases—Rauschenberg's work served as a stimulus, an impetus, and a challenge. Like the mole archaeologist that he encountered in Italy, Rauschenberg created a theater of neo-avant-garde repetition that pushed art and art history forward to the production of something effectively new. What this study has elucidated is some of the specificity of that aesthetic outlook and position, a specificity that will have to be taken into account if the artistic, historical, and even political stakes of its (and our) time are to be more fully understood.

Notes

Introduction

1. Lawrence Alloway, Marcel Duchamp, et al., "The Art of Assemblage: A Symposium" (1961), in *Essays on Assemblage,* ed. James Leggio and Helen M. Franc, Studies in Modern Art, vol. 2 (New York: Museum of Modern Art, 1992), p. 124. This conversation is hereafter cited as "Assemblage Symposium."

2. William C. Seitz, "Problems of 'New Directions' Exhibitions," *Artforum* 2, no. 3 (September 1963): 23.

3. Robert Rauschenberg, "Random Order," *Location* 1, no. 1 (spring 1963); 27–31. "Random Order" is referred to as a "manifesto" by Rosalind Krauss, who has provided the best discussion to date of this enigmatic text. See Krauss, "Perpetual Inventory," in *Robert Rauschenberg: A Retrospective,* ed. Walter Hopps and Susan Davidson (New York: Solomon R. Guggenheim Museum, 1997), pp. 206–223.

4. "Assemblage Symposium," p. 137.

5. "Assemblage Symposium," p. 139.

6. William C. Seitz, *The Art of Assemblage* (New York: Museum of Modern Art, 1961), p. 87. Seitz went on to connect contemporary assemblage to the attitudes manifest in the

beat movement in a way that relates perhaps more closely to Bruce Conner or Edward Kienholz than to Rauschenberg: "Such subjects are often approached in a mystical, aesthetic, or 'arty' way, but just as often they are fearfully dark, evoking horror or nausea: the anguish of the scrap heap; the images of charred bodies that keep Hiroshima and Nagasaki before our eyes; the confrontation of democratic platitudes with the Negro's disenfranchisement; the travesty of the Chessman trial" (p. 89). Seitz refers specifically to the beat movement immediately before the quote above (p. 87).

7. Roger Shattuck, *The Banquet Years* (New York: Harcourt, Brace, 1958), pp. 331ff.

8. Roger Shattuck recalls that Seitz actually assigned the task of opening the symposium with "The Mode of Juxtaposition" to him ("Assemblage Symposium," p. 121).

9. "Assemblage Symposium," p. 128.

10. "Assemblage Symposium," p. 130.

11. "Assemblage Symposium," pp. 130, 150.

12. "Assemblage Symposium," p. 150.

13. "Assemblage Symposium," p. 146.

14. See also Françoise Choay, "Dada, néo-dada, et Rauschenberg," *Art International* 5, no. 8 (20 October 1961): 82–84, 88.

15. "Assemblage Symposium," pp. 148, 127–128.

16. "Assemblage Symposium," p. 145. Rauschenberg specifically questioned whether Duchamp saw in his work any "political significance," by which Rauschenberg seems primarily to have meant critical negation, an idea that he and his associate John Cage would seek to transform along with that of shock. See chapter 1.

17. "Assemblage Symposium," p. 148.

18. "Assemblage Symposium," p. 148. Huelsenbeck, too, seems not to have understood the nature of Rauschenberg's protestations. For the most part, Lawrence Alloway remained silent.

19. Emile de Antonio and Mitch Tuchman, *Painters Painting: A Candid History of the Modern Art Scene, 1940–1970* (New York: Abbeville, 1984), p. 88 (the interviews for this work were conducted in 1970).

20. Alan R. Solomon, *Robert Rauschenberg* (New York: Jewish Museum, 1963), n.p. Seitz's position as stated in the *Art of Assemblage* catalogue was still very much relevant in 1963. See Seitz's comments on the reception of the show in his articles "Assemblage: Problems and Issues," *Art International* 6, no. 1 (February 1962): 26–34, and "Problems of 'New Directions' Exhibitions."

21. Rauschenberg, "How Important Is Surface to Design?" *Print* 13, no. 1 (January–February, 1959): 31, and Solomon, *Robert Rauschenberg,* n.p. The ambiguity in Solomon's analysis of Rauschenberg's work is also seen in his discussion of its possible connections to artistic subjectivity. At one point, Solomon can declare, echoing Rauschenberg's words, that "his intention never becomes biographical," only to conclude later that "Rauschenberg's painting [*Barge*] has become a big statement asserting the intimacy and hermetic privacy of the artist's perceptions and his range of sensibility" (n.p.).

22. Laurie J. Monahan has analyzed the manner in which the same aspects of Solomon's discourse that allowed for Rauschenberg's unproblematic assimilation into the museum reflected, and were thus able to be mobilized by, the overriding political imperatives of the United States' assertion of worldwide cultural hegemony during the 1960s (Monahan, "Cultural Cartography: American Designs at the 1964 Venice Biennale," in *Reconstructing Modernism: Art in New York, Paris, and Montreal, 1945–1964,* ed. Serge Guilbaut [Cambridge, Mass.: MIT Press, 1990], pp. 369–416). While Monahan's own analyses of Rauschenberg's work rely perhaps too heavily on those of Solomon, her discussion of the manner in which Rauschenberg's art was utilized by cultural institutions powerfully reminds one of the effective limitations on the critical dimension of his aesthetic project. See chapter 3, note 60.

23. Brian O'Doherty, "Rauschenberg and the Vernacular Glance," *Art in America* 61, no. 5 (September–October 1973): 84.

24. While coupled historically, these two aspects of Rauschenberg's reception—the inclusion of his works within the museum and their iconographic analysis—do not derive from the same sources. Exhibition catalogues, such as that of the Guggenheim's 1997 retrospective, have generally eschewed iconographic discussions (no doubt largely at the artist's insistence). With each major exhibition, however, comes a revival of the question of iconographic meaning and communicative intention within the pages of the art press. The clearest example is Charles F. Stuckey, "Reading Rauschenberg," *Art in America* 65, no. 2 (March–April 1977): 74–84. The one major museum exhibition catalogue to embrace an iconographic reading of Rauschenberg is Roni Feinstein's *Robert Rauschenberg: The Silkscreen Paintings, 1962–64* (New York: Whitney Museum of American Art, 1990). Martin Duberman and Jonathan D. Katz, who raise important questions about the treatment of Rauschenberg's homosexuality in the Guggenheim retrospective, take for granted that Rauschenberg's subjectivity is clearly readable from his works (Duberman, "Is There Room for Privacy on the Canvas?" *New York Times,* 7 September 1997, sec. 2, p. 89, and Katz, "Rauschenberg's Honeymoon," *Art/Text,* no. 61 [May–June 1998]: 44–47).

25. See Kenneth Bendiner, "Robert Rauschenberg's 'Canyon,'" *Arts Magazine* 56, no. 10 (June 1982): 57–59; Jonathan D. Katz, "The Art of Code: Jasper Johns and Robert Rauschenberg," in *Significant Others: Creativity and Intimate Partnership,* ed. Whitney Chadwick and Isabelle de Courtivron (London: Thames and Hudson, 1993), pp. 189–207 (on the larger import of Katz's work, see chapter 1); and Laura Auricchio, "Lifting the Veil: Robert Rauschenberg's *Thirty-four Drawings for Dante's Inferno* and the Commercial Homoerotic Imagery of 1950s America," in *The Gay 90s: Disciplinary and Interdisciplinary Formation in Queer Studies,* ed. Thomas Foster, Carol Siegel, and Ellen E. Berry, Genders, vol. 26 (New York: New York University Press, 1997), pp. 119–154.

26. Krauss, "Perpetual Inventory," p. 223 n. 60.

27. I do not mean to say that Rauschenberg's work does not traffic in signification, or that he does not, at certain moments, seek to be distinctly illustrational. See the discussions of the Combines in chapter 3 and of the Dante Drawings in chapter 4.

28. Peter Bürger, *Theory of the Avant-Garde,* trans. Michael Shaw (Minneapolis: University of Minnesota Press, 1984). This work is hereafter cited parenthetically in the text.

29. Although Bürger seeks to take up the radical political project of the avant-garde, his own position has been criticized as "transcendental." See Benjamin H. D. Buchloh, "The Primary Colors for the Second Time: A Paradigm Repetition of the Neo-Avant-Garde," *October,* no. 37 (summer 1986): 41–52.

30. Hal Foster has more recently argued that the two moments of the historical avant-garde and the neo-avant-garde can be separated according to their questioning, respectively, of the *conventions* of art and of the *institutions* of art (Foster, "Who's Afraid of the Neo-Avant-Garde?" in *The Return of the Real* [Cambridge, Mass.: MIT Press, 1996], pp. 1–33).

31. Seitz and Shattuck discuss the issue of the institution in "Assemblage Symposium," p. 149.

32. For the most theoretically sophisticated treatments of Rauschenberg's work from a Frankfurt School perspective, see the discussions in Benjamin H. D. Buchloh, "Andy Warhol's One-Dimensional Art, 1956–1966," in *Neo-Avantgarde and Culture Industry: Essays on European and American Art from 1955 to 1975* (Cambridge, Mass.: MIT Press, 2000), pp. 461–529, and Monahan, "Cultural Cartography."

33. See Leo Steinberg, "Other Criteria," in *Other Criteria: Confrontations with Twentieth-Century Art* (New York: Oxford University Press, 1972), pp. 55–91; Rosalind Krauss, "Rauschenberg and the Materialized Image," *Artforum* 13, no. 4 (December 1974): 36–43, and "Perpetual Inventory"; Craig Owens, "The Allegorical Impulse: Toward a Theory of Postmodernism," parts 1 and 2, in *Beyond Recognition: Representation, Power, and Culture,* ed. Scott Bryson et al. (Berkeley: University of California Press, 1992), pp. 52–87; and Douglas Crimp, "On the Museum's Ruins," in *On the Museum's Ruins* (Cambridge, Mass.: MIT Press, 1993), pp. 44–64. Despite his critiques of Rauschenberg, Benjamin H. D. Buchloh contributed to this line of reception in his discussion of the *Erased de Kooning Drawing* in "Allegorical Procedures: Appropriation and Montage in Contemporary Art," *Artforum* 21, no. 1 (September 1982): 43–56. Many of these articles, as well as a brief discussion of Steinberg's essay, are collected in *Robert Rauschenberg,* ed. Branden W. Joseph (Cambridge, Mass.: MIT Press, 2002).

34. Steinberg, "Other Criteria," p. 91.

35. Fredric Jameson, *Postmodernism, or the Cultural Logic of Late Capitalism* (Durham, N.C.: Duke University Press, 1991).

36. Bürger's continuing influence is perhaps most evident in Hal Foster's "Who's Afraid of the Neo-Avant-Garde?" Foster perceptively notes the division of the "1950s" and "1960s" postwar neo-avant-garde. Yet, whereas he staunchly defends minimalism and, to some extent, pop from Bürger's dismissals, Foster grants that "artists in the 1950s"—and Rauschenberg here is paradigmatic—"mostly recycled avant-garde devices" (p. 5). "As the *first* neo-avant-garde recovers the historical avant-garde, dada in particular," he writes, "it does so often literally, through a reprise of its basic devices, the effect of which is *less to transform the institution of art than to transform the avant-garde into an institution.* This is one ruse of history to grant Bürger" (p. 21). Though Foster moves to reevaluate the importance of this first period of the neo-avant-garde as well (see, in particular, his discussion on pp. 16–17), his judgment is ultimately unchanged. We should note, however, that Foster's concession derives from an avowed critical alignment with the 1960s neo-avant-garde. He writes from their position, as it were, and thus productively theorizes that generation's rejection of the earlier period of "1950s" neo-avant-garde.

37. It remains to be seen how Rauschenberg's production informed his more positive reception in the still underresearched areas of happenings, pop, fluxus, neo-realism, and expanded cinema, among others.

38. The concept of "long waves of capitalist development," which played such an important role in Jameson's theorization of postmodernism, is developed in Ernest Mandel, *Late Capitalism,* trans. Joris De Bres (London: Verso, 1978), and reprised in Ernest Mandel, *Long Waves of Capitalist Development: A Marxist Interpretation,* 2nd rev. ed. (London: Verso, 1995).

39. Gilles Deleuze and Félix Guattari, *A Thousand Plateaus: Capitalism and Schizophrenia,* trans. Brian Massumi (Minneapolis: University of Minnesota Press, 1987), p. 20. A broader consideration of the capitalist dynamic of de- and reterritorialization is found in Gilles Deleuze and Félix Guattari, *Anti-Oedipus: Capitalism and Schizophrenia,* trans. Robert Hurley, Mark Seem, and Helen R. Lane (Minneapolis: University of Minnesota Press, 1983), pp. 222–240. My argument here is indebted to Jonathan Crary, who made much the same observation with regard to the limitations of a Frankfurt School perspective in "Eclipse of

the Spectacle," in *Art after Modernism: Rethinking Representation,* ed. Brian Wallis (New York: New Museum of Contemporary Art; Boston: David R. Godine, 1984), pp. 286–287.

40. See Michael Hardt and Antonio Negri's discussion of Jameson's thesis of postmodernism in *Empire* (Cambridge, Mass.: Harvard University Press, 2000), esp. pp. 271–272.

41. The advent of a society of control is discussed in Gilles Deleuze, "Postscript on Control Societies," in *Negotiations, 1972–1990,* trans. Martin Joughin (New York: Columbia University Press, 1995), pp. 177–182.

42. Hardt and Negri, *Empire,* pp. 140–143. Although Michel Foucault, from whom the terms derive, saw the regimes of sovereign and disciplinary power as distinct historical phases, Hardt and Negri argue that discipline is a type or form of modern, sovereign power (p. 88).

43. Hardt and Negri, *Empire,* pp. 217–218.

44. In 1961 the connection between Cage and Rauschenberg would have been especially clear. As briefly referenced by Seitz, Cage's most extended commentary on the work of his friend, "On Robert Rauschenberg, Artist, and His Work," appeared in the Italian art journal *Metro* earlier that year. Seitz included excerpts from this article in the *Art of Assemblage* catalogue alongside reproductions of Rauschenberg's work, and Cage's piece would appear once again that year as the most recent writing in his book *Silence* (John Cage, "On Robert Rauschenberg, Artist, and His Work," in *Silence* [Middletown, Conn.: Wesleyan University Press, 1961], pp. 98–108). In 1961, Cage's article also appeared in Swedish as "On Robert Rauschenberg, konstuär och hans arbete," *Konstrevy* 37, nos. 5–6 (1961): 166–174, and was extensively referenced in the artist Öyvind Fahlström's "En gata full av presenter," *Konstrevy* 37, nos. 5–6 (1961): 176–181.

45. Cage, quoted in Calvin Tomkins, *Off the Wall: Robert Rauschenberg and the Art World of Our Time* (New York: Penguin, 1980), p. 70. Rauschenberg has more recently recalled, "John told me once, 'You know, Bob, it wouldn't have had to be both of us.' And what he meant by that was that we had so much in common, we were such similar spirits" (Julia Brown Turrell, "Talking to Robert Rauschenberg," in *Rauschenberg Sculpture* [Fort Worth, Tex.: Modern Art Museum of Fort Worth, 1995], p. 62).

46. John Cage,"Composition as Process III: Communication"(1958), in *Silence,* p. 44.

47. The relations between Cage and the thinking of Deleuze and Guattari, which will be discussed extensively in later chapters, are multiform. See, to cite only one instance, Deleuze and Guattari's reference to Cage's work in *Anti-Oedipus,* p. 371. The connection of Cage to French poststructuralist thought is also importantly acknowledged in, among other places, Daniel Charles, *Gloses sur John Cage* (Paris: Union Générale d'Éditions, 1978), and throughout the long-standing editorial project of Sylvère Lotringer and Semiotext(e), which cooperated in the publication of John Cage and Daniel Charles, *For the Birds* (New York: Marion Boyars, 1981).

48. John Cage, "History of Experimental Music in the United States" (1959), in *Silence,* p. 75.

49. Cage's reference to "Western commercialism" is found in John Cage, "The East in the West" (1946), in *John Cage: Writer,* ed. Richard Kostelanetz (New York: Limelight Editions, 1993), p. 25. On Cage's relation to Fuller and commercialism, see my "Hitchhiker in an Omni-Directional Transport: The Spatial Politics of John Cage and Buckminster Fuller," *ANY Magazine* 17 (1997): 40–44, and " 'A Therapeutic Value for City Dwellers': The Development of John Cage's Early Avant-Garde Aesthetic Position," in *John Cage: Music, Philosophy, and Intention 1933–1950,* ed. David W. Patterson (New York: Routledge, 2002), pp. 135–175.

50. Cage's understanding of difference is very close to that expressed in a comment by Hardt and Negri: "The modern dialectic of inside and outside has been replaced by a play of degrees and intensities, of hybridity and artificiality" (*Empire,* pp. 187–188).

51. Cage, foreword to *Silence,* p. ix.

52. Cage, "Letter to Paul Henry Lang" (1956), in *John Cage: An Anthology,* ed. Richard Kostelanetz (New York: Da Capo, 1970), p. 117. See also Cage, "45′ for a Speaker" (1954), in *Silence,* p. 162.

53. Cage, foreword to *Silence,* p. ix.

54. Cage "45′ for a Speaker," p. 152.

55. Cage, "Preface to *Indeterminacy*" (1959), in *John Cage: Writer,* p. 79.

56. Rauschenberg, quoted in Dorothy C. Miller, ed., *Sixteen Americans* (New York: Museum of Modern Art, 1959), p. 58.

57. Cage, "On Robert Rauschenberg," p. 107.

1 White on White

1. Rauschenberg's letter to Parsons is reproduced in facsimile in Walter Hopps, *Robert Rauschenberg: The Early 1950s* (Houston: Houston Fine Arts Press, 1991), p. 230. Rauschenberg's idiosyncratic spelling, punctuation, and capitalization have been retained. An unfortunately abridged and somewhat inaccurately transcribed version of the letter appears in Mary Lynn Kotz, *Rauschenberg: Art and Life* (New York: Harry N. Abrams, 1990), p. 78.

2. Although no pieces were sold, it was at the May exhibition that Rauschenberg first briefly met John Cage, to whom he gave *Number 1* (1951), a work later repainted as a black painting in 1953.

3. Rauschenberg, quoted from notes of an interview by Walter Hopps, Captiva Island, Fla., 18–20 January 1991, in Rauschenberg's archives, New York.

4. Rauschenberg does not specifically discuss the signification of the color white in *Mother of God.* He did, however, mention to Hopps that during this period colors were felt to have certain symbolic associations; "Yellow," he noted, "was life" (interview by Hopps). The relationship that Rauschenberg's *Mother of God* bears to the idea of incarnation was suggested to me by Thierry de Duve.

5. Rauschenberg to Parsons, 18 October 1951, in Hopps, *Robert Rauschenberg: The Early 1950s,* p. 230; further quotations from the letter in this discussion are all taken from this page. Lawrence Alloway erroneously substitutes "institutional optimism" for "intuitional optimism" in "Rauschenberg's Development," in *Robert Rauschenberg,* ed. Walter Hopps (Washington, D.C.: National Collection of Fine Arts, 1976), p. 3.

6. Although Thierry de Duve does not discuss Rauschenberg's *White Paintings,* he has explored the imbrication of formalist modernism and the idea of the white monochrome in "The Monochrome and the Blank Canvas," in his *Kant after Duchamp* (Cambridge, Mass.: MIT Press, 1996), pp. 199–279.

7. On Greenberg's teaching at Black Mountain College, see Mary Emma Harris, *The Arts at Black Mountain College* (Cambridge, Mass.: MIT Press, 1987), p. 214.

8. The emphasis on flatness runs throughout Greenberg's criticism. For a particularly clear (although later) presentation, see his "Modernist Painting" (1960), in Clement Greenberg, *The Collected Essays and Criticism,* ed. John O'Brian, vol. 4, *Modernism with a Vengeance, 1957–1969* (Chicago: University of Chicago Press, 1993), pp. 85–93.

9. On the historical avant-garde manifestation of the monochrome, see Yve-Alain Bois, "Malevich, le carré, le degré zéro," *Macula* 1 (1978): 28–49. Despite the extreme position represented by the *White Paintings,* at the moment of their inception Rauschenberg seems to have believed that they existed *within* the framework established by Greenberg. All of Rauschenberg's recollections over the years point to the conclusion that while he saw the *White Paintings* as advancing painting further along its developmental path, they nonetheless maintained a viable presence and quality as paintings. As he recounted his initial enthusiasm to Barbara Rose, "I was so innocently and indulgently excited about the pieces because they worked. I did them as an experiment to see how much you could pull away from an image and still have an image" (Rose, *An Interview with Robert Rauschenberg* [New York: Vintage Books, 1987], pp. 45–46). See similar statements by Rauschenberg in Richard Kostelanetz, "A Conversation with Robert Rauschenberg," *Partisan Review* 35, no. 1 (winter 1968): 94, and Julia Brown Turell, "Talking to Robert Rauschenberg," in *Rauschenberg Sculpture* (Fort Worth, Tex.: Modern Art Museum of Fort Worth, 1995), p. 76.

10. Hubert Crehan, "The See Change: Raw Duck," *Art Digest* 27, no. 20 (15 September 1953): 25.

11. Crehan, "The See Change," p. 25. For a similar evaluation, see James Fitzsimmons, "Art," *Arts and Architecture* 70, no. 10 (October 1953): 9, 32–36. One almost has to pity Hubert Crehan; he had no idea how bad it could get. On the occasion of Rauschenberg's first exhibit of Combine paintings at the Egan Gallery in late 1954, Crehan's annoyed review

would read in its entirety, "Since he is determined to avoid the responsibility of an artist, it is better that he should show blank canvases rather than the contraptions that he has hung in this side show" ("Fortnight in Review: Rauschenberg," *Arts Digest* 29, no. 7 [1 January 1955]: 30).

12. Clement Greenberg, "Recentness of Sculpture" (1967), in *The Collected Essays and Criticism,* 4:251.

13. Michael Fried would most explicitly formulate the role of determinate negation in modernist painting in his "Three American Painters: Kenneth Noland, Jules Olitski, Frank Stella" (1965), in his *Art and Objecthood: Essays and Reviews* (Chicago: University of Chicago Press, 1998), pp. 213–265. Having taken great pains to present Noland's, Olitski's, and Stella's work in terms of a "dialectic of modernism"—in line with the thinking of Hegel, Mark, Lukács, and Merleau-Ponty (p. 217)—Fried found the situation "complicated" by the existence of neo-dada. As he concluded, "there is a superficial similarity between modernist painting and Dada in one important respect: just as modernist painting has enabled one to see a blank canvas, a sequence of random spatters, or a length of colored fabric as a picture, Dada and Neo-Dada have equipped one to treat virtually any object as a work of art—though it is far from clear exactly what this means" (p. 259).

14. Greenberg, "Recentness of Sculpture," pp. 250–256.

15. de Duve, "The Monochrome and the Blank Canvas," and Hal Foster, "The Crux of Minimalism," in *The Return of the Real* (Cambridge, Mass.: MIT Press, 1996), pp. 35–69.

16. Rosalind E. Krauss, *Passages in Modern Sculpture* (Cambridge, Mass.: MIT Press, 1977), esp. pp. 266–267, and Annette Michelson, "Robert Morris: An Aesthetics of Transgression," in *Robert Morris* (Washington, D.C.: Corcoran Gallery of Art, 1969), pp. 7–79.

17. As discussed in the introduction, the thesis that the neo-avant-garde simply recycled earlier avant-garde strategies was developed in Peter Bürger's *Theory of the Avant-Garde,* trans. Michael Shaw (Minneapolis: University of Minnesota Press, 1984).

18. Recently, Douglas Kahn has declared that Cage owned one of Rauschenberg's *White Paintings* as early as 1951, and thus knew of them before the summer of 1952 (Kahn, *Noise*

Water Meat: A History of Sound in the Arts [Cambridge, Mass.: MIT Press, 1999], p. 168). Kahn's source for this information is an e-mail from Cage's friend Irwin Kremin to Larry Solomon, posted on "Silence: The John Cage Discussion List" on 17 June 1997. Although Kremin recalled seeing "not only white canvasses there but also black" as early as December 1951, Kahn fails to mention that Kremin continued, "Neither her [Kremin's wife's] memory nor mine fit a certain set of Rauschenberg white panels that I saw in Chicago at the opening of the Early Rauschenberg show at the Museum of Contemporary Art in 1992." (The panels exhibited in Chicago were Rauschenberg's actual *White Paintings*.) Nor does Kahn mention Kremin's "recollection . . . that they were all quite small." Although Cage did own Rauschenberg's *Number 1* from the artist's exhibition at Parsons's gallery, it is fairly clear that Kremin saw not Rauschenberg's *White Paintings* but rather Mark Tobey's painting *Crystallization* (1944), a small, all-white, abstract panel that Cage owned at the time.

19. In the year 1961 Robert Morris rejected Cage's aesthetic position and began what would become his pursuit of phenomenological formalism. See Morris, "Letters to John Cage," *October,* no. 81 (summer 1997): 70–79. Also in 1961 Yvonne Rainer completed *Satie for Two,* the last of her choreographed works to employ a Cagean chance score. See Rainer, *Work, 1961–73* (Halifax: Press of the Nova Scotia College of Art and Design; New York: New York University Press, 1974), p. 7.

20. John Cage, "On Robert Rauschenberg, Artist, and His Work" (1961), in *Silence* (Middletown, Conn.: Wesleyan University Press, 1961), p. 102.

21. Cage, "On Robert Rauschenberg," p. 108.

22. *Littérature,* n.s., no. 5 (1 October 1922), n.p. The caption reads: "Vue prise en aéroplane par Man Ray—1921."

23. Not only had Cage met and visited with the Arensbergs, but, at the time still pursuing interests in painting as well as musical composition, he reports having discussed his art with Walter Arensberg; see Alan Gillmor, "Interview with John Cage," *Contact,* no. 14 (autumn 1976): 18. On Rauschenberg's exposure to Duchamp, see Calvin Tomkins, *Off the Wall: Robert Rauschenberg and the Art World of Our Time* (New York: Penguin, 1980), pp. 129–130.

24. John Cage, "Reflections of a Progressive Composer on a Damaged Society," *October,* no. 82 (fall 1997): 78. See also John Cage and Joan Retallack, *Musicage: Cage Muses on Words, Art, Music* (Hanover, N.H.: Wesleyan University Press/University Press of New England, 1996), p. 87.

25. During the 1930s, when considering a career as a painter, Cage had been strongly attracted to pure geometric abstraction. Although he reports having been devoted above all to the work of Mondrian, he also recalled liking Malevich's *White on White* (Cage and Retallack, *Musicage,* p. 109; see also Richard Kostelanetz, *Conversing with Cage* [New York: Limelight Editions, 1994], p. 173).

26. László Moholy-Nagy, *The New Vision and Abstract of an Artist,* trans. Daphne M. Hoffmann, 4th rev. ed. (New York: George Wittenborn, 1947), p. 39; this edition is hereafter cited parenthetically in the text. The translation of Moholy-Nagy's book (originally published in German in 1928) was significantly revised in the 1940s. Although Cage claims to have read it in the 1930s, his ideas relate much more integrally to the later translation. As recent research has brought to light, however, Cage's dating of events in the 1930s and 1940s was somewhat unsure even by 1961. See, for instance, the discussion of Cage's recollections in Leta E. Miller, "Cultural Intersections: John Cage in Seattle (1938–1940)," in *John Cage: Music, Philosophy, and Intention, 1933–1950,* ed. David W. Patterson (New York: Routledge, 2002), pp. 47–82.

27. In Moholy-Nagy's discussion, impressionism marks an important turning point, emphasizing the depiction of instantaneous moments in time while maintaining a traditional notion of perspectival space.

28. Moholy-Nagy mentions Duchamp only once, in a footnote, and then only to note that he is being "neglected" (*The New Vision,* p. 40).

29. Cage, quoted in Moira Roth and William Roth, "John Cage on Marcel Duchamp," *Art in America* 61, no. 6 (November–December 1973): 78.

30. See John Cage, "Juilliard Lecture" (1952), in *A Year from Monday* (Middletown, Conn.: Wesleyan University Press, 1967), p. 102; Cage, "Experimental Music" (1957), in *Silence,*

pp. 7–8; Richard Kostelanetz, "Conversation with John Cage," in *John Cage: An Anthology,* ed. Richard Kostelanetz (New York: Da Capo, 1970), pp. 11, 26; and Michael Kirby and Richard Schechner, "An Interview with John Cage," in *Happenings and Other Acts,* ed. Mariellen R. Sandford (New York: Routledge, 1995), p. 64. For a more thorough discussion of Cage's ideas of space and transparency in the realm of architecture, see my "John Cage and the Architecture of Silence," *October,* no. 81 (summer 1997): 80–104.

31. *Stone, Stone, Stone* (ca. 1951) was included in the Parsons exhibition, as was most likely Untitled [with collage and mirror] (ca. 1951) (Hopps, *Robert Rauschenberg: The Early 1950s,* pp. 52–53).

32. John Cage, "45′ for a Speaker" (1954), in *Silence,* p. 161. See also p. 187; his comments in "Where Are We Going? And What Are We Doing?" (1961), in *Silence,* pp. 238–239; and "Happy New Ears!" (ca. 1964), in *A Year from Monday,* p. 31. In addition to Cage's ideas of space and transparency, his understanding of the artwork's registering of external events would have meshed with Rauschenberg's own interest in photography. In their receptivity to the indexical traces of light and shadow, as well as in the idea that they could be reproduced at any time—even existing as multiple copies (Hopps, *Robert Rauschenberg: The Early 1950s,* p. 50)—Rauschenberg's *White Paintings* can be understood as an appropriation of the logic of mechanical reproduction rather than as an autonomous, modernist reaction against it.

33. As Cage wrote in the preface to his article on Rauschenberg in *Silence:* "To Whom It May Concern: The white paintings came first; my silent piece came later" ("On Robert Rauschenberg," p. 98). Rauschenberg has recently stated that "[Cage] wrote the silent piece because of my paintings. And there were lots more" (Turrell, "Talking to Robert Rauschenberg," p. 62).

34. Richard Dyer, "A Refreshing, Surprising Exchange with John Cage," *Boston Globe,* 20 October 1988, p. B8, and Deborah Ann Campana, "Form and Structure in the Music of John Cage" (Ph.D. diss., Northwestern University, 1985), p. 103.

35. Cage, quoted in Kostelanetz, *Conversing with Cage,* p. 67.

36. See, for example, James Pritchett, *The Music of John Cage* (Cambridge: Cambridge University Press, 1993), pp. 59–60.

37. John Cage, "A Composer's Confessions" (1948), in *John Cage: Writer,* ed. Richard Kostelanetz (New York: Limelight Editions, 1993), p. 43.

38. Eric de Visscher, " 'There's no such thing as silence . . . ': John Cage's Poetics of Silence," in *Writings about John Cage,* ed. Richard Kostelanetz (Ann Arbor: University of Michigan Press, 1993), p. 118. See also the discussion of the relations and differences of *Silent Prayer* and *4′33″* in Khan, *Noise Water Meat,* pp. 161–199.

39. See de Visscher, " 'There's no such thing as silence . . . ,' " p. 120.

40. Eckhart's aesthetic philosophy was discussed in the writings of the Indian art historian Ananda Coomaraswamy, also read by Cage. Beginning in the mid-1940s—most likely on the suggestion of the mythologist Joseph Campbell, a close friend at the time—Cage became interested in South Asian and medieval European philosophy and religion. For a discussion of Cage's Eastern influences, see David W. Patterson, "The Picture That Is Not in the Colors: Cage, Coomaraswamy, and the Impact of India," in Patterson, ed., *John Cage,* pp. 177–215. Patterson dates Cage's initial interest in Asian philosophy and aesthetics to the years of World War II (p. 179). James Pritchett has related *Silent Prayer* and *4′33″* (between which he makes little distinction) to Cage's adoption of Eckhart's ideas of "ignorance" or self-negation as a means to perceive the divine (*The Music of John Cage,* pp. 46, 60, 206 n. 11).

41. Eckhart, in Franz Pfeiffer, *Meister Eckhart,* trans. C. de B. Evans (London: John M. Watkins, 1924), p. 284; this collection of Eckhart's writings is cited in Ananda K. Coomaraswamy, "Meister Eckhart's View of Art," in *The Transformation of Nature in Art* (Cambridge, Mass.: Harvard University Press, 1934), p. 83.

42. Eckhart, in Pfeiffer, *Meister Eckhart,* p. 284.

43. Eckhart, in Pfeiffer, *Meister Eckhart,* pp. 284, 283.

44. This pattern—that a reference, after entering his thinking, becomes progressively more complexly understood as he engages with it over a period that may last several years—recurs often in Cage's work.

45. John Cage, "Composition as Process II: Indeterminacy" (1958), in *Silence,* p. 39. See, for example, Eckhart: "Three things are to be noted about the divine essence. First and foremost, it is the principle preserving all things; in his divine essence God is in all things upholding them" (in Pfeiffer, *Meister Eckhart,* p. 284). Pritchett, as noted above, discusses *Silent Prayer* and *4′33″* in terms of an idea, found in Eckhart, of opening oneself up to the universal. However, as de Visscher has indicated, in 1948–1949 Cage still held "a relatively classical position about silence: silence is considered as absolutely necessary to the existence of sound, but still as the absence of sound" (" 'There's no such thing as silence . . . ,' " p. 120). Thus, it would seem that an understanding of *Silent Prayer* as a representation of a stillness rather than as an opening onto the totality of the universe comes closer to Cage's interpretation of *Silent Prayer* as expressed in "A Composer's Confessions." Clearly, this notion of silence has Heideggerian implications as well. For an investigation of Cage's work from that perspective, see Marc Froment Meurice, *Les intermittences de la raison: Penser Cage, entendre Heidegger* (Paris: Klincksieck, 1982).

46. See de Visscher, " 'There's no such thing as silence . . . ,' " p. 121, who also notes that, in that their sounds, soft and somewhat isolated, never seem fully to emerge from their silent surroundings, Cage's compositions of the time served to illustrate this mutual interdependence.

47. de Visscher, " 'There's no such thing as silence . . . ,' " p. 123.

48. Cage, "Lecture on Something" (1951), in *Silence,* p. 135.

49. This story is recounted many times in Cage's writings. See, for example, "Experimental Music," p. 8: "For certain engineering purposes, it is desirable to have as silent a situation as possible. Such a room is called an anechoic chamber, its six walls made of special material, a room without echoes. I entered one at Harvard University several years ago and heard two sounds, one high and one low. When I described them to the engineer in charge, he informed me that the high one was my nervous system in operation, the low one my blood in circulation." See also "Experimental Music: Doctrine" (1955), in *Silence,* pp. 13–14; "Composition as Process I: Changes" (1958), in *Silence,* p. 23; "45′ for a Speaker," p. 168; and "How to Pass, Kick, Fall, and Run" (ca. 1958–1965), in *A Year from Monday,* p. 134.

50. Cage, "Experimental Music: Doctrine," *Silence,* p. 14.

51. Henri Bergson, *Creative Evolution,* trans. Arthur Mitchell (New York: Henry Holt, 1911), pp. 272–298; this work is hereafter cited parenthetically in the text in this discussion. To my knowledge, the impact of Bergson's thinking on Cage has not previously been noted. Cage explicitly refers to Bergson at the end of the article "Experimental Music," where he writes: "Here we are concerned with the coexistence of dissimilars, and the central points where fusion occurs are many: the ears of the listeners wherever they are. This disharmony, to paraphrase Bergson's statement about disorder, is simply a harmony to which many are unaccustomed" (p. 12). This idea forms part of Bergson's larger critique of negation (*Creative Evolution*, pp. 241 ff.).

52. Cage, "45′ for a Speaker," p. 191; Rauschenberg, quoted in Dorothy C. Miller, ed., *Sixteen Americans* (New York: Museum of Modern Art, 1959), p. 58.

53. In his discussion of Cagean silence, de Visscher remarks on an apparent one-year delay in Cage's drawing on the consequences of his experience at Harvard (" 'There's no such thing as silence . . . ,' " p. 125).

54. Despite the decisive impact that Rauschenberg's *White Paintings* had on Cage's thinking, the concept of transparency had already begun to enter Cage's mind. The earliest quotation in which he relates transparency and music occurs in a lecture delivered on 27 March 1952: "It acts in such a way that one can 'hear through' a piece of music just as one can see through some modern buildings or see through a wire sculpture by Richard Lippold or the glass of Marcel Duchamp" (Cage, "Juilliard Lecture," p. 102). The date of this lecture is given in David Wayne Patterson, "Appraising the Catchwords, c. 1942–1959: John Cage's Asian-Derived Rhetoric and the Historical Reference of Black Mountain College" (Ph.D. diss., Columbia University, 1996), p. 336, and in John Holzaepfel, "David Tudor and the Performance of American Experimental Music, 1950–1959" (Ph.D. diss., City University of New York, 1994), p. 223 n. 32.

55. Cage, "45′ for a Speaker," p. 161.

56. The version of the score for *4′33″* dedicated to Kremin initially appeared in *Source* 1, no. 2 (July 1967); it has been published, in a corrected version, by C. F. Peters as Edition 6777a. For a discussion of the important implications of the second version of the score for postwar art, see Liz Kotz, "Post-Cagean Aesthethics and the 'Event' Score," *October,* no. 95

(winter 2001): 55–89. For documentation of the different versions of the score of *4′33″*, see William Fetterman, *John Cage's Theatre Pieces: Notations and Performances* (Amsterdam: Harwood Academic Publishers, 1996), pp. 69–84.

57. Cage, "On Robert Rauschenberg," p. 100; cf. Cage, "Happy New Ears!" p. 31. On Cage's study of Coomaraswamy, see Patterson, "The Picture That Is Not in the Colors."

58. Bergson, *Creative Evolution,* pp. 302, 272, 249; this work is hereafter cited parenthetically in the text in this discussion. Bergson's view contrasts markedly with certain of Coomaraswamy's ideas of nature, largely held to be the source of Cage's own. According to Patterson, Coomaraswamy ultimately felt that all of existence was already present—i.e., that there was nothing actually being created. As Patterson summarizes Coomaraswamy's attitude, "All human activities and extant artifacts throughout all time and within all cultures are merely evidence of the endless cycle of 'rediscoveries' of the same essential, immutable Reality that serves as the basis of all things" ("The Picture That Is Not in the Colors," p. 187).

59. See Gilles Deleuze, "Bergson," in *Les philosophes célèbres,* ed. Maurice Merleau-Ponty (Paris: Editions d'art Lucien Mazenod, 1956), pp. 292–299.

60. For Bergson, science or the scientific attitude was the foremost expression of the limits on perception. We sense reality in the useful form of discrete and stable objects and forms. In fact, perception is nothing other than the separation and isolation of discrete objects out of the interminable flux of reality on which we may act:

> The distinct outlines which we see in an object, and which give it its individuality, are only the design of a certain kind of *influence* that we might exert on a certain point of space: it is the plan of our eventual actions that is sent back to our eyes, as though by a mirror, when we see the surfaces and edges of things. Suppress this action, and with it consequently those main directions which by perception are traced out for it in the entanglement of the real, and the individuality of the body is re-absorbed in the universal interaction which, without doubt, is reality itself. (Bergson, *Creative Evolution,* p. 11, cf. pp. 44–45, 204)

61. Cage refers to the nonanthropocentric point of view as the "outside" in "Morris Graves" (1957), in *John Cage: An Anthology,* p. 126.

62. Cage, "Experimental Music," p. 8. Cage's use of the term "psychological" in this context may also have been derived from Bergson. See, for example, *Creative Evolution,* pp. 257, 299.

63. Cage, "Where Are We Going? And What Are We Doing?" pp. 236–237.

64. Cage, "Robert Rauschenberg" (1953), in *John Cage: An Anthology,* pp. 111–112.

65. Cage, "On Robert Rauschenberg," p. 102 (emphasis added). For a discussion of the historical avant-garde strategy of estrangement and the attempt to attain an unmediated form of perception, see Simon Watney, "Making Strange: The Shattered Mirror," in *Thinking Photography,* ed. Victor Burgin (London: Macmillan, 1982), pp. 154–176.

66. John Cage, "Memoir" (1966), in *John Cage: An Anthology,* p. 77. This idea of immersion within a wholly immanent reality also lies behind Cage's remark, quoted above, that "the water's fine." See Cage, "Lecture on Something," p. 134.

67. As we will see in chapter 4, it was precisely the refusal of Cage's and Rauschenberg's work to separate itself from its temporally changing context that Michael Fried would attack in "Art and Objecthood." There he denigrated the qualitative "degeneration" brought on by their embrace of "theatricality" as he argued for a legitimate modernist art's transcendent "presentness" (see Fried, "Art and Objecthood" [1967], in *Minimal Art: A Critical Anthology,* ed. Gregory Battcock [Berkeley: University of California Press, 1995], esp. pp. 141–142).

68. Lawrence Alloway, Marcel Duchamp, et al., "The Art of Assemblage: A Symposium" (1961), in *Essays on Assemblage,* ed. James Leggio and Helen M. Franc, Studies in Modern Art, vol. 2 (New York: Museum of Modern Art, 1992), p. 137; this conversation is hereafter cited as "Assemblage Symposium." Rauschenberg reiterated these ideas two years later: "Every minute is an assemblage of materials and conflicting ideas and desires" ("Pop Art—Cult of the Commonplace," *Time,* 3 May 1963, p. 72); he made the same points again, much later, at the beginning of his interview with Alain Sayag in *Robert Rauschenberg: Photographs* (New York: Pantheon Books, 1981), n.p.

69. Rauschenberg, quoted in Crehan, "The See Change," p. 25.

70. "Assemblage Symposium," pp. 127–128, 137.

71. Cage, "On Robert Rauschenberg," pp. 99–100.

72. John Cage, "Letter to Paul Henry Lang" (1956), in *John Cage: An Anthology,* pp. 117–118.

73. Rauschenberg, quoted in D. Miller, *Sixteen Americans*, p. 58.

74. Cage, "Lecture on Something," p. 134.

75. "Do you understand this idea?: *Painting relates to both art and life. Neither can be made. (I try to act in that gap between the two.)* The nothingness in between is where for no reason at all every practical thing that one actually takes the time to do so stirs up the dregs that they're no longer sitting as we thought at the bottom" (Cage, "On Robert Rauschenberg," p. 105).

76. Bergson's discussion of memory is developed primarily in *Matter and Memory,* trans. N. M. Paul and W. S. Palmer (New York: Zone Books, 1991), but it is also summarized at the beginning of *Creative Evolution* (see pp. 4–5).

77. See Bergson's description of observing a motionless object (*Creative Evolution,* p. 2).

78. "The implications were so blatantly Freudian, the act itself so obviously a symbolic (if good-natured) patricide" (Tomkins, *Off the Wall,* p. 96).

79. Maxime de la Falaise McKendry, "Robert Rauschenberg Talks to Maxime de la Falaise McKendry," *Interview* 6, no. 5 (May 1976): 36.

80. Rauschenberg, quoted in de la Falaise McKendry, "Robert Rauschenberg," 36.

Despite their connections to a Bergsonian philosophy, Cage's and Rauschenberg's attitudes toward expression nevertheless represent an inversion of Bergson's ideas about art. Bergson portrayed art as opposed to science in that art could grasp the real and science could not. The work of genius, for Bergson, represented the unknowable, the creative. (Bergson even cites Cage's nemesis, Beethoven, as an example in *Creative Evolution,* p. 224.) For Cage and Rauschenberg, art as genius was equivalent to intentional action and cut one off from the true or pure perception of reality; science—understood as an investigation into chaos—would ultimately be seen as supporting their viewpoint.

81. Thomas Crow, "This Is Now: Becoming Robert Rauschenberg," *Artforum* 36, no. 1 (September 1997): 96. Rauschenberg's *Erased de Kooning Drawing* is discussed further in chapter 2.

82. "Assemblage Symposium," p. 138. Once again, this idea of difference resonates profoundly with the thinking of Bergson. On account of our existence in duration, Bergson explained,

> the same reasons may dictate to different persons, or to the same person at different moments, acts profoundly different, although equally reasonable. The truth is that they are not quite the same reasons, since they are not those of the same person, nor of the same moment. That is why we cannot deal with them in the abstract, from outside, as in geometry, nor solve for another the problems by which he is faced in life. Each must solve them from within, on his own account. (*Creative Evolution,* p. 7)

83. "Assemblage Symposium," p. 144.

84. Rauschenberg's objections were raised in the context of his debate with Roger Shattuck:

> Rauschenberg: In the case of shock, don't you have to anticipate a mass reaction?
>
> Shattuck: In most cases this is exactly what was desired. Yes.
>
> Rauschenberg: How can you do that when everybody is different?
>
> Shattuck: I'm afraid people aren't that different when it comes to reacting to certain works.
>
> Rauschenberg: Then that just supports their similarity.
>
> Shattuck: When you put the *Mona Lisa* with a mustache up in front of people, I'm afraid the reaction is very similar.
>
> Rauschenberg: I don't think so. ("Assemblage Symposium," p. 129)

See also Rauschenberg's comments on shock in G. R. Swenson, "Rauschenberg Paints a Picture," *Art News* 62, no. 2 (April 1963): 66. On Rauschenberg's interest in differential collectivity, see his comments in Alloway, "Rauschenberg's Development," p. 18; John Gruen, "Robert Rauschenberg: An Audience of One," *Art News* 76, no. 2 (February 1977): 47–48; and Barbaralee Diamonstein, *Inside New York's Art World* (New York: Rizzoli, 1979), p. 311.

85. Despite its signal importance in opening this line of reception, Moira Roth's "The Aesthetic of Indifference" (1977), reprinted in *Difference/Indifference: Musings on Postmodernism, Marcel Duchamp and John Cage,* by Moira Roth and Jonathan D. Katz ([Amsterdam: G+B Arts International, 1998], pp. 33–47), largely reached the conclusion that silence reflects indifference. For an important discussion of Roth's article, see Jonathan D. Katz, "Identification," in Roth and Katz, *Difference/Indifference,* pp. 49–68. Similar critiques of Cage as essentially apolitical have been extended by, among others, Yvonne Rainer, "Looking Myself in the Mouth . . . ," *October,* no. 17 (summer 1981): 65–76; George J. Leonard, *Into the Light of Things: The Art of the Commonplace from Wordsworth to John Cage* (Chicago: University of Chicago Press, 1994); and Kahn, *Noise Water Meat,* pp. 161–199.

Arguing against them, see Caroline A. Jones, "Finishing School: John Cage and the Abstract Expressionist Ego," *Critical Inquiry* 19, no. 4 (summer 1993): 628–665, and Jonathan D. Katz, who has developed his position through a series of articles. For one of the most sophisticated, see Katz, "John Cage's Queer Silence; or, How to Avoid Making Matters Worse," in *Writings through John Cage's Music, Poetry, and Art,* ed. David Bernstein and Christopher Hatch (Chicago: University of Chicago Press, 2001), pp. 41–61. Katz explicitly extends his reading to Rauschenberg's *White Paintings* in, among other writings, "The Silent Camp: Queer Resistance and the Rise of Pop Art," in *PLOP! Goes the World,* ed. Serge Guilbaut (Durham, N.C.: Duke University Press, forthcoming). An exploration of the origin of Cage's aesthetic from the point of view of his sexuality has also been undertaken in Jill Johnston, *Jasper Johns: Privileged Information* (London: Thames and Hudson, 1996).

86. Katz, "John Cage's Queer Silence," p. 57.

87. Jones argues for viewing Cage's work as the expression of a "specifically homosexual aesthetic" ("Finishing School," p. 639). Despite her efforts to use the term in "a nonessentializing way" (p. 639 n. 33), she largely understands Cage's silence as hiding a specific form

of homosexual subjectivity. Thus, she consistently has recourse to the metaphor of the artist's subjectivity (or body, which she effectively equates with ego) being withdrawn or hidden. She relies on a binary division between a heterosexual and a homosexual aesthetic, which elicits a further set of similar binarisms such as expression/silence, public/private, and dominant social conscious/repressed social unconscious (p. 653); for this reason, Jones rightly sees in Foucault a position that she must argue against (p. 657).

88. Jonathan Katz, arguing from an explicitly Derridean standpoint, sees the importance of Cage's silence as deconstructing binaries in its formulation of a force of resistance that cannot be reduced to dialectical (or "oppositional") negation. Although Katz has, at times, predicated his arguments on the existence of a specifically gay male "core identity" (see Katz, "Passive Resistance: On the Success of Queer Artists in Cold War American Art," *L'Image,* no. 3 [December 1996]: 135), he has more recently maintained that Cage and Rauschenberg's silence initiates a form of "queered reading," closer to the political perspective I attempt to develop here—"one that does not offer a permanent position from which to speak, that does not rely on a pre-scripted identity or subject position, that does not ossify into the other that allows the norm to suture its authority through reference to that which it excludes" (Katz, "Performative Silence and the Politics of Passivity," in *Making a Scene,* ed. Henry Rogers and David Burrows [Birmingham, Eng.: ARTicle Press, 2000], pp. 101–102). It should be noted that such ultimately utopian ideas of subjective transformation are particularly appealing to white males. The limitations imposed by the obstacles of race within the neo-avant-garde legacy of Cage, Rauschenberg, and Johns are addressed perhaps most cogently in David Hammonds's early Body Print works of the 1970s.

89. Eve Kosofsky Sedgwick has strongly argued that the very attempt to make such a move from a discourse centered on homosexuality to a more general discussion of difference is "a phobic form of understanding" (Sedgwick, *Epistemology of the Closet* [Berkeley: University of California Press, 1990], p. 247). Yet it does not seem to me possible to avoid acknowledging that Cage and Rauschenberg themselves made this move. Indeed, in their pivotal positions within the emergence of a postmodern discourse, this move helped give rise to the very forms of "notional 'undecidability' or 'infinite plurality' of 'difference' " that she warns against. I do not deny that the "machinery of heterosexist presumption and homophobic projection" (p. 247) may have played an important role in their own artistic formations and their reticence to discuss their sexuality publicly. But as Katz has eloquently argued, that their position may have developed within repressive (and doubtlessly at least partially internalized)

McCarthyite homophobia does not prevent its resistance to this form of oppression, then or now (Katz, "John Cage's Queer Silence"). While I do not follow Katz's (strategic?) claim to *equate* Derridean indecidability and "queering" (Jonathan Katz, "Dismembership: Jasper Johns and the Body Politic," in *Performing the Body/Performing the Text,* ed. Amelia Jones and Andrew Stephenson [New York: Routledge, 1998], p. 181), I agree that in refusing a stable, gay-identified subject position, their queering of identity renders their work potentially suited for aiding the formulation of a resistant post-identity political position.

90. Michel Foucault, *The History of Sexuality,* vol. 1, *An Introduction,* trans. Robert Hurley (New York: Pantheon, 1978), p. 48. Foucault's provocative quote about silence in the *History of Sexuality* is routinely cited within the literature that explores Cage's or Rauschenberg's sexuality: "Silence itself—the things one declines to say, or is forbidden to name, the discretion that is required between different speakers—is less the absolute limit of discourse, the other side from which it is separated by a strict boundary, than an element that functions alongside the things said, with them and in relation to them within over-all strategies" (p. 27). However, the larger implications of Foucault's perspective (taken up here in chapter 3) have to date been either ignored or explicitly refused. See Jones, "Finishing School," p. 656; Katz, "Performative Silence and the Politics of Passivity," p. 103; and Laura Auricchio, "Lifting the Veil: Robert Rauschenberg's *Thirty-four Drawings for Dante's Inferno* and the Commercial Homoerotic Imagery of 1950s America," in *The Gay 90s: Disciplinary and Interdisciplinary Formation in Queer Studies,* ed. Thomas Foster, Carol Siegel, and Ellen E. Berry, Genders, vol. 26 (New York: New York University Press, 1997), p. 148.

91. Rauschenberg's relationship to spectacle is investigated in chapter 4. On the subversion of stable identity, see, in addition to Cage's famous embrace of "no-mindedness," Rauschenberg's many comments such as "I don't like the single ego. . . . I just don't want to have one" (quoted in Diamonstein, *Inside New York's Art World,* p. 311).

92. Todd May, *The Political Philosophy of Poststructuralist Anarchism* (University Park: Pennsylvania State University Press, 1994), p. 48.

93. Cage, as we have seen, seems to have encountered Bergson between 1950 and 1952, mentioning him in print in 1957. Deleuze's first article on Bergson ("Bergson's Conception of Difference" [1956], trans. Melissa McMahon, in *The New Bergson,* ed. John Mullarkey

[Manchester: Manchester University Press, 1999], pp. 42–65), was initially presented as a lecture in 1954 (as dated in Michael Hardt, *Gilles Deleuze: An Apprenticeship in Philosophy* [Minneapolis: University of Minnesota Press, 1993], p. 2).

94. Gilles Deleuze, *Difference and Repetition,* trans. Paul Patton (New York: Columbia University Press, 1994), p. 55. This work is hereafter cited parenthetically in the text.

95. Deleuze's political position would be developed primarily through his collaborative writings with Félix Guattari, most notably the two volumes subtitled *Capitalism and Schizophrenia: Anti-Oedipus,* trans. Robert Hurley, Mark Seem, and Helen R. Lane (Minneapolis: University of Minnesota Press, 1983), and *A Thousand Plateaus,* trans. Brian Massumi (Minneapolis: University of Minnesota Press, 1987). Jean-François Lyotard developed a related political position, based explicitly on a Cagean critique of negation and dialectics. See, for example, Lyotard, "Several Silences" (1972), trans. Joseph Maier, in his *Driftworks,* ed. Roger McKeon (New York: Semiotext(e), 1984), pp. 91–110.

96. Hopps, *Robert Rauschenberg: The Early 1950s,* p. 32. Cage's relationship to the abstract expressionist clubs is discussed in Jones, "Finishing School," esp. pp. 641–642.

97. Cage, "Experimental Music: Doctrine," p. 14. It is important to note that although Cage and Rauschenberg's understanding of the *White Paintings* is very close to Deleuze's idea of abstraction, the two do not entirely coincide. All parties would have agreed on the role of abstract art in revealing nonrepresentational forces (or "percepts") "to make perceptible," as Deleuze and Guattari write, "the imperceptible forces that populate the world, affect us, and make us become" (Gilles Deleuze and Félix Guattari, *What Is Philosophy?,* trans. Hugh Tomlinson and Graham Burchell [New York: Columbia University Press, 1994], p. 182). However, for Deleuze, what exists on a blank canvas (the *prépictural*) is not the same as Rauschenberg's conception of what inheres in "A canvas [that] is never empty." As he put it in *Francis Bacon,* what crowds onto the unpainted canvas are not the subrepresentational forces of difference but rather "clichés"—reified modes of perception and representation akin to the forms of instrumental reason described by Bergson. What preexists on a blank canvas is not that which is to be identified with but that which must be deformed or opposed (Deleuze, *Francis Bacon: Logique de la sensation* [Paris: La Différence, 1981], p. 14). It is largely through color that the painter is to break with such prepictural clichés. In Deleuze and Guattari's discussion of monochrome painting, they primarily discuss "The colored or, rather,

coloring void [which] is already force," preferring surfaces that evince "subtle imperceptible variations" (p. 181)—a discussion more applicable to Rauschenberg's black paintings (see chapter 2). Deleuze and Guattari would likely have found Rauschenberg's uniformly white paintings not too ascetic but too rich, in that totally wiping away clichés revealed nothing other than unencumbered temporal contingencies (see Deleuze and Guattari's comments about Cage's music deterritorializing too quickly in *A Thousand Plateaus,* p. 344). Yet the forces of difference revealed by the *White Paintings* always interact with the preset forms of perception that, like the clichés crowding Bacon's unpainted canvases, viewers bring from the past. Something similar is implied in the manner in which Rauschenberg's Combines interpenetrate blank "spaces" with appropriated elements of collage (see chapter 3).

For a synthetic discussion of Deleuze's idea of abstraction, see John Rajchman, "Abstraction," in *Constructions* (Cambridge, Mass.: MIT Press, 1998), pp. 55–76. Rajchman obscures the analysis somewhat by translating Deleuze as stating "the canvas is never empty" (p. 61) when Deleuze does not, in fact, so closely approximate Rauschenberg's phraseology (see Deleuze, *Francis Bacon,* p. 57).

98. Cage, quoted in Kostelanetz, *Conversing with Cage,* p. 181.

2 Pedestrian Colors

1. Ellsworth Kelly, quoted in Yve-Alain Bois, "Ellsworth Kelly in France: Anti-Composition in Its Many Guises," in *Ellsworth Kelly: The Years in France, 1948–1954* (Washington, D.C.: National Gallery of Art, 1992), p. 11.

2. Notes of Rauschenberg interview by Walter Hopps, Captiva Island, Fla., 18–20 January 1991, in Rauschenberg's archives, New York.

3. Kelly's sketches for his all-white paintings were published by Roberta Bernstein, who also notes the resemblance to Rauschenberg's works. See Bernstein, "Ellsworth Kelly's Multipanel Paintings," in *Ellsworth Kelly: A Retrospective,* ed. Diane Waldman (New York: Solomon R. Guggenheim Museum, 1996), p. 41.

4. Ellsworth Kelly, conversation with author, Spencertown, New York, 10 April 2002. Kelly retains a photograph of Naudé's white painting in his archives. The statement Kelly recalls making to Rauschenberg—that two so similar ideas could look so different upon

execution—may not have come across as neutral (despite his remembered intent), for to his mind Naudé's panels were the more successful. From Kelly's perspective (and, as we have seen in chapter 1, from that of many others as well), Rauschenberg's *White Paintings,* which could be taken for primed but unpainted canvases, came too close to a dadaist, anti-art gesture.

5. E. C. Goossen, *Ellsworth Kelly* (New York: Museum of Modern Art, 1973), pp. 49–52.

6. *Collection* is Rauschenberg's second Combine painting; the first one, in all probability, was Untitled [with shelf and colored glass light box] (1954) (Walter Hopps, *Robert Rauschenberg: The Early 1950s* [Houston: Houston Fine Arts Press, 1991], p. 166). It was given the title *Collection* by the artist in 1976 on the occasion of his retrospective at the National Collection of Fine Arts in Washington, D.C.

7. Walter Hopps, ed., *Robert Rauschenberg* (Washington: National Collection of Fine Arts, 1976), p. 77. In a recent statement, Rauschenberg confirmed the original tripartite division of *Collection* into red, yellow, and blue panels (unpublished notes from meeting between Robert Rauschenberg and Gary Garrels, David Ross, and Will Shank, San Francisco Museum of Modern Art, 14 August 1999, Conservation Department Files, San Francisco Museum of Modern Art). Since its production, *Collection* has undergone considerable fading. Early reproductions reveal that all of what now appears as pink in the bottom third of the Combine-painting was originally a primary red.

8. Bois, "Ellsworth Kelly in France," pp. 11–12. Both *Painting for a White Wall* and *Red Yellow Blue White and Black,* which are rather modest in size, were intended by Kelly to be realized on a much larger scale, thus providing an even closer possible comparison with the colored panels of *Collection.*

9. Kelly had *La Combe III* (1951) sent from an exhibition at the Boston Museum School to Cage in New York for safekeeping and only recovered it in 1954 (Nathalie Brunet, "Chronology, 1943–1954," in *Ellsworth Kelly: The Years in France, 1948–1954,* p. 191). The irregular lattice of light blue bands on Kelly's painting was a faithful transcription of the patterns of shadows cast on a stairway by a railing. Thus, *La Combe III* has a certain relation (though entirely indistinguishable at the time—Kelly did not make the source of his motif known until 1971) to Cage's famous description of the shadows that play across the surface

of Rauschenberg's *White Paintings*. But as Bois has pointed out, there is all the difference in the world between the near indexicality of Kelly's work of the time and Rauschenberg's interest in the material actuality of the indexical mark (see Bois, "Ellsworth Kelly in France," p. 22). It is in part the distinction between Rauschenberg's interest in materiality and Kelly's investigations of mediation that this chapter explores.

10. Aleksandr Rodchenko, quoted in Yve-Alain Bois, "Painting: The Task of Mourning," in *Painting as Model* (Cambridge, Mass.: MIT Press, 1990), p. 238.

11.

> Abstracted from all content, the pure form around which art has evolved during the last decade has ultimately revealed its insubstantiality; it has exposed the fruitlessness of an art divorced from life and the inability of the typical forms of creativity, suitable only for the graveyard of the museum, to survive in contemporary conditions. In the past, "the picture" was figurative and had its aesthetic and meaning in the milieu of a particular class or social group, as an individualistic expression of the aesthetic consciousness of a class or group. Now, when class and related divisions lose their foundations in all essential characteristics, making aesthetic epicurism fruitless, the "picture" as the typical form of visual art also loses its meaning as social phenomenon. (Nikolai Tarabukin, "From the Easel to the Machine," trans. Christina Lodder, in *Modern Art and Modernism: A Critical Anthology,* ed. Francis Frascina and Charles Harrison [New York: Harper and Row, 1982], p. 141)

12. Such was the theory. In actuality, although Rodchenko and others associated with him did forgo the continuation of art as a purely representational paradigm, their self-effacement into the corps of revolutionary workers was not as complete as Tarabukin urged (a failure on which he based his critique of their activities), nor was the social sphere as homogeneous as his analysis implied. With the reinstatement of capitalist markets under the New Economic Policy came the return of class divisions and the prerevolutionary forms of subjectivity associated with them. In that context, Rodchenko devoted himself to producing advertisements, posters, and other forms of social signification that aimed to play an active, partisan role in defending and even fostering collective, egalitarian institutions (state-run factories, utilities, department stores). Thus, despite the "failure" of the productivist program of moving directly into the productive realm, Rodchenko always worked from the perspective that aesthetic

practice could have a direct, or at least a tangible, impact on actual events, an unshakable tenet underlying any notion of agit-prop.

13. Yve-Alain Bois has discussed this aspect of Rauschenberg's work in relation to Georges Bataille's concept of the *informe:* "From 1951 until his first *Combine Paintings,* Rauschenberg's work is one big celebration of nondialectical, unarticulable waste" (Bois, "Base Materialism, in Yve-Alain Bois and Rosalind E. Kraus, *Formless: A User's Guide* [New York: Zone Books, 1997], p. 59). While Rauschenberg did, as I will argue, pursue a certain strategy of base materialism, he held a notion of natural multiplicity that is not entirely compatible with this understanding of Bataille's *informe.*

14. Rauschenberg began his black paintings before meeting Cage, most likely following from his early interest in paintings as "incarnation" (see chapter 1). Rauschenberg's early matte black triptych without the addition of collage is telling in that he apparently considered it a failure—no doubt because the black paint read as pigment (whereas white signified as its absence, i.e., as blank canvas) and hence restored the representational function of the painting. Despite its lack of figurative representation, the matte black coloration more clearly took on the function of an image. Emphasizing materiality through collage (as Rauschenberg had done in *Mother of God*) was one means of opposing the transcendent status of the image.

15. On Rauschenberg's materialized color, see Rosalind Krauss, "Rauschenberg and the Materialized Image," *Artforum* 13, no. 4 (December 1974): 36–43.

16. This property of the texture of the black paintings has also been noted by Walter Hopps (*Robert Rauschenberg: The Early 1950s,* p. 67).

17. Dore Ashton, "57th Street: Bob Rauschenberg," *Art Digest* 27, no. 20 (15 September 1953): 21. See also John Cage's comments on the aging of Rauschenberg's collage elements in Cage, "On Robert Rauschenberg, Artist, and His Work" (1961), in *Silence* (Middletown, Conn.: Wesleyan University Press, 1961), p. 102.

18. See chapter 1, note 9.

19. Here, Deleuze and Guattari's description of an art of "texture," which they contrast with a Greenbergian, optical flatness, is apposite: "This is painting that no longer has any

background because the 'underneath' comes through: the surface can be furrowed or the plane of composition can take on thickness insofar as the material rises up, independently of depth or perspective, independently of shadows and even of the chromatic order of color (the arbitrary colorist). One no longer covers over; one raises, accumulates, piles up, goes through, stirs up, folds" (Gilles Deleuze and Félix Guattari, *What Is Philosophy?,* trans. Hugh Tomlinson and Graham Burchell [New York: Columbia University Press, 1994], p. 194).

20. Rauschenberg, quoted in Calvin Tomkins, *The Bride and the Bachelors* (New York: Penguin, 1968), pp. 199–200. Rauschenberg further explained, "That's why I ended up doing the all-white and the all-black paintings—one of the reasons, anyway." Rauschenberg related his attitude toward materials to that of "a raw Zen. It was just an attitude about materials that was strong enough not to submit to Albers' dictum of 'It's the *man* who does the painting'" (John Gruen, "Robert Rauschenberg: An Audience of One," *Art News* 76, no. 2 [February 1977]: 46).

21. Rauschenberg calls his works "visual experiences" in Hubert Crehan, "The See Change: Raw Duck," *Art Digest* 27, no. 20 (15 September 1953): 25. See Deleuze and Guattari's comments on the monochrome's being the "bearer of glimpsed forces" (*What Is Philosophy?,* pp. 181–182). This is understood as opening onto the "plane of composition," which is akin to Cage and Rauschenberg's idea of nature as a field of multiplicitous differentiation.

22. Rauschenberg, quoted in Billy Klüver, *On Record: 11 Artists 1963* (New York: Experiments in Art and Technology, 1981), p. 42. Calvin Tomkins quotes this conversation as "without their revealing much" (*Bride,* p. 204, and *Off the Wall: Robert Rauschenberg and the Art World of Our Time* [New York: Penguin, 1980], p. 72). Cage would describe these paintings similarly in terms of "black" becoming "infinite and previously unnoticed" ("On Robert Rauschenberg," p. 102).

23. Rauschenberg, quoted in Dorothy Gees Seckler, "The Artist Speaks: Robert Rauschenberg," *Art in America* 54, no. 3 (May–June 1966): 76.

24. Lawrence Alloway, Marcel Duchamp, et al., "The Art of Assemblage: A Symposium" (1961), in *Essays on Assemblage,* ed. James Leggio and Helen M. Franc, Studies in Modern Art, vol. 2 (New York: Museum of Modern Art, 1992), p. 138. This conversation is hereafter cited as "Assemblage Symposium."

25. Rauschenberg, quoted in Klüver, *On Record,* pp. 42–43. Cf. Rauschenberg's comments in G. R. Swenson, "Rauschenberg Paints a Picture," *Art News* 62, no. 2 (April 1963): 44; Seckler, "The Artist Speaks," p. 76; and Tomkins, *Bride,* p. 212.

26. Rauschenberg, quoted in Seckler, "The Artist Speaks," p. 76.

27. "I've always felt as though, whatever I've used and whatever I've done, the method was always closer to a *collaboration* with materials than to any kind of conscious manipulation and control" (Rauschenberg, quoted in Tomkins, *Bride,* p. 204). Cf. pp. 231–233, and Rauschenberg's statement in *Twelve Americans: Masters of Collage* (New York: Andrew Crispo Gallery, 1977), n.p.

28. Rauschenberg's characterization of Untitled (*Elemental Sculpture*) [block and stones] (1953) is quoted in Hopps, *Robert Rauschenberg: The Early 1950s,* p. 180.

29. The sculptures most notably reflect the influence of ideas already inherent in the French master's work but expressed later in "The Creative Act" (1957) and "Apropos of Readymades," the statement made at the *Art of Assemblage* symposium (1961) (both reprinted in *The Writings of Marcel Duchamp,* ed. Michel Sanouillet and Elmer Peterson [New York: Da Capo, 1973], pp. 138–142).

30. Tomkins, *Off the Wall,* p. 129; Joan Young and Susan Davidson, "Chronology," in *Robert Rauschenberg: A Retrospective,* ed. Walter Hopps and Susan Davidson (New York: Solomon R. Guggenheim Museum, 1997), pp. 552–553.

31. The works included in the Janis exhibition are listed in Arturo Schwarz, *The Complete Works of Marcel Duchamp,* 3rd rev. and expanded ed. (New York: Delano Greenidge Editions, 1997), 2:801. The Arensberg Collection at the Philadelphia Museum would open in the following year, and Rauschenberg, accompanied by Jasper Johns, would visit it then (Tomkins, *Off the Wall,* p. 130).

32. Rauschenberg, quoted in Julia Brown Turrell, "Talking to Robert Rauschenberg," in *Rauschenberg Sculpture* (Fort Worth, Tex.: Modern Art Museum of Fort Worth, 1995), p. 65.

33. Duchamp, quoted in Tomkins, *Off the Wall,* p. 112 n.

34. Rauschenberg, quoted in Françoise Choay, "Dada, néo-dada, et Rauschenberg," *Art International* 5, no. 8 (20 October 1961): 84.

35. Rauschenberg, quoted in Barbaralee Diamonstein, *Inside New York's Art World* (New York: Rizzoli, 1979), p. 307.

36. On the indexical mark in *Tu m',* see Rosalind E. Krauss, "Notes on the Index: Part 1," in *The Originality of the Avant-Garde and Other Modernist Myths* (Cambridge, Mass.: MIT Press, 1985), pp. 196–209.

37. Benjamin H. D. Buchloh, "Allegorical Procedures: Appropriation and Montage in Contemporary Art," *Artforum* 21, no. 1 (September 1982): 43–56.

38. "Duchamp showed the usefulness of addition (mustache). Rauschenberg showed the function of subtraction (De Kooning)" (John Cage, "26 Statements Re Duchamp" [1963], in *A Year from Monday* [Middletown, Conn.: Wesleyan University Press, 1967], p. 71).

39. Buchloh, "Allegorical Procedures," p. 46.

40. "He changes what goes on, on a canvas," Cage noted, "but he does not change how canvas is used for paintings—that is, stretched flat to make rectangular surfaces which may be hung on a wall" ("On Robert Rauschenberg," p. 100). All of Rauschenberg's *Dirt Paintings* were originally intended to be hung from the wall like conventional paintings. Because of its poor condition, the one remaining example, *Dirt Painting (for John Cage),* must be displayed horizontally. Although there were apparently many others, the one tissue paper "painting" recorded in an extant photograph is a clear box that stands upright on a flat surface.

41. Rauschenberg, interview by Hopps. Cf. Rauschenberg's statement about the gold and tissue paper paintings in Seckler, "The Artist Speaks," p. 81: "I did a painting in toilet-paper, then duplicated it in gold-leaf. I studied both very carefully and found no advantage in either: whatever one was saying, the other seemed to be just as articulate. I knew then

that it was somebody else's problem—not mine." In the one documented example of a paper painting, Rauschenberg does not actually use toilet paper but rather employs the tissue used to stuff shoe boxes.

42. On *Tzank Check* and Duchamp's relationship to the flows of capital, see David Joselit, *Infinite Regress: Marcel Duchamp 1910–1941* (Cambridge, Mass.: MIT Press, 1998). Helen Molesworth discusses the interrelation of the black paintings, *Gold Paintings,* and tissue paper paintings by invoking the economic and psychoanalytic tropes of anality in "Before *Bed,*" *October,* no. 63 (winter 1993): 69–82.

43. Rauschenberg, quoted in Emile de Antonio and Mitch Tuchman, *Painters Painting: A Candid History of the Modern Art Scene, 1940–1970* (New York: Abbeville, 1984), p. 88. Duchamp's assertion that he chose his readymades with an attitude of "*visual indifference*" is found in "Assemblage Symposium," p. 135.

44. On the *Red Paintings,* see note 78 below. Rauschenberg reports that red quickly tended to read as gaudy (Klüver, *On Record,* p. 43). More recently, Rauschenberg recalled the effects of red in a discussion with Trisha Brown: "Black and white is a dramatic combination that doesn't allow any side effects. If you use red, a tone is set. Color is a distraction, because it forces an inflexible emotional and psychological affect and reading onto the activity that can't be shrugged off by a quick step or two by the dancers" (Brown, "Collaboration: Life and Death in the Aesthetic Zone," in Hopps and Davidson, eds., *Robert Rauschenberg: A Retrospective,* p. 270).

45. James Meyer, "Art for the City: Sculpture for a Large Wall, 1957," in *Ellsworth Kelly: Sculpture for a Large Wall, 1957* (New York: Matthew Marks Gallery, 1998), pp. 9–11. According to Roberta Bernstein, Kelly became aware of Rodchenko's monochrome triptych only around 1988 (Bernstein, "Ellsworth Kelly's Multipanel Paintings," in *Ellsworth Kelly: A Retrospective,* ed. Diane Waldman [New York: Solomon R. Guggenheim Museum, 1996], p. 51 n. 6).

46. Meyer, "Art for the City," and Michael Plante, "'Things to Cover Walls': Ellsworth Kelly's Paris Paintings and the Tradition of Mural Decoration," *American Art* 9, no. 1 (spring 1995): 37–53.

47. Ellsworth Kelly, letter to John Cage, 4 September 1950, in the John Cage Archive, Northwestern University Music Library, Evanston, Ill. (partially reproduced in Brunet, "Chronology, 1943–1954," pp. 187–188). The passage referred to above reads in full: "[Hans Arp] said that I was courageous, which I don't quite understand. It was courageous for him in 1916 and for Mondrian and Kandinsky. Benefiting their struggle it is very natural today to continue."

48. Kelly, letter to Cage, 4 September 1950.

49. On Cage's early aesthetic, see my "'A Therapeutic Value for City Dwellers': The Development of John Cage's Early Avant-Garde Aesthetic Position," in *John Cage: Music, Philosophy and Intention, 1933–1950,* ed. David W. Patterson (New York: Routledge, 2002), pp. 135–175. On Cage's interest in impersonality and anonymity, as derived from non-Western sources, see David W. Patterson, "The Picture That Is Not in the Colors: Cage, Coomaraswamy, and the Impact of India," in Patterson, ed., *John Cage,* pp. 177–215.

50. Ellsworth Kelly, postcard to John Cage (on an invitation to the *Tendance* exhibition at the Galerie Maeght), ca. October 1952; in the John Cage Archive, Northwestern University Music Library.

51. Kelly's letters echo Cage's sense (which also reached its high point in "Defense of Satie") of the "sickness" of individualistic modern society, against which an ideal of anonymity and collective production would serve as a balm. See John Cage, "Defense of Satie" (1948), in *John Cage: An Anthology,* ed. Richard Kostelanetz (New York: Da Capo, 1970), pp. 77–84. As Kelly wrote, "The dilemma is that in America there are few wise men and because they are few they are bound—and the rest are sick. How can art flourish from a sick humanity[?]" (letter to Cage, 4 September 1950).

52. Ellsworth Kelly, "Project for a Book: *Line, Form and Color*" (1951), in *Line Form Color* (Cambridge, Mass.: Harvard University Art Museums, 1999), n.p.

53. Kelly, letter to Cage, 4 September 1950.

54. Bois, "Ellsworth Kelly in France," and Yve-Alain Bois, *Ellsworth Kelly: The Early Drawings, 1948–1955* (Cambridge, Mass.: Harvard University Art Museums, 1999).

55. Kelly, quoted in Goosen, *Ellsworth Kelly*, p. 29; cited in Bois, "Ellsworth Kelly in France," p. 13.

56. Bois, "Ellsworth Kelly in France," p. 10.

57. Bois, "Ellsworth Kelly in France," p. 28. Michael Plante reports, on the basis of conversations with the artist, "that the unusual pairing of two close hues—pink and orange—came from a chance arrangement of collage papers on the floor of [Kelly's] studio" (" 'Things to Cover Walls,' " p. 42). On the occasion of his 1996 Guggenheim retrospective, Kelly proposed yet another source for this particular color combination: Ambrogio Lorenzetti's *Virgin and Child* (ca. late 1330s–early 1340s), which he saw and copied while a student in Boston (Diane Waldman, "Ellsworth Kelly," in Waldman, ed., *Ellsworth Kelly,* p. 38 n. 11). Before that time, Kelly apparently had no inkling of any such connection. At issue, of course, is not so much where such a color combination may ultimately have come from but how Kelly could have felt that such idiosyncratic color combinations were legitimate in the postwar modern period, especially when pursuing an art that was impersonal, anonymous, and universal.

58. See Harry Cooper's discussion in *An Intense Detachment: Ellsworth Kelly's "Line Form Color"* (Cambridge, Mass.: Harvard University Art Museums, 1999).

59. A photograph of Ann Weber wearing the dress designed by Kelly is reproduced in Brunet, "Chronology, 1943–1954," p. 192, and in Waldman, "Ellsworth Kelly," p. 35.

60. The terms "Imaginary," "Real," and, later, "Symbolic" are used *in analogy with* their original use in the psychoanalytical writings of Jacques Lacan; I follow the deployment made of them in Thierry de Duve, *Pictorial Nominalism: On Marcel Duchamp's Passage from Painting to the Readymade* (Minneapolis: University of Minnesota Press, 1991), and Bois, "Painting: The Task of Mourning," 229–244.

61. Kelly, "Project for a Book: *Line, Form and Color,*" n.p., letter to Cage, 4 September 1950.

62. Bois, "Ellsworth Kelly in France," p. 28. It is only on close inspection that the leftmost panel, which appears black, actually reveals itself to be deep blue. Kelly has stated that in

his mind, he often transposes the child's statement into "bleu foncé—rose—orange—blanc—bleu clair . . . " (Kelly, conversation with author).

63. Bois, "Ellsworth Kelly in France," p. 28.

64. This aspect of Kelly's work was insisted on by the artist after he read an earlier version of this chapter, and confirmed upon the author's visit to Kelly's studio.

65. Yve-Alain Bois, "The Summons," in *Spencertown: Recent Paintings by Ellsworth Kelly* (London: Anthony d'Offay; New York: Matthew Marks, 1994), p. 39.

66. Bois has likened Kelly's art to Mallarmé's attempts to motivate his pictorial "terms" (Bois, "The Summons"), but he does not discuss those aspects of motivation that occurred in Mallarmé's poetry on the level not of the individual term but of the overall poem. (For a discussion of the work of Henri Matisse, with whom Kelly is often compared, from this perspective of Mallermé's poetry, see my "La Sémiologie de Matisse," trans. Nathalie Trouveroy, in *Matisse et Mallarmé* [Vulaines-sur-Seine: Musée départemental Stéphane Mallarmé, 2002], pp. 14–27.) Bois has, however, considered in detail many of the various ways, such as the use of bilateral symmetry, in which Kelly sought to accord his monochrome panel paintings a certain necessity (Bois, "Ellsworth Kelly in France"). In Kelly's later work, both highly individualized color and slightly altered shape are deployed to wrest a necessity out of the contingency of his artistic starting points, motifs often found by chance in the urban environment. For a visual compendium of the starting points out of which Kelly's finished paintings derive, see *Ellsworth Kelly: Tablet, 1948–1973* (New York: Drawing Center, 2002). See also the discussion between Yve-Alain Bois and Benjamin H. D. Buchloh in *Ellsworth Kelly: A Conversation,* Drawing Papers 29 (New York: Drawing Center, 2002), which was published too late for full consideration here.

67. On the seemingly continual, phoenix-like rebirth of modernist painting from the ashes of its own "death," see Bois, "Painting: The Task of Mourning"; Bois does not make the modern/postmodern distinction for which I am arguing here. Yet although the perspective and conditions confronted by Kelly in the 1950s are in some ways typical of the outlook characterizing all of modernism, his recourse to the Symbolic (as well as what we will see as Rauschenberg's very unmodernist reaction to the same historical situation) marks a qualitative change that, in my view, may rightfully be understood as postmodern.

68. Here, of course, I have rehearsed Frederic Jameson's famous description of late capitalism: see Jameson, "Periodizing the 60s," in *The Sixties without Apology,* ed. Sohnya Sayres et al. (Minneapolis: University of Minnesota Press, 1984), pp. 178–209, and *Postmodernism, or the Cultural Logic of Late Capitalism* (Durham, N.C.: Duke University Press, 1991). Leo Steinberg, whose discussion of the "post-Modernist" picture plane will be taken up in the following chapter, seems to have intuited such a relation with regard to Kelly, noting the manner in which certain of his "works suggest a reproducible image . . . , i.e. one which is man-made and stops short at the pigmented surface" (Steinberg, "Other Criteria," in *Other Criteria: Confrontations with Twentieth-Century Art* [New York: Oxford University Press, 1972], p. 80).

69. It is not insignificant that Rauschenberg's work followed closely on the inception, first seen in Helen Frankenthaler's *Mountains and Sea* (1952), of a late-modernist form of painting that involved the staining of paint directly onto canvas, as Pollock's black paintings had done the previous year. The work of Frankenthaler, followed by that of Kenneth Noland, Morris Louis, and Jules Olitski, would attempt to continue the type of artistic autonomy from commercial culture advocated by Clement Greenberg and, increasingly, by Michael Fried. However, the evident restriction and near foreclosure of the space between what Greenberg described as "literal flatness" and "a strictly pictorial, strictly optical third dimension" would also lead a whole generation of artists to seek new spaces of aesthetic practice that were opposed to making—as Allan Kaprow would describe it—"near paintings" in this vein. *Collection,* I am arguing, is one of the first works to take up this foreclosure of the aesthetic realm as problematic and as something to be overcome. Greenberg's famous discussion of flatness is found in "Modernist Painting" (1960), in *The Collected Essays and Criticism,* ed. John O'Brian, vol. 4, *Modernism with a Vengeance, 1957–1969* (Chicago: University of Chicago Press, 1993), p. 90; Kaprow's remark is found in "The Legacy of Jackson Pollock" (1958), in his *Essays on the Blurring of Art and Life,* ed. Jeff Kelley (Berkeley: University of California Press, 1993), p. 7.

70. De Duve, *Pictorial Nominalism.* The term "pictorial nominalism" is found in a 1914 note by Duchamp. See also de Duve, "The Readymade and the Tube of Paint," chap. 3 of *Kant after Duchamp* (Cambridge, Mass.: MIT Press, 1996), pp. 147–196.

71. "Assemblage Symposium," p. 136.

72. Rauschenberg, quoted in de Antonio and Tuchman, *Painters Painting*, p. 89. Cf. Tomkins, *Bride,* p. 215. Mary Lynn Kotz describes Rauschenberg as having bought unlabeled paint, which happened to be red. As no source is provided for this account, we may surmise that she has confused the two otherwise distinct stories; see Kotz, *Rauschenberg: Art and Life* (New York: Harry N. Abrams, 1990), p. 82.

73. The systematic nature of this strategy was unusual for Rauschenberg. For the most part, he rejected such elaborate chance techniques for fear that the painting would become "an intellectual piece" (Rauschenberg, in Barbara Rose, *An Interview with Robert Rauschenberg* [New York: Vintage Books, 1987], p. 65). He explained: "Working with chance, I would end up with something that was quite geometric; I felt as though I were carrying out an idea rather than witnessing an unknown idea taking shape" (p. 81). In other words, the work would become a mere illustration of the process. Reliance on some form of organization meant that the procedure itself would become an a priori meaning or referent for the work, enabling representation to sneak back in. Rauschenberg admitted, "I could never figure out an interesting way to use any kind of programmed activity—and even though chance deals with the unexpected and unplanned, it still has to be organized" (Seckler, "The Artist Speaks," p. 81).

74. Although they are not usually recognized in exhibitions as such, Rauschenberg referred to his "pedestrian color" works as a series, similar to that of the black paintings or the *Red Paintings*. See Seckler, "The Artist Speaks," p. 84.

75. Rauschenberg, quoted in Klüver, *On Record,* p. 43. See also Tomkins, *Bride,* p. 215.

76. Rauschenberg, quoted in André Parinaud, "Un 'misfit' de la peinture newyorkaise se confesse," *Les Arts et Spectat/Arts* (Paris) 821 (10 May 1963): 18. English quotations of Parinaud's text derive from a typescipt translation by staff of the U.S. Department of State titled "Confessions of an Offbeat New York Painter" (a copy is filed in the Smithsonian Institution Archives, in the records of the Department of Twentieth Century Painting and Sculpture, record unit 458, box 25, folder 4). I have corrected all translations where necessary.

77. Throughout his life, Schwitters painted representational landscapes in traditional artistic materials as a counterpoint to his montage activities, thereby revealing the dialectical interdependence between dadaist negation and traditional painting. On Schwitters's continuing to

paint, see Dorothea Dietrich, *The Collages of Kurt Schwitters: Tradition and Innovation* (Cambridge: Cambridge University Press, 1993).

78. The equating of collage with paint begins in the earlier Untitled (*Red Painting*) (1954) in the Broad Collection. There, the multicolored paintstrokes at the top of the work parallel the striped fabric above them; and, at the lower right-hand corner, the vertical stripe of orange material is paired with a paintstroke laid atop the red ground. The equivalence and complementarity of paint and collage were further demonstrated in the alternating stripes of fabric, paint, and collage in *Yoicks* (1954).

79. Rauschenberg, quoted in Dorothy C. Miller, ed., *Sixteen Americans* (New York: Museum of Modern Art, 1959), p. 58.

80. "Everyone knows that the label Modern Art no longer has any relation to the words that compose it. To be Modern Art a work need not be either modern nor art; it need not even be a work. A three thousand-year-old mask from the South Pacific qualifies as Modern and a piece of wood found on a beach becomes art" (Harold Rosenberg, "The American Action Painters" [1952], in *The Tradition of the New* [New York: McGraw-Hill, 1959], p. 36). This work is hereafter cited parenthetically in the text.

81. "A good painting in this mode leaves no doubt concerning its reality as an action and its relation to a transforming process in the artist" (Rosenberg, "The American Action Painters," p. 33).

82. On the connection between Twombly's painting and the analysis of writing, see Rosalind Krauss, "Olympia," in Bois and Krauss, *Formless*, pp. 147–152, and Roland Barthes, "Cy Twombly: Works on Paper," in *The Responsibility of Forms: Critical Essays on Music, Art, and Representation*, trans. Richard Howard (Berkeley: University of California Press, 1985), pp. 157–176.

83. Jacques Derrida, "Signature Event Context" (1977), in *Limited Inc*, trans. Samuel Weber and Jeffrey Mehlman (Evanston, Ill.: Northwestern University Press, 1988), p. 12.

84. Rosenberg, "The American Action Painters," p. 34.

85. Derrida, "Signature Event Context," p. 12.

86. This slide between the Bergsonian/Deleuzian notion of difference elaborated in the previous chapter in relation to the *White Paintings* and the more Derridean idea of *différance* and writing that comes into play with *Collection* characterizes a certain tension within Rauschenberg's production over the next decade. But we should note that the two theorists whose works are most productive in examining this aspect of Rauschenberg's work are not that far from each other at this point. See, for example, Derrida's crucial citation of Deleuze's *Nietzsche and Philosophy* in the essay "Différance" (1972), in *Margins of Philosophy,* trans. Alan Bass (Chicago: University of Chicago Press, 1982), p. 17 n. 20.

87. T. J. Clark, *Farewell to an Idea: Episodes from a History of Modernism* (New Haven: Yale University Press, 1999), pp. 331–332.

88. Clark, *Farewell to an Idea,* p. 314.

89. See Clark's comments on the necessity of abstract expressionism's non-identity with the present in *Farewell to an Idea*, p. 374.

90. T. J. Clark has most provocatively discussed the Beaton photographs as the "bad dream of modernism" (*Farewell to an Idea,* pp. 299–369; quotation, p. 306). On Beaton's photos, see also Thomas Crow, *Modern Art in the Common Culture* (New Haven: Yale University Press, 1996), pp. 39–48.

91. See Cage's comments regarding Pollock and Mark Tobey in Richard Kostelanetz, *Conversing with Cage* (New York: Limelight Editions, 1994), p. 177.

92. Cage's position toward Pollock resembled that toward his former teacher, Arnold Schoenberg. Despite Schoenberg's thoroughgoing embrace of dissonance and negation of harmonic values, Cage rejected his claim to even such a mediated autonomy. "We're chucking this idea too (even though Schoenberg had it): that music enables one to live in a dream world removed from the situation one is actually in (and so the eyes of music lovers, closed or reading scores—fortunate for them they're not crossing city streets)" (Cage, "Mosaic" [1965], in *A Year from Monday,* p. 44). Cage's rejection is directly to the point here, as Clark explicitly likens Pollock's abstraction to Adorno's idea of dissonance (Clark, *Farewell to an Idea,* p. 337), which was, of course, explicitly derived from Schoenberg's music.

93. "Seems Pollock tried to do it—" noted Cage, "paint on glass. It was in a movie. There was an admission of failure. That wasn't the way to proceed. It's not a question of doing again what Duchamp already did. We must nowadays nevertheless at least be able to look through to what's beyond—as though we were in it looking out" ("26 Statements Re Duchamp," p. 71). For Rauschenberg, investigating a difference that did not inhere within the subject must have been appealing because it allowed him to turn Pollock's aesthetic inside out, to invert the abstract expressionist's insistence on "painting out of [his] unconscious" (Pollock, quoted in Selden Rodman, *Conversations with Artists;* quoted in Clark, *Farewell to an Idea,* p. 334). Certainly, there are echoes of Pollock's "I try to stay away from any recognizable image; if it creeps in, I try to do away with it . . . to let the painting come through" in Rauschenberg's "I try to keep wide awake. If I see any superficial subconscious relationships that I'm familiar with . . . I change the picture" (Jackson Pollock, interview for *Life* magazine; quoted in Clark, p. 324; and Seckler, "The Artist Speaks," p. 76) Like Cage, Rauschenberg sought to explode those aspects of subjective autonomy that Pollock's renunciation sought to preserve.

94. Robert Rauschenberg, "How Important Is Surface to Design?" *Print* 13, no. 1 (January–February 1959): 31.

95. Fred Orton has advanced a similar argument apropos of Rauschenberg in "The Object after Theory (Figuring Jasper Johns—Supplement 1: *Flag*)," in *Ex-cavating Modernism,* ed. Alex Coles and Richard Bently, De-, Dis-, Ex, vol. 1 (London: Backless Books, 1996), pp. 24–34.

96. On the deconstructive brushstroke in *Flag,* see Fred Orton, *Figuring Jasper Johns* (Cambridge, Mass.: Harvard University Press, 1994). On its dating, see p. 228 n. 14.

3 Mole Archaeology

1. Irving Sandler, "Reviews and Previews: Robert Rauschenberg," *Art News* 59, no. 2 (April 1960): 14; Alan R. Solomon, *Robert Rauschenberg* (New York: Jewish Museum, 1963), n.p.; Dorothy Gees Seckler, "The Artist Speaks: Robert Rauschenberg," *Art in America* 54, no. 3 (May–June 1966): 74.

2. Leo Steinberg, "Other Criteria," in *Other Criteria: Confrontations with Twentieth-Century Art* (New York: Oxford University Press, 1972), pp. 88, 90.

3. Rauschenberg, quoted in Seckler, "The Artist Speaks," p. 76. The general, and overly simplified, understanding of Rauschenberg's outlook can be found in Richard Kostelanetz's gloss on this quotation: "As formal arrangements, Rauschenberg's paintings are about living in New York" (Kostelanetz, "The Artist as Playwright and Engineer," *New York Times Magazine,* 9 October 1996, p. 122).

4. Brian O'Doherty, "Rauschenberg and the Vernacular Glance," *Art in America* 61, no. 5 (September–October 1973): 82. This work is hereafter cited parenthetically in the text.

5. Walter Benjamin, "Some Motifs in Baudelaire" (1939), trans. Harry Zohn, in *Charles Baudelaire: A Lyric Poet in the Era of High Capitalism* (London: New Left Books, 1973), p. 132.

6. Benjamin, "Some Motifs in Baudelaire," pp. 146–147.

7. Benjamin, "Some Motifs in Baudelaire," p. 117.

8. Walter Benjamin, "The Work of Art in the Age of Mechanical Reproduction" (1936), in *Illuminations,* trans. Harry Zohn (New York: Schocken Books, 1969), pp. 237–238.

9. Benjamin, "The Work of Art," p. 237.

10. See Peter Bürger, *Theory of the Avant-Garde,* trans. Michael Shaw (Minneapolis: University of Minnesota Press, 1984), pp. 52–82.

11. Such an effect is not inevitable. Another possible outcome, as Benjamin H. D. Buchloh points out in relation to Schwitters, is the mere contemplation of the reified state of society (Buchloh, "Allegorical Procedures: Appropriation and Montage in Contemporary Art," *Artforum* 21, no. 1 [September 1982]: 43).

12. That the Combines lack dialectical force is the judgment advanced by Benjamin H. D. Buchloh in "Warburg's model? The End of Collage in Post-War European Art," in *Deep Storage: The Structure of Memory in Contemporary Art,* ed. Hubertus Gassner (Munich: Haus der Kunst, 1997), p. 54 n. 10. Elsewhere, Buchloh has described Rauschenberg's work in terms of a "pictorializing" of the strategies of the historical dadaist avant-garde (Buchloh, "Andy Warhol's One-Dimensional Art, 1956–1966," in *Neo-Avantgarde and Culture Industry:*

Essays on European and American Art from 1955 to 1975 [Cambridge, Mass.: MIT Press, 2000], p. 495).

13. Benjamin, "Some Motifs in Baudelaire," p. 128.

14. Benjamin, "Some Motifs in Baudelaire," pp. 128–129.

15. Benjamin, "Some Motifs in Baudelaire," p. 150.

16. Cf. Hilton Kramer's more damning and derogatory charge that Rauschenberg's work was equivalent to department store window dressing and the "gutter" of commercial detritus. "Frankly, I see no difference between his work and the decorative displays which often grace the windows of Bonwit Teller and Bloomingdale's. The latter aim to delight the eye with a bright smartness, and Rauschenberg's work differs from them only in 'risking' some nasty touches. Fundamentally, he shares the window dresser's aesthetic to tickle the eye, to arrest attention for a momentary dazzle" (Kramer, "Month in Review," *Arts Magazine* 33, no. 5 [February 1959]: 49). See Thomas Crow's discussion of the vicious and homophobic dimensions of Kramer's attack (Crow, "This Is Now: Becoming Robert Rauschenberg," *Artforum* 36, no. 1 [September 1997]: 139).

17. Charles F. Stuckey, "Reading Rauschenberg," *Art in America* 65, no. 2 (March–April 1977): 74. The article to which I refer by Kenneth Bendiner is "Robert Rauschenberg's 'Canyon,'" *Arts Magazine* 56, no. 10 (June 1982): 57–59. Stuckey, Bendiner, and the iconographic reception of Rauschenberg's work are further discussed later in this chapter.

18. Crow, "This Is Now," p. 100. Crow's analysis extends the undisputable references to the *Divine Comedy* in Rauschenberg's Dante Drawings to the production of his 1959 Combines. "*Canyon, Pail for Ganymede,* and *Gift for Apollo,*" Crow writes, "all sort through Greek mythology with evident purpose, shifting Rauschenberg's usual discarded and junk materials into complex reflections on paternal and erotic love between men" (p. 100). The iconographic analyses of Bendiner and others, to whom Crow's argument is indebted, are discussed later in this chapter. For further discussion of the Dante Drawings, see chapter 4.

19. Calvin Tomkins, *Off the Wall: Robert Rauschenberg and the Art World of Our Time* (New York: Penguin, 1980), p. 19. See also Robert Hughes, "The Most Living Artist," *Time,* 29

November 1976, p. 59, and Mary Lynn Kotz, *Rauschenberg: Art and Life* (New York: Harry N. Abrams, 1990), pp. 56, 60.

20. Rauschenberg's status as a "master" within the art world arguably has been recognized since his first retrospective exhibition at the Jewish Museum in New York in 1963; it was ensured by his second major retrospective, held at the National Collection of American Art in Washington, D.C., in 1976. This status was most recently confirmed in the massive Guggenheim Museum retrospective in New York in 1997.

21. Rauschenberg, quoted in James Schuyler, "Is Today's Artist with or against the Past?" *Art News* 57, no. 4 (summer 1958): 56.

22. Rauschenberg, quoted in Schuyler, "Today's Artist," p. 56.

23. Rosalind Krauss, "Rauschenberg and the Materialized Image," *Artforum* 13, no. 4 (December 1974): 41.

24. Krauss, "Materialized Image," p. 43.

25. Benjamin, "Some Motifs in Baudelaire," p. 111. Eduardo Cadava has commented on this relationship most perceptively:

> Describing in photographic terms how history is figured in the movement from Bergson's understanding of memory to Baudelaire's poetics of history, he [Benjamin] suggests that the view of history that emerges in the movement between Bergson's philosophy and Baudelaire's reader follows the principles of a photographic apparatus. This apparatus reveals the traces left by history on Bergson's philosophy in the very gesture through which he attempts to overcome them. The "blinding age" compels him to shut his eyes to the historical dimension of history. If, however, Bergson does not experience experience directly, this nonexperience "indirectly" lets us know what is possible in this "blinding age." (Cadava, *Words of Light: Theses on the Photography of History* [Princeton: Princeton University Press, 1997], p. 88)

For a different discussion of Benjamin's commentary on Bergson, see Jonathan Crary, "Spectacle, Attention, Counter-Memory," *October,* no. 50 (fall 1989): 103–104. In "Rauschenberg and the Materialized Image," Krauss also draws on aspects of Benjamin's studies of Baudelaire, but the text she cites, "Paris—Capital of the Nineteenth Century," does not refer to Bergson. See Walter Benjamin, "Paris—Capital of the Nineteenth Century" (1935), trans. Quintin Hoare, in *Charles Baudelaire,* pp. 155–176.

26. On the surrealist object as harboring a revolutionary potential, see Walter Benjamin, "Surrealism: The Last Snapshot of the European Intelligentsia" (1929), trans. Edmund Jephcott, in *Selected Writings,* vol. 2, ed. Michael W. Jennings, Howard Eiland, and Gary Smith (Cambridge, Mass.: Belknap Press, 1999), pp. 207–221. On Rauschenberg's Italian works in the context of surrealism, see the brief comments by Benjamin Buchloh and Jean-François Chevrier in *Politics, Poetics: Documenta X, the Book* (Ostfildern-Ruit: Cantz-Verlag, 1997), p. 393.

27. Rauschenberg's statement is reproduced in facsimile in Walter Hopps, *Robert Rauschenberg: The Early 1950s* (Houston: Houston Fine Arts Press, 1991), p. 232.

28. Rauschenberg, quoted in Schuyler, "Today's Artist," p. 56.

29. Rauschenberg, quoted in Schuyler, "Today's Artist," pp. 46, 56.

30. Rauschenberg, quoted in Schuyler, "Today's Artist," p. 46. Rauschenberg's "saint's decayed tooth in a frame," visible in the photograph of the shelf in his Fulton Street studio, would later be incorporated into the Combine *Co-Existence* (1961). The red fresco fragment would eventually end up as part of his sculpture *Soles,* ca. 1953.

31. Craig Owens, "The Allegorical Impulse: Toward a Theory of Postmodernism" and "The Allegorical Impulse: Toward a Theory of Postmodernism, Part 2," in his *Beyond Recognition: Representation, Power, and Culture,* ed. Scott Bryson et al. (Berkeley: University of California Press, 1992), pp. 52–87; Buchloh, "Allegorical Procedures."

32. The relationship between allegory and parataxis is discussed in Owens, "The Allegorical Impulse," p. 56.

33. See Walter Benjamin: "The [allegorical] writer must not conceal the fact that his activity is one of arranging, since it was not so much the mere whole as its obviously constructed quality that was the principal impression which was aimed at. Hence the display of the craftsmanship, which . . . shows through like masonry in a building whose rendering has broken away" (Benjamin, *The Origin of German Tragic Drama,* trans. John Osborne [London: Verso, 1977], p. 179; cited in Craig Owens's first consideration of allegory, "Earthwords," in *Beyond Recognition,* p. 43).

34. Lawrence Alloway, Marcel Duchamp, et al., "The Art of Assemblage: A Symposium" (1961), in *Essays on Assemblage,* ed. James Leggio and Helen M. Franc, Studies in Modern Art, vol. 2 (New York: Museum of Modern Art, 1992), p. 148; this conversation is hereafter cited as "Assemblage Symposium."

35. Owens, "The Allegorical Impulse, Part 2," p. 77. Owens proceeds to read this situation in terms of Paul de Man's idea of an allegory of illegibility, the allegorization of the work's own unreadability.

36. "This [archaeological] analysis," writes Michel Foucault, "presupposes that statements are considered in the *remanence* (*rémanence*) that is proper to them, and which is not that of an ever-realizable reference back to the past event of the formulation. To say that statements are residual (*rémanent*) is not to say that they remain in the field of memory" (Foucault, *The Archaeology of Knowledge,* trans. A. M. Sheridan Smith [New York: Pantheon Books, 1972], p. 123).

37. Foucault, *The Archaeology of Knowledge,* pp. 130–131 (emphasis added). The relationship of Rauschenberg's work to Foucault's ideas of the archive (and language) is expanded later in this chapter. In a somewhat different manner from that developed here, Douglas Crimp has also related Rauschenberg's work to a Foucauldian archaeology in "On the Museum's Ruins," in *On the Museum's Ruins* (Cambridge, Mass.: MIT Press, 1993), pp. 44–64. For a different discussion of Rauschenberg in relation to the postwar transformation of the model of the archive, see Rosalind Krauss, "Perpetual Inventory," in *Robert Rauschenberg: A Retrospective,* ed. Walter Hopps and Susan Davidson (New York: Solomon R. Guggenheim Museum, 1997), pp. 206–223, esp. 219.

38. Rauschenberg, quoted in Roberta Bernstein, "Robert Rauschenberg's 'Rebus,'" *Arts Magazine* 52, no. 5 (January 1978): 139.

39. Steinberg, "Other Criteria," p. 84.

40. Solomon, *Robert Rauschenberg*, n.p.; O'Doherty, "Vernacular Glance," p. 85.

41. John Cage, "On Robert Rauschenberg, Artist, and His Work" (1961), in *Silence* (Middletown, Conn.: Wesleyan University Press, 1961), p. 103.

42. Solomon, *Robert Rauschenberg*, n.p.

43. For discussions of this Combine, see Paul Schimmel, "The Faked Gesture: Pop Art and the New York School," in *Hand-Painted Pop: American Art in Transition, 1955–62,* ed. Russell Ferguson (Los Angeles: Museum of Contemporary Art, Los Angeles; New York: Rizzoli, 1993), pp. 31–32, and Caroline A. Jones, "*Coca-Cola Plan* or, How New York Stole the Soul of Giuseppe Panza," in *Panza: The Legacy of a Collector* (Los Angeles: Museum of Contemporary Art, Los Angeles, 1999), pp. 37–38. Rauschenberg had earlier produced another work that similarly related the personal and archival aspects of his production. Titled *Self-made Retrospective,* it contained remade examples of, as Hopps reports, "a red painting, a white lead painting, a growing or dirt painting, a gold painting, a black painting, and a Parsons era painting" (*Robert Rauschenberg: The Early 1950s,* p. 168).

44. Cage, "On Robert Rauschenberg," p. 100. Cage continues, "We know two ways to unfocus attention: symmetry is one of them; the other is the over-all where each small part is a sample of what you find elsewhere. In either case, there is at least the possibility of looking anywhere, not just where someone arranged you should. You are then free to deal with your freedom just as the artist dealt with his, not in the same way but, nevertheless, originally" (p. 100).

45. Rauschenberg, quoted in Seckler, "The Artist Speaks," p. 81.

46. Steinberg, "Other Criteria," p. 84.

47. David Joselit has noted a similar quality in the composition of William S. Burroughs's contemporary notebook collages (Joselit, "Burroughs's Virology," *Art in America* 84, no. 11 [November 1996]: 97–99). In the early 1980s Rauschenberg collaborated with Burroughs in a lithograph series, *American Pewter with Burroughs.*

48. Cage, "On Robert Rauschenberg," pp. 101–102; cf. p. 99. Steinberg also notes Rauschenberg's relationship to the newspaper ("Other Criteria," p. 84).

49. "Its intention is just the opposite," Benjamin continues, "and it is achieved: to isolate what happens from the realm in which it would affect the experience of the reader. The principles of journalistic information (freshness of the news, brevity, comprehensibility, and, above all, lack of connection between the individual news items) contribute as much to this as does the make-up of the pages and the paper's style" ("Some Motifs in Baudelaire," p. 112).

50. See, for instance, *Levee* (1955) with its circular chart, *Memorandum of Bids* (1956), *Factum I* and *II* (1957), *Wager* (1957–1959), and *Collage with Letter* (1957). One work, a small untitled piece of 1956, currently in the collection of Merce Cunningham, consists of practically nothing more than a single sheet of graph paper.

51. Rauschenberg, quoted in "The Emperor's Combine," *Time,* 18 April 1960, p. 92.

52. O'Doherty, "Vernacular Glance," p. 85.

53. Cage, "On Robert Rauschenberg," p. 99.

54. Steinberg, "Other Criteria," p. 88.

55. This analysis of Rauschenberg's "surface" was offered by Toby Mussman, in "A Comment on Literalness, Should the Picture Plane Be Abolished?" *Arts Magazine* 42, no. 4 (February 1968): 14–17. "It is evident that Rauschenberg saw that a Cubist commitment to the theoretical picture plane was no longer relevant. The *White Painting* is a statement without equivocation that a new 'picture plane' had been prepared for investigation, but this time it was not a theoretical one, it was a material, literal one" (p. 17).

56. Cage, "On Robert Rauschenberg," p. 99.

57. As Cage wrote, probably with *Rebus* in mind, "Three stretchers with the canvas on them no doubt already stretched. Fulfilling this plan put the canvas in direct contact with

the floor, the ground thereby activated" ("On Robert Rauschenberg," p. 104). Like *Rebus,* Rauschenberg's *Interview* (1955) is a transitional work, not only because the door gives it a vertical orientation but also because the work is organized primarily into a loosely formulated grid. However, the box at the lower left and the baseball at the upper right appear less as built out from the back plane or suspended above it than as lying unattached upon a horizontal ground.

58. See Rauschenberg's comments on not respecting the limitation of the edges of the canvas in Seckler, "The Artist Speaks," p. 81.

59. O'Doherty, "Vernacular Glance," p. 85. Rauschenberg described the effect of his work as being, "So you would have to keep looking through image after image" (Arthur Perry, "A Conversation between Robert Rauschenberg and Arthur Perry," *Artmagazine* 10, no. 41 [November–December 1978]: 34).

60. Laurie J. Monahan has perhaps provided the most extensive reading of Rauschenberg's work from this perspective, detailing in precise ways how the heterogeneity of his Combines and silkscreen paintings differs from the more abrupt and polarized juxtapositions found in dadaists such as Hannah Höch and Kurt Schwitters (Monahan, "Cultural Cartography: American Designs at the 1964 Venice Biennale," in *Reconstructing Modernism: Art in New York, Paris, and Montreal, 1945–1964,* ed. Serge Guilbaut [Cambridge, Mass.: MIT Press, 1990], pp. 369–416). She refers several times to ways in which Rauschenberg's images might be understood as somewhat critical of or contradictory to the cultural and political deployment to which they were put (specifically by Alan Solomon in the context of the United States Information Agency's sponsorship of the U.S. pavilion at the Venice Biennale in 1964). Ultimately, however, her analysis equates the ambiguity and equivalence of Rauschenberg's imagery with the rise of an affirmative, "Midcult" incarnation of the culture industry. Monahan's analysis is predicated on the two dichotomous poles of a critical, allegorical dadaism and an entropic, affirmative culture industry. I am arguing here that Rauschenberg's production (especially when not understood through the lens of Solomon's discourse) is ultimately inassimilable to either of these two poles. It attempted to form a third position: one that abjured dadaist shock and its attendant critical distance from society's thoroughly commercial saturation, but was also not simply identical to that society, seeking instead to relativize it through notions of difference modeled on indeterminate temporal process or change.

61. Rauschenberg, quoted in Calvin Tomkins, *The Bride and the Bachelors* (New York: Penguin, 1968), p. 199. As in Bergson's famous comment about order cited by Cage (see chapter 1, note 51), what we are faced with in Rauschenberg's "random order" is an instance in which an apparent disorder reveals itself to be an order of a different kind. As I will argue later, this different kind of order is, very specifically, a "multiplicity."

62. John Cage, "45′ for a Speaker" (1954), in *Silence,* p. 190.

63. John Cage, "Juilliard Lecture" (1952), in *A Year from Monday* (Middletown, Conn.: Wesleyan University Press, 1967), p. 100. Though Cage is describing the work of Morton Feldman, the terms he uses apply equally to his own compositions. "Unimpededness" and "interpenetration" are central aspects of Cage's mid-1950s thinking. He explains:

> unimpededness is seeing that in all of space each thing and each human being is at the center and furthermore that each one being at the center is the most honored one of all. Interpenetration means that each one of these most honored ones of all is moving out in all directions penetrating and being penetrated by every other one no matter what the time or what the space. So that when one says that there is no cause and effect, what is meant is that there are an incalculable infinity of causes and effects, that in fact each and every thing in all of time and space is related to each and every other thing in all of time and space. (Cage, "Composition as Process III: Communication" [ca. 1958], in *Silence,* pp. 46-47; see also Cage, "45′ for a Speaker," p. 155)

Cage applied such ideas, elliptically but nonetheless specifically, to Rauschenberg, writing of his collage that each "object is *fact,* not symbol. . . . [T]he farther one goes in this direction the more one sees nothing is in the foreground: each minute point is at the center" ("On Robert Rauschenberg," p. 108).

64. Cage, "45′ for a Speaker," p. 163. Cage is referring to his musical compositions.

65. Cage, "History of Experimental Music in the United States" (1959), in *Silence,* pp. 69–70. Cage is discussing his composition *Music Walk* of 1958.

66. Cage, "Composition as Process II: Indeterminacy" (1958), in *Silence,* p. 40.

67. László Moholy-Nagy, *The New Vision and Abstract of an Artist*, trans. Daphne M. Hoffmann, 4th ed. (New York: George Wittenborn, 1947), pp. 63–64; see chapter 1.

68. Rauschenberg, quoted in Billy Klüver, *On Record: 11 Artists, 1963* (New York: Experiments in Art and Technology, 1981), p. 45; the second ellipsis is found in original. Cf. Rauschenberg's statement to Barbara Rose: "Any tool in my medium tends to stop activity—except for reflective surfaces, lights and anything else that will bring the room and the presence of other activities back into it" (Rose, *An Interview with Robert Rauschenberg* [New York: Vintage Books, 1987], p. 110).

69. Rauschenberg, quoted in Brian O'Doherty, *Object and Idea: An Art Critic's Journal, 1961–1967* (New York: Simon and Schuster, 1967), p. 118. See also Rauschenberg's comments about the "idea," discussed in chapter 4.

70. As Krauss observed in 1974, "In Rauschenberg's work the image is not about an object transformed. It is a matter, rather, of an object transferred. An object is taken out of the space of the world and embedded into the surface of a painting, never at the sacrifice of its density as material" ("Materialized Image," p. 40).

71. See Rauschenberg's comments on the past: "I am in the present. I am trying to celebrate the present, with all my limitations but by using all my resources. The past is not like the future, which is a speculation. The past is a part of the present" (quoted in André Parinaud, "Un 'misfit' de la peinture newyorkaise se confesse," *Les Arts et Spectat Arts (Paris)*, no. 821 [10 May 1961]: 18). And later: "Now we have so much information. A painter a hundred or two hundred years ago knew very little about what was going on in painting in any other place except with his immediate friends or some outstanding event. It wasn't natural for him also to take into consideration cave painting and fold it into his own sense of the present" (quoted in Richard Kostelanetz, "A Conversation with Robert Rauschenberg," *Partisan Review* 35, no. 1 [winter 1968]: 93–94).

72. It is clear that for Rauschenberg, as for Cage, contemporary life was marked by increasing administration, reification, and conformity, closer to Adorno and Horkheimer's idea of culture industry than to Fredric Jameson's idea of postmodern schizophrenia. See Max Horkheimer and Theodor W. Adorno, *Dialectic of Enlightenment,* trans. John Cumming (New

York: Continuum, 1987), and Fredric Jameson, *Postmodernism, or the Cultural Logic of Late Capitalism* (Durham, N.C.: Duke University Press, 1991).

73. Gilles Deleuze has described a somewhat similar dynamic in the operation of the "diagram" against the reified clichés of perception in Francis Bacon's painting (Deleuze, *Francis Bacon: Logique de la sensation* [Paris: La Différence, 1981]). In their more direct incorporation of time, however, Rauschenberg's Combines more closely recall what Deleuze would call the "time-image" of postwar cinema than Bacon's expressionist canvases. Through their spatial interstices, Rauschenberg's collages enact the same reversal as modern cinema, "where the image is unlinked and the cut begins to have an importance in itself. The cut, or interstice, between two series of images no longer forms part of either of the two series: it is the equivalent of the irrational cut, which determines the non-commensurable relations between images. . . . There is thus no longer association through metaphor or metonymy, but relinkage on the literal image; there is no longer linkage of associated images, but only relinkages of independent images" (Gilles Deleuze, *Cinema 2: The Time-Image,* trans. Hugh Tomlinson and Robert Galeta [Minneapolis: University of Minnesota Press, 1989], pp. 213–214). Rauschenberg's relationship to the "time-image" derives not only from his attentiveness to the postwar conditions of spectacle (discussed in chapter 4) but also from the foundations of Deleuze's concept: he draws heavily on Leo Steinberg's discussion of the flatbed picture plane in *Cinema 2* (pp. 265–270).

74. John Cage, "Letter to Paul Henry Lang" (1956), in *John Cage: An Anthology,* ed. Richard Kostelanetz (New York: Da Capo, 1970), p. 118. Cf. Cage's comments in "Where Are We Going? And What Are We Doing?" (1961), in *Silence,* p. 238. Cage refers to New York as "the center and marketplace" in "A Composer's Confessions" (1948), in *John Cage: Writer,* ed. Richard Kostelanetz (New York: Limelight Editions, 1993), p. 38.

75. Rauschenberg, quoted in Seckler, "The Artist Speaks," p. 81. On multiplicity, see Gilles Deleuze, *Bergsonism,* trans. Hugh Tomlinson and Barbara Habberjam (New York: Zone Books, 1988). On the related development of the notion and operation of multiplicity in Cage, see my "Chance, Catastrophe, Indeterminacy," in "Experimental Art: John Cage, Robert Rauschenberg and the Neo-Avant-Garde" (Ph.D. diss., Harvard University, 1999), pp. 87–141.

76. Cage, "On Robert Rauschenberg," p. 102.

77. Stuckey, "Reading Rauschenberg": on the relationship to Ingres, see p. 79; on the autobiographical focus of Rauschenberg's work, see p. 74; and on Rauschenberg's interest in modern history paintings, see pp. 74, 83. Significantly, Stuckey's "Reading Rauschenberg" was written on the occasion of the artist's 1976 retrospective; as Stuckey noted, "This particular exhibition stresses Rauschenberg's more 'classic,' object-making side" (p. 76). Stuckey later distanced himself from the position put forward in "Reading Rauschenberg" (a shift discussed later in this chapter).

78. Stuckey, "Reading Rauschenberg," p. 83.

79. Steinberg also relates Rauschenberg's picture plane to an internal monologue, though not (as did Stuckey) in the interest of shoring up the idea of an iconographic reading (Steinberg, "Other Criteria," p. 88). Recently, Sam Hunter has updated the concept of the internal monologue by positing Rauschenberg's dyslexia as the interpretive key to his work. This explanation, which resembles attempts to explain impressionism as the result of Monet's eye troubles, is specifically used by Hunter to reinforce the idea of Rauschenberg's art as subjective expression (Hunter, *Robert Rauschenberg* [New York: Rizzoli, 1999], p. 39). A more oblique and less reductive reference to Rauschenberg's dyslexia is found in Steve Paxton, "Rauschenberg for Cunningham and Three of His Own," in *Robert Rauschenberg: A Retrospective,* ed. Walter Hopps and Susan Davidson (New York: Solomon R. Guggenheim Museum, 1997), p. 263.

80. Although Jonathan D. Katz argues for the deconstructive "indecidability" of Rauschenberg's *White Paintings* (see chapter 1), his analyses of Rauschenberg's Combines generally reduce the instability of their reading to a similar form of information theory. The signifying multivalence of Rauschenberg's collage is seen as masking a message intentionally placed into the Combines and directed either to a distinct subculture of gay male viewers or, alternately, to a single individual—specifically, whoever was Rauschenberg's partner at the time. Ultimately, it seems that the collaged materials within the Combines follow a deconstructive notion of "undecidability" *unless* they can be decoded as personal or subcultural references; in that case their meaning is understood as indelibly fixed. Such analyses tend to undermine the more radical implications of the queering that Katz at other moments attributes to Rauschenberg and closely related artists such as Jasper Johns and Andy Warhol. See Katz, "The Art of Code: Jasper Johns and Robert Rauschenberg," in *Significant Others: Creativity*

and Intimate Partnership, ed. Whitney Chadwick and Isabelle de Courtivron (London: Thames and Hudson, 1993), pp. 189–207, and "Rauschenberg's Honeymoon," *Art/Text,* no. 61 (May–June 1998): 44–47. Katz explicitly invokes the communicative model of a message transmitted in the midst of noise in "The Silent Camp: Queer Resistance and the Rise of Pop Art," in *PLOP! Goes the World,* ed. Serge Guilbaut (Durham, N.C.: Duke University Press, forthcoming). Like Charles Stuckey, Katz has distanced himself somewhat from such readings that posit the existence of an embedded message (see note 111 below).

81. Bendiner, "Robert Rauschenberg's 'Canyon,'" and Roni Feinstein, *Robert Rauschenberg: The Silkscreen Paintings, 1962–64* (New York: Whitney Museum of American Art, 1990).

82. Bendiner, "Robert Rauschenberg's 'Canyon,'" pp. 59, 57.

83. Bendiner, "Robert Rauschenberg's 'Canyon,'" p. 57. To my knowledge, only Thomas Crow has noted the manner in which such a sexualized interpretation of the image of Rauschenberg's son, as Crow delicately puts it, "thoroughly complicat[es] the account of the ancient god's act of love" ("This Is Now," p. 139).

84. Bendiner, "Robert Rauschenberg's 'Canyon,'" p. 57.

85. Both Alan Solomon and Laurie Monahan, for example, privilege *Canyon*'s more "American" references, such as the Statue of Liberty, and word fragments like "LABOR" (Solomon, *Robert Rauschenberg,* n.p.; Monahan, "Cultural Cartography," p. 388). Bendiner's reading of *Canyon* is seemingly taken for granted in, among others, Crow, "This Is Now"; Katz, "The Art of Code"; and Laura Auricchio, "Lifting the Veil: Robert Rauschenberg's *Thirty-four Drawings for Dante's Inferno* and the Commercial Homoerotic Imagery of 1950s America," in *The Gay 90s: Disciplinary and Interdisciplinary Formation in Queer Studies,* ed. Thomas Foster, Carol Siegel, and Ellen E. Berry, Genders, vol. 26 (New York: New York University Press, 1997), pp. 119–154.

86. Rauschenberg, quoted in Schuyler, "Today's Artist," p. 56. See also Rauschenberg's comment to Richard Kostelanetz: "I think you can see similarities in anything and anything by generalities and warp" (Kostelanetz, "A Conversation with Robert Rauschenberg," p. 93). Cage most fully explained this point. "What do images do?" he asked in his article

on Rauschenberg, "Do they illustrate?" He then recalled a dinner party at which Joseph Campbell discussed the difficulty he had in finding an illustration for his new book. With the conviction that anything could be made to illustrate anything else, Cage made an offhand suggestion: "It was a New Year's Eve party in the country and one of them had written a philosophical book and was searching for a picture that would illustrate a particular point but was having difficulty. Another was knitting, following the rules from a book she had in front of her. The rest were talking, trying to be helpful. The suggestion was made that the picture in the knitting book would illustrate the point. On examination it was found that everything on the page was relevant, including the number" (Cage, "On Robert Rauschenberg," p. 107; the story is retold, with explicit reference to Joseph Campbell, in Cage, "26 Statements Re Duchamp," in *A Year from Monday* [Middletown, Conn.: Wesleyan University Press, 1967], p. 72).

87. In "Perpetual Inventory," Rosalind Krauss has brilliantly analyzed this signifying aspect of Rauschenberg's work with regard to his silkscreen paintings.

88. Cage, "On Robert Rauschenberg," pp. 108, 103.

89. Stuckey, "Reading Rauschenberg," p. 82.

90. Rauschenberg, quoted in Maxime de la Falaise McKendry, "Robert Rauschenberg Talks to Maxime de la Falaise McKendry," *Interview* 6, no. 5 (May 1976): 36.

91. On the relationship between multiplicities and the differential effect of actualization, see Deleuze, *Bergsonism,* esp. pp. 42–43, 96–97, 106. On the relation of actualization to Cage's contemporary compositions, see my "Chance, Catastrophe, Indeterminacy."

92. Robert Rauschenberg, "Note on Painting" (1963), in *Pop Art Redefined,* ed. John Russell and Suzi Gablik (New York: Praeger, 1969), p. 101. The text, which was reproduced in Rauschenberg's handwriting, does not make the distinction between words here signaled by italics, a convention adopted in the 1997 Guggenheim retrospective catalogue. The circumstances of writing the text are given in Joan Young and Susan Davidson, "Chronology," in Hopps and Young, eds., *Robert Rauschenberg: A Retrospective*, p. 563.

93. Benjamin refers to dadaist poetry as a "word salad" in "The Work of Art," p. 237.

94. Stuckey called *Rebus* "one of the most extravagant visual-verbal diagrams in the entire history of art" and referred to the diagrammed sentence found in Rauschenberg's *Wager* ("Reading Rauschenberg," p. 81).

95. Michel Foucault, "Maurice Blanchot: The Thought from Outside" (1966), trans. Brian Massumi, in *Foucault/Blanchot* (New York: Zone, 1990), pp. 11–12 (emphasis added).

96. See Gilles Deleuze, *Foucault,* trans. Seán Hand (Minneapolis: University of Minnesota Press, 1988), p. 84; and, more generally, see the discussion within the chapter "Strategies or the Non-stratified: The Thought of the Outside (Power)," pp. 70–93.

97. Deleuze, *Foucault,* p. 86.

98. Deleuze, *Foucault,* pp. 83–84.

99. Rauschenberg has commented explicitly on the idea of a relationship between forces and remnants in his work: "It's almost as if art, in painting and music and stuff, is the leftovers of some activity. The activity is the thing that I'm most interested in" (in Kostelanetz, "A Conversation with Robert Rauschenberg," p. 94).

100. Robert Rauschenberg, "Öyvind Fahlström" (1964), in Russell and Gablik, eds., *Pop Art Redefined,* pp. 71–72. This comment, I propose, applies to Rauschenberg's work as well.

101. The outside to which Rauschenberg's Combines open is akin to what Deleuze and Guattari have described as the immanent "plane of consistency or composition," in which "There are only relations of movement and rest, speed and slowness between unformed elements, or at least between elements that are relatively unformed, molecules and particles of all kinds. There are only haecceities, affects, subjectless individuations that constitute collective assemblages" (Gilles Deleuze and Félix Guattari, *A Thousand Plateaus: Capitalism and Schizophrenia,* trans. Brian Massumi [Minneapolis: University of Minnesota Press, 1987], p. 266). Not unimportantly, they see this plane as having been approached in music most directly by Cage (p. 267; on the difference of the plane of consistency from the idea of an all-encompassing "ground"—to which, as we have seen, Cage was attracted before 1951 to 1952—see p. 269). I believe that Rauschenberg was attempting to evoke something like

that field of forces with his statement, quoted in the introduction, that "Every minute everything is different, everywhere. It's all flowing" ("Assemblage Symposium," p. 137).

102. Steinberg, "Other Criteria," p. 91.

103. See Jameson, *Postmodernism, or the Cultural Logic of Late Capitalism* (the title essay of this 1991 book was first published in 1984): "In modernism, . . . some residual zones of 'nature' or 'being,' of the old, the older, the archaic, still subsist: culture can still do something to that nature and work at transforming that 'referent.' Postmodernism is what you have when the modernization process is complete and nature is gone for good. It is a more fully human world than the older one, but one in which 'culture' has become a veritable 'second nature' " (p. ix). See also Michael Hardt and Antonio Negri's extended discussion of this loss of an autonomous "outside" in *Empire* (Cambridge, Mass.: Harvard University Press, 2000), esp. pp. 186–190. The term "postmodernization" is not Jameson's but Hardt and Negri's.

104. Foucault, "Maurice Blanchot," pp. 25–26.

105. Cage, "History of Experimental Music," p. 70 (emphasis added).

106. On Cage's relation to "dementation," see David W. Patterson, "The Picture That Is Not in the Colors: Cage, Coomaraswamy, and the Impact of India," in *John Cage: Music, Philosophy, and Intention, 1933–1950,* ed. David W. Patterson (New York: Routledge, 2002), p. 192. As it does not take into account the Bergsonian dimension to Cage's post-1951 thinking, Patterson's discussion emphasizes the mystical over the transformative.

107. Cage, "On Robert Rauschenberg," p. 106.

108. Rauschenberg, quoted in Cage, "On Robert Rauschenberg," p. 106 (italics removed).

109. Charles F. Stuckey, "Rauschenberg's Everything, Everywhere Era," in Hopps and Davidson, eds., *Robert Rauschenberg: A Retrospective,* esp. pp. 38, 41 n. 32.

110. Stuckey, "Reading Rauschenberg," pp. 82–83 (I have here quoted only about half of Stuckey's paragraph).

111. More recently, Caroline Jones has proposed more varied readings of Rauschenberg's Untitled [the man with white shoes] and *Small Rebus.* In these, she recognizes certain aspects of the works' externality and signifying multivalence but does not entirely resist the pull to propose an overarching meaning. "The message," she writes at the end of her discussion of *Small Rebus,* "is clear enough: that only the attempt to make art and culture can stem humanity's propensity for conflict" (Jones, "*Coca-Cola Plan,*" p. 48 n. 56). Somewhat like Charles Stuckey, Jonathan D. Katz has recently distanced himself from his earlier readings of Rauschenberg's work in terms of encoded messages to his lovers. He has come to posit such readings as subjective effects of his own position as a reader, rather than as intentionally encoded keys to the meaning of the works (Katz, "Jasper Johns' *Alley Oop:* On Comic Strips and Camouflage," *Schwule Bildwelten im 20. Jahrhundert,* ed. Thomas Roeske [Berlin: Verlag Rosa Winkel, forthcoming]).

112. Rauschenberg, quoted in Parinaud, "Un 'misfit,'" p. 18.

113. Rauschenberg, quoted in Alain Jouffroy, "Barge," *Quadrum,* no. 15 (1963): 182.

4 SPLIT SCREENS

1. Rauschenberg, quoted in Dorothy Gees Seckler, "The Artist Speaks: Robert Rauschenberg," *Art in America* 54, no. 3 (May–June 1966): 84. Rauschenberg reiterated this position in 1997, commenting that "Attempting Dante was a private exercise in my growth and self-exploration to face my weaknesses. A test" (quoted in Rosalind Krauss, "Perpetual Inventory," in *Robert Rauschenberg: A Retrospective,* ed. Walter Hopps and Susan Davidson [New York: Solomon R. Guggenheim Museum, 1997], p. 215). As I have argued in the previous chapter, however, and as both Rosalind Krauss and Thomas Crow have also argued in different ways, Rauschenberg's work was never as "abstract" and free of connotations as he at times presented it. See Krauss, "Perpetual Inventory," and Crow, "This Is Now: Becoming Robert Rauschenberg," *Artforum* 36, no. 1 (September 1997): 95–96+.

2. See Lawrence Campbell, "Reviews and Previews: Robert Rauschenberg," *Art News* 59, no. 9 (January 1961): 13–14. The Dante Drawings are discussed in more detail in Dore Ashton, "Rauschenberg's Thirty Four Illustrations for Dante's Inferno," *Metro* 2 (1961): 52–61, and Bitite Vinklers, "Why Not Dante?" *Art International* 12, no. 6 (summer 1968): 99–106.

3. In a 1964 interview with David Sylvester, Rauschenberg referred to "associations [that] tend to funnel inwards" while discussing the types of symbolism that he usually tries to avoid (Sylvester, *Interviews with American Artists* [New Haven: Yale University Press, 2001], p. 139).

4. While the silkscreen paintings do not appear representational in the manner of *Election*, Rauschenberg would return explicitly to illustration in "A Modern Inferno," produced for *Life* magazine (17 December 1965, pp. 45–49), as well as (in a different way), in the Bellini prints done in 1986 to 1988.

5. Rauschenberg described such loose thematic associations to Seckler: "If you have strong feelings, these things are expressed over a period of time as opposed to, say, one *Guernica*. That's just a different attitude. When I was doing Dante, the first series, it was election year and a historian would be able to read that this was when it was done" (Seckler, "The Artist Speaks," p. 84). Rauschenberg immediately contrasted this type of expression with those forms of straightforward illustration discussed later in this chapter in terms of the "idea": "When you just illustrate your feelings about something self-consciously—that is for me almost a commercial attitude" (p. 84).

6. Letter from Robert Rauschenberg to the White House, April 1961; quoted in Joan Young and Susan Davidson, "Chronology," in Hopps and Davidson, eds., *Robert Rauschenberg: A Retrospective,* p. 559.

7. Letter from Rauschenberg to the White House, quoted in Young and Davidson, "Chronology," p. 559.

8. John Cage, "On Robert Rauschenberg, Artist, and His Work" (1961), in *Silence* (Middletown, Conn.: Wesleyan University Press, 1961), p. 105.

9. For another treatment of Rauschenberg's relation to television, which reaches conclusions different than mine, see John Alan Farmer, "Art into Television, 1960–65" (Ph.D. diss., Columbia University, 1998), pp. 64–125. Farmer gives an overview of the role of television within the visual arts in "Pop People," in *The New Frontier: Art and Television, 1960–65,* ed. John Alan Farmer (Austin: Austin Museum of Art, 2000), pp. 17–67.

10. In this and the following description of Rauschenberg's transfer drawings, I am indebted to Rosalind Krauss's analysis in "Perpetual Inventory," though I take her observations in a different direction. Both Ashton and Vinklers have related the framing devices within the Dante Drawings to the effects of contemporary cinema (see Ashton, "Illustrations for Dante's Inferno," p. 54, and particularly the excellent and detailed description of *Canto IV* by Vinklers, "Why not Dante?" p. 100.)

11. This characterization of television derives from Paul Virilio, who has noted that although television may appear as a window opening out onto three dimensions, it is actually a "third window" in which perspectival space and depth of field are replaced by a depthless "interface" or "support-surface" that is able to project, resemble, or simulate three-dimensional spaces. In this realm where dimensional appearance is actually only a surface effect, "classical optical perspective" is put to an end by "an image whose formal perfection springs not from an optic convergence but from a commutation of various forms of information" (Virilio, *The Lost Dimension,* trans. Daniel Moshenberg [New York: Semiotext(e), 1991], p. 85). See also Paul Virilio, "The Third Window," trans. Yvonne Shafir, in *Global Television,* ed. Cynthia Schneider and Brian Wallis (New York: Wedge Press; Cambridge, Mass.: MIT Press, 1988), pp. 185–197.

12. Cage, "On Robert Rauschenberg," p. 106.

13. On Rauschenberg's relationship to the old masters and the classical past, see chapter 3. For the idea that Rauschenberg sought to prove himself a serious artist via the Dante Drawings, see Calvin Tomkins, *Off the Wall: Robert Rauschenberg and the Art World of Our Time* (New York: Penguin, 1980), p. 157.

14. The Dante Drawings are described as "orthodox book-illustrations" in Ashton, "Illustrations for Dante's Inferno," p. 53.

15. Cage, "On Robert Rauschenberg," p. 105. He also observed, "Poetry is free-wheeling. You get its impact by thumbing through any of the mass media" (p. 106).

16. Rauschenberg, quoted in Robert Hughes, *The Shock of the New* (New York: Alfred A. Knopf, 1981), p. 345.

17. Despite some controversy, the consensus of opinion seems to be that Warhol was the first to use silkscreened images in his work, and that Rauschenberg learned of the technique from this visit to Warhol's studio. See Young and Davidson, "Chronology," p. 561, as well as Roni Feinstein, *Robert Rauschenberg: The Silkscreen Paintings, 1962–64* (New York: Whitney Museum of American Art, 1990), p. 45, and David Bourdon, *Warhol* (New York: Harry N. Abrams, 1989), p. 132. On the progression of Rauschenberg's work to the silkscreens, see Feinstein, p. 42.

18. Rauschenberg in 1965, quoted in Brian O'Doherty, *Object and Idea: An Art Critic's Journal, 1961–1967* (New York: Simon and Schuster, 1967), p. 116.

19. Guy Debord, *The Society of the Spectacle,* trans. Donald Nicholson-Smith (New York: Zone Books, 1995), p. 34.

20. The phrase "materialized imagery" derives from Rosalind Krauss, "Rauschenberg and the Materialized Image," *Artforum* 13, no. 4 (December 1974): 36–43. In discussing Rauschenberg's representation of male bodies in the Dante Drawings, Laura Auricchio opens up the possible relation of the series to a figuration of desire (Auricchio, "Lifting the Veil: Robert Rauschenberg's *Thirty-four Drawings for Dante's Inferno* and the Commercial Homoerotic Imagery of 1950s America," in *The Gay 90s: Disciplinary and Interdisciplinary Formation in Queer Studies,* ed. Thomas Foster, Carol Siegel, and Ellen E. Berry, Genders, vol. 26 [New York: New York University Press, 1997], pp. 119–154). But Auricchio's argument begins by imputing to the drawings the illustration of a fixed form of gay male subjectivity and desire, and then proceeds to read the illegibility or partial representation of the male bodies in the work as evidence of a repression or veiling of their imputed illustrational content. Auricchio's observation of "The disembodied legs, feet, heads, chests, backs, and areas of innumerable nude or partially clothed men [that] swirl about nearly all of the cantos" (p. 144) might be better understood as evidence of a more multiform, polymorphous figuration of desire—one that moves fluidly among varying part objects rather than individual gay male subjects. Helen Molesworth (whom Auricchio erroneously cites as having discussed Rauschenberg's black paintings in terms of an "anal desire" [p. 152 n. 61]) has suggested that " 'the body' is presented in Rauschenberg's oeuvre as polymorphously perverse" (Molesworth, "Before *Bed,*" *October,* no. 63 [winter 1993], p. 72). Such an understanding of the figuration of desire in Rauschenberg's work (which Molesworth explicitly distances from speculations on

Rauschenberg's sexuality) would not only be in line with Auricchio's observation of fragmented bodies in the Dante Drawings but would also coincide with Rauschenberg's most explicit figurations of sexuality and desire, the *Carnal Clocks* (1969) (see chapter 5).

21. Guy Debord, *Comments on the Society of the Spectacle,* trans. Malcolm Imrie (London: Verso, 1998), p. 3; cited in Jonathan Crary, "Spectacle, Attention, Counter-Memory," *October,* no. 50 (fall 1989): 100.

22. Crary, "Spectacle, Attention, Counter-Memory," pp. 97–107.

23. Debord, *The Society of the Spectacle,* p. 17.

24. Crary, "Spectacle, Attention, Counter-Memory," p. 102.

25. Rauschenberg recalls being exposed to McLuhan's thought as early as 1952 at Black Mountain College. As he told Barbara Rose, "John Cage was trying to read Marshall MacLuhan [*sic*] to me, and I said, 'That's an oversimplification' " (Rose, *An Interview with Robert Rauschenberg* [New York: Vintage Books, 1987], p. 34).

26. Jonathan Crary, "Eclipse of the Spectacle," in *Art after Modernism: Rethinking Representation,* ed. Brian Wallis (Boston: David R. Godine; New York: New Museum of Contemporary Art, 1984), p. 285.

27. Crary, "Spectacle, Attention, Counter-Memory," p. 103; Crary cites Félix Guattari's discussion of "bleak redundancies of representations" in "Les machines conrètes," in *La révolution moléculaire* (Paris: Encres, 1977), pp. 364–376 (published in English as "Concrete Machines," in *Molecular Revolution: Psychiatry and Politics,* trans. Rosemary Sheed [New York: Penguin, 1984], pp. 154–162).

28. Irving Sandler noted in his review of *Broadcast*'s debut exhibition that "the two knobs protruding from the surface of *Radio Piece* [*sic*] control three concealed synchronized radios that flood the room with noise. One's attention is forced to the canvas which gets to resemble a multiple-image TV screen" (Sandler, "Reviews and Previews: Robert Rauschenberg," *Art News* 59, no. 2 [April 1960]: 14). As we will see, Sandler's qualification, "multiple-image," is important.

29. Rauschenberg, quoted in G. R. Swenson, "Rauschenberg Paints a Picture," *Art News* 62, no. 2 (April 1963): 45.

30. David White, Rauschenberg's curator, has confirmed details of the operation of *Broadcast,* noting that its aural effect is one of a "general cacophony" (telephone conversation with author, 16 April 1999).

31. Rauschenberg, quoted in Swenson, "Rauschenberg Paints a Picture," p. 45.

32. The augmentation of the number of radios from three to five no doubt reflects Cage's contention that it was the minimum number at which indeterminacy could occur. "One loud-speaker is insufficient," he wrote in 1954, "and so are two or three or four: five is when it seems to me to begin. What begins is our inability to comprehend" (John Cage, "45′ for a Speaker" [1954], in *Silence,* p. 186). Cf. "For a calculated theatrical activity I would say offhand that the minimum number of necessary actions going on at once is five. Bright people can clear up rather quickly perplexity arising from lower numbers" (p. 173).

33. Robert Rauschenberg, "How Important Is Surface to Design?" *Print* 13, no. 1 (January–February 1959): 31.

34. On the development of *Ace* and its original technological component, see Swenson, "Rauschenberg Paints a Picture," pp. 45–46, and Billy Klüver and Julie Martin, "Working with Rauschenberg," in Hopps and Davidson, eds., *Robert Rauschenberg: A Retrospective,* pp. 310–327.

35. It is interesting to note that printed words, which are so prevalent in Rauschenberg's Combines, largely disappear from the silkscreen paintings.

36. Brian O'Doherty, "Rauschenberg and the Vernacular Glance," *Art in America* 61, no. 5 (September–October 1973): 85.

37. Samuel Weber, "Television: Set and Screen," in *Mass Mediauras: Form, Technics, Media* (Stanford: Stanford University Press, 1996), pp. 117–118.

38. Weber, "Television," p. 120. Weber draws from a developing strand within the analysis of television that includes Jane Feuer, "The Concept of Live Television: Ontology as

Ideology," in *Regarding Television: Critical Approaches—An Anthology,* ed. E. Ann Kaplan (Frederick, Md.: University Publications of America, 1983), pp. 12–22; Mary Ann Doane, "Information, Crisis, Catastrophe," in *Logics of Television: Essays in Cultural Criticism,* ed. Patricia Mellencamp (Bloomington: Indiana University Press; London: BFI, 1990), pp. 222–239; and Deborah Esch, "No Time Like the Present," in *In the Event: Reading Journalism, Reading Theory* (Stanford: Stanford University Press, 1999), pp. 61–70 (cited by Weber as a talk).

39. See, for instance, Tomkins, *Off the Wall,* p. 156, and Kotz, *Rauschenberg*, p. 90. Benjamin Buchloh also briefly discusses this aspect of the *Factums* in "Andy Warhol's One-Dimensional Art, 1956–1966," in *Neo-Avantgarde and Culture Industry: Essays on European and American Art from 1955 to 1975* (Cambridge, Mass.: MIT Press, 2000), pp. 493–495.

40. Rauschenberg, quoted in Richard Kostelanetz, "A Conversation with Robert Rauschenberg," *Partisan Review* 35, no. 1 (winter 1968): 97.

41. Rauschenberg, quoted in Emile de Antonio and Mitch Tuchman, *Painters Painting: A Candid History of the Modern Art Scene, 1940–1970* (New York: Abbeville, 1984), p. 94.

42. Rauschenberg, quoted in Kostelanetz, "A Conversation with Robert Rauschenberg," pp. 96–97. Although I did not realize it at the time of this chapter's original publication as an article, Caroline A. Jones had similarly noted of *Factum I* and *II,* "It is not even exactly a matter of *reproduction* (although collage elements address that condition), for we cannot say, without their Roman numerals to order them, which canvas is the 'original' and which the 'copy' " (Jones, "*Coca-Cola Plan* or, How New York Stole the Soul of Giuseppe Panza," in *Panza: The Legacy of a Collector* [Los Angeles: Museum of Contemporary Art, Los Angeles, 1999], p. 36). Jones goes on, toward the end of her essay, to make conjectures about the emergence of an economy based on electronic technologies that are also in line with the argument developed here (p. 44).

43. This pairing of trees brings to mind comments of Cage's: for example, "If it [one leaf] were the same as another leaf it would be a coincidence from which each leaf would be free because of its own unique position in space" (John Cage, "Juilliard Lecture" [1952], in *A Year from Monday* [Middletown, Conn.: Wesleyan University Press, 1967], p. 99).

44. Rauschenberg said that the repeated images of Gloria Vanderbilt at her wedding in *Gloria* (1956) derived from his finding "several newspapers with the same picture." He continued, "I became captivated and fascinated by, and tried to express, the thought of the innocent, grinning Gloria, reproduced to millions of people" (quoted in Öyvind Fahlström, "En gata full av presenter," *Konstrevy* 37, nos. 5–6 [1961], p. 177; trans. Kris Neville).

45. Such internal pairings were not exclusive to *Factum I* and *II.* In addition to the repeated images of Gloria Vanderbilt in *Gloria* (and the pairing of red cloth and red paint at the work's lower edge), see, for example, the paired photographs at the bottom of the small untitled work of 1955 in the collection of Jasper Johns (reproduced as figure 85 in Hopps and Davidson, eds., *Robert Rauschenberg: A Retrospective,* p. 116), the larger photographic pair at the bottom left of *Photograph* (1959), and the pair of decorated cloth swathes at the upper left of *Wager* (1957–1959), as well as the pair of black squares on orange and white paint toward the center of that work.

46. Cage, "On Robert Rauschenberg," p. 102.

47. Cage, "On Robert Rauschenberg," p. 100.

48. *The Writings of Marcel Duchamp,* ed. Michel Sanouillet and Elmer Peterson (New York: Da Capo, 1973), p. 31. Cage paraphrased this statement many times, apparently first in "Jasper Johns: Stories and Ideas" (1964), in *A Year from Monday,* p. 79.

49. On the "haunting" of difference, discussed in relation to television, see Mark Lewis and Andrew Payne, "The Ghost Dance: An Interview with Jacques Derrida," *Public* 2 (1989): 60–73. In the context of this chapter, it is interesting to note that Derrida's "Signature Event Context" was aimed, in part, against Marshall McLuhan's ideological representation of a transparent, technological, global village (see Jacques Derrida, "Signature Event Context" [1977], in *Limited Inc,* trans. Samuel Weber and Jeffrey Mehlman [Evanston, Ill.: Northwestern University Press, 1988], p. 20).

50. Gilles Deleuze, *Difference and Repetition,* trans. Paul Patton (New York: Columbia University Press, 1994), p. 69.

51. As Deleuze explained on the first page of *Difference and Repetition:*

> Repetition is not generality. . . . The exchange or substitution of particulars defines our conduct in relation to generality. . . . By contrast, we can see that repetition is a necessary and justified conduct only in relation to that which cannot be replaced. Repetition as a conduct and as a point of view concerns non-exchangeable and non-substitutable singularities. . . . If exchange is the criterion of generality, theft and gift are those of repetition. There is, therefore, an economic difference between the two. (p. 1)

52. Cage, "On Robert Rauschenberg," p. 102 (emphasis added).

53. Lawrence Alloway, Marcel Duchamp, et al., "The Art of Assemblage: A Symposium" (1961), in *Essays on Assemblage,* ed. James Leggio and Helen M. Franc, Studies in Modern Art, vol. 2 (New York: Museum of Modern Art, 1992), p. 137.

54. Rauschenberg, quoted in Seckler, "The Artist Speaks," p. 84. Rauschenberg is discussing the multipart sculpture *Oracle* (1962–1965), which contains five radios and was the direct descendant of his initial idea for *Ace.*

55. John Cage, "Questions," *Perspecta* 11 (1967): 71.

56. Deleuze, *Difference and Repetition,* p. 293.

57. Gilles Deleuze, "Letter to Serge Daney: Optimism, Pessimism, and Travel" (1990), in *Negotiations, 1972–1990,* trans. Martin Joughin (New York: Columbia University Press, 1995), p. 72 and n. 8.

58. Deleuze, "Letter to Serge Daney," pp. 72, 74.

59. Deleuze, "Letter to Serge Daney," p. 71. The description of "control" that follows is drawn from Deleuze's discussion in "Control and Becoming" and "Postscript on Control Societies" in *Negotiations,* pp. 169–176, 177–182. On the relationship of Debord to Foucault (and television), see Jonathan Crary's comments in *Suspensions of Perception: Attention, Spectacle, and Modern Culture* (Cambridge, Mass.: MIT Press, 1999), pp. 71–79.

60. Deleuze observes, "We're in the midst of a general breakdown of all sites of confinement—prisons, hospitals, factories, schools, the family. The family is an 'interior' that's breaking down like all other interiors—educational, professional, and so on" ("Postscript on Control Societies," p. 178). (Television, as a force that breaks down interiors, that connects the family room to the outside, is constantly blamed for destroying the family.) Michael Hardt and Antonio Negri have discussed and extended this aspect of Deleuze's thought in *Empire.* They comment, "As the walls of these institutions break down, the logics of subjectification that previously operated within their limited spaces now spread out, generalized across the social field. The breakdown of the institutions, the withering of civil society, and the decline of disciplinary society all involve a smoothing of the striation of modern social space. Here arise the networks of the society of control" (Hardt and Negri, *Empire* [Cambridge, Mass.: Harvard University Press, 2000], p. 329).

61. Deleuze, "Letter to Serge Daney," p. 75.

62. Deleuze, "Letter to Serge Daney," p. 74, and "Postscript on Control Societies," p. 175.

63. Debord, *The Society of the Spectacle,* pp. 26, 16, 110.

64. Andy Warhol and Pat Hackett, *Popism: The Warhol Sixties* (New York: Harcourt Brace Jovanovich, 1980), p. 50. Stephen Heath and Gillian Skirrow make essentially the same observation: "The 'central fact of television experience' is much less flow than *flow and regularity;* the anachronistic succession is also a constant repetition, and these terms of movement and stasis can be found as well within the single programme as within the evening's viewing—or, at least, something of the terms of the latter can be suggested in analysis of the former" (Heath and Skirrow, "Television: A World in Action," *Screen* 18, no. 2 [summer 1977]: 15).

65. Debord, *The Society of the Spectacle,* pp. 26–27.

66. "Visual memory" here must not be understood as the form of cultural memory discussed within a Frankfurt School discourse. From that perspective, the pseudo-repetition of spectacular time is made possible only after an annihilation of cultural memory, reference to which would give the lie to the spectacle's continual proclamation of the new. Rather, this visual memory is more closely related to the comforting recognition that is the handmaiden of

habit—the form of memory that leads an individual to accept and feel comfortable with the repetition of, for example, "the same plots and the same shots and the same cuts" of popular television. On Rauschenberg's understanding of cultural memory (seen as continually piling up and available—though in a mediated fashion—within the present), see chapter 3.

67. Michael Fried, "Art and Objecthood" (1967), in *Minimal Art: A Critical Anthology,* ed. Gregory Battcock (Berkeley: University of California Press, 1995), p. 145. It should be noted that although Fried hypostatizes painting's "essence," he nonetheless regards it as historical (pp. 123–124 n. 4).

68. As James Meyer has indicated, Fried's "Art and Objecthood" is both a certain culmination of and a break with Greenberg's formalist doctrines, "a declaration of independence from Greenberg" that still upheld the main principles of his position (Meyer, *Minimalism: Art and Polemics in the Sixties* [New Haven: Yale University Press, 2001], p. 231). Meyer also stresses the momentary nature of Fried's idea of "presentness" (pp. 234–239), an argument that inflects but does not displace its transcendent metaphysical ideality.

69. For an analysis of the museum as a disciplinary institution, and Rauschenberg's place within it, see Douglas Crimp, *On the Museum's Ruins* (Cambridge, Mass.: MIT Press, 1993).

70. Fried, "Art and Objecthood," p. 139.

71. On minimalism's development into institution critique, see Hal Foster, "The Crux of Minimalism," in *The Return of the Real* (Cambridge, Mass.: MIT Press, 1996), pp. 35–69. Foster also draws on the passage of Deleuze's *Difference and Repetition* cited above to posit the potential of pop and minimalism to mobilize repetition as a force of subversion (pp. 66–68).

72. Fried, "Art and Objecthood," p. 141. This passage occurs within a section titled "Art degenerates as it approaches the condition of theatre."

73. Fried, "Art and Objecthood," p. 141 n. 17. This note was omitted when "Art and Objecthood" was republished in Michael Fried, *Art and Objecthood: Essays and Reviews* (Chicago: University of Chicago Press, 1998), pp. 148–172.

74. Debord, *The Society of the Spectacle,* p. 133.

75. Indeed, I am arguing that in their maintenance of a self-presence, such late-modernist painters actually acquiesced all the more to spectacle's dictates. Rosalind Krauss made a similar argument while discussing the effect of "abstract presence" produced by the postpainterly abstraction championed by Fried (Krauss, "Theories of Art after Minimalism and Pop," in *Discussions in Contemporary Culture,* ed. Hal Foster [Seattle: Bay Press, 1987], p. 61). But Krauss's assimilation of pop art within such an analysis, at least as regards Rauschenberg, runs counter to the position espoused here.

76. Rauschenberg's technological optimism is evident in, for example, his almost entirely positive reaction to the space program as manifest in such work as the *Stoned Moon* series of lithographs of 1969–1970.

5 MOVING IMAGES

1. Other participants included Jack Smith, Angus MacLise, La Monte Young and Marian Zazeela, Nam June Paik, Stan Vanderbeek, Dick Higgins, Larry Rivers, USCO, the Once Group, and Andy Warhol. Rauschenberg performed on a bill with Robert Whitman and Claes Oldenburg. See flier for "New Cinema Festival I" in the text archives of the Anthology Film Archives, New York. The following description of *Map Room II* is taken from accounts in Jill Johnston, "Three Theatre Events," *Village Voice,* 23 December 1965, pp. 11, 25–26; Richard Kostelanetz's interview with Robert Rauschenberg in *The Theatre of Mixed Means: An Introduction to Happenings, Kinetic Environments, and Other Mixed-Means Presentations* (1968; reprint, New York: RK Editions, 1980), pp. 78–99; Steve Paxton, "Rauschenberg for Cunningham and Three of His Own," in *Robert Rauschenberg: A Retrospective,* ed. Walter Hopps and Susan Davidson (New York: Solomon R. Guggenheim Museum, 1997), pp. 261–267; Nina Sundell, *Rauschenberg/Performance, 1954–1984* (Cleveland: Cleveland Center for Contemporary Art, 1984); Nancy Spector, "Rauschenberg and Performance, 1963–67: A 'Poetry of Infinite Possibilities,' " in Hopps and Davidson, eds., *Robert Rauschenberg: A Retrospective,* pp. 227–245; and footage of Rauschenberg's performance included in the video produced by the Guggenheim Museum on the occasion of his 1997 retrospective.

2. Paxton, "Rauschenberg for Cunningham," p. 265.

3. Paxton, "Rauschenberg for Cunningham," p. 265.

4. Paxton, "Rauschenberg for Cunningham," p. 265.

5. Calvin Tomkins, *Off the Wall: Robert Rauschenberg and the Art World of Our Time* (New York: Penguin, 1980), p. 235. Rauschenberg explained to André Parinaud, "After the Grand Prize in the Venice Biennale, . . . I stopped painting to avoid becoming a dollar-machine (*un fabbricante di dollari*)" (Parinaud, "Un Intervista con Rauschenberg," *Le Arti* 19, nos. 1–2 [January–February 1969]: 25; trans. Barry J. McCrea). Another, more cynical reading might conclude that this destruction was meant to ensure or increase the market value of those works already produced. In any case, Rauschenberg's action distinguished him from Andy Warhol, who, even after he had "retired" from painting in favor of cinema, continued to produce canvases from his earlier silkscreens in order to finance his activities as a filmmaker.

6. In the Guggenheim's 1997 retrospective exhibition and catalogue, for example, Rauschenberg's art and technology projects were presented in separate sections and with separate lines of historical development. For another presentation of Rauschenberg's art and technology works as a specific subgenre, see Cornelia Faist and Alfred Kren, eds., *Robert Rauschenberg: Haywire: Major Technological Works of the 1960s* (Ostfildern-Ruit: Hatje, 1997). The third major preoccupation of Rauschenberg's at this time was lithography.

7. Erica Abeel, "Daedalus at the Rollerdrome," *Saturday Review,* 28 August 1965, p. 53.

8. The artist Per Uvelt appeared in the 1963 premiere of *Pelican*. In subsequent performances, his part was taken by Alex Hay.

9. Abeel, "Daedalus at the Rollerdrome," p. 53.

10. Abeel, "Daedalus at the Rollerdrome," p. 53.

11. Sundell, *Rauschenberg/Performance,* p. 14.

12. Paxton, "Rauschenberg for Cunningham," p. 264. Paxton refers not just to the activities in *Pelican* but also to the opening segments of people with shuffled cards in *Map Room II* as an "image" (p. 265). He describes *Spring Training* in similar terms: "The work, of course, yielded many images. First, the eggs. Emerging turtles. Light in darkness, the primordial reptilian shadows, the audition or rehearsal of a tap dance. A sports image in my solo" (p. 264).

13. Rauschenberg, quoted in Kostelanetz, *Theatre of Mixed Means,* pp. 91–92 (emphasis added).

14. For a detailed account of Rauschenberg's work with Merce Cunningham, see Michelle Potter, "'A License to Do Anything': Robert Rauschenberg and the Merce Cunningham Dance Company," *Dance Chronicle* 16, no. 1 (1993): 1–43.

15. On the break between Rauschenberg and the Merce Cunningham Dance Company, see Tomkins, *Off the Wall,* pp. 221–233; it came a couple of years after Rauschenberg's break with Jasper Johns, which occurred in the summer of 1962 (p. 198). Afterward, Johns would come to collaborate more closely with Cage and Cunningham.

16. Sally Banes, *Democracy's Body: Judson Dance Theater, 1962–1964* (Durham, N.C.: Duke University Press, 1993), p. 126.

17. Banes, *Democracy's Body,* p. 112. Earlier Rauschenberg was listed as "advisory" on the flier for the Judson Dance Workshop's Concerts of Dance #3 and #4 (29 and 30 June 1963; p. 82). Included in those concerts, among other pieces, was Rainer's *We Shall Run* (1963).

18. Banes, *Democracy's Body,* p. 116; Jill Johnson notes that *Terrain* was a "culmination" of Rainer's early aesthetic (quoted in Banes, *Democracy's Body,* p. 118).

19. Banes, *Democracy's Body,* pp. 113–114. Throughout the course of *Terrain,* the choreography was fragmented and combined with invented movements in various ways, sometimes left dependent on chance or on the individual dancer's own decisions. On *Terrain* and its relationship to "pop," see pp. 129–130; for a description of the movements, see p. 113.

20. Rauschenberg performed at the Wadsworth Atheneum, 6–7 March 1965, and at the Judson Memorial Church, 23–25 March 1965 (see Joan Young and Susan Davidson, "Chronology," in Hopps and Davidson, eds., *Robert Rauschenberg: A Retrospective,* p. 565).

21. Rauschenberg performed at the Wadsworth Atheneum, 6–7 March 1965 (Young and Davidson, "Chronology," p. 565).

22. Yvonne Rainer, *Work, 1961–73* (Halifax: Press of the Nova Scotia College of Art and Design; New York: New York University Press, 1974), pp. 28–29; Banes, *Democracy's Body,* pp. 113–114.

23. *Duet* is described in Rainer, *Work, 1961–73,* p. 16.

24. *Duet* was performed on its own on 15 February 1963 (Banes, *Democracy's Body,* p. 110).

25. Rainer's relationship to spectacle and "imagery" was not entirely oppositional; see Carrie Lambert, "Moving Still: Mediating Yvonne Rainer's *Trio A,*" *October,* no. 89 (summer 1999): 87–112.

26. Rauschenberg mentioned his admiration of Rainer's *Terrain* (identifiable from his description) to Kostelanetz (*Theatre of Mixed Means,* p. 86).

27. Yvonne Rainer, "Some Retrospective Notes on a Dance for 10 People and 12 Mattresses Called *Parts of Some Sextets,* Performed at the Wadsworth Atheneum, Hartford, Connecticut, and Judson Memorial Church, New York, in March, 1965" (1965), in *Happenings and Other Acts,* ed. Mariellen R. Sandford (New York: Routledge, 1995), p. 166.

28. Score for *Shot Put;* quoted in Spector, "Rauschenberg and Performance," p. 237.

29. Picasso's drawings in light had a tangible impact on postwar artists. On their relation to Pollock, see Rosalind E. Krauss, *The Optical Unconscious* (Cambridge, Mass.: MIT Press, 1993), pp. 301–303. On their relation to Lucio Fontana, see Anthony White, "Lucio Fontana: Between Utopia and Kitsch," *Grey Room,* no. 5 (fall 2001): 65–70.

30. Tomkins, *Off the Wall,* p. 230 (where he quotes Rauschenberg).

31. The nearest analogue to Rauschenberg's amalgam may be the costuming of early dada performance.

32. Rauschenberg, quoted in Kostelanetz, *Theatre of Mixed Means,* p. 91.

33. Performance score for *Map Room II,* Rauschenberg's archives, New York. Because it does not appear to be in Rauschenberg's hand, this copy was most likely used by one of the other performers. Spector does not cite or discuss the score for *Map Room II.* See, however, her discussion of the score for *Linoleum,* which reads in part: "Flag / Simone + chair / Steve + chickens / Alex + bed . . . " (Spector, "Rauschenberg and Performance," p. 235).

34. Rauschenberg, quoted in Kostelanetz, *Theatre of Mixed Means,* p. 93. This avoidance of merger is noted by Spector as well. She observes, "Independent theatrical elements coexisted in each dance, imparting effect through accumulation but not fusion. A Rauschenberg dance was not conceived to transcend its individual components, as a greater sum of its parts, but rather as a mosaic of strange yet allusive images, sounds, and gestures that hovered on the periphery of meaning" ("Rauschenberg and Performance," p. 236). Her characterization resembles Rauschenberg's description of the independent combinations within his visual art (specifically *Oracle*) in terms of a rough-hewn musical chord in which harmonic blending does not drown out the differential specificity of the incorporated notes or tones: "I like the idea of one sound, but I really don't like the idea that it is none of its components. . . . I would like my pictures to be able to be taken apart as easily as they're put together—so you can recognize an object when you're looking at it" (in G. R. Swenson, "Rauschenberg Paints a Picture," *Art News* 62, no. 2 [April 1963]: 46).

35. Rauschenberg, quoted in Kostelanetz, *Theatre of Mixed Means,* p. 91. Kostelanetz: "Was the idea to combine two images in one figure so that neither one could dominate the other?" Rauschenberg: "Yes. It was a kind of combined coexistence to make a single image."

36. Rauschenberg, quoted in Brian O'Doherty, *Object and Idea: An Art Critic's Journal, 1961–1967* (New York: Simon and Schuster, 1967), p. 117. Here, Rauschenberg was referring to lithography. Yet, as he explained to Dorothy Gees Seckler, he approached his performances as he did his other visual art: "I work [in performance] very much the same way—composing in non-sequential relationships—that I do in painting" (Seckler, "The Artist Speaks: Robert Rauschenberg," *Art in America* 54, no. 3 [May–June 1966]: 81).

37. Kostelanetz, *Theatre of Mixed Means,* p. 92.

38. Rauschenberg, quoted in Kostelanetz, *Theatre of Mixed Means,* p. 92.

39. Rauschenberg, quoted in Kostelanetz, *Theatre of Mixed Means,* p. 91.

40. Rauschenberg, quoted in Kostelanetz, *Theatre of Mixed Means,* p. 91.

41. Rauschenberg, quoted in Kostelanetz, *Theatre of Mixed Means,* p. 92 (emphasis added).

42. Rauschenberg, quoted in Kostelanetz, *Theatre of Mixed Means,* p. 92.

43. Cage recounts having come to the evening's performances with Duchamp (although he mentions only Claes Oldenburg's *Moveyhouse*); see Kostelanetz, *Theatre of Mixed Means,* p. 56.

44. See Young and Davidson, "Chronology," p. 568.

45. See Michel Carrouges, *Les machines célibataires* (Paris: Arcanes, 1954), and "Directions for Use," in *Le macchine celibi/The Bachelor Machines* (New York: Rizzoli, 1975), pp. 21–49. Carrouges refers to the bachelor machine as a "system of images" in "Directions for Use," p. 21.

46. Carrouges, "Directions for Use," p. 21.

47. Carrouges, *Les machines célibataires,* p. 36 (he is here writing of Duchamp's *Large Glass* and the disciplinary machine in Franz Kafka's penal colony).

48. *The Writings of Marcel Duchamp,* ed. Michel Sanouillet and Elmer Peterson. (New York: Da Capo, 1973), p. 39 (punctuation altered to coincide with the French version in Marcel Duchamp, *Duchamp du signe: Écrits*, ed. Michel Sanouillet with Elmer Peterson [Paris: Flammarion, 1994], p. 59).

49. Carrouges, "Directions for Use," pp. 22, 24.

50. For a discussion of the initial plan for the *Large Glass,* which remains unrealized, see Jean Suquet, "Possible," in *The Definitively Unfinished Marcel Duchamp,* ed. Thierry de Duve (Halifax: Nova Scotia College of Art and Design; Cambridge, Mass.: MIT Press, 1991), pp. 85–110; he quotes Duchamp on its "definitively unfinished" state (p. 109). The celibate

function of the bachelor machine is elaborated by Carrouges most clearly when he discusses the punishment machine in Kafka's *In the Penal Colony:* "En effet, le célibat, non en tant que fait simple, mais en tant qu'attitude mentale caractéristique se fonde sur une certain perte de sens humain, une impossibilité de participation et de communion avec la femme. . . . [I]l n'y trouve point la déliverance, mais la ruine de la machine et sa propre mort sans issue" (*Les machines célibataires,* p. 44). See also the comments on the "anticonjugal and antifamilial" functions within the literature of Kafka and Proust in Gilles Deleuze and Félix Guattari, *Kafka: Toward a Minor Literature,* trans. Dana Polan (Minneapolis: University of Minnesota Press, 1986), e.g., p. 64. Deleuze and Guattari draw explicitly on the work of Carrouges.

51. Carrouges, "Directions for Use," pp. 39–40. Bataille's *The Accursed Share,* on which he was working at the time of his death in 1962, lies at the heart of the conception of the bachelor machine (Georges Bataille, *The Accursed Share,* trans. Robert Hurley, vol. 1 [New York: Zone Books, 1988]). Carrouges draws attention to the importance of the "remarkably penetrating" works of Bataille and in particular the first volume of *The Accursed Share,* which appeared in 1949, in the first section of *Les machines célibataires,* pp. 18–20. Deleuze and Guattari, for their part, explicitly refer to the theory of consumption within *The Accursed Share* at the very beginning of *Anti-Oedipus,* in the chapter devoted to the celibate and desiring machines (Gilles Deleuze and Félix Guattari, *Anti-Oedipus: Capitalism and Schizophrenia,* trans. Robert Hurley, Mark Seem, and Helen R. Lane [Minneapolis: University of Minnesota Press, 1983], p. 4 n).

52. Bataille, *The Accursed Share,* pp. 63–77.

53. See Jacques Derrida, "From Restricted to General Economy: A Hegelianism without Reserve," in *Writing and Difference,* trans. Alan Bass (Chicago: University of Chicago Press, 1978), pp. 251–277.

54. Bataille, *The Accursed Share,* p. 9.

55. "Humanity exploits given material resources, but by restricting them as it does to a resolution of the immediate difficulties it encounters (a resolution which it has hastily had to define as an ideal), it assigns to the forces it employs an end which they cannot have. Beyond our immediate ends, man's activity in fact pursues the useless and infinite fulfillment of the universe" (Bataille, *The Accursed Share,* p. 21).

56. This characteristic self-consumption is seen most clearly in Carrouges's description of the final demise of the torture machine in Kafka's *In the Penal Colony* (see note 50), where his analysis begins to move in the direction of Deleuze and Guattari's examination of the functioning of "desiring machines" of which the celibate or bachelor machine forms an aspect: "The artist is the master of objects; he puts before us shattered, burned, broken-down objects, converting them to the régime of desiring-machines, breaking down is part of the very functioning of desiring-machines; the artist presents paranoiac machines, miraculating-machines, and celibate machines as so many technical machines, so as to cause desiring-machines to undermine technical machines" (Deleuze and Guattari, *Anti-Oedipus,* p. 32). See also Gilles Deleuze and Félix Guattari, "Balance Sheet: Program for Desiring-Machines," *Semiotext(e)* 2, no. 3 (1977): pp. 117–135. My thanks to Stephen Phillips for bringing this last article to my attention.

57. Carrouges, *Les machines célibataires,* p. 208.

58. On the relation of consummation and production within a bachelor machine, see Deleuze and Guattari:

> A genuine consummation is achieved by the new machine, a pleasure that can rightly be called autoerotic, or rather automatic: the nuptual celebration of a new alliance, a new birth, a radiant ecstasy, as though the eroticism of the machine liberated other unlimited forces.
>
> The question becomes: what does the celibate machine produce? What is produced by means of it? The answer would seem to be: intensive qualities. There is a schizophrenic experience of intensive qualities in their pure state, to a point that is almost unbearable—a celibate misery and glory experienced to the fullest, like a cry suspended between life and death, an intense feeling of transition, states of pure, naked intensity stripped of all shape and form. (*Anti-Oedipus,* p. 18)

On the relation of functioning, breakdown, and totality, see ibid., p. 42.

59. See Rauschenberg's comments on the first performances of *Map Room II* in Kostelanetz, *Theatre of Mixed Means,* p. 96.

60. Allan Kaprow discusses his use of "general" and "archetypal" symbols in his work in, among other places, "A Statement," in *Happenings: An Illustrated Anthology,* ed. Michael Kirby (New York: E. P. Dutton, 1965), pp. 49–50.

61. There is in the work of Rauschenberg and Cage an ongoing embrace of "failure" that can be understood only from the perspective presented here. See, for instance, Rauschenberg's recent comments to Julia Brown Turrell: "I would like to fail, that is something that I can't do. I can't plan to be a failure, but I certainly don't want to be a success" (Turrell, "Talking to Robert Rauschenberg," in *Rauschenberg Sculpture* [Fort Worth, Tex.: Modern Art Museum of Fort Worth, 1995], p. 56). John Cage discussed the failure to achieve predetermined goals in, among other places, the foreword and afterword to *A Year from Monday* (Middletown, Conn.: Wesleyan University Press, 1967), pp. x, 163–164. This aspect of Cage's work is commented on by Gilles Deleuze and Félix Guattari in *A Thousand Plateaus:* "As Cage says, it is of the nature of the plan(e) that it fail" (*A Thousand Plateaus: Capitalism and Schizophrenia,* trans. Brian Massumi [Minneapolis: University of Minnesota Press, 1987], p. 269).

62. Rauschenberg (who, as we have seen, probably knew of the piece through Cage by 1952) saw the *Large Glass* in the Philadelphia Museum with Jasper Johns in 1954 (Tomkins, *Off the Wall,* pp. 129–130).

63. See Billy Klüver, "The Garden Party" (1960), in *The Machine as Seen at the End of the Mechanical Age,* ed. K. G. Pontus Hultén (New York: Museum of Modern Art, 1968), pp. 169–171. Klüver also understood the notion of "failure" and unproductive expenditure at stake in Tinguely's bachelor machine. He described *Homage to New York* as "a machine that has rejected itself and become humor and poetry. New York has humor and poetry, in spite of the presence of the machine, whereas in a purely technocratic society the machine must always be a functional object. Failures of the machine can therefore never be allowed, because control is the necessary element of that society. It is when the machine must function at any cost that there can be no 'Homage to New York' " (p. 171). Hultén briefly cites Carrouges in the catalogue's introduction (pp. 6–13).

64. See Billy Klüver and Julie Martin, "Working with Rauschenberg," in Hopps and Davidson, eds., *Robert Rauschenberg: A Retrospective,* p. 313.

65. Klüver and Martin, "Working with Rauschenberg," p. 312.

66. Rauschenberg, quoted in Kostelanetz, *Theatre of Mixed Means,* p. 99.

67. Rauschenberg, quoted in Seckler, "The Artist Speaks," p. 84.

68. Rauschenberg, quoted in Seckler, "The Artist Speaks," p. 84.

69. Klüver and Martin, "Working with Rauschenberg," p. 312. The first recorded voicing of this idea seems to have been Rauschenberg's 1961 interview with André Parinaud; he spoke of his "intention to paint without the physical presence of the objects that I integrated in the paintings or to do it to such a degree that one can no longer call them paintings but rather an environment, a milieu" (André Parinaud, "Un 'misfit' de la peinture newyorkaise se confesse," *Les Arts et Spectat/Arts* [Paris], no. 821 [10 May 1961]: 18).

70. Rauschenberg, quoted in Seckler, "The Artist Speaks," p. 84. See also similar statements in Richard Kostelanetz, "The Artist as Playwright and Engineer," *New York Times Magazine,* 9 October 1966, p. 109, and Andrew Forge, *Robert Rauschenberg* (New York: Abrams, 1978), p. 14. The first meeting for "9 Evenings" took place on 14 January 1966.

71. Rauschenberg, quoted in Henry R. Lieberman, "Art and Science Proclaim Alliance in Avant-Garde Loft," *New York Times,* 11 October 1967, p. 49; quoted in Klüver and Martin, "Working with Rauschenberg," p. 318. The *Revolvers* were made in early spring 1967 and were first exhibited from 13 May to 10 June 1967.

72. Lewis Ellmore, quoted in *A Report on the Art and Technology Program of the Los Angeles County Museum of Art, 1967–1971* (Los Angeles: Los Angeles County Museum of Art, 1971), p. 280.

73. Frank LaHaye, quoted in Klüver and Martin, "Working with Rauschenberg," p. 322.

74. Rauschenberg, quoted in Richard Kostelanetz, "A Conversation with Robert Rauschenberg," *Partisan Review* 35, no. 1 (winter 1968): 98–99. Rauschenberg would return to investigate the use of air currents and pressure differentials in the work he would briefly explore with the engineers at Teledyne (see *A Report on the Art and Technology Program,* p. 280).

75. Rauschenberg, quoted in Kostelanetz, *Theatre of Mixed Means,* p. 94. Rauschenberg's characterization of a subject in constant change reveals certain historical limitations of his project, which was still largely established against a mass production- and commodity-based economy (see the conclusion).

76. The idea of the "mega-machine," as developed by Lewis Mumford, was strictly contemporary with this period in Rauschenberg's pursuits. Mumford gave lectures on "The Myth of the Machine" in 1962 and finished the second volume of *The Myth of the Machine,* titled *The Pentagon of Power,* in 1970 (New York: Harcourt Brace Jovanovich). Mumford's idea was adopted by Deleuze and Guattari in *Anti-Oedipus* (see p. 141).

77. Rauschenberg suggested this polarity despite rejecting the notion of "two cultures," science and art (see his comments in Kostelanetz, *Theatre of Mixed Means,* p. 98). He usually used the term "technology" neutrally, but he casts the distinction between "industry" and "humanity" as that between "technology" and "man" in Robert Rauschenberg, "A Collage 'Comment' by Robert Rauschenberg on His Latest Suite of Prints," *Studio International* 178, no. 917 (December 1969): 246–247.

78. Rauschenberg, quoted in *A Report on the Art and Technology Program,* pp. 285, 287. He reiterated the final point in Barbara Rose, *An Interview with Robert Rauschenberg* (New York: Vintage Books, 1987), p. 67.

79. Rauschenberg, quoted in *A Report on the Art and Technology Program,* p. 285; "broader" is bracketed in the original.

80. Rauschenberg, quoted in Kostelanetz, *Theatre of Mixed Means,* pp. 99, 94.

81. This description, of course, summarizes the general thesis of Louis Althusser, "Ideology and Ideological State Apparatuses (Notes towards an Investigation)" (1969), in *Lenin and Philosophy,* trans. Ben Brewster (New York: Monthly Review Press, 1971), pp. 127–186.

82. Rauschenberg, quoted in Kostelanetz, *Theatre of Mixed Means,* p. 94.

83. Rauschenberg, quoted in Seckler, "The Artist Speaks," pp. 81, 84.

84. Lawrence Alloway, Marcel Duchamp et al., "The Art of Assemblage: A Symposium" (1961), in *Essays on Assemblage,* ed. James Leggio and Helen M. Franc, Studies in Modern Art, vol. 2 (New York: Museum of Modern Art, 1992), p. 137. This conversation is hereafter cited as "Assemblage Symposium."

85. Rauschenberg, quoted in Seckler, "The Artist Speaks," p. 84.

86. Rauschenberg, quoted in Turrell, "Talking to Robert Rauschenberg," p. 68.

87. Rauschenberg, quoted in Kostelanetz, "The Artist as Playwright and Engineer," p. 109.

88. Rauschenberg, quoted in Turrell, "Talking to Robert Rauschenberg," p. 58: "The public is predictable. . . . I think that the public has to be educated to risk." This risk is synonymous with Rauschenberg's pursuit of *indeterminate* subjective transformation; it thus differs markedly from an Enlightenment form of progress, which would be fully in line with the technological pursuits of industry.

89. Tomkins, *Off the Wall,* p. 269. Catherine Craft discusses these works in detail, including their relation to the growth of a newly visible pornography industry (Craft, "Grand Central: Rauschenberg's *Carnal Clocks* and Other Experiments with Collaboration," in Faist and Kren, eds., *Robert Rauschenberg: Haywire,* pp. 11–40).

90. Calvin Tomkins considered the *Carnal Clocks* a "low ebb" in Rauschenberg's career (*Off the Wall,* p. 270). Gregory Battcock, in contrast, reviewed the works positively as "socially provocative and thus . . . important social documents" (Battcock, "Rauschenberg's New Clocks at Castelli," *Arts Magazine* 43, no. 7 [May 1969]: 69).

91. Roland Barthes, "The Metaphor of the Eye" (1963), in *Critical Essays,* trans. Richard Howard (Evanston, Ill.: Northwestern University Press, 1972), p. 242. The description of Bataille's story as an "image system" appears on p. 240.

92. Rauschenberg, quoted in *Art Now: New York* 1, no. 5 (May 1969): n.p.; quoted in Craft, "Grand Central," p. 26.

93. As Craft writes,

> an essential element of the Clocks' functioning as pictures is the way in which images themselves pun and couple with one another. Breasts, buttocks, or fruit? Erections, fire hydrants or turtles? When we see all these images as part of the functioning clock, the occasionally obvious visual jokes become something different and unsettling. With the dim and uneven lighting, their formal rhyming intensifies to a polymorphic perversity in which we—through the unavoidable presence of our reflection—are implicated. Sometimes it's difficult to tell what, exactly, we see, perhaps only that it is an oval form, surrounded by folds of flesh and hair. But buffalo's eye or vulva? Object of desire or revulsion? ("Grand Central" p. 15)

Though apparently explicitly aimed against the commercial representations of eroticism in commercial pornography, Rauschenberg's *Carnal Clocks,* like all of his actually produced technological works, ultimately fail to escape the type of circulation characteristic of the commodity (as discussed later in this chapter).

94. Fredric Jameson, "Periodizing the 60s," in *The Sixties without Apology,* ed. Sohnya Sayres et al. (Minneapolis: University of Minnesota Press, 1984), p. 190.

95. See Maurice Berger, *Labyrinths: Robert Morris, Minimalism, and the 1960s* (New York: Harper and Row, 1989).

96. Hal Foster, "The Crux of Minimalism," in *The Return of the Real* (Cambridge, Mass.: MIT Press, 1996), p. 58. Foster is here the necessary corrective to Jameson, providing a genealogy of the oppositional strain of postmodernism to which Jameson refers only in passing. See Fredric Jameson, *Postmodernism, or the Cultural Logic of Late Capitalism* (Durham, N.C.: Duke University Press, 1991), pp. 158–159. Recently, Foster's work has been explicitly paired with Jameson's; see Perry Anderson, *The Origins of Postmodernity* (London: Verso, 1998).

97. Yvonne Rainer, "Don't Give the Game Away," *Arts Magazine* 41, no. 6 (April 1967): 47.

98. Rainer discusses *Performance Demonstration* in *Work, 1961–73,* pp. 109–115.

99. Rauschenberg, Claes Oldenburg, the Living Theater, Allan Kaprow, Dick Higgens, and George Brecht, as well as other artists who took Cage's courses in "composition" at the New School in the late 1950s, were all exposed to Artaud either directly or at some remove. This exposure was also fostered, as P. Adams Sitney pointed out to me, by the appearance of Antonin Artaud's *Artaud Anthology,* ed. Jack Hirschman (San Francisco: City Lights Books, 1965).

100. Antonin Artaud, *The Theater and Its Double,* trans. Mary Caroline Richards (New York: Grove Weidenfeld, 1958), p. 13. See Jacques Derrida, "The Theater of Cruelty and the Closure of Representation," in *Writing and Difference,* pp. 232–250.

101. Artaud, *The Theater and Its Double,* p. 51. This text is hereafter cited parenthetically in the text.

102. Georges Bataille, "Formless," in *Visions of Excess: Selected Writings, 1927–1939,* ed. Allan Stoekl, trans. Allan Stoekl with Carl R. Lovitt and Donald M. Leslie, Jr. (Minneapolis: University of Minnesota Press, 1985), p. 31.

103. See Derrida, "The Theater of Cruelty," p. 235.

104. See Derrida, "The Theater of Cruelty"; Jacques Derrida, "La parole soufflée," in *Writing and Difference,* pp. 169–195; and Derrida, "To Unsense the Subjectile," in *The Secret Art of Antonin Artaud,* by Jacques Derrida and Paule Thévenin, trans. Mary Ann Caws (Cambridge, Mass.: MIT Press, 1998), pp. 59–157.

105. Mary Emma Harris, *The Arts at Black Mountain College* (Cambridge, Mass.: MIT Press, 1987), p. 228.

106. See the excellent discussion of the importance of Artaud for Tudor and Cage in John Holzaepfel, "David Tudor and the Performance of American Experimental Music, 1950–1959" (Ph.D. diss., City University of New York, 1994). The presence of Artaud within the postwar American avant-garde is further sketched in Douglas Kahn, "Artaud in America," in *100 Years of Cruelty: Essays on Artaud,* ed. Edward Scheer (Sydney: Power Publications and Artspace, 2000), pp. 237–262. For another discussion of Artaud and his (more Deleuzian)

reception by Cage, see the chapter "Chance, Catastrophe, Indeterminacy," in my "Experimental Art: John Cage, Robert Rauschenberg, and the Neo-Avant-Garde" (Ph.D. diss., Harvard University, 1999), pp. 87–141.

107. For discussions of *Theater Piece #1,* see Harris, *The Arts and Black Mountain College*, pp. 226–228; Spector, "Rauschenberg and Performance," pp. 229–230; and William Fetterman, *John Cage's Theatre Pieces: Notations and Performances* (Amsterdam: Harwood Academic Publishers, 1996), pp. 97–104.

108. John Cage, "On Robert Rauschenberg, Artist, and His Work" (1961), in *Silence* (Middletown, Conn.: Wesleyan University Press, 1967), p. 100.

109. Rauschenberg, quoted in Billy Klüver, *On Record: 11 Artists, 1963* (New York: Experiments in Art and Technology, 1981), p. 45.

110. Rauschenberg and Cage differ from Artaud in that force, for them, is from the "outside," not the individual. That is why Rauschenberg was interested, as he told Klüver, in "getting the room into the picture" rather than himself. Nevertheless, the ongoing discussion of the "excremental" nature of Rauschenberg's art could very productively be expanded by relating it to the "fecal" concerns of Artaud. On the excremental aspect of Rauschenberg's early production, see Helen Molesworth, "Before *Bed*," *October,* no. 63 (winter 1993): 69–82. On Rauschenberg's refusal to sketch, see his comments in Swenson, "Rauschenberg Paints a Picture," p. 46.

111. *Urban Round* was a chaotic performance that took place about the audience and through the aisles in much the same manner as Cage's *Black Mountain College Event.*

112. Rauschenberg, quoted in Suzi Gablik, "Light Conversation," *Art News* 67, no. 7 (November 1968): 60.

113. See Debord: "The self-movement of the spectacle consists in this: it arrogates to itself everything that in human activity exists in a fluid state so as to possess it in a congealed form—as things that, being the *negative expression* of living value, have become exclusively abstract value" (Guy Debord, *The Society of the Spectacle,* trans. Donald Nicholson-Smith [New York: Zone Books, 1995], p. 26).

114. Rauschenberg, quoted in Seckler, "The Artist Speaks," p. 81. In *Proust and Signs* (1964), Deleuze uses a similar example to describe the force of time as it affects forms: "It is a revelation to see again those who were familiar to us, for their faces, no longer a habit, bear in a pure state the signs and effects of time, which has modified this feature, elongated, blurred, or crushed that one. Time, in order to become visible, 'seeks bodies and everywhere encounters them, seizes them to cast its magic lantern upon them'" (Gilles Deleuze, *Proust and Signs: The Complete Text,* trans. Richard Howard [Minneapolis: University of Minnesota Press, 2000], p. 18). As we have seen in chapter 4, Jonathan Crary develops this aspect of Deleuze and Guattari's work specifically to characterize spectacle. After discussing the perception of the "face" in terms of "bleak redundancies of representations" that closely resemble Rauschenberg's idea of a painting's being a "facsimile of itself," Crary concludes: "That kind of redundancy of representation, with its accompanying inhibition and impoverishment of memory, was what Benjamin saw as the standardization of perception, or what we might call an effect of spectacle" (Crary, "Spectacle, Attention, Counter-Memory," *October,* no. 50 [fall 1989]: 103).

115. Derrida, "The Theater of Cruelty," p. 238.

116. Rauschenberg, quoted in Seckler, "The Artist Speaks," p. 84. On this aspect in Artaud and the nonseparation of force and form, see Derrida, "The Theater of Cruelty," pp. 238–240.

117. Rauschenberg, quoted in Kostelanetz, "The Artist as Playwright and Engineer," p. 109.

118. Rauschenberg, quoted in Dorothy C. Miller, ed., *Sixteen Americans* (New York: Museum of Modern Art, 1959), p. 58.

119. Temporal movement is key, for Rauschenberg is still as thoroughly indebted to Bergson as to Artaud. The forces of change, as he makes clear during this period, are temporal. "Time works things so that you can't recognize yourself," he said to Alain Jouffroy; "Time comes and changes you while you are planning" (Jouffroy, "Barge," *Quadrum,* no. 15 [1963]: 182).The idea of the "diagram," as an articulation of forces, is found in Gilles Deleuze, *Foucault,* trans. Seán Hand (Minneapolis: University of Minnesota Press, 1988), pp. 23–44, and Gilles Deleuze, *Francis Bacon: Logique de la sensation* (Paris: La Différence, 1981), pp. 65–71.

120. Rauschenberg, quoted in Jouffroy, "Barge," p. 182. Hal Foster has noted a similar moment of deconstructive "testing" in others of Rauschenberg's remarks (see Foster, "Who's Afraid of the Neo-Avant-Garde?" in *The Return of the Real,* pp. 16–17).

121. Rauschenberg's statement is found in an unreleased film, *Mostly about Rauschenberg* (produced by Reiner Moritz, 1974–1975); cited in Lawrence Alloway, "Rauschenberg's Development," in *Robert Rauschenberg,* ed. Walter Hopps (Washington: National Collection of Fine Arts, 1976), p. 18. This deconstructive impulse separates the outlooks of Cage and Rauschenberg—who, as we have noted, had become estranged from the composer during this period. Cage commented in 1972: "I think there's a slight difference between Rauschenberg and me. And we've become less friendly, although we're still friendly. We don't see each other as much as we did. . . . I have the desire to just erase the difference between art and life, whereas Rauschenberg made that famous statement about working in the gap between the two. Which is a little Roman Catholic, from my point of view" (in Richard Kostelanetz, *Conversing with Cage* [New York: Limelight Editions, 1994], p. 181). Interestingly, it was precisely Cage's desire to so fully collapse the distinction of art and life, to forgo form for a direct immersion in force, that would draw the sole criticism of him from Deleuze and Guattari (see *A Thousand Plateaus,* p. 344).

122. In the final two sentences of this paragraph, I have explicitly adopted Derrida's phraseology from "From Restricted to General Economy," p. 274. The "next to nothing" of an emerging minimalist position is articulated by Robert Morris in a letter to John Cage of 27 February 1961 (Morris, "Letters to John Cage," *October,* no. 81 [summer 1997]: 72).

123. Rauschenberg's characterization of his " 'blowing fuses' period" is found in Rose, *An Interview with Robert Rauschenberg*, p. 65.

124. Rauschenberg, quoted in Kostelanetz, *Theatre of Mixed Means,* p. 99.

125. Importantly, these forces could be technological, as in Rauschenberg's interactions with the neon tubes in *Map Room II.* On a subjectivity understood through its relation to forces of the outside, see Deleuze's discussion of the "Formation of the Future" toward the end of *Foucault,* pp. 129–132.

126. "Still, I have never been particularly interested in improvisation, because trusted to improvise, people very rarely move out of their own particular clichés and habits. Or, if they do, they are using their own pre-manufactured disguises of those habits" (Rauschenberg, quoted in Kostelanetz, *Theatre of Mixed Means,* p. 88). Both Artaud and Cage were opposed to improvisation for much the same reasons.

127. Rauschenberg, quoted in Barbaralee Diamonstein, *Inside New York's Art World* (New York: Rizzoli, 1979), p. 311.

128. Such impotence is signaled in the prologue to *Map Room II,* where the grammatically correct sentences spelled out by the blindfolded "chorus" fail to attain a comprehensible meaning, and where the Austrian travelogue is broken up by its projection on a sea of moving cards.

129. Artaud, *The Theater and Its Double,* pp. 125, 89.

130. Rauschenberg, quoted in Parinaud, "Un 'misfit,'" p. 18 (emphasis added).

131. Duchamp, *The Writings of Marcel Duchamp,* p. 140 (emphasis added).

132. Rauschenberg, quoted in Parinaud, "Un 'misfit,'" p. 18.

133. Duchamp, *The Writings of Marcel Duchamp,* p. 139.

134. In their acceptance of this semiosis, Rauschenberg (and Duchamp) would also differ from Artaud, who tended to lament such dissemination as the spiriting away of his thought (see Derrida, "La parole soufflée," esp. pp. 178–179).

135. Duchamp, "Assemblage Symposium," p. 144. As Rauschenberg noted in his interview with Kostelanetz, "your audience is not a familiar thing. It is made up of individual people who have all led different lives" (*Theatre of Mixed Means,* p. 85).

136. On the policing use of iconography to bring all unknown aspects of representation back into the known, there is no better example than Erwin Panofsky's famous "Introductory" to

Studies in Iconology: Humanistic Themes in the Art of the Renaissance (Oxford: Oxford University Press, 1939), pp. 3–31.

137. Robert Rauschenberg, "Note on Painting" (1963), in *Pop Art Redefined,* ed. John Russell and Suzi Gablik (New York: Praeger, 1969), p. 101. On the ultimate foreclosure of Rauschenberg's work within the realm of signification and clichés, see, once again, Rosalind Krauss, "Perpetual Inventory," in Hopps and Davidson, eds., *Robert Rauschenberg: A Retrospective,* pp. 206–223.

138. Rauschenberg, "Note on Painting," p. 101 (interjected words removed).

139. Rauschenberg, quoted in John Gruen, "Painter Dancing in the Dark," *Sunday Herald Tribune Magazine, NY Herald Tribune,* 2 January 1966, p. 34; quoted in Spector, "Rauschenberg and Performance," p. 233 (final emphasis added). See Rauschenberg's further comments on "contact" from 1966, also cited in Spector, p. 233. In the Kostelanetz interview, Rauschenberg specifically opposed "contact" to linguistic communication: "I've been with people who have speech problems. At first it made me quite nervous, later I found myself listening to it and being quite interested in just the physical contact; it can be a very dramatic thing" (*Theatre of Mixed Means,* p. 85).

140. Cage, "On Robert Rauschenberg," p. 103.

141. See Calvin Tomkins, *The Bride and the Bachelors* (New York: Penguin, 1968), p. 204.

142. Harold Rosenberg, "The American Action Painters" (1952), in *The Tradition of the New* (New York: McGraw-Hill, 1959), p. 25. Although Rosenberg was ostensibly describing abstract expressionism, his observations about the painter's attempt to leave behind representation in favor of actions were partly rooted in a meditation on "unpainted canvases." That meditation was probably a response to Rauschenberg's *White Paintings* (exhibited at Black Mountain College in that year), as Fred Orton argues in "The Object after Theory (Figuring Jasper Johns—Supplement 1: *Flag*)," in *Ex-cavating Modernism,* ed. Alex Coles and Richard Bentley, De-, dis-, ex-, vol. 1 (London: Backless Books, 1996), pp. 24–34.

143. See chapter 2. Cage knew Rosenberg and worked with him, along with Robert Motherwell, in editing the journal *Possibilities* (1947–1948).

144. Rosenberg, "The American Action Painters," p. 27. Cage and Rauschenberg might agree with Rosenberg only if biography is understood as continual transformation and growth. It is from such a perspective that Rauschenberg could answer Barbaralee Diamonstein's question "How much of your work is autobiographical?" with "Probably all of it" (Diamonstein, *Inside New York's Art World,* p. 310).

145. John Cage, "Experimental Music" (1957), in *Silence,* p. 10.

146. That Cage, through a "misplaced positivism," viewed sounds as existing in a state of unmediated facticity is the position advanced by Theodor W. Adorno in, among other places, "Vers une musique informelle" (1961), in *Quasi una fantasia: Essays on Modern Music,* trans. Rodney Livingstone (London: Verso, 1994), pp. 269–322. For a discussion, see my "Chance, Catastrophe, Indeterminacy."

147. Cage, "Experimental Music," p. 10.

148. The overly didactic responses given in the course of Cage's lecture to the Music Teachers National Association are misleading, for they seem initially to point to his viewing nature as a repository of meaning (see Cage, "Experimental Music," p. 10).

149. Rauschenberg, quoted in Parinaud, "Un 'misfit,'" p. 18.

150. Indeed, Rauschenberg's performances are the only works of his that have for the most part escaped iconographic readings, although Paxton has recently made a rather weak attempt at one ("Rauschenberg for Cunningham," p. 267).

151. In 1964 Gilles Deleuze began to develop his own, very similar theorization of "encounter" in *Proust and Signs* and later, as the epigraph to this chapter demonstrates, in *Difference and Repetition* (trans. Paul Patton [New York: Columbia University Press, 1994], p. 139). See Deleuze, *Proust and Signs:*

> What forces us to think is the sign. The sign is the object of an encounter, but it is precisely the contingency of the encounter that guarantees the necessity of what it leads us to think. The act of thinking does not proceed from a

simple natural possibility; on the contrary, it is the only true creation. Creation is the genesis of the act of thinking within thought itself. This genesis implicates something that does violence to thought, which wrests it from its natural stupor and its merely abstract possibilities. (p. 97)

152. Cage, quoted in Kostelanetz, *Conversing with Cage,* p. 173.

153. Rauschenberg, quoted in O'Doherty, *Object and Idea,* p. 116, and in Seckler, "The Artist Speaks," p. 76. As we have seen, Rauschenberg was probably referring less to surrealism directly than to surrealist practices of automatism as filtered through Pollock. See chapter 2, n. 93.

154. Rauschenberg, quoted in Parinaud, "Un 'misfit,'" p. 18.

155. An excerpt from *Linoleum* was included on an 8mm film reel in *Aspen: The Magazine in a Box,* nos. 5/6 (fall–winter 1967). Other film segments were by Hans Richter, László Moholy-Nagy, and Robert Morris.

156. Rauschenberg's terms are quoted in "The Emperor's Combine," *Time,* 18 April 1960, p. 92.

157. Despite his preoccupation with the mediatized televisual or spectacular image (discussed in the previous chapter), Rauschenberg, unlike Warhol, never entered into the production of either television or film as an autonomous form but always incorporated them into his live performances. His treatment of them as components is perfectly consistent with the aesthetic outlook I have been chronicling. Film and video, as reproductive media, are like the recorded tape that Rauschenberg had refused to use in *Oracle.* Because they are removed from real time, they are renditions of the "idea"; hence, in Rauschenberg's words, they are "commercial art."

158. Rauschenberg is criticized for having reduced spectators to the role of a "switch" in David Antin, "Art and the Corporations," *Art News* 70, no. 5 (September 1971): 26. This criticism is reiterated in Leo Steinberg, "Other Criteria," in *Other Criteria: Confrontations with Twentieth-Century Art* (New York: Oxford University Press, 1972), p. 81.

159. In the end, *Mud Muse* is activated by a sort of hermetic feedback device. See the description in Klüver and Martin, "Working with Rauschenberg," pp. 323–324.

160. Rauschenberg, quoted in *A Report on the Art and Technology Program,* pp. 286, 285. Rauschenberg's conception of *Mud Muse* clearly differs from Klüver's subsequent description of it: "It presents in a simple and legible way what sophisticated technology can do" (Klüver and Martin, "Working with Rauschenberg," p. 324).

Conclusion

1. The "A Modern Inferno" spread that Rauschenberg did for *Life* magazine in 1965 conveys much the same pessimism. At the time, however, Rauschenberg presented it as a willfully limited reflection of the mass media. "Someone asked me yesterday," he told Dorothy Gees Seckler about the work, " 'Do you really see modern life as all made up of hell?' Of course not. But if one is illustrating hell one usually uses the properties of hell" (Seckler, "The Artist Speaks: Robert Rauschenberg," *Art in America* 54, no. 3 [May–June 1966]: 84).

2. Rauschenberg began making obviously "classical" works in vegetable dye on frescoed panels in a series titled *Arcadian Retreats* (1996). With these, some of his most successful recent works, Rauschenberg seems to have accepted the mantle of old master with the same wit and generosity that characterized his earlier production. Previously, however, Rauschenberg had largely continued what had become an increasingly futile resistance to such canonization. A particularly telling instance can be found in his lengthy interview with Barbara Rose, who refuses Rauschenberg's protestations that he does not attempt to make his works "add up to something that is coherent" (Rose, *An Interview with Robert Rauschenberg* [New York: Vintage Books, 1987], p. 111).

3. Rauschenberg's successes often appear in pieces where least expected. One of the revelations of the Guggenheim Museum retrospective was the effect of actually encountering *Cardboards* such as *Volon* and *Castelli/Small Turtle Bowl* (both 1971) in full scale—works that, to my eye, have little or no interest in reproduction.

4. Calvin Tomkins, *Off the Wall: Robert Rauschenberg and the Art World of Our Time* (New York: Penguin, 1980), p. 301.

5. I have addressed some of the implications of such a realization in my " 'My Mind Split Open': Andy Warhol's *Exploding Plastic Inevitable,*" *Grey Room,* no. 8 (summer 2002): 80–107.

6. For a discussion of the discourses of the 1940s, see Jackson Lears, "A Matter of Taste: Corporate Cultural Hegemony in a Mass-Consumption Society," in *Recasting America: Culture and Politics in the Cold War,* ed. Larry May (Chicago: University of Chicago Press, 1989), pp. 38–57.

7. Such anticipation is somewhat characteristic of postmodern discourses in general. As Michael Hardt and Antonio Negri write, "The danger is that postmodernist theories focus their attention so resolutely on the old forms of power they are running from, with their heads turned backward, that they tumble unwittingly into the welcoming arms of the new power. . . . However confusedly or unconsciously, they indicate the passage toward the constitution of Empire" (Hardt and Negri, *Empire* [Cambridge, Mass.: Harvard University Press, 2000], pp. 142–143).

8. Michel Foucault, "The Subject and Power," in Hubert L. Dreyfus and Paul Rabinow, *Michel Foucault: Beyond Structuralism and Hermeneutics* (Chicago: University of Chicago Press, 1982), pp. 210–211.

9. See Hal Foster's comments in "Who's Afraid of the Neo-Avant-Garde?" in *The Return of the Real* (Cambridge, Mass.: MIT Press, 1996), p. 14.

10. Gilles Deleuze, *Difference and Repetition,* trans. Paul Patton (New York: Columbia University Press, 1994), p. 10.

Bibliography

Abeel, Erica. "Daedalus at the Rollerdrome." *Saturday Review,* 28 August 1965, 51–53.

Adorno, Theodor W. "Vers une Musique Informelle." In *Quasi Una Fantasia: Essays on Modern Music,* translated by Rodney Livingstone, pp. 269–322. London: Verso, 1994.

Alloway, Lawrence. "Rauschenberg's Development." In *Robert Rauschenberg,* edited by Walter Hopps, pp. 3–23. Washington: National Collection of Fine Arts, 1976.

Alloway, Lawrence, Marcel Duchamp, Richard Huelsenbeck, Robert Rauschenberg, Roger Shattuck, and William C. Seitz. "The Art of Assemblage: A Symposium." In *Essays on Assemblage,* edited by James Leggio and Helen M. Franc, pp. 118–159. Studies in Modern Art, vol. 2. New York: Museum of Modern Art, 1992.

Althusser, Louis. "Ideology and Ideological State Apparatuses (Notes towards an Investigation)." In *Lenin and Philosophy,* translated by Ben Brewster, pp. 127–186. New York: Monthly Review Press, 1971.

Anderson, Perry. *The Origins of Postmodernity.* London: Verso, 1998.

Antin, David. "Art and the Corporations." *Art News* 70, no. 5 (September 1971): 22–26, 52–56.

Artaud, Antonin. *Artaud Anthology*. Edited by Jack Hirschman. San Francisco: City Lights Books, 1965.

———. *The Theater and Its Double*. Translated by Mary Caroline Richards. New York: Grove Weidenfeld, 1958.

Ashton, Dore. "57th Street: Bob Rauschenberg." *Art Digest* 27, no. 20 (15 September 1953): 21, 25.

———. "Rauschenberg's Thirty Four Illustrations for Dante's Inferno." *Metro* 2 (1961): 52–61.

Auricchio, Laura. "Lifting the Veil: Robert Rauschenberg's *Thirty-four Drawings for Dante's Inferno* and the Commercial Homoerotic Imagery of 1950s America." In *The Gay 90s: Disciplinary and Interdisciplinary Formation in Queer Studies,* edited by Thomas Foster, Carol Siegel, and Ellen E. Berry, pp. 119–154. Genders, vol. 26. New York: New York University Press, 1997.

Banes, Sally. *Democracy's Body: Judson Dance Theater, 1962–1964*. Durham, N.C.: Duke University Press, 1993.

Barthes, Roland. "Cy Twombly: Works on Paper." In *The Responsibility of Forms: Critical Essays on Music, Art, and Representation,* translated by Richard Howard, pp. 157–176. Berkeley: University of California Press, 1985.

———. "The Metaphor of the Eye." In *Critical Essays,* translated by Richard Howard, pp. 239–247. Evanston, Ill.: Northwestern University Press, 1972.

Bataille, Georges. *The Accursed Share*. Translated by Robert Hurley. Vol. 1. New York: Zone Books, 1988.

———. *Visions of Excess: Selected Writings, 1927–1939*. Edited by Allan Stoekl. Translated by Allan Stoekl with Carl R. Lovitt and Donald M. Leslie, Jr. Minneapolis: University of Minnesota Press, 1985.

Battcock, Gregory. "Rauschenberg's New Clocks at Castelli." *Arts Magazine* 43, no. 7 (May 1969): 69.

Bendiner, Kenneth. "Robert Rauschenberg's 'Canyon.'" *Arts Magazine* 56, no. 10 (June 1982): 57–59.

Benjamin, Walter. *The Origin of German Tragic Drama.* Translated by John Osborne. London: Verso, 1977.

———. "Paris—Capital of the Nineteenth Century." Translated by Quintin Hoare. In *Charles Baudelaire: A Lyric Poet in the Era of High Capitalism,* pp. 155–176. London: New Left Books, 1973.

———. "Some Motifs in Baudelaire." Translated by Harry Zohn. In *Charles Baudelaire: A Lyric Poet in the Era of High Capitalism,* pp. 107–154. London: New Left Books, 1973.

———. "Surrealism: The Last Snapshot of the European Intelligentsia." In *Selected Writings,* edited by Michael W. Jennings, Howard Eiland, and Gary Smith, 2:207–221. Cambridge, Mass.: Belknap Press, 1999.

———. "The Work of Art in the Age of Mechanical Reproduction." In *Illuminations,* translated by Harry Zohn, pp. 217–251. New York: Schocken Books, 1969.

Berger, Maurice. *Labyrinths: Robert Morris, Minimalism, and the 1960s.* New York: Harper and Row, 1989.

Bergson, Henri. *Creative Evolution.* Translated by Arthur Mitchell. New York: Henry Holt, 1911.

———. *Matter and Memory.* Translated by N. M. Paul and W. S. Palmer. New York: Zone Books, 1991.

Bernstein, Roberta. "Ellsworth Kelly's Multipanel Paintings." In *Ellsworth Kelly: A Retrospective,* edited by Diane Waldman, pp. 40–55. New York: Solomon R. Guggenheim Museum, 1996.

———. "Robert Rauschenberg's 'Rebus.'" *Arts Magazine* 52, no. 5 (January 1978): 138–141.

Bois, Yve-Alain. "Base Materialism." In *Formless: A User's Guide,* by Yve-Alain Bois and Rosalind E. Krauss, pp. 51–62. New York: Zone Books, 1997.

———. *Ellsworth Kelly: The Early Drawings, 1948–1955.* Cambridge, Mass.: Harvard University Art Museums, 1999.

———."Ellsworth Kelly in France: Anti-Composition in Its Many Guises." In *Ellsworth Kelly: The Years in France, 1948–1954,* pp. 9–36. Munich: Prestel Verlag, 1992.

———. "Malevich, le carré, le degré zéro." *Macula* 1 (1978): 28–49.

———. "Painting: The Task of Mourning." In *Painting as Model,* pp. 229–244. Cambridge, Mass.: MIT Press, 1990.

———. "The Summons." In *Spencertown: Recent Paintings by Ellsworth Kelly,* pp. 33–50. London: Anthony d'Offay; New York: Matthew Marks, 1994.

Bois, Yve-Alain, and Benjamin H. D. Buchloh, *Ellsworth Kelly: A Conversation.* Drawing Papers 29. New York: Drawing Center, 2002.

Bois, Yve-Alain, and Rosalind E. Krauss. *Formless: A User's Guide.* New York: Zone Books, 1997.

Bourdon, David. *Warhol.* New York: Harry N. Abrams, 1989.

Brown, Trisha. "Collaboration: Life and Death in the Aesthetic Zone." In *Robert Rauschenberg: A Retrospective,* edited by Walter Hopps and Susan Davidson, pp. 269–274. New York: Solomon R. Guggenheim Museum, 1997.

Brunet, Nathalie. "Chronology, 1943–1954." In *Ellsworth Kelly: The Years in France, 1948–1954,* pp. 177–194. Munich: Prestel Verlag, 1992.

Buchloh, Benjamin H. D. "Allegorical Procedures: Appropriation and Montage in Contemporary Art." *Artforum* 21, no. 1 (September 1982): 43–56.

———. "Andy Warhol's One-Dimensional Art, 1956–1966." In *Neo-Avantgarde and Culture Industry: Essays on European and American Art from 1955 to 1975,* pp. 461–529. Cambridge, Mass.: MIT Press, 2000.

———. "The Primary Colors for the Second Time: A Paradigm Repetition of the Neo-Avant-Garde." *October,* no. 37 (summer 1986): 41–52.

———. "Warburg's Model? The End of Collage in Post-War European Art." In *Deep Storage: The Structure of Memory in Contemporary Art,* edited by Hubertus Gassner, pp. 50–60. Munich: Haus der Kunst, 1997.

Bürger, Peter. *Theory of the Avant-Garde.* Translated by Michael Shaw. Minneapolis: University of Minnesota Press, 1984.

Cadava, Eduardo. *Words of Light: Theses on the Photography of History.* Princeton: Princeton University Press, 1997.

Cage, John. "26 Statements Re Duchamp." In *A Year from Monday,* pp. 70–72. Middletown, Conn.: Wesleyan University Press, 1967.

———. "45′ for a Speaker." In *Silence,* pp. 146–193. Middletown, Conn.: Wesleyan University Press, 1961.

———. Afterword to *A Year from Monday,* pp. 163–167. Middletown, Conn.: Wesleyan University Press, 1967.

———. "A Composer's Confessions." In *John Cage: Writer,* edited by Richard Kostelanetz, pp. 27–44. New York: Limelight Editions, 1993.

———. "Composition as Process I: Changes." In *Silence,* pp. 18–34. Middletown, Conn.: Wesleyan University Press, 1961.

———. "Composition as Process II: Indeterminacy." In *Silence,* pp. 35–40. Middletown, Conn.: Wesleyan University Press, 1961.

———. "Composition as Process III: Communication." In *Silence,* pp. 41–56. Middletown, Conn.: Wesleyan University Press, 1961.

———. "Defense of Satie." In *John Cage: An Anthology,* edited by Richard Kostelanetz, pp. 77–84. New York: Da Capo, 1970.

———. "The East in the West." In *John Cage: Writer,* edited by Richard Kostelanetz, pp. 21–25. New York: Limelight Editions, 1993.

———. "Experimental Music." In *Silence,* pp. 7–12. Middletown, Conn.: Wesleyan University Press, 1961.

———. "Experimental Music: Doctrine." In *Silence,* pp. 3–17. Middletown, Conn.: Wesleyan University Press, 1961.

———. Foreword to *Silence,* pp. ix–xi. Middletown, Conn.: Wesleyan University Press, 1961.

———. Foreword to *A Year from Monday,* pp. ix–x. Middletown, Conn.: Wesleyan University Press, 1967.

———. "Happy New Ears!" In *A Year from Monday,* pp. 30–34. Middletown, Conn.: Wesleyan University Press, 1967.

———. "History of Experimental Music in the United States." In *Silence,* pp. 67–75. Middletown, Conn.: Wesleyan University Press, 1961.

———. " How to Pass, Kick, Fall, and Run." In *A Year from Monday,* pp. 133–140. Middletown, Conn.: Wesleyan University Press, 1967.

———. "Jasper Johns: Stories and Ideas." In *A Year from Monday,* pp. 73–84. Middletown, Conn.: Wesleyan University Press, 1967.

———. *John Cage: An Anthology.* Edited by Richard Kostelanetz. New York: Da Capo, 1970.

———. "Juilliard Lecture." In *A Year from Monday,* pp. 95–111. Middletown, Conn.: Wesleyan University Press, 1967.

———. "Lecture on Nothing." In *Silence,* pp. 109–126. Middletown, Conn.: Wesleyan University Press, 1961.

———. "Lecture on Something." In *Silence,* pp. 128–145. Middletown, Conn.: Wesleyan University Press, 1961.

———. "Letter to Paul Henry Lang." In *John Cage: An Anthology,* edited by Richard Kostelanetz, pp. 116–118. New York: Da Capo, 1970.

———. "Memoir." In *John Cage: An Anthology,* edited by Richard Kostelanetz, pp. 76–77. New York: Da Capo, 1970.

———. "Morris Graves." In *John Cage: An Anthology,* edited by Richard Kostelanetz, pp. 124–126. New York: Da Capo, 1970.

———. "Mosaic." In *A Year from Monday,* pp. 43–49. Middletown, Conn.: Wesleyan University Press, 1967.

———. "On Robert Rauschenberg, Artist, and His Work." In *Silence,* pp. 98–108. Middletown, Conn.: Wesleyan University Press, 1961.

———. "On Robert Rauschenberg, Konstuär och hans arbete." *Konstrevy* 37, nos. 5–6 (1961): 166–174.

———. "Preface to *Indeterminacy.*" In *John Cage: Writer,* edited by Richard Kostelanetz, pp. 75–79. New York: Limelight Editions, 1993.

———. "Questions." *Perspecta* 11 (1967): 65–71.

———. "Reflections of a Progressive Composer on a Damaged Society." *October,* no. 82 (fall 1997): 77–93.

———. "Robert Rauschenberg." In *John Cage: An Anthology,* edited by Richard Kostelanetz, pp. 111–112. New York: Da Capo, 1970.

———. *Silence.* Middletown, Conn.: Wesleyan University Press, 1961.

———. "Where Are We Going? And What Are We Doing?" In *Silence,* pp. 194–259. Middletown, Conn.: Wesleyan University Press, 1961.

———. *A Year from Monday.* Middletown, Conn.: Wesleyan University Press, 1967.

Cage, John, and Daniel Charles. *For the Birds.* New York: Marion Boyars, 1981.

Cage, John, and Hans G. Helms. *John Cage Talking to Hans G. Helms on Music and Politics.* Munich: S-Press Tapes, 1975. Audiocassette.

Cage, John, and Joan Retallack. *Musicage: Cage Muses on Words, Art, Music.* Hanover, N.H.: Wesleyan University Press/University Press of New England, 1996.

Campana, Deborah Ann. "Form and Structure in the Music of John Cage." Ph.D. diss., Northwestern University, 1985.

Campbell, Lawrence. "Reviews and Previews: Rauschenberg and Twombly." *Art News* 52, no. 5 (September 1953): 50.

———. "Reviews and Previews: Robert Rauschenberg." *Art News* 59, no. 9 (January 1961): 13–14.

Carrouges, Michel. "Directions for Use." In *Le macchine celibi / The Bachelor Machines,* pp. 21–49. New York: Rizzoli, 1975.

———. *Les machines célibataires.* Paris: Arcanes, 1954.

Charles, Daniel. *Gloses sur John Cage.* Paris: Union Générale d'Éditions, 1978.

Choay, Françoise. "Dada, néo-dada, et Rauschenberg." *Art International* 5, no. 8 (20 October 1961): 82–84, 88.

Clark, T. J. *Farewell to an Idea: Episodes from a History of Modernism.* New Haven: Yale University Press, 1999.

Cole, Mary. "Fifty-seventh Street in Review: Bob Rauschenberg." *Art Digest* 25, no. 17 (1 June 1951): 18.

Coomaraswamy, Ananda K. "Meister Eckhart's View of Art." In *The Transformation of Nature in Art,* pp. 59–95. Cambridge, Mass.: Harvard University Press, 1934.

Cooper, Harry. *An Intense Detachment: Ellsworth Kelly's "Line Form Color".* Cambridge, Mass.: Harvard University Art Museums, 1999.

Craft, Catherine. "Grand Central: Rauschenberg's *Carnal Clocks* and Other Experiments with Collaboration." In *Robert Rauschenberg: Haywire: Major Technological Works of the 1960s,* edited by Cornelia Faist and Alfred Kren, pp. 11–40. Ostfildern-Ruit: Hatje, 1997.

Cranshaw, Roger, and Adrian Lewis. "Re-Reading Rauschenberg." *Artscribe* 29 (1981): 44–51.

Crary, Jonathan. "Eclipse of the Spectacle." In *Art after Modernism: Rethinking Representation,* edited by Brian Wallis, pp. 283–294. New York: Museum of Contemporary Art; Boston: David R. Godine, 1984.

———. "Spectacle, Attention, Counter-Memory." *October,* no. 50 (fall 1989): 97–107.

———. *Suspensions of Perception: Attention, Spectacle, and Modern Culture.* Cambridge, Mass.: MIT Press, 1999.

Crehan, Hubert. "Fortnight in Review: Rauschenberg." *Arts Digest* 29, no. 7 (1 January 1955): 30.

———. "The See Change: Raw Duck." *Art Digest* 27, no. 20 (15 September 1953): 25.

Crimp, Douglas. "On the Museum's Ruins." In *On the Museum's Ruins,* pp. 44–64. Cambridge, Mass.: MIT Press, 1993.

———. *On the Museum's Ruins.* Cambridge, Mass.: MIT Press, 1993.

Crow, Thomas. *Modern Art in the Common Culture.* New Haven: Yale University Press, 1996.

———. "This Is Now: Becoming Robert Rauschenberg." *Artforum* 36, no. 1 (September 1997): 95–96 +.

De Antonio, Emile, and Mitch Tuchman. *Painters Painting: A Candid History of the Modern Art Scene,* 1940–1970. New York: Abbeville, 1984.

De Visscher, Eric. " 'There's no such thing as silence . . .': John Cage's Poetics of Silence." In *Writings about John Cage,* edited by Richard Kostelanetz, pp. 117–133. Ann Arbor: University of Michigan Press, 1993.

Debord, Guy. *Comments on the Society of the Spectacle.* Translated by Malcolm Imrie. London: Verso, 1998.

———. *The Society of the Spectacle.* Translated by Donald Nicholson-Smith. New York: Zone Books, 1995.

Deleuze, Gilles. "Bergson." In *Les philosophes célèbres,* edited by Maurice Merleau-Ponty, pp. 292–299. Paris: Editions d'art Lucien Mazenod, 1956.

———. *Bergsonism.* Translated by Hugh Tomlinson and Barbara Habberjam. New York: Zone Books, 1988.

———. "Bergson's Conception of Difference." Translated by Melissa McMahon. In *The New Bergson,* edited by John Mullarkey, pp. 42–65. Manchester: Manchester University Press, 1999.

———. *Cinema 2: The Time-Image.* Translated by Hugh Tomlinson and Robert Galeta. Minneapolis: University of Minnesota Press, 1989.

———. "Control and Becoming." In *Negotiations, 1972–1990,* translated by Martin Joughin, pp. 169–176. New York: Columbia University Press, 1995.

———. *Difference and Repetition.* Translated by Paul Patton. New York: Columbia University Press, 1994.

———. *Foucault.* Translated by Seán Hand. Minneapolis: University of Minnesota Press, 1988.

———. *Francis Bacon: Logique de la sensation.* Paris: La Différence, 1981.

———. "Letter to Serge Daney: Optimism, Pessimism, and Travel." In *Negotiations, 1972–1990,* translated by Martin Joughin, pp. 68–79. New York: Columbia University Press, 1995.

———. *Negotiations, 1972–1990.* Translated by Martin Joughin. New York: Columbia University Press, 1995.

———. "Postscript on Control Societies." In *Negotiations, 1972–1990,* translated by Martin Joughin, pp. 177–182. New York: Columbia University Press, 1995.

———. *Proust and Signs: The Complete Text.* Translated by Richard Howard. Minneapolis: University of Minnesota Press, 2000.

Deleuze, Gilles, and Félix Guattari. *Anti-Oedipus: Capitalism and Schizophrenia.* Translated by Robert Hurley, Mark Seem, and Helen R. Lane. Minneapolis: University of Minnesota Press, 1983.

———. "Balance Sheet: Program for Desiring-Machines." *Semiotext(e)* 2, no. 3 (1977): 117–135.

———. *Kafka: Toward a Minor Literature.* Translated by Dana Polan. Minneapolis: University of Minnesota Press, 1986.

———. *A Thousand Plateaus: Capitalism and Schizophrenia.* Translated by Brian Massumi. Minneapolis: University of Minnesota Press, 1987.

———. *What Is Philosophy?* Translated by Hugh Tomlinson and Graham Burchell. New York: Columbia University Press, 1994.

Derrida, Jacques. "Différance." In *Margins of Philosophy,* translated by Alan Bass, pp. 1–27. Chicago: University of Chicago Press, 1982.

———. "From Restricted to General Economy: A Hegelianism without Reserve." In *Writing and Difference,* translated by Alan Bass, pp. 251–277. Chicago: University of Chicago Press, 1978.

———. "La parole soufflée." In *Writing and Difference,* translated by Alan Bass, 169–195. Chicago: University of Chicago Press, 1978.

———. "Signature Event Context." In *Limited Inc,* translated by Samuel Weber and Jeffrey Mehlman, pp. 1–23. Evanston, Ill.: Northwestern University Press, 1988.

———. "The Theater of Cruelty and the Closure of Representation." In *Writing and Difference,* translated by Alan Bass, pp. 232–250. Chicago: University of Chicago Press, 1978.

———. "To Unsense the Subjectile." In *The Secret Art of Antonin Artaud,* by Jacques Derrida and Paule Thévenin, translated by Mary Ann Caws, pp. 59–157. Cambridge, Mass.: MIT Press, 1998.

———. *Writing and Difference.* Translated by Alan Bass. Chicago: University of Chicago Press, 1978.

Diamonstein, Barbaralee. *Inside New York's Art World.* New York: Rizzoli, 1979.

Dietrich, Dorothea. *The Collages of Kurt Schwitters: Tradition and Innovation.* Cambridge: Cambridge University Press, 1993.

Doane, Mary Ann. "Information, Crisis, Catastrophe." In *Logics of Television: Essays in Cultural Criticism,* edited by Patricia Mellencamp, pp. 222–239. Bloomington: Indiana University Press; London: BFI, 1990.

Duberman, Martin. "Is There Room for Privacy on the Canvas?" *New York Times,* 7 September 1997, sec. 2, p. 89.

Duchamp, Marcel. *Duchamp du signe: Écrits.* Edited by Michel Sanouillet, with Elmer Peterson. New ed. Paris: Flammarion, 1994.

———. *The Writings of Marcel Duchamp.* Edited by Michel Sanouillet and Elmer Peterson. New York: Da Capo, 1973.

Duve, Thierry de. "The Monochrome and the Blank Canvas." In *Kant after Duchamp,* pp. 199–279. Cambridge, Mass.: MIT Press, 1996.

———. *Pictorial Nominalism: On Marcel Duchamp's Passage from Painting to the Readymade.* Minneapolis: University of Minnesota Press, 1991.

———. "The Readymade and the Tube of Paint." In *Kant after Duchamp,* pp. 147–196. Cambridge, Mass.: MIT Press, 1996.

———, ed. *The Definitively Unfinished Marcel Duchamp.* Halifax: Nova Scotia College of Art and Design; Cambridge, Mass.: MIT Press, 1991.

Dyer, Richard. "A Refreshing, Surprising Exchange with John Cage." *Boston Globe,* 20 October 1988, p. B8.

Ellsworth Kelly: Tablet, 1948–1973. New York: Drawing Center, 2002.

"The Emperor's Combine." *Time,* 18 April 1960, p. 92.

Esch, Deborah. "No Time Like the Present." In *In the Event: Reading Journalism, Reading Theory,* pp. 61–70. Stanford: Stanford University Press, 1999.

Fahlström, Öyvind. "En gata full av presenter." *Konstrevy* 37, nos. 5–6 (1961): 176–181.

Faist, Cornelia, and Alfred Kren, eds. *Robert Rauschenberg: Haywire: Major Technological Works of the 1960s.* Ostfildern-Ruit: Hatje, 1997.

Farmer, John Alan. "Art into Television, 1960–65." Ph.D. diss., Columbia University, 1998.

———. "Pop People." In *The New Frontier: Art and Television, 1960–65,* edited by John Alan Farmer, pp. 17–67. Austin: Austin Museum of Art, 2000.

Feinstein, Roni. "The Early Work of Robert Rauschenberg: The White Paintings, the Black Paintings, and the Elemental Sculptures." *Arts Magazine* 61, no. 1 (September 1986): 28–37.

———. "Random Order: The First Fifteen Years of Robert Rauschenberg's Art: 1949–1964." Ph.D. diss., New York University, 1990.

———. *Robert Rauschenberg: The Silkscreen Paintings, 1962–64.* New York: Whitney Museum of American Art, 1990.

———. "The Unknown Early Robert Rauschenberg: The Betty Parsons Exhibition of 1951." *Arts Magazine* 59, no. 5 (January 1985): 126–131.

Ferguson, Russell, ed. *Hand-Painted Pop: American Art in Transition, 1955–62.* Los Angeles: Museum of Contemporary Art, Los Angeles; New York: Rizzoli, 1993.

Fetterman, William. *John Cage's Theatre Pieces: Notations and Performances.* Amsterdam: Harwood Academic Publishers, 1996.

Feuer, Jane. "The Concept of Live Television: Ontology as Ideology." In *Regarding Television: Critical Approaches—An Anthology,* edited by E. Ann Kaplan, pp. 12–22. Frederick, Md.: University Publications of America, 1983.

Fitzsimmons, James. "Art." *Arts and Architecture* 70, no. 10 (October 1953): 9, 32–36.

Forge, Andrew. *Robert Rauschenberg*. New York: Harry N. Abrams, 1978.

Foster, Hal. "The Crux of Minimalism." In *The Return of the Real,* pp. 35–69. Cambridge, Mass.: MIT Press, 1996.

———. "Who's Afraid of the Neo-Avant-Garde?" In *The Return of the Real,* pp. 1–33. Cambridge, Mass.: MIT Press, 1996.

Foucault, Michel. *The Archaeology of Knowledge*. Translated by A. M. Sheridan Smith. New York: Pantheon Books, 1972.

———. *The History of Sexuality*. Vol. 1, *An Introduction*. Translated by Robert Hurley. New York: Pantheon, 1978.

———. "Maurice Blanchot: The Thought from Outside." Translated by Brian Massumi. In *Foucault/Blanchot,* pp. 7–58. New York: Zone Books, 1990.

———. "The Subject and Power." In *Michel Foucault: Beyond Structuralism and Hermeneutics,* by Hubert L. Dreyfus and Paul Rabinow, pp. 208–226. Chicago: University of Chicago Press, 1982.

Fried, Michael. "Art and Objecthood." In *Art and Objecthood: Essays and Reviews,* pp. 148–172. Chicago: University of Chicago Press, 1998.

———. "Art and Objecthood." In *Minimal Art: A Critical Anthology,* edited by Gregory Battcock, pp. 116–147. Berkeley: University of California Press, 1995.

———. "Three American Painters: Kenneth Noland, Jules Olitski, Frank Stella." In *Art and Objecthood: Essays and Reviews,* pp. 213–265. Chicago: University of Chicago Press, 1998.

Gablik, Suzi. "Light Conversation." *Art News* 67, no. 7 (November 1968): 58–60.

Gillmor, Alan. "Interview with John Cage." *Contact,* no. 14 (autumn 1976): 18–25.

Goossen, E. C. *Ellsworth Kelly*. New York: Museum of Modern Art, 1973.

Greenberg, Clement. "Modernist Painting." In *The Collected Essays and Criticism*. Edited by John O'Brian. Vol. 4, *Modernism with a Vengeance, 1957–1969*, pp. 85–93. Chicago: University of Chicago Press, 1993.

———. "Recentness of Sculpture." In *The Collected Essays and Criticism*. Edited by John O'Brian. Vol. 4, *Modernism with a Vengeance, 1957–1969*, pp. 250–256. Chicago: University of Chicago Press, 1993.

Gruen, John. "Robert Rauschenberg: An Audience of One." *Art News* 76, no. 2 (February 1977): 44–48.

Guilbaut, Serge, ed. *Reconstructing Modernism: Art in New York, Paris, and Montreal, 1945–1964*. Cambridge, Mass.: MIT Press, 1990.

Hardt, Michael. *Gilles Deleuze: An Apprenticeship in Philosophy*. Minneapolis: University of Minnesota Press, 1993.

Hardt, Michael, and Antonio Negri. *Empire*. Cambridge, Mass.: Harvard University Press, 2000.

Harris, Mary Emma. *The Arts at Black Mountain College*. Cambridge, Mass.: MIT Press, 1987.

Heath, Stephen, and Gillian Skirrow. "Television: A World in Action." *Screen* 18, no. 2 (summer 1977): 7–59.

Holzaepfel, John. "David Tudor and the Performance of American Experimental Music, 1950–1959." Ph.D. diss., City University of New York, 1994.

Hopps, Walter, ed. *Robert Rauschenberg*. Washington: National Collection of Fine Arts, 1976.

———. *Robert Rauschenberg: The Early 1950s*. Houston: Houston Fine Arts Press, 1991.

———. Interview with Robert Rauschenberg, Captiva Island, Fla., 18–20 January 1991, Rauschenberg's archives, New York.

Hopps, Walter, and Susan Davidson, eds. *Robert Rauschenberg: A Retrospective.* New York: Solomon R. Guggenheim Museum, 1997.

Horkheimer, Max, and Theodor W. Adorno. *Dialectic of Enlightenment.* Translated by John Cumming. New York: Continuum, 1987.

Hughes, Robert. "The Most Living Artist." *Time,* 29 November 1976, 54–62.

———. *The Shock of the New.* New York: Alfred A. Knopf, 1981.

Hunter, Sam. *Robert Rauschenberg.* New York: Rizzoli, 1999.

Jameson, Fredric. "Periodizing the 60s." In *The Sixties without Apology,* edited by Sohnya Sayres et al., pp. 178–209. Minneapolis: University of Minnesota Press, 1984.

———. *Postmodernism, or the Cultural Logic of Late Capitalism.* Durham, N.C.: Duke University Press, 1991.

Johnston, Jill. *Jasper Johns: Privileged Information.* London: Thames and Hudson, 1996.

———. "Three Theatre Events." *Village Voice,* 23 December 1965, 11, 25–26.

Jones, Caroline A. "*Coca-Cola Plan* or, How New York Stole the Soul of Giuseppe Panza." In *Panza: The Legacy of a Collector,* pp. 22–87. Los Angeles: Museum of Contemporary Art, Los Angeles, 1999.

———. "Finishing School: John Cage and the Abstract Expressionist Ego." *Critical Inquiry* 19, no. 4 (summer 1993): 628–665.

Joselit, David. "Burroughs's Virology." *Art in America* 84, no. 11 (November 1996): 97–99.

———. *Infinite Regress: Marcel Duchamp, 1910–1941.* Cambridge, Mass.: MIT Press, 1998.

Joseph, Branden W. "Chance, Catastrophe, Indeterminacy." In "Experimental Art: John Cage, Robert Rauschenberg, and the Neo-Avant-Garde," pp. 87–141. Ph.D. diss., Harvard University, 1999.

———. "Hitchhiker in an Omni-Directional Transport: The Spatial Politics of John Cage and Buckminster Fuller." *ANY Magazine* 17 (1997): 40–44.

———. "John Cage and the Architecture of Silence." *October,* no. 81 (summer 1997): 80–104.

———. " 'My Mind Split Open': Andy Warhol's *Exploding Plastic Inevitable.*" *Grey Room,* no. 8 (summer 2002): 80–107.

———. "Robert Morris and John Cage: Reconstructing a Dialogue." *October,* no. 81 (summer 1997): 59–69.

———. "La sémiologie de Matisse." Trans. Nathalie Trouveroy. In *Matisse et Mallarmé,* pp. 14–27. Vulaines-sur-Seine: Musée départemental Stéphane Mallarmé, 2002.

———. " 'A Therapeutic Value for City Dwellers': The Development of John Cage's Early Avant-Garde Aesthetic Position." In *John Cage: Music, Philosophy, and Intention, 1933–1950,* edited by David W. Patterson, pp. 135–175. New York: Routledge, 2002.

———, ed. *Robert Rauschenberg.* Cambridge, Mass.: MIT Press, 2002.

Jouffroy, Alain. "Barge." *Quadrum,* no. 15 (1963): 99–106, 182.

Kahn, Douglas. "Artaud in America." In *100 Years of Cruelty: Essays on Artaud,* edited by Edward Scheer, pp. 237–262. Sydney: Power Publications and Artspace, 2000.

———. *Noise Water Meat: A History of Sound in the Arts.* Cambridge, Mass.: MIT Press, 1999.

Kaprow, Allan. "The Legacy of Jackson Pollock." In his *Essays on the Blurring of Art and Life,* edited by Jeff Kelley, pp. 1–9. Berkeley: University of California Press, 1993.

———. "A Statement." In *Happenings: An Illustrated Anthology,* edited by Michael Kirby, pp. 44–52. New York: E. P. Dutton, 1965.

Katz, Jonathan D. "The Art of Code: Jasper Johns and Robert Rauschenberg." In *Significant Others: Creativity and Intimate Partnership,* edited by Whitney Chadwick and Isabelle de Courtivron, pp. 189–207. London: Thames and Hudson, 1993.

———. "Commies, Cold War, and Queers." In *Out of the Cold,* edited by Renny Pritikin with René de Guzman, pp. 12–14. San Francisco: Center for the Arts at Yerba Buena Gardens, 1993.

———. "Dismembership: Jasper Johns and the Body Politic." In *Performing the Body/Performing the Text,* edited by Amelia Jones and Andrew Stephenson, pp. 170–185. New York: Routledge, 1998.

———. "Identification." In *Difference/Indifference: Musings on Postmodernism, Marcel Duchamp, and John Cage,* by Moira Roth and Jonathan D. Katz, pp. 49–68. Amsterdam: G+B Arts International, 1998.

———. "Jasper Johns' *Alley Oop:* On Comic Strips and Camouflage." In *Schwule Bildwelten im 20. Jahrhundert,* edited by Thomas Roeske. Berlin: Verlag Rosa Winkel, forthcoming.

———. "John Cage's Queer Silence; or, How to Avoid Making Matters Worse." In *Writings through John Cage's Music, Poetry, and Art,* edited by David Bernstein and Christopher Hatch, pp. 41–61. Chicago: University of Chicago Press, 2001.

———. "Opposition, Inc.: The Homosexualization of Postwar American Art." Ph.D. diss., Northwestern University, 1995.

———. "Passive Resistance: On the Success of Queer Artists in Cold War American Art." *L'Image,* no. 3 (December 1996): 119–142.

———. "Performative Silence and the Politics of Passivity." In *Making a Scene,* edited by Henry Rogers and David Burrows, pp. 97–103. Birmingham, England: ARTicle Press, 2000.

———. "Rauschenberg's Honeymoon." *Art/Text,* no. 61 (May–June 1998): 44–47.

———. "The Silent Camp: Queer Resistance and the Rise of Pop Art." In *Plop! Goes the World,* edited by Serge Guilbaut. Durham, N.C.: Duke University Press, forthcoming.

Kelly, Ellsworth. *Line Form Color.* Cambridge, Mass.: Harvard University Art Museums, 1999.

Kirby, Michael, and Richard Schechner. "An Interview with John Cage." In *Happenings and Other Acts,* edited by Mariellen R. Sandford, pp. 51–71. New York: Routledge, 1995.

Klüver, Billy. "The Garden Party." In *The Machine as Seen at the End of the Mechanical Age,* edited by K. G. Pontus Hultén, pp. 169–171. New York: Museum of Modern Art, 1968.

———, ed. *On Record: 11 Artists 1963.* New York: Experiments in Art and Technology, 1981.

Klüver, Billy, and Julie Martin. "Working with Rauschenberg." In *Robert Rauschenberg: A Retrospective,* edited by Walter Hopps and Susan Davidson, pp. 310–327. New York: Solomon R. Guggenheim Museum, 1997.

Kostelanetz, Richard. "The Artist as Playwright and Engineer." *New York Times Magazine,* 9 October 1966, pp. 32–33+.

———. *Conversing with Cage.* New York: Limelight Editions, 1994.

———. "Conversation with John Cage." In *John Cage: An Anthology,* edited by Richard Kostelanetz, pp. 6–35. New York: Da Capo, 1970.

———. "A Conversation with Robert Rauschenberg." *Partisan Review* 35, no. 1 (winter 1968): 92–106.

———. *The Theatre of Mixed Means: An Introduction to Happenings, Kinetic Environments, and Other Mixed-Means Presentations.* 1968. Reprint, New York: RK Editions, 1980.

———, ed. *Writings about John Cage.* Ann Arbor: University of Michigan Press, 1993.

Kotz, Liz. "Post-Cagean Aesthetics and the 'Event' Score." *October,* no. 95 (winter 2001): 55–89.

Kotz, Mary Lynn. *Rauschenberg: Art and Life.* New York: Harry N. Abrams, 1990.

Kramer, Hilton. "Month in Review." *Arts Magazine* 33, no. 5 (February 1959): 48–51.

Krauss, Rosalind E. "Notes on the Index: Part 1." In *The Originality of the Avant-Garde and Other Modernist Myths,* pp. 196–209. Cambridge, Mass.: MIT Press, 1985.

———. "Olympia." In *Formless: A User's Guide,* by Yve-Alain Bois and Rosalind Krauss, pp. 147–152. New York: Zone Books, 1997.

———. *The Optical Unconscious.* Cambridge, Mass.: MIT Press, 1993.

———. *Passages in Modern Sculpture.* Cambridge, Mass.: MIT Press, 1977.

———. "Perpetual Inventory." In *Robert Rauschenberg: A Retrospective,* edited by Walter Hopps and Susan Davidson, pp. 206–223. New York: Solomon R. Guggenheim Museum, 1997.

———. "Rauschenberg and the Materialized Image." *Artforum* 13, no. 4 (December 1974): 36–43.

———. "Theories of Art after Minimalism and Pop." In *Discussions in Contemporary Culture,* edited by Hal Foster, pp. 59–64. Seattle: Bay Press, 1987.

Lambert, Carrie. "Moving Still: Mediating Yvonne Rainer's *Trio A.*" *October,* no. 89 (summer 1999): 87–112.

Lears, Jackson. "A Matter of Taste: Corporate Cultural Hegemony in a Mass-Consumption Society." In *Recasting America: Culture and Politics in the Cold War,* edited by Larry May, pp. 38–57. Chicago: University of Chicago Press, 1989.

Leggio, James. "Robert Rauschenberg's *Bed* and the Symbolism of the Body." In *Essays on Assemblage,* edited by James Leggio and Helen M. Franc, pp. 79–117. Studies in Modern Art, vol. 2. New York: Museum of Modern Art, 1992.

Leonard, George J. *Into the Light of Things: The Art of the Commonplace from Wordsworth to John Cage.* Chicago: University of Chicago Press, 1994.

Lewis, Mark, and Andrew Payne. "The Ghost Dance: An Interview with Jacques Derrida." *Public* 2 (1989): 60–73.

Lieberman, Henry R. "Art and Science Proclaim Alliance in Avant-Garde Loft." *New York Times,* 11 October 1967, p. 49.

Lyotard, Jean-François. "Several Silences." Translated by Joseph Maier. In his *Driftworks,* edited by Roger McKeon, pp. 91–110. New York: Semiotext(e), 1984.

Mandel, Ernest. *Late Capitalism.* Translated by Joris De Bres. London: Verso, 1978.

———. *Long Waves of Capitalist Development: A Marxist Interpretation.* 2nd ed. London: Verso, 1995.

May, Todd. *The Political Philosophy of Poststructuralist Anarchism.* University Park: Pennsylvania State University Press, 1994.

McKendry, Maxime de la Falaise. "Robert Rauschenberg Talks to Maxime de la Falaise McKendry." *Interview* 6, no. 5 (May 1976): 34–36.

Meurice, Marc Froment. *Les intermittences de la raison: Penser Cage, entendre Heidegger.* Paris: Klincksieck, 1982.

Meyer, James. "Art for the City: Sculpture for a Large Wall, 1957." In *Ellsworth Kelly: Sculpture for a Large Wall, 1957,* pp. 5–38. New York: Matthew Marks Gallery, 1998.

———. *Minimalism: Art and Polemics in the Sixties.* New Haven: Yale University Press, 2001.

Michelson, Annette. "Robert Morris: An Aesthetics of Transgression." In *Robert Morris,* pp. 7–79. Washington, D.C.: Corcoran Gallery of Art, 1969.

Miller, Dorothy C., ed. *Sixteen Americans.* New York: Museum of Modern Art, 1959.

Miller, Leta E. "Cultural Intersections: John Cage in Seattle (1938–1940)." In *John Cage: Music, Philosophy, and Intention, 1933–1950,* edited by David W. Patterson, pp. 47–82. New York: Routledge, 2002.

Moholy-Nagy, László. *The New Vision and Abstract of an Artist.* Translated by Daphne M. Hoffmann. 4th rev. ed. New York: George Wittenborn, 1947.

Molesworth, Helen. "Before *Bed.*" *October,* no. 63 (winter 1993): 69–82.

Monahan, Laurie J. "Cultural Cartography: American Designs at the 1964 Venice Biennale." In *Reconstructing Modernism: Art in New York, Paris, and Montreal, 1945–1964,* edited by Serge Guilbaut, pp. 369–416. Cambridge, Mass.: MIT Press, 1990.

Morris, Robert. "Letters to John Cage." *October,* no. 81 (summer 1997): 70–79.

Mumford, Lewis. *The Myth of the Machine: The Pentagon of Power.* New York: Harcourt Brace Jovanovich, 1970.

Mussman, Toby. "A Comment on Literalness, Should the Picture Plane Be Abolished?" *Arts Magazine* 42, no. 4 (February 1968): 14–17.

O'Doherty, Brian. *Object and Idea: An Art Critic's Journal, 1961–1967.* New York: Simon and Schuster, 1967.

———. "Rauschenberg and the Vernacular Glance." *Art in America* 61, no. 5 (September–October 1973): 82–87.

Orton, Fred. *Figuring Jasper Johns.* Cambridge, Mass.: Harvard University Press, 1994.

———. "The Object after Theory (Figuring Jasper Johns—Supplement 1: *Flag*)." In *Ex-Cavating Modernism,* edited by Alex Coles and Richard Bentley, pp. 24–34. De-, dis-, ex-, vol. 1. London: Backless Books, 1996.

Owens, Craig. "The Allegorical Impulse: Toward a Theory of Postmodernism." In *Beyond Recognition: Representation, Power, and Culture,* edited by Scott Bryson, Barbara Kruger, Lynne Tillman, and Jane Weinstock, pp. 52–69. Berkeley: University of California Press, 1992.

———. "The Allegorical Impulse: Toward a Theory of Postmodernism, Part 2." In *Beyond Recognition: Representation, Power, and Culture,* edited by Scott Bryson, Barbara Kruger, Lynne Tillman, and Jane Weinstock, pp. 70–87. Berkeley: University of California Press, 1992.

———. "Earthwords." In *Beyond Recognition: Representation, Power, and Culture,* edited by Scott Bryson, Barbara Kruger, Lynne Tillman, and Jane Weinstock, pp. 40–51. Berkeley: University of California Press, 1992.

Panofsky, Erwin. *Studies in Iconology: Humanistic Themes in the Art of the Renaissance.* Oxford: Oxford University Press, 1939.

Parinaud, André. "Un intervista con Rauschenberg." *Le Arti* 19, nos. 1–2 (January–February 1969): 25–26.

———. "Un 'misfit' de la peinture newyorkaise se confesse." *Les Arts et Spectat/Arts* (Paris), no. 821 (10 May 1961): 18.

Patterson, David Wayne. "Appraising the Catchwords, c. 1942–1959: John Cage's Asian-Derived Rhetoric and the Historical Reference of Black Mountain College." Ph.D. diss., Columbia University, 1996.

———. "The Picture That Is Not in the Colors: Cage: Coomaraswamy, and the Impact of India." In *John Cage: Music, Philosophy, and Intention, 1933–1950,* edited by David W. Patterson, pp. 177–215. New York: Routledge, 2002.

Paxton, Steve. "Rauschenberg for Cunningham and Three of His Own." In *Robert Rauschenberg: A Retrospective,* edited by Walter Hopps and Susan Davidson, pp. 261–267. New York: Solomon R. Guggenheim Museum, 1997.

Perry, Arthur. "A Conversation between Robert Rauschenberg and Arthur Perry." *Artmagazine* 10, no. 41 (November–December 1978): 31–35.

Pfeiffer, Franz. *Meister Eckhart.* Translated by C. de B. Evans. London: John M. Watkins, 1924.

Plante, Michael. " 'Things to Cover Walls': Ellsworth Kelly's Paris Paintings and the Tradition of Mural Decoration." *American Art* 9, no. 1 (spring 1995): 37–53.

Politics, Poetics: Documenta X, the Book. Ostfildern-Ruit: Cantz, 1997.

"Pop Art—Cult of the Commonplace." *Time,* 3 May 1963, pp. 69–72.

Potter, Michelle. " 'A License to Do Anything': Robert Rauschenberg and the Merce Cunningham Dance Company." *Dance Chronicle* 16, no. 1 (1993): 1–43.

Pritchett, James. *The Music of John Cage.* Cambridge: Cambridge University Press, 1993.

Rainer, Yvonne. "Don't Give the Game Away." *Arts Magazine* 41, no. 6 (April 1967): 44–47.

———. "Looking Myself in the Mouth: Sliding Out of Narrative and Lurching Back In, Not Once but . . . Is the 'New Talkie' Something to Chirp About? From Fiction to Theory (Kicking and Screaming) Death to the Maiden, I Mean Author, I Mean Artist . . . No, I Mean Character A Revisionist Narrativization of/with Myself as Subject (Still Kicking) via John Cage's Ample Back." *October,* no. 17 (summer 1981): 65–76.

———. "Some Retrospective Notes on a Dance for 10 People and 12 Mattresses Called *Parts of Some Sextets,* Performed at the Wadsworth Atheneum, Hartford, Connecticut, and Judson Memorial Church, New York, in March, 1965." In *Happenings and Other Acts,* edited by Mariellen R. Sandford, pp. 160–167. New York: Routledge, 1995.

———. *Work, 1961–73.* Halifax: Press of the Nova Scotia College of Art and Design; New York: New York University Press, 1974.

Rajchman, John. "Abstraction." In *Constructions,* pp. 55–76. Cambridge, Mass.: MIT Press, 1998.

Rauschenberg, Robert. "A Collage 'Comment' by Robert Rauschenberg on His Latest Suite of Prints." *Studio International* 178, no. 917 (December 1969): 246–247.

———. "How Important Is Surface to Design?" *Print* 13, no. 1 (January–February 1959): 25–36.

———. "A Modern Inferno." *Life,* 17 December 1965, pp. 45–49.

———. "Note on Painting" (1963). In *Pop Art Redefined,* edited by John Russell and Suzi Gablik, pp. 101–102. New York: Praeger, 1969.

———. "Öyvind Fahlström." In *Pop Art Redefined,* edited by John Russell and Suzi Gablik, 71–72. New York: Praeger, 1969.

———. "Random Order." *Location* 1, no. 1 (spring 1963): 27–31.

———. [Statement]. In *Twelve Americans: Masters of Collage.* New York: Andrew Crispo Gallery, 1977.

A Report on the Art and Technology Program of the Los Angeles County Museum of Art, 1967–1971. Los Angeles: Los Angeles County Museum of Art, 1971.

Rose, Barbara. *An Interview with Robert Rauschenberg.* New York: Vintage Books, 1987.

Rosenberg, Harold. "The American Action Painters." In *The Tradition of the New,* pp. 23–39. New York: McGraw-Hill, 1959.

Roth, Moira. "The Aesthetic of Indifference." In *Difference/Indifference: Musings on Postmodernism, Marcel Duchamp and John Cage,* by Moira Roth and Jonathan D. Katz, pp. 33–47. Amsterdam: G+B Arts International, 1998.

Roth, Moira, and William Roth. "John Cage on Marcel Duchamp." *Art in America* 61, no. 6 (November–December 1973): 72–79.

Russell, John, and Suzi Gablik, eds. *Pop Art Redefined.* New York: Praeger, 1969.

Sandford, Mariellen R., ed. *Happenings and Other Acts.* New York: Routledge, 1995.

Sandler, Irving. "Reviews and Previews: Robert Rauschenberg." *Art News* 59, no. 2 (April 1960): 14.

Sayag, Alain. "Interview with Robert Rauschenberg." In *Robert Rauschenberg: Photographs.* New York: Pantheon, 1981.

Schimmel, Paul. "The Faked Gesture: Pop Art and the New York School." In *Hand-Painted Pop: American Art in Transition, 1955–62,* edited by Russell Ferguson, pp. 19–65. Los Angeles: Museum of Contemporary Art, Los Angeles; New York: Rizzoli, 1993.

Schuyler, James. "Is Today's Artist with or against the Past?" *Art News* 57, no. 4 (summer 1958): 46, 56.

Schwarz, Arturo. *The Complete Works of Marcel Duchamp.* 3rd rev. and expanded ed. 2 vols. New York: Delano Greenidge Editions, 1997.

Seckler, Dorothy Gees. "The Artist Speaks: Robert Rauschenberg." *Art in America* 54, no. 3 (May–June 1966): 72–84.

———. "Exhibition at Betty Parsons' Gallery." *Art News* 50, no. 3 (May 1951): 59.

Sedgwick, Eve Kosofsky. *Epistemology of the Closet.* Berkeley: University of California Press, 1990.

Seitz, William C. *The Art of Assemblage.* New York: Museum of Modern Art, 1961.

———. "Assemblage: Problems and Issues." *Art International* 6, no. 2 (February 1962): 26–34.

———. "Problems of 'New Directions' Exhibitions." *Artforum* 2, no. 3 (September 1963): 23–25.

Shattuck, Roger. *The Banquet Years.* New York: Harcourt, Brace, 1958.

Solomon, Alan R. *Robert Rauschenberg.* New York: Jewish Museum, 1963.

———. *XXXII International Biennial Exhibition of Art, Venice 1964, United States of America.* New York: Jewish Museum, 1964.

"Speaking of Pictures." *Life,* 9 April 1951, pp. 22–24.

Spector, Nancy. "Rauschenberg and Performance, 1963–67: A 'Poetry of Infinite Possibilities.'" In *Robert Rauschenberg: A Retrospective,* edited by Walter Hopps and Susan Davidson, pp. 227–245. New York: Solomon R. Guggenheim Museum, 1997.

Steinberg, Leo. *Encounters with Rauschenberg.* Houston: Menil Collection; Chicago: University of Chicago Press, 2000.

———. "Footnote." *Arts* 32, no. 8 (May 1958): 9.

———. "Month in Review: Contemporary Group at Stable Gallery . . ." *Arts* 30, no. 4 (January 1956): 46–48.

———. "Other Criteria." In *Other Criteria: Confrontations with Twentieth-Century Art,* pp. 55–91. New York: Oxford University Press, 1972.

———. "Reflections on the State of Criticism." *Artforum* 10, no. 7 (March 1972): 37–49.

Stuckey, Charles F. "Rauschenberg's Everything, Everywhere Era." In *Robert Rauschenberg: A Retrospective,* edited by Walter Hopps and Susan Davidson, pp. 31–41. New York: Solomon R. Guggenheim Museum, 1997.

———. "Reading Rauschenberg." *Art in America* 65, no. 2 (March–April 1977): 74–84.

Sundell, Nina. *Rauschenberg/Performance, 1954–1984.* Cleveland: Cleveland Center for Contemporary Art, 1984.

Suquet, Jean. "Possible." In *The Definitively Unfinished Marcel Duchamp,* edited by Thierry de Duve, pp. 85–110. Halifax: Nova Scotia College of Art and Design; Cambridge, Mass.: MIT Press, 1991.

Swenson, G. R. "Rauschenberg Paints a Picture." *Art News* 62, no. 2 (April 1963): 44–47; 65–67.

Sylvester, David. *Interviews with American Artists.* New Haven: Yale University Press, 2001.

Tarabukin, Nikolai. "From the Easel to the Machine." Translated by Christina Lodder. In *Modern Art and Modernism: A Critical Anthology,* edited by Francis Frascina and Charles Harrison, pp. 135–144. New York: Harper and Row, 1982.

Taylor, Paul. "Robert Rauschenberg." *Interview* 20, no. 12 (December 1990): 142–147.

Tomkins, Calvin. *The Bride and the Bachelors.* New York: Penguin, 1968.

———. *Off the Wall: Robert Rauschenberg and the Art World of Our Time.* New York: Penguin, 1980.

Turrell, Julia Brown. *Rauschenberg Sculpture.* Fort Worth, Tex.: Modern Art Museum of Fort Worth, 1995.

———. "Talking to Robert Rauschenberg." In *Rauschenberg Sculpture,* pp. 49–82. Fort Worth, Tex.: Modern Art Museum of Fort Worth, 1995.

Twelve Americans: Masters of Collage. New York: Andrew Crispo Gallery, 1977.

Vinklers, Bitite. "Why Not Dante?" *Art International* 12, no. 6 (summer 1968): 99–106.

Virilio, Paul. *The Lost Dimension.* Translated by Daniel Moshenberg. New York: Semiotext(e), 1991.

———. "The Third Window." In *Global Television,* edited by Cynthia Schneider and Brian Wallis, pp. 185–197. New York: Wedge Press; Cambridge, Mass.: MIT Press, 1988.

Waldman, Diane. "Ellsworth Kelly." In *Ellsworth Kelly: A Retrospective,* edited by Diane Waldman, pp. 10–39. New York: Solomon R. Guggenheim Museum, 1996.

Wallis, Brian, ed. *Art after Modernism: Rethinking Representation.* New York: New Museum of Contemporary Art; Boston: David R. Godine, 1984.

Warhol, Andy, and Pat Hackett. *Popism: The Warhol Sixties.* New York: Harcourt Brace Jovanovich, 1980.

Watney, Simon. "Making Strange: The Shattered Mirror." In *Thinking Photography,* edited by Victor Burgin, pp. 154–176. London: Macmillan, 1982.

Weber, Samuel. "Television: Set and Screen." In *Mass Mediauras: Form, Technics, Media,* pp. 108–128. Stanford: Stanford University Press, 1996.

Weinberg, Jonathan. "It's in the Can: Jasper Johns and the Anal Society." *Genders,* no. 1 (spring 1988): 40–56.

White, Anthony. "Lucio Fontana: Between Utopia and Kitsch." *Grey Room,* no. 5 (fall 2001): 54–77.

Young, Joan, and Susan Davidson. "Chronology." In *Robert Rauschenberg: A Retrospective,* edited by Walter Hopps and Susan Davidson, pp. 550–587. New York: Solomon R. Guggenheim Museum, 1997.

Index

Page numbers in boldface indicate illustrations.